This collection of contemporary essays by a group of well-known philosophers and legal theorists covers various topics in the philosophy of law, focusing on issues concerning liability in contract, tort, and criminal law. The book is divided into four sections. The first is a conceptual overview of the issues at stake in a philosophical discussion of liability and responsibility. The second, third, and fourth sections present, in turn, more detailed explorations of the roles of notions of liability and responsibility in contracts, torts, and punishment.

The collection not only presents some of the most challenging work being done in legal philosophy today, it also demonstrates the interdisciplinary character of the field of philosophy of law, with contributors taking into account recent developments in economics, political science, and rational choice theory. This thought-provoking volume will help to shed light on the under-explored ground that lies between law and morals.

This volume will prove of great interest to philosophers of law, moral philosophers, political philosophers, and legal theorists.

CAMBRIDGE STUDIES IN PHILOSOPHY AND LAW

Liability and responsibility

Cambridge Studies in Philosophy and Law

GENERAL EDITOR: JULES L. COLEMAN
(YALE LAW SCHOOL)

ADVISORY BOARD

David Gauthier (University of Pittsburgh)
David Lyons (Cornell University)
Richard Posner (Judge in the Seventh Circuit Court of Appeals, Chicago)
Martin Shapiro (University of California, Berkeley)

This exciting new series will reflect and foster the most original research currently taking place in the study of law and legal theory by publishing the most adventurous monographs in the field as well as rigorously edited collections of essays. It will be a specific aim of the series to traverse the boundaries between disciplines and to form bridges between traditional studies of law and many other areas of the human sciences. Books in the series will be of interest not only to philosophers and legal theorists but also to political scientists, sociologists, economists, psychologists, and criminologists.

OTHER BOOKS IN THE SERIES

Jeffrey G. Murphy and Jean Hampton: *Forgiveness and mercy*
Stephen R. Munzer: *A theory of property*

Liability and responsibility

Essays in law and morals

Edited by

R.G. FREY and CHRISTOPHER W. MORRIS

BOWLING GREEN STATE UNIVERSITY

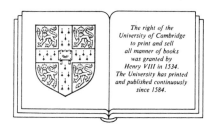

The right of the
University of Cambridge
to print and sell
all manner of books
was granted by
Henry VIII in 1534.
The University has printed
and published continuously
since 1584.

CAMBRIDGE UNIVERSITY PRESS

CAMBRIDGE

NEW YORK   PORT CHESTER   MELBOURNE   SYDNEY

Published by the Press Syndicate of the University of Cambridge
The Pitt Building, Trumpington Street, Cambridge CB2 1RP
40 West 20th Street, New York, NY 10011, USA
10 Stamford Road, Oakleigh, Melbourne 3166, Australia

First published 1991

Printed in the United States of America

Library of Congress Cataloging-in-Publication Data
Liability and responsibility : essays in law and morals / edited by
R. G. Frey and Christopher W. Morris.
p.   cm. – (Cambridge studies in philosophy and law)
Based upon a conference on liability and responsibility sponsored
by the Department of Philosophy of Bowling Green State University in
1988" – Pref.
ISBN 0-521-39216-0 (hardcover)
1. Law – Philosophy.   2. Law and ethics.   3. Liability (Law)
I. Frey, R. G. (Raymond Gillespie)   II. Morris, Christopher W.
III. Bowling Green State University. Dept. of Philosophy.
IV. Series.
K230.F74L53   1991
340'.1 – dc20   90–40997
                                                    CIP

British Library Cataloguing in Publication Data
Liability and responsibility : essays in law and morals. –
(Cambridge studies in philosophy and law)
1. Law. Ethical aspects
I. Frey, R. G. (Raymond G.)   II. Morris, Christopher W.
340.112

ISBN 0-521-39216-0 hardback

Contents

Contents

Preface

This volume of essays is based upon a conference on liability and responsibility sponsored by the Department of Philosophy of Bowling Green State University in 1988. Other invited essays have been added.

Our aims in holding a conference on the theme of liability and responsibility in law and morals were twofold. First, we hoped that our participants, from different viewpoints and with different emphases, would be able to shed light on this most troublesome area of interconnection between law and morals. The whole concept of responsibility in morals is a difficult one, and problems there seep into and infect the discussion of liability in law. In order to avoid a scattering of essays upon all sorts of issues to do with responsibility and so to focus our considerations, we decided to concentrate upon four areas. One, of course, had to be conceptual in character, even though all contributors could be expected in part to be attempting conceptual clarification; the remaining three areas – contract, torts, and punishment – we chose because some of the most interesting work being done in legal philosophy today occurs there.

Our second aim in holding our conference, and in inviting additional contributions, was to show the interdisciplinary character of much of the work in our four areas of concentration. No longer is it true that moral philosophers and legal theorists generally go about their business in ignorance of work done in economics, political science, and rational choice theory, and we hoped that our participants and contributors would make this manifest in their discussions. This is not to disparage conceptual analysis, which remains the centrally important tool of the philosopher; it is simply to acknowledge that application and analysis no longer remain apart, assigned to different disciplines, with different standards of argumentation and rigor.

A great many people helped us in holding our conference and preparing this volume, especially among the graduate students, staff, and faculty of the Department of Philosophy at Bowling Green, and we are grateful to them all. Our series editor, Jules Coleman, deserves special mention for his constant advice and encouragement. Our Cambridge editor, Terence Moore, proved particularly forthcoming and helpful.

Bowling Green, Ohio   R.G.F.
                                                                     C.W.M.

Contributors

Randy E. Barnett, Professor of Law and Norman and Edna Freehling Scholar, Chicago-Kent College of Law

Jules L. Coleman, John A. Garver Professor of Jurisprudence and Philosophy, Yale Law School

Richard A. Epstein, James Parker Hall Distinguished Service Professor of Law, University of Chicago

John Finnis, Professor of Law and Legal Philosophy, University of Oxford

George P. Fletcher, Professor of Law, Columbia University

Robert E. Goodin, Professorial Fellow of Philosophy, Research School of Social Sciences, Australian National University

Jean Hampton, Professor of Philosophy, University of California, Davis

Douglas D. Heckathorn, Associate Professor of Sociology and Economics, University of Missouri, Kansas City

Anthony Kenny, Warden, Rhodes House, University of Oxford

Steven M. Maser, Professor, Atkinson Graduate School of Management, Willamette University

Jeffrie G. Murphy, Professor of Law and Philosophy, Arizona State University

Glen O. Robinson, John C. Stennis Professor of Law, University of Virginia

Contributors

Ernest J. Weinrib, Professor of Law and Special Lecturer in Classics, University of Toronto

Alan R. White, Professor of Philosophy, University of Hull

R.G. Frey, Professor of Philosophy, Bowling Green State University

Christopher W. Morris, Associate Professor of Philosophy, Bowling Green State University

Introduction

R.G. FREY AND CHRISTOPHER W. MORRIS

The concept of responsibility would appear to oscillate among (at least) three meanings. On one, to be responsible for P is to be guilty of having done P; on another, to be responsible for P is to be the cause of P; and, on still another, to be responsible for P is to say that there is a case to be put and so a case to be answered. With this last, though guilt is not ascribed, there is present the implication that we shall look into the answer that is forthcoming. Different aspects of these three meanings of the term, particularly the last two, which readers may well think of prime importance, are explored in this volume. Here, we touch only upon some of the pertinent issues.

I. RESPONSIBILITY:
SOME CONCEPTUAL PROBLEMS

To be responsible, in a sense that matters in law and morals, is minimally to be accountable or answerable for one's actions (or omissions). We are responsible for some consequences of our acts (or omissions), but not for others. The bases of the distinctions that we draw, and those that we ought to draw, are matters of great controversy, not least because of the obscurity of the notions of act and intention. The contributors to this section address three important matters of controversy, each of which attempts to resolve issues central to a theory of responsibility.

In "Can Responsibility Be Diminished?", Anthony Kenny is critical of various legal devices that have recently been

1

introduced which permit the rendering of verdicts which reduce or diminish criminal responsibility, while not altogether eliminating it. He defends the insanity defense in the face of recent attacks on both sides of the Atlantic. Against recent trends in the United States, Kenny criticizes recent reforms following the Hinckley case that make it harder to secure an acquittal by reason of insanity; he argues that such reforms increase the likelihood of the conviction of the innocent. In England, by contrast, proposals for reform aimed at reducing the likelihood that mentally disordered individuals will be convicted of murder may have an effect opposite to that of American reforms, in that the former would increase the likelihood that those guilty of murder would not be convicted of that crime.

In his essay, "Intention and Side-Effects", John Finnis wants to rescue from what he takes to be confusion and sceptical doubt the distinction between what is intended and what is merely brought about as a side-effect. This distinction is the basis for the criminal law's distinction between murder and manslaughter, as well as the law of tortious liability in negligence, and it has long been discussed by moral philosophers in connection with the doctrine of double effect. Finnis criticizes standard accounts of the distinction and claims that the errors to be found in these have two main sources: (1) the failure to distinguish free choice from spontaneity, and rational from subrational motivation, and (2) the failure in moral theory to distinguish norms bearing only on what one intends (and does) from norms bearing on what one foresees (the side-effects of what one intends). Finnis discusses a recently clarified English judicial doctrine of intention and side-effect, one which allows (1) that one may intend to achieve a certain result without desiring that it come about and (2) that one may foresee a certain result as likely (or even certain) to follow from one's action without intending that result. Such a doctrine permits juries to convict of murder only if the accused had the requisite intention. It allows a determination of intent where desire is not present and of lack of intent where the death was merely foreseen; the conclusion of intent based upon foresight is to be understood as evidential and not conceptual. Finnis' defense of the moral significance of these distinctions is in terms of the importance of free choice from the perspective of his natural law account of morality.

Can one attempt the impossible? Many legal jurisdictions allow that one can (e.g., attempting to steal from an empty pocket, attempting to kill someone who is already dead). But the issue remains a matter of controversy; a perplexity over it arguably explains conflicting judicial decisions on such attempts. In "Attempting the Impossible", Alan White addresses this controversy. He analyzes the concept of an attempt and suggests that it is indeed possible to attempt the impossible. Attempts, whether successful or not, are doings with intention. An important ambiguity in the notion of attempting (and those of intending, desiring, hoping, etc.), White argues, is that between what the attempt (intention, etc.) is *aimed at* and what it *amounts to*. Awareness of this ambiguity helps resolve some of the legal and philosophical confusions about impossible attempts. For the fact that what one attempts to do (e.g., steal from an empty pocket, kill what is in fact a corpse) *amounts to* the impossible does not entail that one's attempt is *aimed at* the impossible.

II. CONSENT, CHOICE, AND CONTRACTS

The law of contracts has in recent decades been proclaimed dead, or at least dying. The contributors to this section of the volume would each endorse a stay of execution. One of the factors leading to contract law being overshadowed by other areas of law has been the general problem of understanding the nature of contractual obligation and the related problem of determining the content and justification of principles governing default. The three essays included in this section address these issues in ways that make evident the distinct nature of the law of contract.

Contracts fail to cover all contingencies that might arise, notes Richard Epstein, in "Beyond Foreseeability: Consequential Damages in the Law of Contract", and contract interpretation consequently involves addressing matters of uncertainty and ambiguity that could have been, but actually are not, resolved by explicit provisions. While the common law has typically allowed contracting parties great freedom in specifying the terms of agreement, judicial practice with regard to remedies for breach of contract is frequently very different: the view that damage rules are to be viewed as determined by general principles external to the contract itself, rather than as default rules of construction, has become prevalent. Epstein is critical not only of the dominant expectation measure of damages, but of the received understanding of contract damages generally. They should not, he argues, be construed as derived from contract-independent principles of fairness or justice but should instead be understood to be default provisions in the absence of express provisions. Epstein thus wishes to deny that "the choice of proper remedial rules is largely a judicial function." He argues that "damage rules are no different from any other term of a contract. They should be understood as default provisions subject to variation by contract."

From a perspective congenial to that of Epstein, Randy Barnett addresses the matter of remedies for breach of contract from the perspective of a consent theory of contract law. In his essay, "Rights and Remedies in a Consent Theory of Contract", he argues that contract law, understood from this perspective, is part of a larger system of legal entitlements that specifies the conditions for valid consensual transfers of alienable rights. On Barnett's account contractual duties are not derived from those of promise-keeping (and contract law is not embedded in tort law). Rather, they are derived from more fundamental notions of rights and of their legitimate acquisition and transfer. The distinction between alienable and inalienable rights and the notion of consent, the manifested intent to alienate rights, he suggests, are the key to understanding contracts and remedies for breach.

Agreeing with Epstein's view that "the art of contract interpretation requires the application of a general theory of bargaining to particular contractual provisions", Jules Coleman,

Douglas Heckathorn, and Steven Maser, in their essay, "A Bargaining Theory Approach to Default Provisions and Disclosure Rules in Contract Law", address the foundational issues raised by Epstein and Barnett and related approaches to contract law by developing a detailed account of rational bargaining. They distinguish between two approaches to the justification of the default rule in contracts, both of which appeal to what would be a rational, *ex ante* bargain. One approach, the consent theory, appeals to such a bargain to provide evidence of what the parties to a contract would have agreed to; the other approach, that of rational choice theory, understands such a bargain to specify what is rational for the parties to accept (and, with some additional assumptions, what is morally required of them). Without attempting to settle the dispute between these approaches, Coleman et al. develop, with the aid of contemporary game theory, a detailed account of the notion of an *ex ante* rational bargain. They claim that appeals to rational bargains have been insufficiently detailed or systematic to be of much use, and their essay seeks to remedy that defect.

III. RISK, COMPENSATION, AND TORTS

The nature of private law, in particular the law of torts, has always been the source of perplexities. Much recent scholarship has been devoted to discovering the foundations of tort law and the features that distinguish it from criminal law and contract law. The essays in this section address various questions that are central to these efforts.

The notion of compensation is clearly central to the law of torts, as well as to other areas of law and of policy generally. If, as Robert Goodin states, "compensation serves to right what would otherwise count as wrongful injuries . . . ", then the question arises why we may not do anything we like to people as long as we compensate them for their losses. One answer is that some losses cannot be compensated, at least fully, perhaps because their value is infinite or because of problems of incommensurability. Eschewing this type of answer, Goodin develops an alternative account in his essay, "Theories of Compensation". He distinguishes between two kinds of compensation – "means-replacing" and "ends-displacing" views – and argues that certain state policies are impermissible, not because the losers cannot be compensated, but because the only compensation available is the wrong kind given the loss. The first type of compensation, means-replacing compensation, provides people with equivalent means for pursuing the same ends (e.g., an artificial limb). Ends-displacing compensation, by contrast, seeks to help people to pursue some other end in a way that leaves them as well off as they would have been had they not suffered the loss (e.g., a Mediterranean cruise after having suffered a bereavement). The former sort of compensation, Goodin argues, is superior to the latter. He then suggests that it is wrong for states to do certain things to people, even if it compensates them, since the compensation possible in such cases – the second sort – is incapable of restoring the *status quo ante*. Policies that impose losses on people that cannot be compensated in the first way might still be justified; but what cannot be assumed is that just because compensation (of the second sort) has been provided, the losers have no grounds for complaint.

Ernest Weinrib, in "Liberty, Community, and Corrective Justice", understands private law as the realization of corrective justice. Interaction in corrective justice is immediate: there is a doer and a sufferer of a wrong, related causally, as equals. By contrast, distributive justice understands human relations as mediated by a criterion of distribution. Recent attempts to understand the law of torts in distributive terms, Weinrib argues, are consequently mistaken. Equally importantly, in view of recent fashion, he is critical as well of the application of substantial notions of community to private law. It is corrective justice's abstraction from the particular aspects of the parties' situation or character, not any relation of community, that makes bare recognition of each agent's equal standing relevant. Lastly, Weinrib is sceptical of Richard Epstein's well-known defense of strict liability.

The latter's defense of liability without fault is one-sided in its conception of liberty, he urges, and is inconsistent both with the bilateral nature of corrective justice and with the conception of action underlying moral personality.

Causation in tort law is deterministic. The appropriate characterization of the relevant relations (e.g., that of proximate cause) is a matter of considerable controversy. There is, however, relative agreement that the relevant notions of cause are not probabilistic, but deterministic. Probabilities, as Glen Robinson argues in his contribution, "Risk, Causation, and Harm", are treated as evidential and do not otherwise affect liability. Recent cases involving "toxic torts" (e.g., Agent Orange, asbestos) suggest that the assumption of deterministic notions of causation in the determination of liability may be misguided. Without wishing to commit himself to probabilistic accounts, Robinson argues for a consideration of liability based on risk, that is, on the (significant) probability of harm. While he considers some legal precedents for such an extension of liability rules, his main arguments stem from considerations of aggregate utility and corrective justice. In the case of the latter, Robinson argues that the *creation* of risk is the wrong to be corrected in the cases under consideration, and he criticizes the view of others, such as Judith Jarvis Thomson, that culpability is dependent on outcomes. Robinson is critical as well of Weinrib's account of corrective justice and of his endorsement of Cardozo's view in *Palgraf* that risk requires an identifiable set of victims.

IV. PUNISHMENT

Several decades ago deterrence and, to a lesser degree, rehabilitative accounts dominated the theory of punishment in moral and legal philosophy. While many of the criticisms of these accounts were retributive in nature, it would be fair to say that retributivism, as an account or theory of punishment, was not influential. The focus of the debate was primarily upon the ways in which the deterrence theory would have to be modified and amended in order to be fully satisfactory. In recent years, all this has changed. Rehabilitation has to a great extent ceased to be a serious contender among accounts of punishment, and deterrence has become but one among a number of theories in a crowded field. New accounts of punishment have been proposed (focusing upon paternalism, moral education, the morality of threats, etc.), and they are often difficult to classify using the traditional categories. Significantly, retributivism has been resurrected as a serious account of punishment.

The essays in Part IV reflect this new interest in the theory of punishment. Jeffrie Murphy's essay, "Retributive Hatred: An Essay on Criminal Liability and the Emotions", is a defense of a form of hatred as the appropriate response to certain forms of wrongdoing. Building on work he has done with Jean Hampton, Murphy argues that a certain type of hatred, which has as one of its central elements a desire to diminish and hurt another relative to oneself, is motivated by sentiments that are retributive in nature. He argues a case for not dismissing this type of hatred out of hand, as is often done in treatments of retributive (and vengeful) emotions. Murphy's central argument rests upon the idea that if hurt is a retributively justified and consequently permissible response to wrongdoing, then a desire to hurt the wrongdoer is also permissible; retributive hatred can then be seen as a strategy that helps to ensure that wrongdoers get what they deserve. There remains, of course, much that can be said against such hatred, and Murphy concludes with a discussion of cautionary considerations.

It is often said that theories of retribution fail to distinguish retribution from revenge, much less provide a justification of retributive attitudes. In her essay, "A New Theory of Retribution", Jean Hampton claims that Murphy's defense of retribution as involving a type of hatred plays into the hands of such critics of retributivism. Drawing upon discussions with Murphy, Hampton proposes an alternative account of retribution. She argues that someone wrongs another to the extent that the former objectively *demeans* the latter. Wrongdoers thus reveal disrespect of the worth of others. Retribution, in her view, then, is not so much a form of hatred as it is, first of all, the imposition of *defeat* on the wrongdoer: the aim of the retributive infliction of suffering on the wrong-doer-is the annulment of the latter's assertion of superiority over the victim. Punishment thus aims to humble the wrong-doer and express a prior and correct impression of the latter's worth relative to that of the victim. Secondly, considering punishment from a social perspective, Hampton argues that as a form of protection, society's punishment of a wrongdoer is a reflection of its understanding of the victim's value. To some degree modifying her earlier views of punishment as moral education, Hampton develops a novel account of re-tributive punishment as a communicative act designed to show that the act punished was wrong; punishment conveys this message by affirming the worth of the victim.

George Fletcher, in his essay, "Punishment and Self-Defense", is critical of the connections that have been drawn between self-defense and punishment in the recent litera-ture. He contrasts our ordinary views with those of Robert Nozick and others who view the harm inflicted in self-defense as a "down-payment" on deserved punishment. In-voking Kant's distinction between *Recht* and justice, he seeks to explain the differences between self-defense and punish-ment. The former has as its end the defense of the rightful order of cooperation among autonomous beings; as such, considerations of desert are not relevant to justifications of self-defense. By contrast, punishment is not defended by reference to the theory of *Recht*; rather, it seeks to fulfill a requirement of justice, namely the avoidance of the injustice of suffering unsanctioned crime.

It is clear that the concept of responsibility, not merely at its edges but even in its central cases, needs further work. We hope this volume addresses this need, even as we realize that it cannot totally fulfill it. New thinking on some of the relevant issues, however, is never amiss.

Part I

Responsibility:
some conceptual problems

Chapter 1

Can respons;bility be diminished?

ANTHONY KENNY

The theme of this essay is the relation between mental abnormality and criminal responsibility. One particular topic
will be the insanity defence, which if successful altogether
relieves of responsibility. But I wish to devote my major
consideration to the devices which in various jurisdictions
have been introduced to permit a verdict which while not
eliminating criminal responsibility reduces or diminishes it.

At the present time the full insanity defence is under threat
in English-speaking jurisdictions on both sides of the Atlantic, but for different reasons in the different places. When
John Hinckley, having shot the President and three other
people, was found not guilty by reason of insanity, there
was a widespread sense of outrage in the U.S. This has led
to changes in the law in many states, all designed to make
a plea of insanity less likely to be successful, and some going
so far as to eliminate altogether insanity as a separate defence. As a result of what seemed an inappropriate acquittal,
reforms have been made which increase the likelihood of the
innocent being found guilty.

In England, on the other hand, the insanity defence has
become almost obsolete for opposite reasons. A homicide
who is mentally ill now very rarely – not more than once or
twice a year – will receive a verdict of not guilty by reason
of insanity (see Dell, 1986, 30). For a variety of reasons, such
an accused is likely to offer instead a plea of guilty to the
lesser crime of manslaughter on the basis of diminished responsibility. Such pleas are very commonly accepted without

13

being contested in the courts. In one or two rare and spectacular cases they have been refused. Peter Sutcliffe, a highly disordered person who killed a number of prostitutes and others, claiming divine authorization, was not allowed to plead diminished responsibility and was convicted of murder. The verdict in the Sutcliffe case fuelled pressure from liberals for further reform in the law of England, designed to make it less likely that mentally disordered persons will be convicted of murder. Some of these reforms, I shall argue, are ill-conceived. The situation in England is the mirror image of that in the U.S. As a result of what seemed an inappropriate conviction, reforms are being proposed which increase the likelihood that those guilty of murder will not be convicted of that crime.

Most of this essay will be devoted to the recent developments in English law. But I shall begin by giving a summary of the present state of American reform, which will be based on R.D. Mackay's recent article in the *Criminal Law Review* (Mackay, 88–96).

Since the acquittal of Hinckley more than half the States have reconsidered the status of the insanity plea. All the changes introduced have been in the direction of making it more difficult to secure an acquittal by reason of insanity. But the changes made have been of various kinds.

(1) Three states, Montana, Idaho and Utah, have effectively abolished the insanity defence. Psychiatric evidence is allowable only to establish whether the accused had or did not have the relevant *mens rea*.

(2) Twelve states, following a lead given by Michigan in 1975 before the Hinckley verdict, have enacted provisions offering an alternative verdict of "guilty but mentally ill" (GBMI). This verdict may be brought in, according to the Michigan law, if it is proved "that the defendant (i) is guilty of the offence charged, (ii) was mentally ill at the time of the commission of the offence, (iii) was not legally insane at the time of the commission of the offence". The issue is complicated because different states accept different definitions of insanity. Some states, e.g. Pennsylvania, accept Mc-

14

Naghten insanity; others, such as Michigan, accept the ALI test which allows an accused to be regarded as insane if he "lacks substantial capacity . . . to conform his conduct to the requirements of law". Pennsylvania, in its GBMI statute, defines mental illness in a way similar to the Michigan definition of insanity, so that on the same facts an accused might be not guilty but insane in Michigan, while guilty but mentally ill in Pennsylvania.

(3) Many states have adjusted the law concerning the burden and quantum of proof in the insanity defence. When Hinckley was tried, the law in Washington, D.C., required the prosecution, if the insanity defence was to be rebutted, to prove beyond reasonable doubt that he was sane at the time he shot President Reagan. At the present time about two-thirds of the states which accept the insanity plea place the burden of proof on the accused. (The standard of proof is usually the balance of probability.)

(4) A number of states have changed the definition of insanity, moving away from the volitional test of the ALI back towards the cognitive test of the McNaghten rules. Thus the Federal Law was altered by the Insanity Defense Reform Act, so that the defence requires that "the defendant as a result of severe mental disease or defect was unable to appreciate the nature and quality or the wrongfulness of his act". California and Alaska have taken this course.

(5) New Federal Rules of Evidence expressly prohibit expert witnesses from testifying to the "ultimate issues [which] are matters for the triers of fact alone". This limits the scope of psychiatric intervention in defence of accused persons who are mentally ill.

Of these five changes the last three deserve welcome. The use of the volitional test in insanity rests on philosophical confusion about the relationship between the intellect and the will (see Kenny, 1978, 38–44). The usurpation by expert witnesses of the roles of judge and jury has long been objectionable (see Kenny, 1985, 52–62). The adjustment of the burden of proof seems reasonable, and consistent with the law's attitude to other general defences.

Changes of the first two types, however, give very real cause for concern.

The total abolition of the insanity defence is repugnant to any defensible theory of responsibility. In 1953 the British Royal Commission on Capital Punishment spoke of the "ancient and humane principle . . . that if a person was at the time of his unlawful act mentally so disordered that it would be unreasonable to impute guilt to him, he ought not to be held liable to conviction and punishment . . . under the criminal law . . .". This principle seems to me deserving of continuing respect.

It may be argued that the abolition of a separate insanity defence does not contravene this principle since in the relevant cases the mental disorder will render the accused incapable of forming the *mens rea* required for the crime. In the words of Norval Morris (quoted by Mackay, 89), "in the broad run of cases, certainly in those where the special defence [of insanity] is not pleaded, ordinary *mens rea* principles can well carry the freight".

But to restrict consideration of mental disorder to the *mens rea* element is very much to narrow the insanity defence from the scope which it has had in the century and a half during which it has been based in England and most of the U.S. on the McNaghten rules. To bring this out I would like to quote those rules a little more fully than is commonly done.

> The jurors ought to be told in all cases that every man is to be presumed to be sane, and to possess a sufficient degree of reason to be responsible for his crimes, until the contrary be proved to their satisfaction; and that to establish a defence on the ground of insanity, it must be clearly proved that at the time of committing the act, the party accused was labouring under such a defect of reason, from disease of the mind, as not to know the nature and quality of the act he was doing, or, if he did know it, that he did not know he was doing wrong.

The judges added, in a clause which is too often overlooked by critics of the rules, that if the accused labours under [a] partial delusion only, and is not in all respects insane . . . he must be considered in the same situation as to responsibility as if the facts with respect to which the delusion exists were real.

Now the first limb of the McNaghten defence – that the accused did not know the nature and quality of the acts he was doing – will correspond more or less with the cases where *mens rea* will be lacking. For instance, the accused believes he is strangling a snake, when in fact he is killing his wife, and therefore does not know the nature of his act; or he does not realize that throwing a lighted match into a gas-filled room is dangerous, and therefore he does not realize the quality of his act. Accordingly, he may be acquitted of murder or arson.

But there are two other limbs to the McNaghten rules; there is the "right–wrong" test, and there is what we may call the delusional justification test. Both of these deserve greater consideration than they are normally given. The right–wrong test is commonly interpreted in the most limited way, so that only lack of knowledge that something is a crime will suffice for the defence. But even so interpreted, the second limb gives to the insane a protection not given to the sane; because a sane defendant cannot plead ignorance of the law as an excuse for crime.

The Michigan GBMI verdict offers the jury a compromise position between acquitting a mentally ill defendant from all responsibility for his action, on the one hand, and, on the other hand, treating him in all respects like a normal person. I have not studied the considerable literature on the operation of this alternative verdict, but I understand that it is criticized on both conceptual and functional grounds. Conceptually it is argued that the distinction between "guilty and mentally ill" and "not guilty by reason of insanity" is an unclear one. Juries find it difficult, and it does not seem susceptible of being made precise by judicial clarification. In practice, it seems, the introduction of the defence has not had the hoped-for effect of reducing the number of insanity verdicts.

ANTHONY KENNY

While it has, by contrast, reduced the number of guilty verdicts it has often done so with effects which have actually
been prejudicial to the defendants (see Mackay, 92–3).
In the U.K. the equivalent of GBMI is the verdict introduced by section 2 of the Homicide Act of 1957. This Act, in
cases of murder, offers a mentally ill accused the alternative
of pleading guilty to manslaughter rather than pleading
guilty to murder or offering the insanity defence. The English
Homicide Act and the GBMI provision have it in common
that they operate with a concept of responsibility which is
diminished: a *tertium quid* between being held, and not being
held, responsible for one's actions.

The defence of diminished responsibility had been allowed
in Scots law since early in the nineteenth century (Higgins,
10–11). It was introduced into English law by the 1957 Act
as a result of dissatisfaction with the purely cognitive nature
of the tests set out in the McNaghten rules. The rules had
been criticized because they allowed only for defects of
knowledge, and not for defects of the emotions or the will;
they took no account of the possibility of "irresistible im-
pulse". (Similar preoccupations in the U.S. led to the redefi-
nition of insanity in the ALI model penal code.) (See Butler
Report, 18.5–18.6.)

In 1953 the British Medical Association suggested to the
Royal Commission on Capital Punishment that it should be
a defence to a mentally diseased person that owing to a
disorder of emotion he did not possess sufficient power to
preserve himself from committing an act he knew was
wrong. But the Commission preferred to abolish any such
test as the rules, and to leave it to the jury, without guidance,
to determine whether the accused when he acted was mentally diseased "to such a degree that he ought not to be held
responsible" (*Royal Commission,* section 324).

The Homicide Act of 1957 gave partial effect to the Commission's proposals. Without abolishing the McNaghten
rules Parliament introduced a defence of diminished responsibility which enabled the accused in a murder case to be
convicted of the lesser crime of manslaughter if the jury find

18

that he is "suffering from such abnormality of mind . . . as substantially impaired his mental responsibility for his acts and omissions in doing or being a party to the killing".

Since its introduction, the defence of diminished responsibility has become very popular. Many defendants are brought within its terms who would be difficult to bring within the McNaghten definition. The insanity defence can only be established by a jury verdict, whereas courts are often willing to accept pleas of guilty to diminished responsibility manslaughter. Thirdly, a finding of diminished responsibility leaves a judge with total discretion as to sentence, up to and including a conditional discharge, whereas one acquitted on ground of insanity will be hospitalized under secure conditions for an indefinite period at the discretion of the Home Secretary.

Despite its popularity with mentally ill defendants, their lawyers and their doctors – and indeed with many prosecutors and judges – section 2 of the Homicide Act has been the subject of severe criticism by philosophers, by academic lawyers and, increasingly, by psychiatrists themselves.

Some years ago, in a Blackstone lecture entitled "The Expert in Court", I tried to summarize the philosophical objections to the wording of the Act.

> The term "mental responsibility" is a curious one. Whether someone is to be held responsible for his acts seems to be either a legal question – is a man acting in such and such a way in such and such a mental condition guilty of a legal offence? – or a moral question – should people who act thus in such and such mental conditions be convicted and sentenced by the laws? The word "mental" seems to belong with "capacity" or "disorder" or "disease" rather than with "responsibility". In practice "mental responsibility" has come to mean something very close to "a mental state such that psychiatrists believe he ought to be convicted". Because the word "mental" precedes the word "responsibility" the matter seems to be one proper for the expert evidence of the experts on mental health and disease: namely the psychiatrists. Because the matter at issue is responsibility, i.e. whether the accused is to be re-

garded as suitable for conviction and punishment, the expert is being asked to testify, in a case where there is no dispute about the acts and omissions of the accused, whether in his opinion the accused should be convicted . . . The question whether an individual should be convicted should be a question, not for the psychiatrists, but for the jury; the question whether persons of a certain kind should be punished is a question not for the psychiatrists but for the legislature. But a psychiatrist who is asked to give expert evidence when a defence of diminished responsibility is led can hardly avoid giving his opinion on these two matters. (Kenny, 1985, 54)

Psychiatrists who are called on to testify as expert witnesses are placed in an anomalous position because of the wording of the Act.

There are three ways in which experts may usurp the functions of others. They may usurp the functions of the jury, by testifying to the naked conclusion, instead of providing information about the accused to assist the jury in making the ultimate judgement about guilt or innocence. In another way the juridical process is distorted if experts act like judges, tacitly imposing on the jury a meaning of their own for statutory terms such as "responsibility". Finally, experts can usurp the functions of the legislature by testifying on the basis of convictions of general policy, e.g. that people who are sick in a certain way should not be sent to prison. (Kenny, 1985, 52)

Many psychiatrists with long experience of the courts find very painful the position in which they are placed by the requirements of this section of the Act and the questionings of judge and counsel. The position can be equally painful whether it turns into that of extra barrister or thirteenth juror.

But the evil effects of the statute are not restricted to their effects on witnesses. They operate unfairly upon defendants and upon society. To illustrate the unfairness upon defendants Dell (Dell, 1986, 24) offers the example of a youth brought up in Northern Ireland. "He came from a good background, and there was no history of deviance, maladjustment or psychiatric disorder of any kind. He killed, with some premeditation, a person whose behaviour was causing much unhappiness in the family."

Prison doctor, independent psychiatrist, and defence doctor all noted absence of mental disorder, and gave similar accounts of family and social background. But the defence psychiatrist, alone, argued that the facts amounted to a defence against a murder charge. Because of the boy's constant exposure to sectarian violence, he argued, he had not attained a mature regard for the sanctity of life; and this constituted a "significant abnormality...amounting to an incomplete development of the moral aspects of the mind" (Dell, 1986, 24). The jury brought in a verdict of manslaughter, and the judge gave a three-year sentence.

Whether or not one thinks the sentence an appropriate one, it is, Dell says, arbitrary and unfair that the difference between life imprisonment and the short sentence should depend on the chance happening that a psychiatrist was willing to help the judge to circumvent the mandatory sentence – by a kind of help which has nothing to do with psychiatry. She says:

> In this case, for example, there was no disagreement about psychiatric matters, nor about the social background. The disagreement was about whether the agreed findings of all the doctors could amount to a defence under Section 2. And that, as Butler and others have pointed out, is a legal, or more accurately a moral question; certainly not a psychiatric one. (Dell, 1986, 30)

The case cited illustrates the way in which the present system operates unfairly against those who are accused of murder: on very similar facts some will be convicted of murder and be sentenced to life imprisonment; others will be convicted of manslaughter and receive a much lighter sentence.

A series of other cases illustrates an opposite defect, where the present system operates unfairly against society as a whole, by allowing courts to avoid convicting those who, as the law stands, should clearly count as guilty.

These cases are described by Dell, a little tendentiously, as "cases where the defendant was so deserving that it made up for the total absence of mental disorder":

> I refer to the cases of family mercy killing: people who killed a loved member of the family in order to put an end to suffering. Here not only the defence and the doctors but the judge and prosecution, are anxious to avoid the mandatory sentence. In my sample, there were cases where the doctors were unable to find any signs of disorder in such defendants but where they nevertheless unanimously reported that they inferred from the circumstances that abnormality must have been present at the time of the offence ... Thus sentencing in homicide comes to depend on how psychiatrists view the issues of Section 2. In most killings, strong emotion, unhappiness and stress play a part. All can be cited in aid of section 2 ... (Dell, 1986, 30)

Could there be an anomaly more bizarre, asks Dell, than for medical people to have been manoeuvred into performing this sentencing function?

Dissatisfaction with section 2 of the 1957 Act has given rise to a number of proposals for reform. The most substantial treatment of the status of mentally abnormal offenders, the report of the Butler Committee of 1975, proposed a rewriting of section 2. There should be no conviction for murder, the Butler Committee said, "if there is medical or other evidence that [the accused] was suffering from a severe form of mental disorder and if, in the opinion of the jury, the mental disorder was such as to be an extenuating circumstance which ought to reduce the offence to manslaughter."

Turning to the same topic in 1980 the Criminal Law Revision Committee (CLRC) in its report *Offences Against the Person* had some misgivings about the final clause of this proposal and substituted, as a description of the necessary degree of mental disorder, "such as to be a substantial enough reason to reduce the offence to manslaughter". This has since formed the basis of the definition of diminished responsibility in the draft Criminal Code Bill of 1985.

It is a welcome element in each of these formulations that it is made clear that the relevant opinion about responsibility is that of the jury, not of the expert witness. However, these new proposals simply turn the jury adrift in a difficult area without sufficient guidance as to how they should form their opinion. The statute will give them no help; and all the judge will be able to tell them is that manslaughter is what the jury thinks is manslaughter.

It will be open to the jury to draw the line between murder and manslaughter where it is now drawn (so that roughly 90 percent of those who raise the diminished responsibility defence are successful). But it will also be open to them to draw the line on the verge of insanity, so that of mentally disordered killers less than 10 percent might escape conviction for murder. (If juries showed themselves disposed to behave in that way, of course, the insanity defence itself might recover from its present unpopularity, and there might be more acquittals.)

To be fair to the Butler Committee, it should be said that rewriting of section 2 was not its most favoured reform. It thought that section 2 needed rewriting if the McNaghten rules were to remain in force, but it would have preferred a total review of the insanity plea and the special verdict.

The special verdict should remain, the Butler Committee concluded, but not on the basis of the McNaghten rules. A special verdict, it proposed, could be reached in two ways. In the first place, evidence of mental disorder might go to show that the accused lacked the *mens rea* for the crime with which he was charged. In the second place, evidence of mental disorder should prevent the conviction of someone who performed the prohibited act with the relevant *mens rea* if the jury believe that at the time of the act or omission charged the defendant was suffering from severe mental illness or severe subnormality (Butler, 18.17–36).

To escape conviction it would not be necessary to show

that the accused's unlawful act was the product of his mental disorder. The Butler Committee regarded this as unnecessary, since it is difficult to be certain how much of a person's behaviour is affected by mental disease or defect.

I have argued more than once that this proposal is misguided (Kenny, 1978, 81–4; 1985, 57–8). It is rash to proceed from the difficulty of being sure that there is no connection between mental disorder and a particular crime to the very sweeping generalization that mental disorder has a causal effect on every single action of the affected person. To illustrate the radical nature of the Butler proposal, I put forward the following imaginary case.

Let us suppose that an academic suffers from paranoid delusions that his colleagues are constantly plagiarizing his work, and that they are denying him the promotion which is due to his talents (which in his own deluded opinion amount to genius). This will bring him within the Butler Committee's definition of a severely mentally disordered person. Let us suppose that while subject to these delusions he makes careful and efficient plans for the secret poisoning of his mother-in-law, so that he can enjoy the large fortune which he stands to inherit at her death. It does not seem obvious that his mental disorder should excuse him from criminal responsibility for a premeditated murder which has no connection with it, in the sense that the topics of his delusions form no part of his reasons for committing it. No doubt his mental disorder entitles him to sympathy; he would be equally entitled to sympathy if he was blind or had lost the use of his legs; but that would not exempt him from criminal responsibility (Kenny, 1975, 83).

The most substantial objection to the Butler Committee's proposals is that they treat insanity, not as a factor in determining responsibility, but as a status exempting from responsibility. This is a return to the policy of the eighteenth century and earlier, when the mentally disordered were regarded as a category outside the bounds of responsibility in the same way as children or brute beasts. Treating madness as a status rather than a factor has two bad effects. On the one hand, it gives a certified mental patient a license which is not given to others: he knows that there are certain things which he may do without being held criminally responsible, while all others not of the same status will be held responsible. On the other hand, it attaches a stigma to insanity by assuming, without any need of proof, that insanity as such predisposes to criminal action.

If section 2 is unsatisfactory as it stands, and if the Butler proposals for reforming it and the insanity defence are unsatisfactory, what should replace the defence of diminished responsibility? I believe that it should not be replaced at all, and that the insanity defence should be the only way of avoiding conviction in a case where it is clear that the accused caused death with the relevant *mens rea* of intention or recklessness. And I believe that despite all the criticism levelled at them, the McNaghten rules do provide the basis for a workable insanity defence.

There are three things to be distinguished when we apply the judicial process to those accused of an offence, and in particular to mentally disordered offenders. The first is the attachment of a stigma to what has been done. The second is the detention of the offender once convicted and sentenced. The third is the place and style of his incarceration while he is detained as sentenced. In my view it is important to unite stigma and detention more than we now do; but to separate detention from conditions of incarceration, and indeed to remove the third from the courts altogether.

In my view there is no injustice in attaching a stigma to mentally disordered offenders, provided they do not come within the McNaghten rules. Nor is there any injustice in, after conviction, sentencing them to loss of liberty in the same way as normal offenders are sentenced. If the mandatory life sentence were ended, then in appropriate cases the mental disorder could be taken into account when deciding the appropriate length of loss of liberty. Mental illness sufficient to nullify the *mens rea* necessary for a crime should, as now, totally remove criminal responsibility. The only reason for giving a special verdict rather than a complete acquittal is to give the court the standing to enforce loss of liberty on an innocent person who may be highly dangerous if left at large.

But where someone has been sentenced to detention it is not at all clear why it should be the court which decides whether the detention should be served in prison or in a secure hospital. If a convicted criminal suffers from a physical illness or handicap, it is not the court which convicts him that decides whether he should move to the prison hospital, or what provisions should be made in the penal system for handicapped detainees. Why should it not be the same with mental illness and mental handicap?

I have argued that the McNaghten rules do provide the basis for a just criterion to discriminate where responsibility should be assigned in criminal cases. But I do not claim that they are completely in order as they stand and as they have been interpreted. In particular, the rule that an accused can escape liability if he is under such a defect of reason, from a disease of the mind, as not to know what he was doing was wrong is, in itself, an excellent one; but it has been nullified by the confused decision in *Windle* ([1952] 2 All E.R.1) which is commonly taken to show that "wrong" means "against the law". If that is what it means (which is not clear because the Lord Chief Justice's references to "the law of God and man" make it unclear what is meant by "law" here) then Windle should be overruled.

I believe also that greater emphasis should be placed on the third, "delusional justification" arm of the McNaghten defence. It is sometimes said that any case which can be brought under this defence would clearly be caught by the first or second limb of the McNaghten rules, but I do not believe that this is true.

To illustrate the possibility of a case falling under the third McNaghten categorisation but not within the first or second, consider the following imaginary case, suggested by W.S. Gilbert's libretto to *Iolanthe*.

Let us suppose that the accused, a male of twenty-five, had intercourse with a girl of twelve, under the delusional belief that she was his mother; and let us suppose that in the relevant jurisdiction son–mother incest is not criminal, but that intercourse with a girl under sixteen is a serious offence, and responsibility is strict with respect to the circumstance of age. Now would the accused, assuming that his delusion was the result of mental disease or defect, be protected by the McNaghten rules?

He would not be protected by the first limb of the rules: he has the necessary *mens rea* of knowing that he was having intercourse with a particular person who, unknown to him, was under sixteen. Nor would he be protected by the second limb: he did know that what he was doing was wrong, because he believed it to be the hideous sin of incest. However, he would be protected by the third limb because, if his delusion were true, the woman with whom he had intercourse, being his mother, could not possibly have been under sixteen. Therefore, no crime would have been committed had his delusion been true.

There will, it must be admitted, be few cases where the third limb will apply without the second being applicable. But the third test is far easier to apply, and is exempt from the criticisms made against the second test in the Butler Committee's report. In general, the third limb will concern justification: if the circumstances were as the accused deludedly thought them to be, would the otherwise illegal act have been justified?

The most difficult cases where an acquittal seems clearly called for, and yet the circumstances are difficult to bring within the McNaghten rules, are the cases described by psychiatrists as non-insane automatism, such as epilepsy.

In *R. v. Sullivan*, 1983, the accused assaulted an elderly neighbour during an epileptic fit (Hamilton, 15). The automatism of his action was undisputed. At first instance he was told that he could either plead guilty or not guilty by reason of disease of the mind – he could not plead non-insane automatism. The Court of Appeal, dismissing an appeal, said that the special verdict had to be returned if the defendant had "total lack of understanding and memory due to a morbid inherent condition of the brain". In the House of Lords

Lord Diplock said that if reason, memory and understanding were so impaired by disease of the mind that the accused did not know the nature and quality of his acts, or pass the right–wrong test, then the special verdict should be given whether the aetiology was organic or functional and whether it was permanent or transient.

The decision in *Sullivan* was unpopular because psychiatrists are reluctant to call epilepsy a disease of the mind. But this is not just a matter of psychiatrists being pedantically professional about diagnostic terminology, or being unhappy about having their epileptic patients, whether dangerous or not, stigmatized as "insane". Some patients, who are dangerous, can be committed to secure hospitals by other procedures. But the non-dangerous ones are innocent of crime and should not be treated on a par with those who, within living memory, were called "guilty but insane". Sullivan's defence lawyers claimed that he would do better to plead guilty (to assault) than plead not guilty by reason of insanity with the consequence, if his plea was successful, that he would be disposed of by committal to a special secure hospital.

To my mind, the judges are right in thinking that non-insane automatism should rule out guilt. But so too are the psychiatrists right in thinking that non-dangerous epileptics should not be sent to Broadmoor. The solution is not to tamper with the insanity defence, but to give greater discretion on disposal when it is successfully pleaded. The special verdict is needed to give the court the right to commit the innocent to a secure hospital; it need not inflict on the court an obligation to do so.

Along with many others, I have been critical of section 2 of the English Homicide Act (most recently in Kenny, 1986). The criticisms I have made of it have recently been contested by Dr. Ranaan Gillon (Gillon, 3–4). The concept of responsibility, he argues, is ambiguous. It need not be taken to mean a moral or legal evaluation. The *Shorter Oxford English Dictionary* gives, as one definition of "responsibility", "the state of fact" of being "capable of rational conduct". Let us suppose, suggests Gillon, that this was the sense intended by Parliament.

Suppose further that the very purpose of calling it "mental" responsibility was precisely to indicate that it was this sense of responsibility which was intended rather than the moral–legal evaluative sense. Such suppositions seem not unreasonable. If they are made, does section 2 then still suffer from the sort of incoherence alleged by its critics? Surely not. Under this reading the word "mental" as a qualifier of "responsibility" does indeed also belong with "capacity", as Prof. Kenny says it ought to belong – notably, with a capacity for rational conduct. Under this reading, section 2 offers reduction of a verdict of murder to a verdict of manslaughter if the defendant's capacity for rational conduct was, in relation to the killing in question, substantially impaired by an abnormality of mind.

Gillon argues that it does not force psychiatrists to go beyond their proper role if they are asked to assess the degree of impairment of the mental component of responsibility in the sense of capacity for rational conduct. Certainly it does not ask them to do more in the case of homicide than they are already, uncontentiously, asked to do in the case of the voluntariness of a tort, the soundness of mind needed for making a valid will or contract and the degree of mental disorder required for compulsory admission to hospital under the Mental Health legislation. "Given a more sympathetic interpretation", Gillon says, "perhaps section 2 of the 1957 Homicide Act may be judged not guilty after all."

There are two difficulties here. The first, serious but comparatively minor, difficulty is that Gillon's interpretation of the phrase "mental responsibility" as "capacity for rational conduct" is impossible to reconcile with the wording of the Act. The Act speaks of "such an abnormality of mind . . . as substantially impaired his mental responsibility for his acts and omissions in doing or being a party to the killing". One cannot simply substitute the *definiens* for "mental responsibility" to read "his capacity for rational conduct for his acts

29

and omissions . . . ". "Capacity for rational conduct" does not admit of being followed by "for". This is not a mere grammatical point: the grammatical difficulty beings out that capacity for rational conduct is a general state; responsibility relates to particular acts and omissions.

Gillon shows he appreciates this point when he says, in the passage quoted above, that section 2 addresses the question whether "the defendant's capacity for rational conduct was, *in relation to the killing in question*, substantially impaired". But the matter cannot be glossed over in this way. For the second, more serious, objection to Gillon's proposal is that, like the Butler proposal on insanity, it makes mental abnormality not a factor in assessing the accused's responsibility for a particular crime, but rather a status giving general exemption from criminal responsibility.

My essay has been a defence of the insanity defence. It has defended it, on the one hand, against those in the U.S. who wish to eliminate it from the statute book in order to make it harder for the mentally ill to secure an acquittal on charges such as murder. It has defended it, on the other hand, from those in the U.K. who welcome its virtual suspension in the practice of the courts since this has made it easier for mentally ill killers to avoid the consequences of a murder conviction.

The fact that my position is in the middle between the two extremes is not, of course, sufficient to prove that it is in the golden mean. But my argument may perhaps serve to convince the reader that a defence of the insanity defence need not be an insane defence.

REFERENCES

Butler Report: Home Office & Department of Health and Social Security, *Report of the Committee on Mentally Abnormal Offenders*, Cmnd. 6244, HMSO 1975.

Criminal Law Revision Committee, Fourteenth Report, *Offences Against the Person*, Cmnd. 7844, HMSO 1980.

Dell, Susanne, *Murder into Manslaughter*, Oxford University Press, 1984.

Dell, Susanne, "The Mandatory Sentence and Section 2", *Journal of Medical Ethics*, 1986, 12, 28–31.

Can responsibility be diminished?

Gillon, Raanan, "Murder, Manslaughter and Responsibility", *Journal of Medical Ethics*, 1986, 12, 3–4.

Hamilton, John, "Insanity Legislation", *Journal of Medical Ethics*, 1986, 12, 13–17.

Higgins, J., "The Origins of the Homicide Act 1957", *Journal of Medical Ethics*, 1986, 12, 8–12.

Kenny, Anthony, *Freewill and Responsibility*, Routledge and Kegan Paul, 1978.

Kenny, Anthony, *The Ivory Tower*, Blackwell, 1985.

Kenny, Anthony, "Anomalies of Section 2 of the Homicide Act 1957", *Journal of Medical Ethics*, 1986, 12, 24–27.

Mackay, R.D., "Post-Hinckley Insanity in the U.S.A.", *Criminal Law Review*, February 1988, 88–96.

Royal Commission on Capital Punishment, Cmnd 8932, HMSO 1953.

Chapter 2

Intention and side-effects

JOHN FINNIS

The distinction between what is intended and what is not intended but brought about as a side-effect is at the basis of the vast modern law of tortious liability in negligence; it is the focus, too, of the criminal law's long-accepted distinction between murder and manslaughter. As those facts suggest, it is not the esoteric preserve of some sectarian moral teaching, but a morally significant distinction which is intrinsic to practical reasonableness.

But accounts of it, judicial, legal-academic, and philosophical, remain deeply confused. The confusion can be traced to two main sources: (i) failure to distinguish free choice from spontaneity, and rational from subrational motivation, and (ii) lack of an ethical theory clear enough to identify the variety of different moral norms which human conduct is required to satisfy, some norms bearing only on what one intends (and does) but others bearing, in other ways, on what one foresees and thus somehow controls as the side-effect(s) of what one intends (and does).

It would be good to show how several philosophical accounts of modern tort law – notably those inspired by economic analysis – overlook the significance of the intention/side-effect distinction for the entire structure of tort. But in this essay I shall attend only to criminal law. In that restricted context, I shall try to advance a clarification of issues by discussing a newly, though not wholly, clarified judicial understanding of intention and side-effect. One can summarise this understanding in two propositions:

32

Intention and side-effects

(i) one may intend to achieve a certain result without desiring it to come about; and

(ii) one's foresight of a certain result as likely (or even, perhaps, as certain) to follow from one's action(s) does not entail that one intends that result.

So juries can convict of murder, this English judicial doctrine holds, only if they find that the accused intended to kill (or to cause grievous bodily harm). Juries should be directed that he can intend to kill without desiring to kill, and that they are legally free to find he foresaw death as certain but did not intend it. Though they may consider his foresight that his actions would cause death a sufficient and compelling ground for inferring intent to kill, the inference is entirely for them to make or not make, on a consideration of all the evidence about what the accused said and did.[1]

In Part I, then, I discuss intention and "desire", and in Part II, intention and foreseen consequences. In Part III, I sketch some abstract but fundamental grounds for accepting the human and moral importance of the distinction between intending ends and means and accepting the side-effects which one knowingly causes.

I

Intention and desire

The first element of the newly clarified English judicial doctrine is its distinction between intention and desire: one may intend to achieve a certain result without desiring it to come about.[2]

1 Glanville Williams, *The Mental Element in Crime* (Jerusalem & Oxford, 1965), 10, reports that (to his regret) "no English judgment defines intention as involving desire". What is new is the explicit rejection of invitations to use such a definition, and the insistence that juries be warned against such an account of intention.

2 See *R* v. *Nedrick* [1986] 3 All ER 1 at 3–4 (CA per Lord Lane CJ); *R* v. *Hancock* [1986] 1 All ER 641 at 645e (CA per Lord Lane CJ); 649, 651b (HL per Lord Scarman); *R* v. *Moloney* [1985] 1 All ER 1025 at 1027f (Lord

This salutary assertion contradicts the principal academic criminal lawyers and legal theorists of the mid-twentieth century. Almost unanimously, these have adopted *desire* as the middle or fundamental term of their explanation of intention: to intend a consequence is to desire it, whether as end or as means; so, for example, consequences which are merely foreseen as probable, but are not desired, are not intended.[3]

Now the same writers, equally unanimously, go on to assert that the "legal concept of intention" includes among intended consequences all results which are foreseen as *certain*, even results which are in no way desired by the agent. This aspect of academic legal doctrine is the theme of Part II below. Here I wish only to make a concession: that *one* reason why some judges have distinguished sharply between intention and desire seems to have been their acceptance of the same notion, viz. that consequences foreseen as certain are, or count as, intended.[4] That said, however, it seems

Hailsham), 1037c, 1038c–h (HL per Lord Bridge); *A-G* v. *Newspaper Publishing plc* [1987] 3 All ER 276 at 304c (CA per Donaldson MR). Likewise, Lord Goff of Chieveley, "The Mental Element in the Crime of Murder" (1988) 104 L.Q.R. 30 at 42–3.

3 See the analysis of texts in Alan White, *Grounds of Liability* (Oxford, 1985), 72–3; also Glanville Williams, *Textbook of Criminal Law* (London, 1983), 74. This account of intention has been disputed, rightly, by virtually all the recent philosophers who have interested themselves in the law: for helpful discussions, see White, *Grounds of Liability*, 75–82; Anthony Kenny, *Will, Freedom and Power* (Oxford, 1975), 46–69; R. A. Duff, "The Obscure Intentions of the House of Lords" [1986] Crim. L.R. 771 at 772–3; also Michael Moore, "Intentions and *Mens Rea*", in Gavison (ed.), *Issues in Contemporary Legal Philosophy* (Oxford, 1987), 245–70 at 246.

4 Thus *D.P.P.* v. *Smith* [1961] AC 290 at 302 (CCA per Byrne J): "intent and desire are different things and . . . once it is proved that an accused man knows that a result is certain the fact that he does not desire that result is irrelevant". The judgment of the Court of Criminal Appeal in *Smith* was approved, but particularly insofar as it denies that foresight of *probable* consequences amounts to intention, in the Court of Appeal in *Hancock* [1986] 1 All ER at 645a per Lane LCJ. But in stating later (at 645e) that "desire and intent are two different things", Lane LCJ does not reassert that to foresee consequences as certain is to intend them; rather, he insists that the jury must be left to find intention with no more explanation of the meaning of "intention" than the negative clarification that "if you are sure [that the accused intended to cause

34

clear that usually the judicial purpose in distinguishing intention from desire has been much wider: not merely to deal with the special case of consequences undesired but foreseen as certain, but to insist quite generally that "intention is something quite distinct from motive or desire."[5]

In the confused conflict between the judges and the legal academics, both sides are in important ways right. But the truth asserted by the judges is the more important for an understanding of intention. The academics are right insofar as "desire" (like "want") is indeed equivocal – as they fail, however, to make clear – between (i) one's response to an intelligible good *qua* intelligible and understood to be good (whether or not morally good), i.e., *qua* rationally motivating, and (ii) one's response to what, as a concrete and experienced or otherwise imaginable possibility, appeals to one's feelings; and one cannot intend without in some way desiring in at least one of these senses. The judges are right insofar as "intention", "intend" and "with intent" unequivocally belong with sense (i) of "desire"; these terms refer to what is *freely chosen* just insofar as it is *chosen* as an intelligent and rationally appealing option, desirable in sense (i), whether it is also desired in sense (ii) *or not*. One can choose and intend to do what is utterly repugnant to one's dominant feelings – that is the important reality (or the most important of the realities) which judges recall when they state, at large, that one can intend what one does not desire.

(I shall be relying upon these sharp distinctions – between intelligible factors and factors contributed by sense and imag-

death or really serious bodily injury,] the fact that he may not have desired that result is irrelevant." The House of Lords (651g) deprecated even this degree of "generalisation" in directing juries as to intention, and did not repeat Lane LCJ's approval of the dicta in *Smith*. Glanville Williams, "Oblique Intention" [1987] C.L.J. 417 at 430 n. 49, concedes that it is "still unclear" that the judicial understanding of intention extends (as he would wish it) to "known certainties". See also n. 17 below.

5 *Moloney* [1985] 1 All ER at 1037c per Lord Bridge; see also *Lynch* v. *DPP* [1975] 1 All ER 913 at 934e per Lord Simon (dissenting; but the majority decision was overruled in *R* v. *Howe* [1987] 1 All ER 771 [HL]).

ination, and correspondingly between volitions, including choices, and feelings. This may give the impression that I hold a dualistic view of human personality and action. But I do not. All the distinctions are made, for analytic purposes, among the dynamic aspects of one reality, the acting person, who alone is properly said to imagine, understand, feel and will. It may be helpful, however, to note that "feeling" and "emotion" have some unwelcome connotations of conscious experience and intensity. The motivations consequent on sensory cognition, and generically common to human beings and brute animals, are in fact normally effective without one's being aware of them. But for want of better words, I use "feeling" and "emotion"; the unwelcome connotations are in any case, perhaps, less troublesome in the more or less dramatic context of criminal offences, in which these not-specifically-human motivations do usually, even in the heat of "unselfconscious" action, become more or less intense and rise to consciousness.)

The conception of intention used in moral and legal reasoning, properly understood, is tightly linked to sense (i) of "desire" precisely because it is tightly linked to the moral significance of *choice*. To choose, in the relevantly rich sense of "choice", is essentially to *adopt a plan or proposal* which one has put to oneself in one's practical reasoning and deliberation on the merits of alternative options, i.e., of alternative plans or proposals which one sees some reason to adopt – i.e., understands as desirable. Whatever, then, is included within one's chosen plan or proposal, whether as its end or as a means to that end, is *intended*, i.e., is included within one's intention(s).[6] What one does is done "with intent to

6 What I call "proposal" is called by some "goal" or "purpose" – the context making it clear that they do not mean end as distinct from means, but rather everything one is trying to do (considered not as being done but as being envisaged). Thus, for example, George Fletcher, *Rethinking Criminal Law* (Boston & Toronto, 1978), 442, rightly says: "The basic cleavage in the states of mind used in criminal legislation is between those that focus on the actor's goal (willfullness, intention, purposefulness) and those that focus on the risk that the actor creates in acting (recklessness and negligence)." Similarly, the

X" (or: "with intent that X") if X is a state of affairs which is *part of one's plan* either as its end (or a part of its end, or one of its ends) or as a means.[7]

(It goes without saying that "plan" and "proposal" must not be understood as connoting some ponderous or formal process of deliberation. One can form and act on an intention in a moment. But if the choice so to act was intelligent and free, one will always be able to identify the plan or proposal thus instantly and informally conceived and opted for, and that plan or proposal will always be analysable in terms of ends and means. It should also be understood that means are not always materially distinct from ends – for example, when one chooses something for its intrinsic value, e.g. to give a gift as an act of friendship, with no ulterior purpose.)

In sense (i) of "desire" – what I call volitionally desiring – it is analytically true that what one intends one desires. But it remains true that one often chooses, intends and does what one does not desire, i.e., what one's dominant desire – one's strong or strongest emotional desire – is *not* to do or *not* to bring about. The Hobbesian or Spinozist conception – adopted with more or less philosophical consciousness by legal theorists such as John Austin and Glanville Williams – according to which action necessarily manifests one's dominant desire,[8] is equivalently a denial of the reality of free

Model Penal Code's "conscious object": MPC 2.02(2) (a): "A person acts purposely with respect to a material element of an offense when: (i) if the element involves the nature of his conduct or a result thereof, it is his conscious object to engage in conduct of that nature or to cause such a result; . . . ".

7 And one's will bears upon X in a morally equivalent way if one chooses *not* to do something, precisely in order to bring about X (whether as an end one considers worthwhile in itself or as a means to bringing about some further state of affairs). That is to say, there are omissions which correspond to the action which carries about a proposal adopted by choice.

8 Hobbes, *Human Nature* (1651), ch. 12.2; *Leviathan* (1651), ch. 6, s.v. Deliberation (a passage reproduced in Austin, *Lectures on Jurisprudence* [1869], addenda to lect. 18); Spinoza, *Ethics* (1677), Part III, note to prop. ii.; Glanville Williams, *Criminal Law: The General Part* (London, 1961), 36: "Intention is, by definition, the desire that prevails and issues in action." See also Glanville Williams, "The *Mens Rea* of Murder: Leave

choice; choice between rationally appealing, incompatible alternative practical proposals such that there is *no factor* but the choosing itself which settles which alternative is chosen. But free choice (whose reality I shall not defend here)[9] is a central presupposition of the importance attributed to intention in the moral theory which the criminal law as we know it more or less steadily embodies and enforces. Still, even those philosophers who deny that choice can be free can recognise the reality, and something of the importance, of distinguishing between desire and intention, provided that they have a fairly clear concept of *reasons for acting* and *acting for a reason*.[10]

The distinction between desire and intention – i.e., between what is desired emotionally and what is desired volitionally – is not to be understood as expressing some rationalistic conception of human motivation. The central case of action done with intention is rationally motivated action, but even rationally motivated actions are never done – or even deliberated about – without emotional motives as well. In a full account of human action, it is therefore important to distinguish between two aspects of one's *purpose* in acting, i.e., of that for the sake of which, and in the hope of realizing which, one acts. Though such an account is not necessary for the purposes of this essay, it may be of interest for me to digress for two or three paragraphs to sketch my understanding of the relation between (rational) volition and (emotional) desiring in purposive action.[11]

It Alone" (1989) 105 L.Q.R. 387 at 390. (But cf. his more cautious formulation in *Textbook of Criminal Law* [1983], 74: "*if I decide to try to achieve my desire* . . . the desire becomes the intention with which I act" [emph. added].)

9 It is defended adequately in Joseph Boyle, Germain Grisez and Olaf Tollefsen, *Free Choice: A Self-Referential Argument* (Notre Dame, Ind., 1976); see also John Finnis, *Fundamentals of Ethics* (Oxford & Washington, 1983), 137.

10 Thus Moore, "Intentions and *Mens Rea*", at 245–6.

11 The account follows that in Germain Grisez, Joseph Boyle and John Finnis, "Practical Principles, Moral Truth, and Ultimate Ends" (1987) 32 Am. J. Juris. 99–151 at 102–6.

Rational and subrational motivation in purposive action

By "purpose" I mean a state of affairs – something concrete which can exist or not exist in reality. That about one's purpose which makes one *rationally* interested in it is some intelligible good, whether instrumental or basic. Achieving the purpose will instantiate the good which is the reason for which one acts for that purpose. Thus, in going to the doctor, one's purpose is to regain one's health; regaining one's health is a state of affairs instantiating the intelligible good of health, an intelligible good which doctors hope all their patients will participate in, and which is not exhausted by its instantiation in any concrete state of affairs which it could be one's purpose to realize. In short, one's purpose is in one aspect desired, volitionally, by reason of an intelligible good; in this aspect, the purpose, while remaining a concrete state of affairs, is proposed by intellectual, propositional knowledge which commends acting for the purpose by reason of that intelligible good (and ultimately by reason of a basic good, some basic aspect of human flourishing which the agent hopes to share in or to help another or others to share in).

But in another aspect, every purpose is desired, emotionally, as concrete and imaginable. In this aspect, the purpose is just the particular objective, a state of affairs envisaging which arouses the feelings the agent needs to act for it. (Sometimes these feelings are aroused by something linked by psychological association with the objective.) Whereas rational motives motivate toward some fulfilment of some person as a whole, emotional motives motivate toward some fulfilment of the agent's sentience. But though they are distinct from one another, emotional and rational motives are dynamically united – so much so that it is easy to confuse emotional motives with reasons for acting. (*Common talk about "reasons" for action often manifests this confusion*, or want of differentiation.) The goal of some emotional motivation – say, eating a particular meal – can be understood and generalized; one thinks of eating in general as a good, in which one is interested. But as a reason for acting, such an intelligible good can never be more than instrumental, since a fulfilment of sentient nature just as such is not yet a fulfilment of the person as a whole. So eating can be *deliberately chosen* only insofar as it is instrumental to basic goods such as life and fellowship, goods one's anticipation of which renders one's choice not merely instrumental to the satisfaction of feelings but rational in its ultimate motivation.

There are, moreover, intelligently ordered performances whose only ultimate motives are feelings – i.e., whose motivation is not specifically human. For example, a traveller spontaneously responding to nature's call may follow signs towards a toilet. Common speech, attending to the fact that he is pursuing an intelligently guided causal process, will say he is acting intentionally (and "rationally"). But his actions, insofar as they are spontaneous (rather than deliberately chosen by him for a reason, in preference to some rationally appealing alternative such as catching his plane), do not instantiate choice and intention in their focal senses and should not be confused with rationally motivated action; he is not acting for a reason, in the strict sense used here and in Part III below.

Common speech will also say that the signs which our traveller is following are "means" he is using or employing to reach his "end" or destination. But technical "means" (objects), such as signs or other tools, are not to be confused with means in the sense relevant to the analysis of the central cases of intention. Means, in the latter sense, are states of affairs – one's actions and, often, certain resulting states of affairs – which one chooses to bring about for the sake of some further purpose (one's end), and which figure accordingly in the plan or proposal one adopts by choice. Means, then, are purposes. But they are instrumental purposes, adopted for their intelligible appeal as promising to bring about the further purposes. In the paradigm cases of intention, means are instrumental to purposes adopted for the human fulfilment they are taken to instantiate – i.e., purposes adopted, like the means, for their appeal to reason.

The law may have to allow uses of its terms which go

beyond their paradigm senses. It would be futile to object to a judge or jury finding that our traveller *intended* to find a toilet. But if there is to be any *explanation* offered to guide the judge's or jury's deliberations (and wherever there is a question whether someone's intention was *this rather than that*), it must respect the distinctions which are important to understanding the paradigms that give the law its shape, even if they are lost in some of the peripheral extensions of terms.

Intention and side-effects: some interim payoffs

I have distinguished intention from desire by suggesting that intention includes all that is *chosen* whether as end or as means, and noting that what is chosen as means is often strongly repugnant to desire in the sense of feelings and emotion. I conceded that there is no action without some emotional motivation, some appeal to feeling. But the appeal to feeling may often come entirely from the end, leaving the means – perhaps deeply repugnant to one's feelings – with nothing motivating but its bare appeal to reason, i.e., its bare promise of bringing about the end. And even the end may, and in cases of fully intentional action will, have been adopted not *for* its appeal to feeling but for its appeal to reason. For choice, in the full sense, is of proposals which link (a) the intelligible benefit(s) that make more or less ultimate purposes (ends) appealing to reason with (b) the intelligible empowerments (instrumental goods) that make immediate purposes (means) appealing to reason.

The analysis so far yields several payoffs in relation to "side-effects".

First payoff. There are states of affairs which stand to some *technique* or *technical process* as side-effects, but which those who choose the technical process adopt as means (or even, sometimes, as end) and thus intend.

A simple example: A commander orders the instant destruction of a city by nuclear bombing, in order to shock the

41

adversary out of the war or to deter escalation by the adversary. The targeters select some purely military installation in the city as their aim-point, and tell themselves that what they intend is the destruction of that target; "all else is side-effect". But they merely deceive themselves. For side-effects, in the sense relevant to morals (and law), are effects which are not intended as end or means, i.e., which figure neither as end nor as means in the plan adopted by choice. And the plan in whose execution the targeters choose to participate is a plan which includes the destroying of the entire city and very many of its inhabitants, as a means adopted precisely for the sake of achieving the desired further effects (on the adversary's willingness to continue and/or to escalate the war). Intent is determined not by the technical processes of targeting (aiming a bomb, and delivering it onto its aim-point – its "Desired Ground Zero"), but by the more or less strategic plan which directs that those techniques (technical means) be employed to effect the means and thus, it is hoped, the end. The targeters' and bomb-aimers' "objective" is the target; but the tactical/strategic objective is the destruction of the city; the more ultimate strategic objective is the hoped-for change in the adversary's will and operations; and both tactical and strategic objectives are fully intended and in no morally relevant sense are side-effects.[12]

A slightly more complex example: On 30 October 1940, RAF Bomber Command was ordered to adopt a new bombing policy, in which objectives such as "centres of communication" would be selected precisely because they were "suitably placed in the centres of towns or populated districts", and incendiary bombs were to be used with the aim of causing fires "either on or in the vicinity of the targets". On 9 July 1941, Bomber Command was ordered to carry out its night attacks with the double aim of economic dislocation and reduction of civilian morale, by attacking targets described as "suitably located for obtaining incidental effect on the morale

---

12 See John Finnis, Joseph Boyle and Germain Grisez, *Nuclear Deterrence, Morality and Realism* (Oxford, 1987), 92–6, 102–3, 165.

of the industrial population".[13] Thus, even at this early stage of the city-bombing campaign, the policy was one which included the destruction of civilians and civilian housing among its *intended* effects, notwithstanding that both the *targets* and the *primary objects* of attack still remained military (i.e., non-civilian) in a fairly strict sense. A secondary and in that sense "incidental" effect can be a fully intended effect; a secondary or supplementary means is still a means.

Second payoff. What states of affairs are means and what are side-effects depends on the description which they have in the proposal or plan adopted in the choice which brings them about, i.e., in the clear-headed practical reasoning which makes that plan seem a rationally attractive option.

For example: Suppose that Minsk is attacked by British nuclear missiles in retaliation for a Soviet attack on Birmingham, and in order both to dissuade the Soviets from making any more attacks on British cities and to manifest British resolve not to surrender. The British attack may be targeted on military installations and personnel in Minsk (because the

13 See ibid., 40–1. In 1942, the orders were changed again, authorising Bomber Command to employ its forces "without restriction"; their "primary object" was to be "focused on the morale of the enemy civil population"; commanders were specifically instructed that, because the policy now included attack on enemy morale, the rule applicable to enemy-*occupied* territory (e.g. occupied France), forbidding "the intentional bombardment of civilian populations, as such", did not apply to the bombing of enemy territory (e.g. Germany itself). It would be very naive to think that those who gave and received these orders supposed that the desired effects on morale would be achieved simply by moving the destruction of military–industrial targets into close proximity with civilians who would thus be more shocked and depressed by that destruction than if they saw it on the horizon or read about it in the newspaper; or by an impressive and frightening fireworks display. Fireworks displays become frightening and thus morale-depressing only when they are carried out in such a way as to make all who see them fear for the destruction of themselves, their friends and their most treasured possessions. There is no way to make people develop a lasting fear for themselves, their friends or their possessions other than by destroying some of the people and possessions in question. *That* was therefore the relevant though secondary objective and intention.

targeters have conceptions of decency and like to "direct their intention" in that way) and it may well have some significant impact on Soviet military operations. History might (or might not) relate that that particular effect – on Soviet military targets and operations – turned out to be decisive in subsequent military campaigns. But if that effect did not enter into the practical reasoning of those who ordered the attack, then it was a mere side-effect, and those Soviet military personnel killed in the attack were killed not as – i.e., under the description of – combatants but simply as inhabitants of a city which, with its inhabitants, is intended to be destroyed in a terrific act of threatening (and perhaps of "punishment"): that is to say, these Soviet combatants were killed as non-combatants. The intention was to kill them as non-combatants.

Third payoff. Any who welcome and rejoice in an effect of their actions, but who in *no* way adapt their practical reasoning (and thus the plan they adopt and execute) with a view to bringing about that effect, do not intend it.

This payoff follows from the distinction between intention and the emotions which, in one form or another, always accompany it. But, since such bonus side-effects can be genuinely *side*-effects even when foreseen (if they are in no way provided for in the chosen proposal), a full understanding and acceptance of this payoff must depend upon the issue to which I now turn: intention and foresight.

II

The second element in the new English judicial understanding of intention is its sharp distinction between intention and foresight: the fact that one foresees a certain result as likely or even certain to follow from one's action(s) does not entail that one intends that result.

As I noted in Part I, legal academic writers have virtually unanimously asserted that the "legal concept of intention" includes among intended consequences all results which are foreseen as *certain*, even results in no way desired by the agent.[14] I have also noted that it remains rather uncertain quite how far the judges have confronted and rejected this view. Certainly they have rejected the view – to be found "in legal systems across the Western world"[15] – that an agent who foresees consequences as *probable*, or at least as highly probable, intends those consequences.[16] But that was a view long campaigned against by Glanville Williams, yet he simultaneously campaigned for the view that to foresee consequences of one's act as certain, or "morally certain", or "virtually certain" or "practically certain", *is* to intend them ("obliquely"). Still, it seems to me that the English judges, at the highest level, have decided not to encumber the understanding of "intention" with a distinction as tenuous and artificial as that thus drawn between "highly probable" (and so *not* necessarily intended) and "virtually certain" (and so *necessarily* intended) consequences.[17]

14 And not merely the legal academics: see e.g. Henry Sidgwick, *The Methods of Ethics* ([1874], 7th ed., London, 1907), 202; Roderick Chisholm, "The Structure of Intention" (1970) 67 J. Phil. 636.

15 Fletcher, *Rethinking Criminal Law*, 443; but cf. 445 on the "important doctrinal difference between German and Soviet law, on the one hand, and Anglo-American (and possibly French) law on the other. The former systems draw the distinction between intentional and negligent conduct by including *dolus eventualis* within the contours of intending a particular result."

16 See especially *R. v. Hancock* [1986] 1 All ER 641 at 649g–j; likewise, Lord Goff, "The Mental Element", at 43–7. Thus they have clearly, if implicitly, overruled the direction in *R. v. Desmond & Barrett, The Times* 28 April 1868 (that it is murder "if a man did [an] act not with the purpose of taking life but with the knowledge or belief that life was *likely* to be sacrificed by it"), on which H.L.A. Hart founded his view that "for the law, a foreseen outcome is enough . . . the law does not require in such cases that the outcome should have been something intended in the sense that the accused set out to achieve it, either as a means or an end": Hart, *Punishment and Responsibility* (Oxford, 1968), 119–20. Equally clearly, the judges have rejected Sidgwick's claim that "for purposes of exact moral or *jural discussion*, it is best to include under the term 'intention' all the consequences of an act that are foreseen as certain *or probable*": *The Methods of Ethics*, 202 (emph. added).

17 The House of Lords' approval, in *Moloney* at 1039d, of the judgment of the Court of Criminal Appeal in *R. v. Steane* [1947] KB 997 at 1004,

JOHN FINNIS

The essence of the new judicial doctrine is that intent is a commonsense concept which must be left to the jury without any attempt to give directions imposing or even suggesting some special legal meaning of "intend", "intention", "with intent", etc. This being so, it is well to recall how foreign to the commonsense concept of intention is the academics' notion that what is foreseen as certain is intended.

One who hangs curtains knowing that the sunlight will make them fade does not thereby intend that they shall fade. Those who wear shoes don't intend them to wear out. Those who fly the Atlantic foreseeing certain jetlag don't do so with the intention to get jetlag; those who drink too heavily rarely intend the hangover they know is certain. Those who habitually stutter foresee with certainty that their speech will create annoyance or anxiety, but do not intend those side-effects.[18] Indeed, we might well call the academics' extended notion of intent the Pseudo-Masochist Theory of Intention – for it holds that those who foresee that their actions will have painful effects upon themselves *intend* those effects.

Moreover, common morality attributes considerable importance to the distinction between what is intended and what is foreseen as certain. Throughout the Second World War, the British Government felt constrained by this morality to preserve for public consumption the wholly false pretence that its bombing policy did not include attacks intended to kill and injure civilians as such; ministers consistently deceived Parliament by insisting that the bombing of dwellings located near factories was no more than a side-effect, though *admittedly certain*, of night-bombing of the factories and other

entails (as Glanville Williams implicitly concedes, "Oblique Intention", at 428) a rejection of the doctrine that certain consequences are intended.
18 See further Joseph Boyle and Thomas Sullivan, "The Diffusiveness of Intention Principle: A Counter-Example" (1977) 31 Phil. Studies at 357–60 (giving citations to other counter-examples advanced by Anscombe, J.L. Austin, Kenny, B.N. Fleming, and G. Pitcher. Boyle and Sullivan's own counter-example: stuttering as a vividly foreseen and struggled-against side-effect of trying to defend one's father's reputation).

"military objectives". When the commander of Bomber Command secretly protested to the Air Ministry about this sort of deception, and asked the Ministry to stop its public denials that the intention of the bombing campaign was "the obliteration of German cities and their inhabitants as such" and to cease claiming that the wiping out of German cities was only an "inevitable acompaniment of all-out attack on the enemy's means and capacity to wage war", the Ministry refused, and insisted that "this distinction is in fact one of great importance in the presentation to the public of the aims and achievements of the bomber offensive".[19] The distinction in question was, of course, simply that between effects foreseen as certain and effects intended.

Against all this, the theorists of "oblique intention" offer a very restricted diet of unanalysed examples. The pièce de résistance, invented by Glanville Williams and everywhere repeated,[20] is the blowing up of an aircraft in flight in order to collect the cargo or hull insurance, thereby killing the pilot; this, it is said, is a clear case of (obliquely) intending to kill. What should be said?

It is in no sense a case of intending to kill, intention to kill or intent to kill – and adding the qualifier "oblique" is to no effect, save in a jargon driven not by the insights reflected in common speech but by a theory which, as an analysis of

19 See Finnis, Boyle and Grisez, *Nuclear Deterrence*, 42–4. It must be borne in mind that the distinction was preserved only for public consumption: the secret standing orders to Bomber Command made it unambiguously clear, from at latest 14 February 1942, that attacks were to be made against civilian dwelling houses *in preference to* war-related factories; accordingly, for example, the massive and repeated attacks in 1943 on Hamburg included in the planned bombing area *none* of Hamburg's war-related facilities and *only* its residential districts; and the operational orders began "Intention: To destroy Hamburg": ibid., 41.

20 Williams, *The Mental Element in Crime*, 34–5; [English] Law Commission, "Imputed Criminal Intent", Law Comm. No. 10 (HMSO, 1967), para. 18; *Hyam* [1975] AC at 77C per Lord Hailsham; Law Reform Commission of Canada, *Report on Recodifying Criminal Law*, vol. 1 (1986), 20. Cf. Law Reform Commission of Canada, Working Paper 29, *Criminal Law. The General Part: Liability and Defences* (1982), 181–2; Williams, "The *Mens Rea* of Murder" at 388.

intention, has nothing to be said for it. One must immediately add, however, that by a nuance of our language, it *is* a case in which the accused cannot be said to have killed *unintentionally* – for "unintentionally" connotes accident or mistake or lack of foresight.[21] By another nuance of our language, it is also a case, I think, of "wilfully" killing – for "wilfully", to my ear, means not unintentionally. But the bomb's effects on the pilot, though not unintentional, are not intended, for they are no part of the accused's end or means as these figure in the proposal he adopted by choosing to blow up the plane. They are side-effects, in the morally relevant sense.

Compare another aircraft case. Terrorists hijack a plane. One of them is carrying a timing device primed to detonate a bomb in a city; the instrument can be destroyed only by free-fall from a great height. They call for a parachute to be prepared, so that the woman among them can exit during the flight. The steward selects two parachutes and cuts off the ripcord of one of them, planning (a) to give over the dud parachute if the exiting terrorist is carrying the timing device, but (b) *to give over the good parachute if she is not;* the steward's sole concern is that the timing device be destroyed. In the event, the terrorist who asks for the parachute is carrying the device, so she is given the dud chute and falls to her death. Glanville Williams, the "theorist of oblique intention", says (of any case in which a flight steward deliberately gives an exiting criminal a dud parachute):

> it seems clear that, as a matter of law, the steward must be credited with an intention to kill the criminal. He foresees the certainty of the criminal's death if the events happen as he sees they may, even though he does not desire that death.[22]

To me it seems clear that my story's steward (whose practical reasoning has a content overlooked by Glanville Williams)

21 It is thus a killing which is both intentional and not intentional, for "intentional(ly)" is equivocal between "intended" and "not unintentional(ly)".
22 Williams, *The Mental Element in Crime*, 52–3.

manifestly did not intend to kill the terrorist, though he foresaw and accepted that his own choice would certainly bring
about her death. Her free fall and death are side-effects of
the steward's plan to destroy the timing device.

Of course, the steward does the terrorist no injustice; one
going about to kill others is not treated unfairly by lethal
counter-measures. The pilot killed by the cargo-bomber, on
the other hand, is treated with gross injustice; his life is
simply treated as if it were of less value than the insurance
moneys gained by the bomber; the bomber violates the
Golden Rule since he would not wish his own life to be thus
wilfully destroyed by others acting not pursuant to any moral
responsibility (e.g., of defence of self or others) but to desire
for gain.

In a legal system which divides all criminal homicide into
two sharply distinguished categories – murder and manslaughter – ranked in gravity, it is easy to sympathise with
the pressure to assign the cargo-bomber to the more serious
category, notwithstanding that the categorisation centres on
the distinction between the intended and the non-intended
but reckless or culpably negligent causing of death, and that
the cargo-bomber's killing is not a case of intending to cause
death. But the clear-headed way of acceding to this pressure
is, I suggest, to broaden the definition of murder to include
not only (i) killing with intent to kill but also (ii) doing without
lawful justification or excuse an act which one is sure will
kill.[23]

Such a definition would have the same reach as those

---

23 Doesn't this reintroduce a distinction (between certainty and aware-
    ness of high probability) which I said the judges seem to have rejected
    as tenuous and artificial? Yes. But here it is employed not in the
    explication of the key *explanans* of murder (intent) but in an indepen-
    dent definition of a distinction which is inevitably artificial (that be-
    tween murder and manslaughter, as exhaustive and exclusive
    categories of criminal homicide). For the conceptually chaotic travails
    of legal systems which attempt to expand "intention" artificially to
    include *dolus eventualis*, see Fletcher, *Rethinking Criminal Law*, 325–6,
    445–9. For other techniques for defining a class of murders-without-
    intent-to-kill, see ibid., 264–7.

proposed by the Law Reform Commissioners of England and Canada in 1985 and 1986. But each of these proposals involves imposing an artificial legal meaning on the deceptively common-language terms "intention" and "purpose", used to pick out the mental element in their definitions of murder. The English Commissioners define murder (in its main limb) as intending to kill, and they define *intending* an element of an offence as (a) wanting it to exist or occur, or (b) being aware that it exists, or (c) being almost certain that it exists or will exist or occur.[24] They distinguish acting "intentionally" (i.e., with intention) from acting "purposely", which is that subclass of acting intentionally (in their artificially extended sense) where one *wants* the relevant element of the offence to exist or occur. The Canadians, however, select "purposely" as the term to be artificially extended. They define murder as purposely killing, and define acting "purposely", as to a consequence, as acting "in order to effect either that consequence or another consequence" which one "knows involves that consequence".[25]

The strains imposed by these special definitions of common-language terms show up even before the proposed Codes are applied to particular cases. The Canadians, when giving the extended definition of purpose, say that "oblique or indirect intent" extends to consequences which, to one's knowledge, are "entailed by" the consequences which are one's aim. But when recalling this extension of "purposely", on the occasion of defining murder, their only illustration of "oblique or indirect purpose" is of causing death, which one does not desire, "as a *necessary step to* some other objective", which one does desire. They thus give unwitting testimony to the pull of intention's (or purposive action's) true analysis in terms of means to ends, steps to objectives. Meantime, the English Commissioners have equipped themselves with a similarly factitious definition of "intention(ally)", an arte-

24 Law Commission, *Codification of the Criminal Law*, H.C. 270 (London, 1985), 202 (draft Code s. 56), 183 (draft Code s. 22).
25 Law Reform Commission of Canada, *Recodifying Criminal Law*, vol. 1 (1986), 54 (murder), 20 ("purposely").

fact constructed simply by tacking the whole of their definition of "knowingly" onto the whole of their definition of "purposely". Hence my modest proposal: to define the mental element in murder disjunctively, as either intention in its ordinary sense or certainty ("knowledge") that death would be brought about by an act which one does without lawful justification or excuse.

The last-mentioned qualification is needed to accommodate not merely my perhaps fanciful case of the steward and the parachute, but the most elementary and commonplace example of the vital distinction between intention and foresight of certainty: the administration of drugs in order to suppress the pain of the dying with the knowledge that they will hasten death. It is in relation to *this* case, and in explicit contradiction of "the Roman Church's doctrine of 'double effect' ", that Glanville Williams in 1956 first said: "When a result is foreseen as certain, it is the same as if it were desired or intended."[26]

The contrary view, he claimed, involved the artificiality and/or hypocrisy of distinguishing between a doctor who has "in the forefront of his mind the aim of ending his patient's existence" and a doctor who gives the same dose *in order to relieve pain* and who "keeps his mind steadily off the consequence which his professional training teaches him is inevitable" and who does not "welcome his patient's death as a merciful release".[27] Thus Williams manifested the most thoroughgoing misunderstanding of the so-called doctrine of double effect, which in the aspects here relevant is nothing more than an analysis of intention in terms of chosen means and ends. Such an analysis of intention has nothing to do with "keeping one's mind off" the unintended but foreseen consequences, nor with whether one emotionally welcomes that consequence. It is entirely concerned with what figures in the rational proposal (moral or immoral) which one adopts

26 Glanville Williams, *The Sanctity of Life and the Criminal Law* (London, 1958 [Carpentier Lectures at Columbia, 1956]), 286.
27 Ibid., 286, 288.

by choice and which thus constitutes one's immediate reason for acting as one does. On Williams' own account, it is clear that the second doctor is acting "in order to relieve pain" by giving a dose which is "the minimum necessary to deaden pain";[28] all that figures in this doctor's proposal is his responsibility to relieve pain, and the fulfilling of that responsibility by administering a dose calculated not so as to bring relief *by* bringing death but so as to relieve pain. Such a doctor can realistically and resolutely resolve never to intend to kill, or intentionally bring about death, and yet welcome the patient's death just insofar as it is a relief from suffering. This is not a "direction of intention", artificial, hypocritical, or at all.

Difficult moral questions do, however, appear at the margins of this clarity. What if the person carrying the timing device, whom the steward therefore treats to the dud parachute, is an innocent passenger? What if the person suffering agonising pain which could be relieved only by *de facto* lethal doses has years more expectation of fairly normal life? That which is done "for a lawful purpose" may yet be in some respects unreasonable. The law could mark this by means analogous to the category of manslaughter by "excessive self-defence".

That was a category invented by the Australian courts in the late 1950s and proposed by the English Law Commissioners for adoption in England and by the Canadians for Canada. But the Australian High Court has now rejected its own progeny, denouncing the intermediate category as a practically unworkable source of excessive refinements in directing juries who should be left to make a broad judgment, facing only the alternatives of convicting of murder and acquitting outright.[29] No one will imagine that these arguments about the workability and consequent procedural fairness of directions to juries are arguments which helpfully trace the relevant *moral* boundaries, i.e., the boundaries relevant to the deliberations of the upright conscience.

28 Ibid., 286, 285.
29 *Zecevic* v. *DPP* (1987) 61 ALJR 375, overruling *R.* v. *Howe* (1958) 100 CLR 448 and *Viro* v. *R.* (1978) 141 CLR 88.

Private defence and intent to kill

The common law of private defence, as recently stated by the High Court of Australia, departs from morality in another important respect. For, according to the High Court, those who act reasonably in private defence are not guilty of murder even if they acted with intent to kill.[30] But the classic moral doctrine, stated by Aquinas in the passage which is the principal historical source of the so-called doctrine of double effect, is that while private defence justifies *behaviour known to be death-dealing* (provided that it does not go beyond what is needed to protect from serious assault), it does not justify *acting to kill*, i.e., the same behaviour executed with the intent to kill.[31]

Nor is the latter a theologian's refinement foreign to the conscience of practical people; on the contrary, it finds a place in moral thought wherever that is not corrupted by feelings of antipathy or of discriminatory superiority (or by bad philosophy). Let me illustrate popular moral thought in its uncorrupt and corrupt forms, by two examples from the British colonial empire.

In 1854, the legislature of Western Australia enacted an ordinance "for the suppression of violent crimes committed by Convicts illegally at large" – the said convicts being, of course, of the same stock as the legislators. Having recited that "the lives of officers of justice and their assistants, while in the execution of their duty in endeavouring to apprehend such offenders, have been perilled by resistance with deadly weapons", the ordinance provided that when an armed convict is challenged to surrender himself but refuses to do so and instead

> give[s] reasonable cause to believe that he is about to use [his weapon] for the purpose of preventing his apprehension, then, and in such case, it shall be lawful for such Justice, policeman, constable, or officer . . . or for any free person acting in aid . . .

30 *Zecevic* at 381.
31 Aquinas, *Summa Theologiae* II–II, q. 64 a. 7.

by the discharge of any loaded firearms . . . *to disable and over-power such convict, with a view to his apprehension*, without bodily injury to his captor; and in case the death of such convict shall be thereby caused, the same shall be deemed an act of justifiable homicide.[32]

Less than three years later, the legislature of Hong Kong – under Governor Sir John Bowring LL.D., the editor of Bentham's *Works* – enacted an ordinance "for better securing the Peace of the Colony". A key provision:

Every person lawfully acting as a sentry or patrol at any time between the hour of eight in the evening and sunrise is hereby authorized, whilst so acting, to fire upon, *with intent* or effect *to kill,* any *Chinaman* whom he shall meet with or discover abroad and whom he shall have reasonable ground to suspect of being so abroad for an improper purpose, and who being challenged by him shall neglect or refuse to make proper answer to his challenge.[33]

There is, I think, no need to comment on these two lucid provisions.

"But doing X just is doing Y!"

Some will be impatient with the distinction drawn by Aquinas. Some acts, they will say, just *are* killing, whether done in self-defence or not; one who chooses to do such an act just is, willy nilly, intending to kill. Intentionally firing a shotgun at close range directly at robbers just is acting with

---

32 No. 7 of 1854 (W.A.), preamble and s. 5 (emphasis added). Section 6 similarly provided that convicts attempting to escape might be shot by sentries or guards "for the purpose of preventing such escape".

33 No. 2 of 1857 (Hong Kong), s. 11. After being in force for seven months, this ordinance was suspended (evidently on the instructions of the Colonial Office in London) and was replaced on the same date (15 July 1857) by an ordinance (No. 9 of 1857) substantially identical but omitting the provision I have quoted. Ordinance No. 2 remained in suspense until repealed by a Statute Law Revision Ordinance in 1887.

intent to kill them, even if done as the only way of stopping their violent assault. And this sort of claim is made, or at least conceded, by many who otherwise acknowledge that one's intention is defined by one's practical reason, in terms of the desirability characterisation under which one wills the end and the description under which one judges one's chosen means appropriate to that end.[34]

Thus Anscombe, in relation to the fat man blocking the escape of pot-holers (cave-explorers) threatened by rising waters, speaks of a proposal to make an exit by moving a rock, the moving of which will crush the fat man's head:

> At this point the Doctrine of Double Effect helps itself to an absurd device, of choosing a description under which the action is intentional, and giving the action under that description as *the* intentional act. "I am moving what blocks that egress", or "I am removing a rock which is in the way". The suggestion is that that is *all* I am doing as a means to my end.[35]

I interject. *First:* The description under which what is done is intended is not "chosen" as a "device", or "given" as some kind of defence devised to satisfy an examining tribunal. It is settled by one's practical reasoning as an agent, by the intelligible benefit one seeks and the means one chooses under the description which promises to yield that benefit. *Second:* To speak of "the suggestion . . . that that is *all* I am doing as a means to my end" is equivocal, since "doing", like every other term in this area, is equivocal as between the action *qua* intentional (intended) and the behaviour *qua* humanly interesting pattern of movements and results. The "suggestion" is true in the sense that that is all one is *doing intentionally* (reading "intentionally" as the strict cognate of "intention" and "intend", not as the contrary of the collo-

---

34 E.g., A.J.P. Kenny, "Intention and *Mens Rea* in Murder", in P.M.S. Hacker and J. Raz (eds.), *Law, Morality and Society* (Oxford, 1977), at 165, 173 (but contrast 165); Duff, "Obscure Intentions", at 774, 778.

35 G.E.M. Anscombe, "Action, Intention and 'Double Effect'" [1982] Proc. Am. Cath. Phil. Ass. 12–25 at 23.

quial "unintentionally", i.e., accidentally). The suggestion is false if it is taken to deny that one has moral responsibility for what one knowingly causes as the fully foreseen and inevitable side-effect of one's chosen means. But the "doctrine of double effect", properly understood, makes no such denial.

Anscombe continues:

> This is as if one could say "I am merely moving a knife through such-and-such a region of space" regardless of the fact that that space is manifestly occupied by a human neck, or by a rope supporting a climber.

I interject: The doctrine of double effect in no way suggests that one can choose "regardless" of the certain side-effects. One's acceptance of the side-effects must satisfy all moral requirements (must "be proportionate", as it was often vaguely put). That something is a side-effect rather than an intended means entails the satisfaction of one, important, but only one, moral requirement: that one never *choose* – intend – to destroy, damage or impede any instantiation of a basic human good.

> "Nonsense", we want to say, "doing that is doing this, and so closely that you can't pretend only the first gives you a description under which the act is intentional." For an act does not merely have many descriptions, under some of which it is indeed not intentional: it has several under which it is intentional. So you cannot just choose one of these, and claim to have excluded others by that.

I interject again. *First*: It is true that an act will have several descriptions under which it is intentional, even recalling the ambiguity of "intentional" to which Anscombe does not attend – i.e., several descriptions under which it is intended, corresponding to the several parts of one's plan.[36] Thus, one

36   As Anscombe says, *Intention* (Blackwell, 1957), 46 (para. 26): "So there is one action with four descriptions, each dependent on wider circumstances, and *each related to the next as description of means to end . . .*" (emph. added).

who is moving a rock to clear an egress from a cave is, in the strong sense, intentionally (i) moving a rock, (ii) cooperating in a team effort, (iii) clearing an escape route and so forth. One cannot choose just one of these and claim to have excluded the others. But *second*: The "doctrine" of double effect is not about choosing descriptions, let alone just one description. It holds rather that what is *being done* is not settled simply by looking at behaviour, to see what movements are being made, with what awareness and what results. Rather, that is settled by what one chose, under the description which made it attractive to choice (not: the description which makes it acceptable to onlookers, or to "conscience"). And this is not some "doctrine" got up for a special, evasive purpose. Rather, it is the implication of a quite general conception that the one factor which cannot but settle what kind of act, morally speaking, a human act is is the intention with which what is done is done.[37]

Anscombe continues:

37 See, e.g., Aquinas, *Summa Theol.* I–II, q. 18, aa. 2, 4, 5, 6, 7, 10 (acts are morally specified by their "objects"); q. 12, a. 4 ad 2, and q. 19, a. 5c (the "object" of will is the end and the means taken together in the agent's reason's proposal); q. 72, a. 3 ad 1 & 2 (means as objects of effort are ends and thus intended); also II–II, q. 64, a. 7c; see Joseph Boyle, "*Praeter Intentionem* in Aquinas" (1978) 42 The Thomist 649 at 653–4, 663–5. Philippa Foot, "The Problem of Abortion and the Doctrine of Double Effect", in her *Virtues and Vices* (Oxford, 1978), at 21, and Moore, "Intentions and *Mens Rea*", at 261, consider that to analyse intention in the way I do here would "make nonsense of [the doctrine of double effect] from the beginning". On the contrary, the doctrine in its origins (*Summa Theol.* II–II, q. 64, a. 7) and in many of its plausible and important applications depends on drawing distinctions as fine-grained as this. What Foot and Moore may have in mind is that such distinctions yield the result that a certain type of abortion condemned by common Catholic teaching is not an intended killing – and they may assume (a) that sustaining this condemnation is the main point of the doctrine, and (b) that the condemnation depends on the killing being intended. The first assumption is wholly mistaken, and the second quite questionable (see Finnis, "The Rights and Wrongs of Abortion" (1973) 2 Phil & Pub. Aff. at 138–41, though my discussion on these and nearby pages fails to distinguish adequately between the means v. side-effect issue and the justified v. unjustified side-effect issue).

Nor can you simply bring it about that you intend *this* and not *that* by an inner act of "directing your intention".

I agree.

Circumstances, and the immediate facts about the means you are choosing to your ends, dictate what descriptions of your intention you must admit . . . Suppose for example that you want to train people in habits of supporting the Church with money. If you exact money from them as a condition of baptism you cannot say that you are not making them pay for it.

I interject: What is said about this example is right, but cannot support Anscombe's argument against the account of intention which I have proposed. For "exacting money from people as a condition of baptism" and "making people pay money for baptism" express one and the same proposition. So, since intention is propositional, there here cannot but be an intention to make people pay for baptism (as a means to training them in supporting the Church financially).

All this is relevant to our pot-holer only where the crushing of his head is an immediate effect of moving the rock . . . if you do know [that in moving the rock you would crush his head], then where the crushing is immediate you cannot pretend not to intend it if you are willing to move the rock . . . [But] consider the case where the result is not so immediate – the rock you are moving has to take a path after your immediate moving of it, and in the path it will take it will crush his head. Here there is indeed room for saying that you did not intend that result, even though you could foresee it.

I think this attempt to distinguish the intended from the unintended by reference to sheer physical "immediacy" of cause and effect is unsound, a confusion of categories, of human behaviour with human action. I know of no *argument* that Anscombe has brought against her own analysis, twenty-five years earlier in her book *Intention*, of the intentions of the man who pumps poisoned water into a house.

In one variant of the situation, "the man's intention might not be to poison [the inhabitants] but only to earn his pay", by doing his usual job:

> In that case, although he knows concerning an intentional act of his – for it, namely replenishing the house water-supply, is intentional by our criteria – that it is *also* an act of replenishing the house water-supply with *poisoned* water, it would be incorrect, by our criteria, to say that his act of replenishing the house supply with poisoned water was intentional. And I do not doubt the correctness of the conclusion; it seems to shew that our criteria are rather good.[38]

Notice how fine-grained is the analysis which Anscombe accepted as correct: not merely that the poisoning of the inhabitants – which is not physically "immediate" – is not intentional, but that the *replenishing of the house water-supply with poisoned water* is not intentional (because that the water be poisoned is not part of the pumper's proposal, viz. to do-his-usual-job-of-replenishing-the-water-supply). Nothing could be more "immediate" than the known presence of the poison in the water supply: as *behavior*, replenishing the supply with water *just is*, in this case, replenishing it with poisoned water. Yet the criteria for a sound analysis of intention(ality) and thus of *action* require that we distinguish knowingly pumping in poisoned water from intentionally pumping in poisoned water (or: pumping water with intent to contaminate the water supply). That the water-supply be poisoned was, for this man on this occasion, a side-effect.

Anscombe, in 1957, had a final reflection:

> The question arises: what can be the interest of the intention of the man we have described, who was only doing his usual job, etc.? It is certainly not an ethical or legal interest; if what he said was true, *that* will not absolve him from guilt of murder! We just *are* interested in what is true about a man in this kind of way.[39]

---

38 Anscombe, *Intention*, 42 (para. 25)
39 Ibid., 45 (para. 25).

But how can we be so sure that law and ethics are indifferent to an admittedly interesting truth about human persons? Anscombe has not, I think, offered an ethical theory which would show that ethics must be indifferent to such true and interesting distinctions. And the fact that the water-pumper would, in all readily imaginable circumstances, be found guilty of murder in English law only goes to show that murder in law extends beyond its main limb, killing with intent to kill (or to do grievous bodily harm), and includes also, in effect, a secondary limb: doing without lawful justification or excuse an act which one knows will kill.

But surely this is all unrealistic! Surely there are cases where the known physical character of one's behaviour just does define what one is intending and doing! Glanville Williams reverts to this case:

> If an eccentric surgeon, while operating on an appendix, re-moved his patient's heart for the purpose of a later experiment, we should not listen with much sympathy to the surgeon's argument that he did not intend to cause the patient's death, but was quite happy that the patient should go on living if he could do so without a heart.[40]

In an earlier version of the "eccentric surgeon" paradigm, Glanville Williams concluded that "such a case would clearly be murder".[41] Indeed it would. But not because D intends to kill P. As Anscombe has elsewhere remarked, such killings may be more callous and heinous than some that are intentional.[42] The surgeon intends to and does deal with the body, i.e., the very person of the patient, as his own to dispose of.

40 Williams, *The Mental Element in Crime*, 13.
41 Williams, *Criminal Law: The General Part* (1961), 39.
42 As Anscombe and I have joined in observing: "intention and foresight are distinct, and . . . the intention (i.e. the purpose) of harm or danger to the victim is not a necessary part of the mental element in murder. Even without such intent, unlawful acts can be murderous. 'Unlawful' is closer in sense to 'wrongful' than to 'illegal', and the unlawfulness of an act may reside in its endangering someone's life without excuse": *Euthanasia and Clinical Practice: Trends, Principles and Alternatives*, A Report of a Working Party (London, 1982), 26.

Though his choice is not, precisely, to kill or even, perhaps, to impair the functioning of the patient/victim – i.e., though death and impairment of functioning are side-effects – the surgeon's choice *is* precisely to treat the bodily substance and reality of that other human person as if that person were a mere subhuman object. The moral wrong, on a precise analysis of the surgeon's intent, is a form of *knowingly death-dealing enslavement;* one who inflicts death, even as a side-effect, in order to effect such an instrumentalisation of another has, in the fullest sense, "no excuse" for thus knowingly causing death. We should not complain if both law and common moral thought treat this as murder. But nor should we distort our understanding of intention so as to bring this within the category of murder supposed, too casually, to be limited to *intent* to kill (or seriously harm).

III

The distinction between what one intends (and does) and what one accepts as foreseen side-effect(s) is significant because free choice matters.[43] For there is a free choice (in the sense that matters morally) only when one is rationally motivated towards incompatible alternative possible purposes (X and Y, or X and not-X) which one considers desirable by reason of the intelligible goods (instrumental and basic) which they offer – and when nothing but one's choosing itself *settles* which alternative is chosen. Now, in choosing, one adopts a proposal to bring about certain states of affairs. And the states of affairs which one commits oneself to bringing about – one's instrumental and basic purposes – are precisely those identified under the intelligible description which made them seem rationally appealing and choosable. And what one thus adopts is, so to speak, synthesised with one's will, i.e., with oneself as an acting subject; one *becomes*

---

43 For a more detailed account of the issues touched on in this part, see Joseph Boyle, "Toward Understanding the Principle of Double Effect" (1980) 90 Ethics 527–38; also Finnis, Boyle and Grisez, *Nuclear Deterrence*, 288–94.

what one saw reason to do and chose and set oneself to do
– in short, what one intended. Nothing but contrary free
choice(s) can reverse this manifold self-constitution.

And no form of voluntariness other than intention – e.g.,
the voluntariness involved in knowingly causing the side-
effects one could have avoided causing by not choosing what
one chose – can accomplish the self-constitution effected by
the very fact of really forming an intention. Forming an intention, in choosing freely, is not a matter of having an internal feeling or impression; it is a matter of *setting oneself* to
do something. Thus, for example, if one fails to do what one
set oneself to do, *one has failed*. (Of course, one is not committed to the means in the same way that one is committed
to the end. If an alternative and less repugnant means became
available, one might change one's choice and adopt the new
means without any vivid sense of changing one's project.
But many ends are also means, and even ends valued for
their own sake can be set aside without a strong *sense* of
having changed one's personality. The significance of willing
is not determined by one's "sense", i.e., one's feelings.)

The distinction between the intended and the side-effect
is *morally* significant. For, one who chooses (intends) to destroy, damage or impede some instantiation of a basic human
good chooses and acts contrary to the reason constituted by
that basic human good. It can never be reasonable – and
hence it can never be morally acceptable – to choose contrary
to a reason, unless one has a reason to do so which is rationally preferable to the reason not to do so. But where the
reason *not* to act is a *basic* human good, there cannot be a
rationally preferable reason to choose so to act. (For the basic
goods are aspects of the human persons who can participate
in them, and their instantiations in particular persons cannot,
as reasons for action, be rationally commensurated with one
another. If they could be – i.e., if there were a rational method
of ranking such reasons for action – the reason ranked lower
and thus identified as rationally less preferable would, by
that very fact, cease to be a *reason*; the higher ranked reason
would be rationally unopposed, and the situation would

cease to be a situation of rationally motivated choice, of free choice between rationally appealing alternatives.) Thus one who *intends* to destroy, damage or impede some instantiation of a basic human good necessarily acts contrary to reason, i.e., immorally.

But every choice and action has some more or less immediate or remote negative impact on – in some way tends to damage or impede, or blocks the impeding of the damaging or impeding of – some instantiation(s) of basic human good(s). So, while one can refrain from the *choice* to harm an instance of a good, one *cannot* avoid *harming* some instances of human goods; that there will be some such harm is inevitable, and so cannot be excluded by reason's norms of action. For, moral norms exclude irrationality over which we have some control; they do not exclude accepting the inevitable limits we face as rational agents. Accepting – knowingly causing – harms caused to basic human goods as side-effects will be contrary to reason (immoral) only if doing so is contrary to a reason of another sort, viz. a reason which bears not on choosing precisely as such but rather on knowing acceptance, awareness and causation. There certainly are reasons of this other sort – particularly reasons of impartiality and fairness (the Golden Rule), and reasons arising from role-responsibilities and prior commitments. These moral norms, while not excluding absolutely actions in virtue of aspects of those actions which are unavoidable if one is to act at all, do recognise that we have some discretion about *which* bad side-effects to accept. Save in a relatively few kinds of case, where the acceptance of the side-effect is clearly unfair or wanton, there can be no absolute moral norms here. For in many cases, the side-effects of alternatives will be equally harmful to some human goods, or harmful to very important but incommensurable goods.

Very often, then, options should be rejected because bringing about the side-effects would be unfair or unfaithful. The only situation in which one can be, so to speak, *a priori* certain that harmful side-effects are *not* such as to give reason to reject an option is (i) the situation in which the feasible alternative option(s) involves *intending* to destroy, damage or impede some instantiation of a basic human good, or (ii) the situation (if any) in which any feasible alternative option, while not involving such an intention, is necessarily accompanied by harmful side-effects which it could not be reasonable to accept.

Chapter 3

Attempting the impossible

ALAN R. WHITE

Our relations to the impossible have long been of consuming interest to philosophers. Though everyone is agreed not only that the impossible cannot exist and also that we cannot do the impossible, there has been much speculation and divergence of opinion about which other relations one can have to the impossible. Thus, it has been maintained by some and denied by others that one can conceive of the impossible,[1] that one can imagine the impossible,[2] that one can believe the impossible,[3] and that one can intend the impossible.[4] It is also much disputed – and this is our present problem – not only by philosophers, but by both courts of law and by the text book writers on the law, whether one can *attempt the impossible.*

1 Allowed by H. Putnam, 'Meaning and Reference', *Journal of Philosophy,* 70 (1973), 699–711; C. Kirwan, *Logic and Argument* (1978), 242; Thomas Reid, *Essays on the Intellectual Powers,* IV. iii.4, V. vi.2; and denied by Berkeley, *Principles,* s. 5; *Three Dialogues,* II. 125; Hume, *Treatise,* I.ii.2; Descartes, *Meditation* V; G. Ryle, *Concept of Mind* (1949), 75; M. Tye, 'The Subjective Qualities of Experience', *Mind,* 95 (1986), 2–6.
2 Allowed by B. Williams, *Problems of the Self* (1973), 45; C. Peacocke, 'Imagination, Experience and Possibility', in *Essays on Berkeley,* eds. J. Foster and H. Robinson (1985), 35; Putnam (1973); Kirwan (1978); and denied by Berkeley, Hume, Descartes, *op. cit.;* Ryle (1949); Tye (1986); Wittgenstein, *Blue and Brown Books* (1958), 53–4.
3 Allowed by A. R. White, 'Belief Sentences', *Mind,* 67 (1958), 527–32; and denied by A. Stroll, 'A Problem Concerning the Analysis of Belief Sentences,' *Analysis,* 14 (1953), 15–19.
4 Allowed by I. Thalberg, *Enigmas of Agency* (1972), chs. IV and V; and denied by A. C. Baier, 'Act and Intent', *Journal of Philosophy,* 67 (1970), 648–58.

ALAN R. WHITE

Though the Criminal Codes, where any exist, of many, or perhaps most, countries allow the possibility of attempting the impossible, on almost every kind of example of attempting the impossible and in almost every jurisdiction, cases can be quoted of opposing judicial decisions.[5] Thus, attempting to steal from an empty pocket or room was allowed as a possibility in England in *Brown*[6] in 1889 and in *Ring*[7] in 1892, in Scotland in *Lamour* v. *Strathern*[8] in 1933, in France in a 1876 case,[9] in the United States in *State* v. *Meisch*[10] in 1965 and *Gargan* v. *State*[11] in 1968, and in Canada in *Reg* v. *Scott*[12] in 1964; but denied in England in *McPherson*[13] in 1857, in *Collins*[14] in 1864, in *Partington* v. *Williams*[15] in 1975, and in Prussia in an 1854 case.[16] Attempting to receive as stolen goods something which was in fact not stolen was allowed as a possibility in the United States in *People* v. *Rojas*[17] in 1961 and in England in *Miller and Page*[18] in 1965; but denied in the United States in *People* v. *Jaffe*[19] in 1906, in England in *Haughton* v.

---

5 Law Commission Report 102, paras. 2.53–2.84, quotes various Codes and relevant cases in various jurisdictions; cp. G. P. Fletcher, *Rethinking Criminal Law* (1978), 169, note 101; for many U.S. cases, see J. B. Elkind, 'Impossibility in Criminal Attempts: A Theorist's Headache', *Virginia Law Review*, 54 (1968), 20.
6 (1889) 24 Q.B.D. 357; cp. *Curbishley* (1971) 55 Cr. App. R. 310, attempting to assist in removal of stolen goods already removed.
7 (1892) 17 Cox C.C. 491.
8 (1933) J.C. 33.
9 Nov. 4, 1876 Rec. Sir. 1877 I. 48.
10 (1965) 86 N.J. Super. 279.
11 (1968) 436 P. 2d 968 (Alaska 1968); for further U.S. cases, see Elkind (1968), 21, note 8.
12 (1964) 2 C.C.C. 257.
13 (1857) Dears and B. 197.
14 (1864) 9 Cox C.C. 497.
15 (1975) 62 Cr. App. 220; cp. *DPP* v. *Nock* [1978] A.C. 979, attempting to extract cocaine from a chemical substance not containing it.
16 Prussian High Court, Feb. 22, 1854, 1854 G.A. 548.
17 (1961) 55 Cal. 2d 252; 358 P. 2d 921.
18 (1965) 49 Cr. App. R. 241, attempted larceny.
19 (1906) 185 N.Y. 497; 78 N.E. 169; cp. *U.S.* v. *Berrigan* (1973) 482 F. 2d 171, attempting to smuggle letters out of prison unknown to and without consent of Warden, though Warden did know but had not consented.

Smith[20] in 1975 and in *Anderton* v. *Ryan*[21] in 1985, and in New Zealand in *R.* v. *Donnelly*[22] in 1970. Attempting to kill someone who was not there or already dead was allowed as a possibility in the United States in *People* v. *Lee Kong*[23] in 1892 and in *State* v. *Mitchell*[24] in 1902, in Germany in an 1880 case,[25] in France in an 1877 case,[26] and in England in *Anderton* v. *Ryan*[27] in 1985; but denied in England in *Lovel*[28] in 1837, in *McPherson*[29] and in *Gaylor*[30] in 1857. Attempting to use as a noxious substance what was innocuous or to possess, import or supply as a prohibited substance what was not prohibited was allowed as a possibility in the United States in *Commonwealth* v. *Kennedy*[31] in 1897, in *People* v. *Sui*[32] and *People* v. *Gill*[33] in 1954, in Germany in an 1880 case,[34] and in England in *Brown*[35] in 1899, in *Rowsell*[36] in 1970, in *Haggard* v. *Mason*[37] in 1976, and in *Shivpuri*[38] in 1985; but denied in England in *Osborn*[39] in 1919, in *Mieras* v. *Rees*[40] in 1975 and in *Chatwood*[41] in 1980, in the United States in *State* v. *Clarissa*[42] in 1847, and

20 [1975] A.C. 476.
21 [1985] A.C. 560.
22 [1970] N.Z.L.R. 980.
23 (1892) 95 Calif. 666; 30 Pac. 800.
24 (1902) 170 Mo. 633; 71 S.W. 175.
25 June 10, 1880, 1 R.G. St. 451.
26 Crim. 12 April 1877; R.S. 1877 I. 329.
27 [1985] A.C. 560, *obiter per* Lord Roskill.
28 (1837) 174 E.R. 206.
29 (1857) 169 E.R. 975.
30 (1857) 169 E.R. 1011, *obiter per* Pollock C.B. at 1012.
31 (1897) 170 Mass. 18; 48 N.E. 770.
32 (1954) 126 Cal. App. 2d 41; 271 P. 2d 575.
33 (1954) 126 Cal. App. 2d 291.
34 May 24, 1880; 1 R.G. St. 439.
35 (1899) 63 J.P. 790.
36 [1970] Crim. L. R. 15.
37 [1976] 1 W.L.R. 187.
38 [1986] 2 All E.R. 334.
39 (1919) 84 JP 63.
40 [1975] Crim. L. R. 224.
41 [1980] 1 All E.R. 467; cp. attempting to steal one's own umbrella, *Collins* (1864) 9 Cox C.C., 497, *obiter per* Bramwell, B., *Anderton* v. *Ryan* [1985] A.C. 560 *per* Lord Bridge, *Haughton* v. *Smith* [1975] A.C. 476 *per* Lords Morris and Dilhorne at 502 and 506.
42 (1847) 11 Ala. 57.

in France in an 1859 case.[43] Attempting to procure a miscarriage or abortion in a non-pregnant woman was allowed as a possibility in England in *Goodchild*[44] in 1846 and in *Whitchurch*[45] in 1890, in South Africa in *R. v. Davies*[46] in 1956, in Canada in *Young*[47] in 1949 and in Germany in a 1901 case,[48] but denied in England in *Gaylor*[49] in 1857, in Scotland in *H.M. Adv. v. Anderson*[50] in 1928, and in France in an 1859 case.[51]

The courts have not always distinguished clearly between the question whether to attempt the impossible is itself impossible and the question whether such an attempt, if possible, would be non-criminal. Though one could logically hold that attempting the impossible is non-criminal even though such attempts are in themselves possible – as, indeed, is held by those who argue that to do the impossible cannot, since it is impossible to do the impossible, be a crime, and that it cannot be a crime to attempt what is not a crime – usually those who have held that attempting the impossible is non-criminal have done so because they held that such an attempt is in itself impossible, while those who have held that attempting the impossible can be a crime have done so because they denied that it is impossible to attempt the impossible. On the other hand, the distinction is clearly made by those who, though arguing that one can, for example, attempt to steal what is in fact one's own umbrella, attempt to kill by witchcraft or magic,[52] or attempt to have unlawful

---

43 (1859) Jan. 6 Rec. Stir. 1859. I. 362.
44 (1846) 2 Car. and Kir. 293.
45 (1890) 24 Q.B. 420; cp. Using impossible means on pregnant woman, *R. v. Spicer* (1955) 39 Cr. App. R. 189.
46 (1956) (3), S.A. 52 (A.D.).
47 (1949) 94 C.C.C. 117 (Que.).
48 (1901) R.G. St. 34. 218.
49 (1857) 169 e.r. 1011.
50 1928. J.C. 1.
51 (1859) Crim. 8 Jan. 1859. R.S. 1859. I. 362.
52 Cp. Fletcher (1978), 166, for cases and text book writers. He himself seems to shift, because of the black magic example, from taking 'aptness' as relevant to a theory of attempt to taking it as relevant to the liability of an attempt. Similarly, partly because of a shift from expressing the subjectivist position on attempt in terms of the actor's

sexual intercourse with a girl under sixteen who is in fact eighteen, nevertheless advocate that such attempts either not be criminally liable or not be prosecuted.[53] It could also be, though I doubt it was,[54] that the judge who declared it would be asinine if the law made it criminal to attempt to murder a man who was in fact already dead nevertheless thought such an attempt possible.[55]

This disagreement among philosophers, lawyers and the courts, the frequent explicit recourse by the courts to logical argument and such remarks as that of Rowlatt J. in *Osborn* (1919) that 'when you come to analyse it it becomes a little difficult', namely 'to say what amounts to an "attempt" ', all suggest that the root of the problem is basically a conceptual puzzle about the nature of an attempt.[56] I shall, therefore, try to make clear what an attempt is, to argue that it is perfectly possible to attempt the impossible, and to lay bare what I think to be fallacies in those arguments of the courts which deny this.

The two ingredients necessary to, but neither in itself suf-

intent to expressing it in terms of what the actor thinks, and partly because of a shift from the conceptual to the legal problem, he supposes, wrongly, that the subjectivist theory cannot cope with superstitious or legal attempts, e.g. 174 fl.

53   E.g. Glanville Williams, 'The Lords and Impossible Attempts', *Cambridge Law Journal*, 45 (1986), 42–3; Law Commission Report 102, paras. 2.97–2.100.

54   As does Williams (1986), 69.

55   Lord Reid in *Haughton* v. *Smith* [1975], 476.

56   Cp. Law Commission Report 102, para. 2.8, which advocates an agreement of the legal and non-legal use of 'attempt'; cp. Fletcher (1978), 160: 'The concepts of "trying" and "attempting" are rooted in English usage and therefore we should probe the semantic rules that generate the boundaries of those concepts'; and similarly, he adds, for French *tenter* and German *Versuchen;* cp. at 161, 'the source of Anglo-American legal terms – namely the English language'. Lord Reid in *Haughton* v. *Smith* [1975] A.C. 476 at 499 seems to agree, though he considers as wrong the ordinary man's view that one can attempt the impossible. On the other hand, even those who argue the case for attempting the impossible on logical grounds think also that there are general principles in their favour, e.g. Fletcher (1978), s. 3.3.6; H. L. A. Hart, 'The House of Lords on Attempting the Impossible', in *Essays in Philosophy and Jurisprudence* (1983), 388–91; Williams (1986).

ficient for, an attempt are action and intention.[57] In the law the action is the *actus reus* and the intention the *mens rea*.

One attempts or tries to do something *by* doing something else, as when one tries to open a door by turning the handle and pushing, to kill someone by stabbing him, or to cure him by giving him a medicine. That *by* which we attempt to do so and so is the means or, as the courts commonly say, the steps we take to do it. Not to try is to take no steps, make no effort. An attempt to do something is, therefore, itself a doing; it is the taking of such steps or the using of such means. And this doing must be intentional. One cannot try to V by unintentionally, absent-mindedly, accidentally, etc., doing something, though what one does may be an intentional omission, as when attempting to kill someone by deliberately starving him.[58] An attempt may be successful or unsuccessful. When unsuccessful it is still a doing, though it is not and cannot be doing what was attempted to be done. When successful the attempt to do so and so becomes the doing of so and so; the turning of the handle and pushing is opening the door, the stabbing is killing, the administration of medicine is a cure. So the orders 'Try to do this' and 'Do this' are obeyed in the same way.

But whether what one does in attempting to do so and so is in fact the same as what one attempts, as it necessarily is in successful attempts, or different, as it necessarily is in unsuccessful attempts, the two are logically distinct, though both are what one does. The waving by which one tries to attract attention is not what one attempts, whether or not it amounts to attracting attention. Much less is the taking of the wrong path by which one tries to reach one's destination what one is trying to do. One can attempt, vigorously or feebly, successfully or unsuccessfully, to attract attention, but

57 E.g. Glanville Williams, *Criminal Law: The General Part* (1961), ss. 199–200; Smith and Hogan, *Criminal Law* (1973), 191; Law Commission Report 102, paras. 2.14–2.18, 2.69–2.70; Criminal Attempts Act 1981; *R.* v. *Eagleton* (1855) Dears C.C. 515; *Haughton* v. *Smith* [1975] A.C. 476; *R.* v. *Mohan* [1976] Q.B. 1.
58 Cp. Williams (1961), s. 200 note 2: ALI M.P.C. 5.501 'purposely does or omits to do . . .'.

one does not attract attention, vigorously or feebly, success- fully or unsuccessfully, even if one's attempt to do it succeeds and therefore becomes doing it. Hence, the fact that what one does in an attempt to handle stolen goods is actually to handle goods which are not stolen does not show that one has not attempted to do something forbidden, if it is forbid- den to handle stolen goods.

Lord Reid, in *Haughton* v. *Smith*,[59] makes this mistake in moving from 'The only possible attempt would be to do what Parliament has forbidden. But Parliament has not forbidden that which the accused did, i.e., handling goods which had ceased to be stolen goods.' But the criminal attempt is not the *doing* of what is forbidden – which admittedly the accused did not do – but the *attempting to do* what is forbidden – which he did do. What the accused does in attempting to V is the *actus reus* of the attempt, though only in successful attempts is it the same as the *actus reus* of V-ing itself.

But though all attempts are doings, either – when suc- cessful – the doing of what was attempted to be done or – when unsuccessful – a step taken to do what was attempted, not all doings are attempts, even successful attempts. For there may be nothing we can take as a step towards so and so, as, perhaps, when what we do is something basic like moving one's muscles[60] or something which happens to us when we choke or tremble, hope or fear, feel pain or plea- sure. A blind man, perhaps, cannot try to see. Or there may be no steps we actually took towards what we did, as when we unintentionally drop a vase or absent-mindedly leave the door open. Similarly, it has been argued that there are crimes, such as perjury, demanding money with menaces or driving carelessly, which one can commit, but not just attempt to commit.[61] Sometimes too the means or steps we take may be

---

59 [1975] A.C. 476 at 498.
60 Difficulties about the analysis of 'basic' or 'non-instrumental' tryings, like moving one's muscles – on which see, e.g., B. O'Shaughnessy, *The Will* (1980), chs. 10–11; O. R. Jones, 'Trying', *Mind* 92 (1983), 368– 85 – do not arise in the law, where criminal acts are all non-basic.
61 Cp. cases cited in Smith and Hogan (1973), ch. 10, 5.10.

71

so effortless, unhindered or lucky that, as we say, we succeed without trying or don't even speak of trying at all.[62] That *by* doing which we attempt to V, that is, the step we take to reach our intended result, need not be a step which would in fact bring about either the intended result or some unintended characteristic of that result. What one takes *as* a step or means, like what one takes *as* a precaution or a cure, need not be a step or means, or a precaution or a cure. They are, as Hart[63] calls them, 'steps intended' or, as the A.L.I. Model Penal Code 5.501 calls them, 'steps planned' to achieve what is attempted. Clearly, nothing can in fact be a step towards picking an empty pocket or towards squaring the circle, yet various moves can be, and commonly are, taken *as* steps towards these. It is, therefore, a fallacy to argue, as Lord Reid did in *Haughton* v. *Smith*,[64] that because no act can be 'proximate' to what is impossible, therefore there can be no attempt at the impossible. Even when what is attempted is possible, the steps or means one takes may be incapable of achieving that end, as when a burglar uses an inefficient jemmy or a would-be murderer a jammed gun.[65] Furthermore, the fact that what one takes *as* steps to so and so may actually *be* steps to such and such and not to so and so does not mean that they cannot be part of an attempt to do so and so. Not all failed attempts need be due to interruptions of what would have been a successful attempt.[66] We commonly try to do so and so *by* doing something which, unknown to us, will not or cannot succeed. The

---

62 E.g. Wittgenstein, *Philosophical Investigations* (1953), s. 622–3. Contrast O'Shaughnessy's (1980), ch. 9, distinction between speech-conditions and truth-conditions of trying.
63 Hart (1983).
64 (1975) A.C. 476 at 500; cp. New York, Penal Law, s. 110.00.
65 Cp. impossible means to procure miscarriage, *R.* v. *Spicer* (1955) 39 Cr. App. R. 189; Williams (1986), 34, suggests that impossibility for such reasons has never been a defence; but contrast some of the innocuous substance cases, e.g. *Osborn* (1919) 84 J.P. 63.
66 Contrast Stephen, *Digest* 50; *R.* v. *Percy Dalton* (London) Ltd. (1949) 33 Cr. App. R. 102 *per* Birkett J. at 110; *Davey* v. *Lee* [1967] 2 All E.R. 423 *per* Lord Hailsham at 497. *R.* v. *Linneker* [1906] 2 K.B. 99 *per* Kennedy J. Hart (1983), 371 fl., makes this point.

means or steps by which we attempt to do things can be as unsuccessful, in practice or in principle, as the attempts themselves.

There is a crucial difference between Lord Cockburn's tautologically true remark in *McPherson* (1857) 169 ER 975 that 'An attempt must be to do that which, if successful, would amount to the felony charged' and his false claim in *Collins* (1864) 9 Cox C.C. 497 that 'an attempt to commit a felony can only be made out when, if no interruption had taken place, the attempt could have been carried out successfully . . .', which explains why in neither case did he allow an attempt at the impossible. Though I cannot be attempting to reach a certain destination or to square the circle unless reaching my destination or squaring the circle would count as the success of my attempt, I can be attempting these when my attempt consists in taking the wrong path or an invalid proof, steps which could not be successful. When we give someone good or bad marks for trying, we are not necessarily judging how near or far he was from success, nor whether success was possible.

Attempts, whether successful or not, are not only doings, they are doings with intention. To attempt to V implies to do something X with the intention of V-ing; for example, to attempt to kill may be to strike with intent to kill, to try to open a door may be to turn the handle and push with the intention of opening the door. Attempts are defined, not in terms of what is done in the attempt, but in terms of the intended result. Though something must be done in an attempt, for example the door handle grasped or the victim struck, this deed is not mentioned in the characterisation of the attempt, but only in how the attempt is made. The same thing may be done in attempting different things, as when someone makes a certain remark in an attempt to interest one person, provoke a second, annoy a third, insult a fourth, etc.[67] It's the intention with which a deed is done which

---

67 Cp. *Davey* v. *Lee* [1976] 2 All E.R. 423; *Campbell and Bradley* v. *Ward* [1955] N.Z.L.R. 471.

73

identifies the attempt made.[68] As Salmond put it, 'A criminal attempt bears criminal intent upon its face.'[69] To attempt to V is to do something unspecified with the intention of V-ing. In this respect attempting is just a particular example of the way in which what is done is identified not by the action taken but by the psychological characteristic which the action manifests, as in an act of generosity, kindness, malice, jealousy, etc.[70] But this does not have the consequence, feared by some of the courts, that punishing for an attempt, defined in this way, would merely be punishing for an intention.[71] Attempting is not just intending, but it implies it. Intention is a necessary, but not a sufficient, condition of attempting.[72]

Hence, though what is done in the attempt may be, for example, legal or illegal, moral or immoral, this does not make what is attempted legal or illegal, moral or immoral. What I do in my attempt to gain a knighthood may be admirable without such an attempt being admirable; and *vice versa*. I may illegally attempt to murder my wife either by mistakenly and illegally stabbing an innocent stranger or by mistakenly but legally stabbing a corpse or a pillow.[73] Lord Hailsham was mistaken in arguing in *Haughton* v. *Smith*,[74] 'I do not think it is possible to convert a completed act of handling, which is not itself criminal because it was not the handling of stolen goods, into a criminal act by the simple device of alleging that it was an attempt to handle stolen goods on the ground that at the time of handling the accused falsely believed them still to be stolen.' This is analogous to

68 Cp. *R.* v. *Whybrow* (1951) 35 Cr. App. R. 141 at 147; *Jones* v. *Brooks and Brooks* (1968) 52 Cr. App. R. 614.
69 *Jurisprudence* (1920), 346; cp. *R.* v. *Easom* [1971] 2 All E.R. 945 *per* Lord Edmund-Davies at 948–9.
70 Cp. Lord Mansfield in *Scofield* (1784) Cald. 397 at 402: 'the intent may make an act, innocent in itself criminal'.
71 E.g. Lords Coleridge and Cockburn in *McPherson* (1857) 169 E.R. 975 and Lords Reid and Morris in *Haughton* v. *Smith* [1975] A.C. 476 at 500 and 511.
72 Cp. *R.* v. *Linneker* [1906] 2 K.B. 99 *per* Kennedy J.: 'although an attempt implies the intent, an intent does not necessarily imply an attempt'.
73 Cp. hypothetical examples in Williams (1986), 49–50, 66–70.
74 [1975] A.C. 476 at 490.

saying that a blow which is not criminal because it was not murder could not be made criminal by being an instance of attempted murder.

On the other hand, not every characteristic of the intended result is relevant to the identification of the attempt; but only the intended characteristics. Though what is done in an attempt to V may in fact amount to W, the actor did not attempt W if his intention was only to V.[75] Since intended characteristics are known or believed characteristics, any characteristics of the attempt which are unknown to or unthought of by the actor, for example that the attacked victim is already dead, that the picked pocket is empty or that the received goods are not stolen, cannot be intended and, therefore, cannot be part of his *attempt*, though, as we shall see, they are, in one aspect, part of *what he attempted*. Thus, a devout Moslem who is caught in the act of climbing through the broken window of a Mosque is caught attempting to break and enter not only a particular building, but also a Mosque, though, if his intention was only to break and enter a Catholic Church, his attempt cannot have been to break-and-enter-a-Mosque. When, as in peculiar circumstances, one confesses that one does not know what one is trying to do, it is only because one is confused about one's exact intentions.

But though the intended characteristics of what one does must be known or believed characteristics, not all the known or believed characteristics need be intended. When someone in authority promulgates a law or rule which he knows or thinks will make him unpopular, he is not usually intending, much less attempting, to make himself unpopular. It is not logically impossible, however implausible it may sometimes be, that strikers do not intend that innocent bystanders should suffer from their actions, though they realise that this is an inevitable consequence of their strike action. Hence, it

---

75 Cp. *Churchill* v. *Walton* [1967] 1 All E.R. 497 *per* Viscount Dilhorne: 'An agreement which is not to do an unlawful act will not be converted into an unlawful act by the fact that, unknown to the accused, gas oil is used in respect of which the required repayment has not been made.'

does not follow that when in attempting to receive goods which are in fact stolen, because the receiver also knows or thinks them to be stolen, therefore he intends to receive stolen goods and, hence, his attempt is to receive stolen goods. Similarly, because a man who attempts to have unlawful sexual intercourse with a girl knows or thinks that the girl is under sixteen, it does not follow that he intends to have or that it is part of his attempt to have intercourse with a girl under sixteen. A *fortiori*, someone who attempts to V believing wrongly that to V is a crime, for example to have sexual intercourse with a girl between sixteen and eighteen years of age, does not necessarily either intend or *attempt* to commit a crime, nor, if to V is not a crime, is *what* he attempts a crime.

It is a defect of the 'putative fact' theory of attempt that it attributes to someone an attempt to Z just because he knows or thinks that the V he attempts is Z.[76] Such a theory also makes unnecessary difficulties for itself by not distinguishing between 'attempting, in circumstances Z, to V' and 'attempting-to-V-in-circumstances-Z' when it asks whether someone who mistakenly thinks the circumstances to be Z has attempted to V-in-Z.[77] But such charges as attempting to drive while disqualified or intoxicated, attempting to enter without permission, attempting to aid the enemy while a British citizen, attempting to serve drinks after hours, etc. are really examples of the former, not the latter. Whether one, rightly or wrongly, thinks that the circumstances are such and such is not necessarily relevant to what one intends or attempts to do, though what makes the attempt illegal or not depends on whether it was made in such and such circumstances.

76 E.g. Williams (1986), 39, 78. At 61, he seems to assume that one must either intend what one thinks or intend the opposite. At 42 he tries to save the 'putative fact' theory in such a case as that of the under age girl by introducing non-logical reasons. At 81–3 he himself raises certain difficulties in the theory. Similarly, Fletcher (1978), 174, sometimes expresses the 'subjectivist' theory in terms of what the actor thinks rather than of what he intends.

77 E.g. Williams (1986), 80–3.

The legitimate distinction between what someone thinks or knows his actions to be and what he intends them to be also makes it irrelevant to propose that a basis for taking account of what the attempter, perhaps mistakenly, thinks should be his 'purpose', as J. C. Smith suggests,[78] or his 'rational motivation', as G. Fletcher suggests.[79] So and so cannot be either someone's purpose, rational motivation, or intention in doing such and such if he does not think that so and so is the case, though his thinking so and so to be the case does not make it either his purpose, rational motivation, or intention. But it is his intention, not his purpose or rational motivation, in doing such and such which makes so and so his attempt. The role that purpose and rational motivation play here is at best only evidence for his intention.[80]

Nor is it necessary to appeal[81] to any alleged confusion between a mistake of fact and a mistake of law in order to distinguish between the person who is not guilty of attempting a crime when he imports sugar, rightly thinking it is sugar but wrongly thinking its importation is a crime, and the person who is guilty of attempting a crime[82] when he imports a harmless powder, wrongly thinking that it is heroin and rightly thinking its importation is a crime. Neither the importation of sugar nor that of a harmless substance is a crime, nor is it either man's intention or attempt to commit a crime as such, though each thinks he is doing so, but what

---

78 J. C. Smith, 'Two Problems in Criminal Attempts Re-examined, II', [1962], Crim. L. R. 212.

79 Fletcher (1978), 161 fl., who seems to think that rational motivation is less subjective than intention.

80 Williams (1986), 78–80, brings other objections to the motivation theory. Fletcher's (1978), 183, preference for rational motivation may be because he thinks its test is a counter-factual condition, while that of intention is a state of mind. But this is a mistaken view of the latter, whose test is just as counter-factual as the former, e.g. Wittgenstein (1953), ss. 628–48.

81 E.g. Williams (1986), 55–6; Williams (1961), s. 205; Law Commission Report 102, para. 2.98; Smith and Hogan (1976), ch. 10. 3.6.

82 E.g. *Shivpuri* [1986] 2 All E.R. 334, where, contrary to Williams's (1986), 56, prediction, the House of Lords did not reverse the Court of Appeals's decision of guilty.

the latter does intend and attempt is to import heroin and this is a crime, whereas what the former intends and attempts is to import sugar and this is not a crime. Equally the only relevant question in distinguishing the attempt at adult consensual homosexual acts of the man in England and the man in Northern Ireland is that the former's attempt is not illegal. Ignorance of the law can save as well as condemn. People do not generally desire, intend or attempt to commit crimes as such, but attempt to do certain things, which they may well think, rightly or wrongly, or even know to be crimes. Contrast someone who, wanting for some reason to be arrested and thinking and knowing that committing a crime will get him arrested, attempts to commit a crime. Similarly, a man can, for example, succeed or fail in an attempt to break the rules of an institution either because he does or does not manage to do what he thinks he is doing and what would be such a breach or because what he manages to do is or is not in fact a breach of the rules.

But though attempting to V implies doing something with the intention of V-ing, the converse is not the case. This is clearly so where the intention is not also one's purpose. The man who steals money with the intention of returning it before the theft is discovered is not thereby attempting to return the money, nor is the traveller who goes to Australia with the intention of returning in a month's time thereby attempting to return within the month. Even where one's intention and one's purpose coincide, the thief who steals the money with the intention and for the purpose of buying a car is not thereby attempting to buy a car, nor is the traveller who visits Australia with the intention and for the purpose of seeing his grandchildren thereby attempting to see them, nor is he who loiters, who buys or who possesses the appropriate articles, with intent to burgle, thereby attempting to burgle. What one does preparatory to, in preparation for, for the purpose of, or even with the intention of, V-ing is not necessarily a part of an attempt to V.[83] Hence, the 'in-

83   As the Law Commission Report 102, paras. 2.30–2.37, recognized. Cp.

tended steps' theory, even coupled with an intention for a goal, is not sufficient to categorise an attempt.[84] Nor do any of the oft suggested tests of 'substantial', 'unequivocal' or 'proximate' steps seem to do the job.[85] I suggest, therefore, the logical-linguistic criterion that what one does with the intention of V-ing must, in order to be an attempt, be something describable as that *by* which one attempts to V, where 'by' signifies a believed in causal link between the steps and the intended result.[86] One's action must be such that *thereby* one attempts to V. Whether in a given case one is *by* X-ing attempting to V might, as the Law Commission Report 102 recommends, be in the courts left to the jury as a question of fact.

Our interest, both inside and outside the law, in attempts is usually only in unsuccessful attempts, since an interest in a successful attempt would be identical with an interest in the accomplished deed. A successfully attempted crime would be the crime itself. Yet it is a logical mistake to assert that an attempt implies a failure[87] or that successful attempts are only called 'attempts' when the actor is doubtful of success.[88]

Unsuccessful attempts may have either possible or impos-

R. v. *Eagleton* (1855) Dears C.C. 515; R. v. *Taylor* (1859) F. and F. 511; R. v. *Robinson* (1915) 2 K.B. 342; *Comer* v. *Bloomfield* (1970) 55 Cr. App. R. 305; *People* v. *Rizzo* 264 N.Y. 334; 158 N.E. 888 (1927). Contrast *Dugdale* (1853) 118 E.R. 499; *Roberts* (1855) 169 E.R. 836. Fletcher (1978), 167, seems, wrongly, to think that the difference between preparation and attempt 'dissolves' into a question of intent.

84   Suggested by Hart (1983), 373 and *passim*.
85   Cp. the examination and criticisms of these by Law Commission Report 102, paras. 219–2.49, though they plump in the end (para. 2.86) for 'sufficiently proximate'; cp. Williams (1961), ss. 201–4; Fletcher (1978), s. 3.3.2.
86   O'Shaughnessy (1980), ch. 12, suggests that trying is 'the immediate act-expression of a desire to act'. But, firstly, one need no more desire to do what one tries to do than one need desire to do what one does. Secondly, what one does with a desire to do so and so may be a preparation for doing so and so, not a trying to do it.
87   J. Hall, *General Principles of Criminal Law* (1947), 577; Fletcher (1978), s. 3.3; *Commonwealth* v. *Crow* (1931) 303 Pa. 91.
88   E.g. O'Shaughnessy (1980), 43.

sible goals. When the goal is possible, they may be unsuccessful because the means are insufficient, as when I try to poison someone but I use an innocuous substance, or because my use of the means is inefficient, as when I try to shoot someone but my marksmanship is poor, or because of some deficiency in the actor, as when I try to lift a rock which is too heavy for me, or because my efforts are interrupted or frustrated, as when someone interferes while I am trying to do so and so. When the goal is circumstantially or logically impossible, it will be because of some self-contradiction in the defined goal, as when scientists try to square the circle or build a perpetual motion machine or the accused tries to steal his own umbrella, pick an empty pocket or kill someone already dead, or when anyone tries to make water run uphill or stop the ageing process. An impossible goal also arises when there is a contradiction between it and its means, as when one tries to turn on the light though the switch is disconnected, to poison with an innocuous substance or to kill by shooting with an unloaded gun.

Both the possibility and the actuality of attempting the impossible are shown not only from such common examples, but also from our normal idioms. As well as instancing mathematicians who have tried to square the circle, scientists who have tried to build a perpetual motion machine and Sisyphus who was condemned to eternal attempts to roll a stone to the summit of a hill, we often know about the efforts of others and come to realise about our own that what they are attempting is impossible. It is a common part of the learning process to find out not only what can and cannot be done, but also what steps can and cannot succeed by trying to do it and by trying out these steps. Testing is a type of trying. We convince others that they cannot do what they think they can by inviting them to try to do it just as the paralysed man discovers he is paralysed by trying to move his limbs. Among the many of us who try and don't succeed, there are some who can't succeed.

We can try or think worth trying what we also think is almost certain to fail. Furthermore, we do sometimes say, perhaps in order to please or show willingness, such things as 'I will try it, though I know it won't work' or 'I will try it on, though I know it won't fit', and even, perhaps because of convention, make attempts to escape which we know won't succeed; yet it seems that we cannot genuinely try to do what we know or even think to be impossible.[89] The impossibility of attempts is connected with their steps and their achievement, not with their intention.

The difference between an impossible goal such as squaring the circle or building a perpetual motion machine and an impossible goal such as picking an empty pocket or killing someone already dead alerts us to a crucial difference between what someone's attempt is and what he is attempting to do analogous to the difference between someone's intention, desire, hope, etc. and what he intends, desires, hopes, etc. This difference is disguised by an ambiguity in such a phrase as 'what he attempts, intends, desires, hopes, etc.' between expressing, on the one hand, what his attempt, intention, desire or hope is aimed at and, on the other, what his attempt, intention, desire or hope amounts to. An attempt, intention, desire or hope is defined in terms of what the attempt, intention, desire or hope is aimed at, not in terms of what it amounts to. Thus, my attempt and what, in one sense, I attempt is to open the door, my intention and what I intend is to give up smoking, my desire and what I desire is an interesting well paid job, my hope and what I hope for is a happy retirement.

An important consequence of this is that what someone attempts (intends, desires or hopes) may be judged differently depending on whether it is what his attempt (intention, etc.) is aimed at or what his attempt (intention, etc.) amounts to which is being judged. It is this ambiguity in 'what he attempts (intends, etc.)' which explains our wish both to accept and deny that if what someone attempts (intends, etc.) is to V and to V is, quite unknown to him, W, then

89 E.g. S. Hampshire, *Thought and Action* (1959), 134; contrast Thalberg (1972), ch. V.

ALAN R. WHITE

what he attempts (intends, etc.) is W. We feel inclined to deny, for example, that if we attempt to pick a pocket and the pocket is empty, what we are attempting is to pick an empty pocket, because that was not our attempt, that is what our attempt was aimed at. So Hamlet attempted, successfully, to kill the man behind the arras, but, though he did kill Polonius, he was not attempting to kill Polonius. If, as everyone agrees, an intention to V is necessary for an attempt to V, we must deny that our attempt can include any unintended characteristics of what we do. Yet we also feel inclined to accept that if the pocket was empty what we were doing was attempting to pick an empty pocket. So one philosopher, who has written extensively about trying, has argued that, if someone intending to ring and thinking that he is ringing bell number six in fact presses the adjacent bell number four, then he is trying to ring number four.[90] And was not our Moslem intruder trying to break and enter a Mosque? If I stab a disguised figure, thinking it is my wife's lover, when in fact it is my wife, my attempt, what my attempt is aimed at, is to kill a man, since that is my intention; but what I am in fact attempting, and may be stopped in the act of, as an observer might put it, is to kill a woman. On occasion of doing something I may protest that I was only trying to help, though I realise now that what I was trying to do may be harmful. Similarly, someone may not intend to do anything dangerous, illegal, hurtful or with fatal consequences, yet what he intends to do may be all of these; he may not desire to do anything risky, arduous or time-consuming, yet what he desires to do may be just this; he may hope for something rewarding, lasting and beneficial, yet what he hopes for may be unrewarding, ephemeral and harmful. I may be looking for a man without a beard, though the particular man I am looking for now has a beard. It is this ambiguity which led Rowlatt J. in *Osborn* (1919)[91] to say,

90 O'Shaughnessy (1980), II.84.
91 (1919) 84 J.P. 63 at 64; contrast *D.P.P.* v. *Morgan* [1975] 2 All E.R. 347 *per* Lord Simon of Glaisdale at 363: ' "an intention to have sexual intercourse with a woman without her consent" is ambiguous. It can

in what Smith and Hogan regard as a defensible conclusion,[92] 'If the thing was not noxious though he thought it was, he did not attempt to administer a noxious thing by administering the innocuous thing.'

This ambiguity also accounts for the fact that the actor not only thinks, but knows, what it is he is attempting (intends, desires, hopes) to do in the sense that he knows what his attempt (intention, etc.) is, that is, what it is aimed at, but does not necessarily know all the characteristics which what he is attempting, intends, etc. possesses, that is, what it amounts to. Hence the actor's description of 'what he attempts' etc., though perfectly correct, can be different from or even inconsistent with an observer's perfectly correct description of what the actor attempts, intends, etc.[93]

This ambiguity in 'what he attempts (intends, desires, hopes)' can be displayed in terms well-known to logicians as that between 'He attempts (intends, etc.) something-with-such-and-such-a-characteristic' and 'There is something which he attempts (intends, desires, etc.), and it has such and such a characteristic.' Though he attempts (intends, etc.) to pick a pocket which is in fact empty, to kill a man who is in fact dead, to administer a substance which is in fact innocuous, his attempt (intention, etc.) was merely to pick a (non-empty) pocket, kill a (live) man, administer a (noxious) substance. On the other hand, for the scientist who attempts

denote either, first, an intention to have intercourse with a woman who is not in fact consenting to it . . . or, secondly, it can mean an intention to have sexual intercourse with a woman with knowledge that she is not consenting to it (or reckless as to whether or not she is consenting).'

92 *Smith and Hogan* (1973), 205.
93 I think Williams (1986), 36, is making this point in his distinction between 'attempting to handle what one thinks to be stolen goods' and 'attempting to handle goods when they are stolen'. Fletcher's (1978), 150 fl., 'theory of aptness' seems to depend rather arbitrarily on distinguishing not between the actor's intended act and the act's actual qualities, but between qualities within the act itself, so that, e.g., whether one is attempting to rape when the victim is thought to be alive but is in fact dead is made to depend on whether or not the attempt takes place in a funeral parlour.

(intends, etc.) to square the circle or build a perpetual motion machine and for the man who attempts to poison by sugar or to make water run uphill, his attempt (intention, etc.), that is, what his attempt is aimed at, and what his attempt (intention, etc.) amounts to, coincide, for example to square a circle or poison by sugar.

The prime importance of this distinction is that the fact that what one attempts (intends, desires, hopes) to do amounts to the impossible – and, therefore, in one sense one is attempting (intends, etc.) to do the impossible – does not imply that one's attempt (intention, etc.) is aimed at the impossible – and, therefore, does not imply that, in another sense, one is attempting (intends, etc.) the impossible. Those courts and those text book writers who take what Fletcher[94] calls an 'objectivist' and Williams[95] calls an 'actual fact' theory of attempt count as the accused's attempt what the attempt amounts to, while those who take what Fletcher calls a 'subjectivist' and Williams a 'putative fact' theory count as the attempt what it was aimed at. Each is emphasizing a different aspect of 'what is attempted'. They are not, despite what is commonly thought, giving rival theories of attempt.

Another distinction of importance for our problem is this. Though for any characteristic X it is tautologically true that it is not-X *to do* what it is not-X *to do* and tautologically true that it is not-X *to attempt (intend, desire, hope) to do* what it is not-X *to attempt (attempt, intend, desire, hope) to do*, it does not follow, and indeed is not always true, that it is not-X *to attempt (intend, desire, hope) to do* what it is not-X *to do*. Thus, there is no logical rule that it should be impossible to attempt (intend, etc.) to do what it is impossible to do or that an attempt to do so and so should be non-existent just because doing so and so is non-existent, any more than that it should be difficult, uncommon, unusual, to attempt (intend, etc.) to do what it is difficult, uncommon, unusual to do. It need not, for example, be unusual and uncommon to attempt (in-

94 Fletcher (1978), 138 fl.
95 Williams (1986), 36.

tend, etc.) to climb Mount Everest, though it is unusual and uncommon to climb it. It may be easy to attempt (intend, etc.) to avoid someone whom it is not easy to avoid. Similarly, it can be quite possible – and indeed not uncommon – to attempt (intend, etc.) to square the circle, build a perpetual motion machine or poison someone with sugar, though none of these is possible to do. Equally, it can be quite possible – and, indeed, not uncommon – to attempt (intend, etc.) to do something which, though possible under one description of it as your attempt (intention, etc.), for example picking a pocket or killing a man, is impossible under the description of what it in fact is, for example picking an empty pocket or killing a corpse. The fact that I cannot kill a man who is already dead, pick a pocket which is empty, take what is not there or scale a mountain which is unscalable is no reason why I cannot attempt to do these. Detective stories and films commonly feature someone attempting to arouse an apparently sleeping man who is in fact dead. Hence Lord Cockburn was mistaken in saying in *Collins*,[96] 'No larceny would have been committed and therefore no attempt to commit larceny could have been committed.'

For the same reason, whether or not it is true that it is moral or immoral, legal or illegal, a crime or not a crime to try to do what is moral or immoral, legal or illegal, a crime or not a crime, it is not a necessary truth. There cannot be an attempt to commit such an offence as careless driving; and, though an intention to inflict grievous bodily harm is sufficient *mens rea* for murder, it is not sufficient for attempted murder.[97] Furthermore, it is a matter for legal debate whether it should be an offence to attempt to commit a summary offence,[98] whether, if an offence is strictly liable, an attempted offence should be strictly liable,[99] or whether one should be

96 (1864) 9 Cox C.C. 497 at 499. Hart (1983), 377–8, seems to confuse this fallacy with another which the judge made, namely that if stealing X implies X, then an attempt to steal X implies X. This is the intentional fallacy.
97 E.g. *R. v. Whybrow* (1951) 35 Cr. App. R. 141 *per* Lord Goddard.
98 Cp. Law Commission Report 102, paras. 2.102 and 2.105.
99 *R. v. Mohan* [1970] Q.B. 1.

85

vicariously liable for someone else's attempt to commit an offence for which one can be vicariously liable.[100] Conversely, it may be criminal to conspire to do something which is not itself criminal.[101]

Even if it is good or bad to attempt to do what is good or bad, it is generally agreed that it is not as good or bad as actually doing what is good or bad. So the law frequently punishes attempted offences less than completed offences, just as we generally praise and reward failed attempts to do what is good less than successful attempts. Some people who stick pins into wax images of their enemies are undoubtedly trying to kill them, but the law does not usually hold them liable for attempted murder, though killing one's enemies by sticking pins into their wax images, if it were possible, would be murder.[102]

Whether attempts to commit what is in fact a crime, which, for whatever reason, are impossible of success, should be criminally liable is not a purely conceptual question, but an evaluative one about, for example, the relative importance of punishing dangerous people or dangerous deeds.[103] It is not a question about which I am competent to say or wish to say anything.

100 Law Commission Report 102, para. 2.118; *Gardner* v. *Akeroyd* [1952] 2 Q.B. 743 *obiter per* Lord Goddard.
101 E.g. *R.* v. *DeBerenger and Others* (1814) 3 M and S 67, *Quinn* v. *Leathem* [1901] A.C. 495, *Shaw* v. *D.P.P.* [1962] A.C. 220.
102 In *Att. Gen.* v. *Sillem* (1863) 159 E.R. 178 at 221, it was held there was no attempt.
103 Fletcher (1978), s. 3.3.6; Hart (1983), 388–91; cp. Lord Hailsham in *Haughton* v. *Smith* [1975] A.C. 476 at 497; Law Commission Report 102, para. 129; J. Temkin, 'Impossible Attempts – Another View', *Modern Law Review*, 39 (1976), 55; M. S. Rowell, 'Impossible Attempts – An Alternative Solution', *New Law Journal*, 128 (1978), 716; Elkind (1968), 28 fl.

Part II

Consent, choice, and contracts

Chapter 4

Beyond foreseeability: consequential damages in the law of contract

RICHARD A. EPSTEIN

I. INTRODUCTION

The image of the Garden of Eden both before and after the Fall plays a powerful role in religious and literary theory. It also has its precise, if humbler, analogue in modern law and economics scholarship. Eden before the Fall is the complete contingent state contract: the relationship between parties is so specified that nothing that has not been anticipated can occur during the life of the contract. Each possible breach is known in advance, as are the elements of the appropriate remedy. In such a world, a common-law judge need only consult the sacred text of the contract in order to resolve all doubts about the rights and duties of the parties.

The Fall from Eden is the world we live in, where contracts never cover all the contingencies that might arise. This world necessarily arises whenever the cost of contracting is positive, for now it no longer pays to draft contracts to envision what will happen in all possible states of the world, even if such were technically possible. Now contract interpretation be-

Earlier versions of this article were delivered at the Conference on Liability in Law and Morals, held at Bowling Green State University, April 15–17, 1988, and at the Brooklyn Law School on April 20, 1988. I should like to thank Richard Craswell and Alan Schwartz for their most insightful comments on an earlier draft. Sean Smith and James Fiero provided their helpful research assistance.

This essay first appeared in the *Journal of Legal Studies*, vol. 18 (January 1989), © 1989 by The University of Chicago. It is reprinted here with the kind permission of the journal.

comes a second-best proposition that addresses the uncertainty and ambiguity that explicit provisions could have resolved but did not.

Redemption after the Fall is only partial, and lies in the sound rules of contract construction. Of necessity, the possible techniques are divided into two basic types.[1] First, it is possible to read those portions of the contract that are explicit in order thereafter to decide how the contested issue should be resolved in light of what the parties themselves have decided. Second, it is possible to resort to some general theory of contracting behavior that tries to reconstruct the "rational" bargain that self-interested parties would have made in order, ex ante, to maximize their joint gains from the agreement. This second technique requires courts to understand not only the circumstances of any immediate dispute but also the larger business and institutional context in which the contract was formed. Invariably, these two methods of contract interpretation tend to reinforce each other in practice. What parties have, in fact, agreed to is strong evidence of what rational parties would have agreed to: indeed, one function of bargaining theory is to understand why certain contract provisions have been included when their relevant terms are clear and unambiguous. Similarly, what rational parties would have agreed to is, in turn, strong evidence of what these parties did, in fact, agree to where there is silence or ambiguity. There is, accordingly, a complete congruence between the "efficient" identification of the proper contract terms and honoring what the parties did, or would have agreed to do, under contract.[2]

The art of contract interpretation, then, requires the application of a general theory of bargaining to particular contractual provisions. Accordingly, one critical question is, What is the mix between the discrete inquiry into the par-

1 For a further defense of this consumer sovereignty model, see Alan Schwartz. Proposals for Products Liability Reform: A Theoretical Synthesis, 97 Yale L. J. 353, 357 (1988).
2 See Richard Craswell, Contract Remedies, Renegotiation, and the Theory of Efficient Breach, 61 So. Calif. L. Rev. 630, 633 (1988).

ticular facts and the reliance on the general theory of contracting? In this context, the common law (of both England
and the United States) has exhibited something of an uneasy
dualism. With regard to the primary obligations of the parties
– to buy, to ship, to work – the tendency has been to allow
the parties themselves to specify the subject matter of the
agreement, including any price term. This inquiry is case
specific. After breach, the opposite tendency has emerged
for the selection of remedy. While the judicial practice is far
from uniform, courts and commentators often treat the required damage rules as though they were generated by some
normative theory external to the contract itself. From this
premise, the implicit understanding has grown up that damages are resolved more by "rules of law" and less by default
rules of construction.

This attitude is most evident in typical statements about
the function and purpose of damage awards for breach of
contract. Here discussions of the damage rules often begin
from a social norm that the innocent party should be made
whole after breach. The question whether it is possible to
contract out of the rules is suppressed, so that it is often
unclear how the issue of contracting out would be resolved
if raised expressly. Samuel Williston articulated the classical
position as follows. "In fixing the amount of these damages,
the general purpose of the law is, and should be, to give
compensation: that is to put the plaintiff in as good a position
as he would have been in had the defendant kept his contract."[3] The statement takes a stance external to the will of
the parties, for it is the purpose the law "should" have that
seems dispositive. Countless cases take much the same view.
Thus it has been rendered axiomatic that "the function of
the award of damages for a breach of contract is to put the
plaintiff in the same position he would have been in had
there been no breach."[4] Charles Fried has argued for the

---

3 Samuel Williston, A Treatise on the Law of Contracts, § 1338 (1920).
   The statement is picked up in much of the modern literature. See, for
   example, Craswell, *supra* note 2, at 636.
4 See, for example, Spang Industries, Inc. v. Aetna Casualty & Surety

normative power of this position on fairness grounds: "If I make a promise to you, I should do as I promise; and if I fail to keep my promise, it is fair that I should be made to hand over the equivalent of the promised performance. In contract doctrine this proposition appears as the expectation measure of damages for breach."[5]

The dominance of the expectation interest is sometimes challenged, but usually on the wrong ground. Lon Fuller, in his classic study, "The Reliance Interest in Contract Damages,"[6] takes it as "obvious" that the expectation measure of damage is entitled to less protection than the reliance interest – that is, compensation that places the plaintiff in the same position he would have enjoyed had there been no contract. In addition, he further claims that the reliance interest is entitled to less protection than the restitution interest, by which the defendant is made to surrender the gains obtained under the contract. "It is as a matter of fact no easy thing to explain why the normal rule of contract recovery should be that which measures damages by the value of the promised performance."[7] Fuller's criticism rests on the supposed superiority of one legal norm over another. His position does not challenge the (implicit) assumption that the choice of proper remedial rules is largely a judicial function. Yet as a matter of basic contract theory, there is, in principle, no abstract way to resolve this battle of intuitions. Damage rules are no different from any other terms of a contract. They should be understood solely as default provisions subject to

Corp., 512 F. 2d 365 (2d Cir. 1975). See also Hawkins v. McGee, 84 N.H. 114, 117, 146 A. 641, 643 (1929), quoting the Williston passage, *supra* note 3.

5   Charles Fried, Contract as Promise 17 (1981).
6   L. L. Fuller & William R. Perdue, Jr., The Reliance Interest in Contract Damages, 46 Yale L. J. 52, 56 (1936).
7   *Id.* at 57. Fuller's doubt rests on the alleged circularity of the expectation principle. The contract has value only if the law decides to enforce it, so the contract cannot be enforced only because it has value, *Id.* at 59–60. The best answer to this point is to note that, from a system perspective, the choice of legal rule is made to maximize joint benefits of the parties so that the evaluation of the individual case rests on the application of some prior accepted social norm.

variation by contract. The operative rules should be chosen by the parties for their own purposes, not by the law for its purposes.

The received wisdom on contract damages is flawed, then, both in its methodology and in its concomitant elevation of the expectation measure of damages. Accordingly, the first section argues that in contract the damages payable should be set by agreement and not by any abstract principles of justice, however pleasing and symmetrical they might appear to judges. On matters of both liability and remedy, the principle of freedom of contract should control so that all legal damage rules should be understood routinely as default provisions in lieu of express provisions, not as general rules of fairness or natural justice entitled to independent respect.

The second section then gives reasons why the range of damage solutions to which parties might agree is more varied than the canonical treatment of the subject suggests. The familiar expectation, reliance, and restitution all share a certain intellectual elegance, scope, generality, and versatility that a liquidated damage provision calling for a $100 payment cannot hope to match.[8] Together they seem to exhaust the logical possibilities. Nonetheless, in fact, these three measures do not begin to capture the full array of remedial provisions that are expressly incorporated into standard form contracts. The disjunction between observed practice and general theory is especially evident in the rules that govern consequential damages, that is, damages for lost profits, or damages to property or person. In this context, the expectation measure seems to call for full compensation, subject to such tort-like limitations as speculation and foresight, and mitigation of damages. Yet most contractual provisions seem to provide otherwise. This pattern holds in three separate areas: warranties for the sale of goods, liability for employees'

8 Charles J. Goetz & Robert E. Scott, Liquidated Damages, Penalties, and the Just Compensation Principle: Some Notes on an Enforcement Model and a Theory of Efficient Breach, 77 Colum. L. Rev. 554 (1977); Samuel A. Rea, Jr., Efficiency Implications of Penalties and Liquidated Damages, 13 J. Legal Stud. 147 (1984).

accidents, and damages for delayed shipment of goods. The second section discusses reasons why the rule of expectation damages, good in some contexts, need not carry over to consequential damages.

The third section of the article then uses the insights gathered from the examination of express damage provisions to evaluate the general default rules of contract damage as they derive from *Hadley v. Baxendale.*[9] To the extent that *Hadley* leads courts to follow the classical "tacit" assumption-of-risk test, it provides an accurate mirror for the express contractual provisions observed in contracts. In many instances, however, the courts act as though the same damage rules applicable to stranger cases in torts should carry over without modification to the law of contract. At this point, the emphasis shifts to some linguistic variation of the "foreseeability"-of-damage test that leads to incorrect default rules that call for a systematic overexpansion of contract damages, relative to the voluntary norm. This mistaken chain of reasoning can be usefully – but not exclusively – illustrated by cases where carriers make late delivery of goods. A brief conclusion then assesses the dangers of the wrong approach toward contract damages.

II. FREEDOM OF CONTRACT
AND THE MEASURE OF DAMAGES

The provisions of a standard contract are not an arbitrary assemblage of words and phrases with no business and social function. Anyone who drafts a complex contract knows that provisions on delivery, payment, product quality, warranties, and a thousand other terms matter. Provisions directed toward remedies when things go wrong are every bit as important as those terms that are directed toward routine performance. Even if contract breach is, as a matter of relative frequency, the exception instead of the rule, breach can be a very expensive exception. For parties who draft contracts

9 9 Ex. 341, 156 Eng. Rep. 145 (1854).

that must work in thousands or millions of standard transactions, the wording of every provision is of critical importance. It is just not credible to assume that commercial parties draft toward performance but ignore breach in ways that justify more vigorous judicial intervention on remedial questions. The extensive negotiation over explicit limitations on consequential damages tells a different story. Let the terms on damages or other remedy be too restrictive, and it will be difficult to obtain business. Let them be too generous, and the business that is obtained will be a losing proposition. The drafting of contract terms is a constant search for getting the business that is wanted, and for wanting the business that is gotten. Fine-tuning in drafting is the order of the day.

An important object lesson emerges from this discussion. The importance of the written contract itself should not be forgotten in the constant quest for contract theories of greater abstraction. If the contract measure of damages functions as a default provision, then the methodology for handling these cases should be clear: first, look for express provisions on damages, and only as a last resort adopt some general principle of law. While the parties may not have entered into a complete contingent-state contract, their fall from grace need not be complete if they have taken into account the contingencies that did, in fact, occur.

Consistent with the heavy bias toward state control in this area, the cases have often done the opposite.[10] One influential illustration of the wrong methodology is *Kerr S.S. Co. v. Radio Corporation of America.*[11] The defendant telegraph company failed to transmit a message delivered in code to its Manila office by the plaintiff steamship company, in consequence of which the plaintiff sought the recovery of some $6,675 for "the freight that would have been earned if the message had been carried."[12] Judge Cardozo, speaking for a unanimous

10 See also, Charles J. Goetz & Robert E. Scott, The Limits of Expanded Choice: An Analysis of the Interactions between Express and Implied Contract Terms, 73 Calif. 261 (1985), chiding the courts for their unwillingness to accept the benefits of contracting out.
11 245 N.Y. 284, 157 N.E. 140 (1927).
12 245 N.Y. at 287, 157 N.E. At 141.

court, limited the plaintiff's recovery to a refund of the return of the tolls, or some $26.78. His case discussion was couched in terms of the general damage rules found in *Hadley v. Baxendale*,[13] with specific attention to the question whether the defendant had sufficient knowledge from the cipher of the nature of the plaintiff's business, which would make the recovery of lost freight appropriate. Cardozo denied that the defendant could get the needed information from the unintelligible cipher but, on receipt of the message, "might infer that the message had relation to business of some sort. Beyond that it could infer nothing."[14] The message could have related to the carriage of cargo, the employment of an agent, or to nameless transactions "as divergent as the poles."[15] There was not enough information to impress on the defendant the nature of the risk. Cardozo did not say what outcome would have been correct had the telegram been in plain English, but it is possible that he might have seen fit to accept some higher award, perhaps the full $6,675. One cannot say.

To generalize his conclusion, however, Cardozo then launched into a more abstract discussion about the distinction between general and special damages. He noted that these categories were not fixed by nature but depended heavily on the identity of the parties to the transaction. Matters, then, were "not absolute but relative."[16] As between buyer and seller, general damages normally include the difference between contract and market price, but as between the sender of a telegram and a carrier, even with reference to that same sale, the general damages on default are "the cost of carriage and no more."[17] The functional reason for limiting damages was understood by Cardozo. There was a risk of cross-subsidization between senders of messages, where the telegraph company was unable to charge different premia to

---

13 See discussion in Section IVA *infra*.
14 245 N.Y. 288, 157 N.E. at 141.
15 *Id.*
16 *Id.*
17 *Id.* at 289, 157 N.E. at 141.

different customers to reflect the differences in anticipated consequential damages.[18] What is so striking is that nowhere in his analysis does Cardozo once rely on the *explicit* provision in this contract that, in fact, generally limited damages to a return of the charges collected.[19] Indeed, the last clause of the agreement identified the difference between ordinary messages and ciphers, but it did not use the distinction in order to prevent the recovery of lost profits for coded messages while allowing

18 "The loss of a cipher message to load a vessel in the Philippines may mean to one the loss of freight, to another an idle factory, to another a frustrated bargain for the sale or leasing of cargo" (*id.*). To be more accurate, the true problem lies not in the different types of loss but in their different magnitudes, which could vary as much within these classes as across them. But even with this emendation, it is clear that Cardozo has identified a key element in restricting damages. This is one of the reasons why the privity limitation in products liability cases is important as well. It prevents careless plaintiffs from obtaining subsidies from careful ones. See Richard A. Epstein. Products Liability as an Insurance Market, 14 J. Legal Stud. 645 (1985). And Cardozo had strong intuitions about the point in other cases. See, for example, Moch Co. v. Rensselaer Water Co., 247 N.Y. 160, 159 N.E. 896 (1928), which was defended on insurance grounds in Charles Gregory, Gratuitous Undertakings and the Duty of Care, 1 DePaul L. Rev. 30 (1951).

19 245 N.Y. at 293–94, 157 N.E. at 143. The clause reads as follows. "It is agreed between the sender of the message on the face hereof and this company, that said company shall not be liable for mistakes or delays in transmission or delivery, nor for nondelivery to the next connecting telegraph company or to the addressee, of any unrepeated message, beyond the amount of that portion of the tolls which shall accrue to this company; and that this company shall not be liable for mistakes or delays in the transmission or delivery, nor for delay or nondelivery to the next connecting telegraph company, or to the addressee, of any repeated message beyond the usual tolls and extra sum received by this company from the sender for transmitting and repeating such message; and that this company shall not be liable in any case for delays arising from interruption in the working of its system, nor for errors in cipher or obscure messages."

Note, too, that his cavalier dismissal of the agreement has been carried over into the casebook tradition. See, for example, Friedrich Kessler, Grant Gilmore, & Anthony Kronman, Contracts: Cases and Materials 1152 (3d ed. 1986). The opinion is so edited to eliminate both Cardozo's brief discussion of the contract language and the text of the actual provision.

them otherwise, as the logic of Cardozo's opinion seems to suggest. The last clause of the contract provides explicitly "that this company shall not be liable in any case for . . . errors in cipher or obscure messages." The contract therefore appears to place the risk of mistransmission of these messages on the sender, doubtless in recognition of the greater possibility for error. Yet given that the message was not sent at all, the last clause, which governs only *errors* in cipher or obscure messages, does not seem to relieve the company from all liability for a coded message that is not sent at all; rather, cases of nondelivery of coded messages are treated like nondelivery of uncoded ones. The problem of ciphers was doubtless a common one because of the need to preserve secrecy for important business messages. The contract thus provides for an authoritative and sophisticated answer to the question that Cardozo chose not to face.[20]

In a sense, Cardozo reached the right result in the case after all, given that his abstract solution comports with the standard voluntary contract solution – in this instance at least, restitution damages. The result in *Kerr* thus minimizes the cost of recontracting that the parties would otherwise have to bear. But the decision rests in very large measure on a clever interpretation of *Hadley* instead of on an understanding of the relevant business practices. An adequate theory of contract analysis should begin with transactions, not with doctrine. It is to some transactions with explicit contract provisions that the doctrine now turns.

III. DAMAGE SOLUTIONS

In order to understand how damages are selected, it is critical to abandon the ex post approach to the subject and to ask

---

20 Note the plaintiff argued that "this provision (that is, the full clause) is inapplicable where the telegraph company has omitted to transmit the telegram at all, and moreover that it is unreasonable and oppressive in the limitation affixed to liability where the message is repeated. We leave these questions open." 245 N.Y. at 294, 157 N.E. at 143. The contract seems to resolve them in favor of the refund.

the single question. Which default rule promises, under the known circumstances of the transaction, to maximize the joint gain of the parties? In order to make that judgment, it is critical not only to look at the contracting process after the breach has occurred but also at the full range of prospects and perils that the contract itself addresses at formation. When all these circumstances are taken into account, the expectation measure of damage makes perfectly good economic sense in some contexts but not in others.[21] Where the damage measures chosen by the law tend to meet the needs of the parties in standard transactions, there will be little contracting out. But where there is a tension between the rules set by the legal system and the economic interests of the parties, contracting out will take place, at least when the anticipated gains exceed the costs of negotiating and drafting the voluntary provisions. In this section, I consider a number of contexts to which the damage rules apply and contrast, where applicable, the explicit provisions observed in standard contracts with the presumed measures created by operation of law.[22]

A. Seller's remedies: nonpayment
of price and nonacceptance of goods

Suppose the seller has delivered, and the buyer has accepted, all the promised conforming goods. The expectation measure calls for the buyer to pay the price, as the Uniform Commercial Code (U.C.C.) now requires.[23] This result seems to make perfectly good sense for the parties, even from the ex ante perspective. Any lesser measure of damage would allow the buyer to renege on the contract and, in effect, to purchase

---

21 For the relevant formulas, see E. Allan Farnsworth, Contracts § 12.9–12.11 (1982).
22 For general discussions of contract remedies, see William Bishop, The Choice of Remedy for Breach of Contract, 14 J. Legal Stud. 299 (1985); Lewis A. Kornhauser, An Introduction to the Economic Analysis of Contract Remedies, 57 Colo. L. Rev. 683 (1986).
23 See U.C.C. § 2–709 (1).

the goods for less than what had been promised while pocketing the difference between the original contract price and the lesser award of contract damages. The system of credit would be undone by opportunistic behavior.

Similarly, where a buyer does not accept the goods or repudiates the contract before delivery, the expectation measure of damage also works well. Here the seller's measure of damage "is the difference between the market price at the time and place for tender and the unpaid contract price together with any incidental damage provided in this Article, but less expenses saved in consequence of the buyer's breach,"[24] subject to further qualifications where the contract/market differential does not "put the seller in as good a position as performance would have done," in which case lost profits (including allowance for reasonable overhead) are allowed.[25]

Whatever the differences between the two measures of damages used for repudiation or nonacceptance, four features remain constant. First, the seller is to receive only money, so any consequential losses attributable to the want of money alone can generally be avoided by resort to the capital markets. It follows that the price term is the upper bound on damages, so the buyer can never complain that he is required to bear losses far in excess of the amounts he has agreed to pay. The prospect of mitigation eliminates the possibility of enormous consequential damages. Second, the seller is required to take into account the *benefits received* from breach, that is, the value of the goods in his hands, as a set-off against any liability. Third, the insistence on the contract/market differential imposes on the seller perfect incentive to mitigate damages, for he assumes the risk, good or bad, in any movement in prices after breach. He will thus have, after breach, the incentive to act as a single owner intent on maximizing his own gain. Fourth, the administrative or litigation

---

24   *Id*. at § 2–708 (1).
25   *Id*. at § 2–708 (2).

costs necessary to determine contract-market differentials are relatively low, given the ease of getting the relevant data and the relatively small size of the damages. Calculations of this sort can be done routinely, say, in ordinary exchanges or other active markets. In principle, these damage rules should be subject to variation by contract, but as the fit between the default rules and the optimal contract rules seems very close, very little recontracting should be expected.

B. Consequential damages

The expectation measure of damages for nonpayment or non-acceptance of goods offers a useful foil for the cases of consequential damages of primary interest here. The rules governing seller's remedies illustrate the importance of taking into account the gains that the seller retains in the event of breach. They also point to several key variables relevant to the overall desirability of any given rule. At a minimum, it is necessary to take into account (*a*) the incentives for the defendant to perform, (*b*) the incentives for the plaintiff to perform and to mitigate the losses consequent upon breach, and (*c*) the anticipated costs of resolving the differences between the parties through either litigation or settlement.

1. Buyer's remedy for seller's breach of promise. The difficulties with the expectation measure of damages become more acute when we shift from the seller's remedy for buyer's breach to the buyer's remedy for seller's breach. The question of consequential damages can arise when goods are not delivered on time, or when they misfunction once delivered. Now the action against the seller is not obviously limited to an amount less than the price term of the contract. There is no ability to prevent losses by obtaining money – a fungible good from capital markets. The cost of putting the buyer in exactly the same position he would have been in had the contract been performed properly could be enormous, whether we deal with lost profits, personal injury, or property damage. To

make matters more difficult, the consequential damages typically do not arise solely because of the seller's breach but
usually depend on a combination of factors, some of which
are in control of the buyer.

With consequential damages, the superiority of the expectation measure of damages is far from self-evident. Whatever the abstract law of contract, many ordinary sales
contracts contain warranty provisions that specify both the
obligation of the supplier and the remedy in the event of
breach. The provisions widely adopted across different industries stipulate for liquidated damages or call for the repair

26 See, for example, the survey of warranty provisions undertaken by
Bogert & Fink, Business Practices Regarding Warranties in the Sale of
Goods, 25 Ill. L. Rev. 400, 408–9 (1929).
   Thus the standard tire warranty reads as follows. "Every pneumatic
tire of our manufacture bearing our name and serial number is warranted by us against defects in material and workmanship during the
life of the tire to the extent that if any tire fails because of such defect,
we will either repair the tire or make reasonable allowance on the
purchase of a new tire."
   The standard automobile warranty provides:

   WARRANT each new motor vehicle manufactured by us, whether passenger car or commercial vehicle, to be free from defects in material
and workmanship under normal use and service, our obligation under
this warranty being limited to making good at our factory any part or
parts thereof which shall, within ninety (90) days after delivery of
such vehicle to the original purchaser, be returned to us with transportation charges prepaid, and which our examination shall disclose
to our satisfaction to have been thus defective; this warranty being
expressly in lieu of all other warranties expressed or implied and of
all other obligations or liabilities on our part, and we neither assume
nor authorize any other person to assume for us any other liability in
connection with the sale of our vehicles.
   This warranty shall not apply to any vehicle which shall have been
repaired or altered outside of our factory in any way so as, in our
judgment, to affect its stability, or reliability, nor which has been
subject to misuse, negligence or accident, nor to any commercial vehicle made by us which shall have been operated at a speed exceeding
the factory rated speed, or loaded beyond the factory rated load
capacity.
   We make no warranty whatever in respect to tires, rims, ignition
apparatus, horns or other signalling devices, starting devices, gen-
erators, batteries, speedometers or other trade accessories inasmuch

While the full expectation measure of damage may require the seller to bear the cost of delivery to the firm, contracts often leave that loss on the buyer, who likewise may receive no compensation for any interim loss of use. Often the warranty is voided where the product was damaged by excessive or impermissible use by the buyer.[27] Most notably, all liability for personal injury or property damages is excluded. Without question, these warranties call for a risk-sharing arrangement, which leaves the buyer worse off when the seller honors the warranty in full than he, the buyer, would have been if the product had worked perfectly in the first place. Warranty restrictions similar to these led the New Jersey Court in *Henningsen v. Bloomfield Motors, Inc.*[28] to invalidate these warranties as limitations on recovery for personal injury and to usher in the modern age of product liability law by imposing full tort liability for consequential damages.

Against this backdrop of express contractual provisions, there is ample reason to doubt that the expectation measure of damage of the classical common law maximizes the joint gains of the parties ex ante. If it did, we should expect to observe it frequently in practice, which is decidedly not the case. The failure to observe this standard in practice cannot easily be attributed to the systematic ignorance of buyers and sellers in all product markets, for someone must have the incentive to break the logjam if making the plaintiff whole on breach is the ideal contract measure of damages. The better approach, therefore, is to ask why it is that informed parties might not choose to use this damage measure. A closer inspection of the expectation measure of damages reveals some costs of its application.

First, under the orthodox view, the basic rule provides for

as they are usually warranted separately by their respective manufacturers.

For a discussion of the functions of these warranties, see George L. Priest, A. Theory of the Consumer Product Warranty, 90 Yale L. J. 1297 (1981).

27   Priest, *supra* note 26.
28   32 N.J. 358, 161 A.2d 69 (1960).

full consequential damages, but (like the tort rules of contributory negligence it parallels)[29] it then allows the defendant an affirmative defense, where the plaintiff is in breach of some condition precedent. The two halves of this rule thus raise two high-stakes issues (plaintiff's and defendant's breach) on which enormous liabilities can turn. As a general matter, the parties' investment in litigation increases with both the uncertainty of the outcome and the size of the stakes.[30] Ex ante, the parties wish to avoid this cost, as it represents a deadweight loss to both sides. In addition, full consequential damages raise the real risk that the plaintiff, while in the better position to avoid the loss, will, in fact, not take the right steps to do so. Any money that is spent on further loss reduction is his own, while the money that is saved is the defendant's. The temptation to maximize private gain results in the systematic externalization of losses: why should I spend my money to reduce his damages? The law recognizes this and imposes a duty of mitigation of damages to counter this all-too-tenacious human tendency.[31] But that duty is a very imprecise tool to use against so persistent a business practice, for defendant's monitoring of plaintiff conduct, whether under a misuse or a mitigation doctrine, is both costly and error prone. The expectation rules with affirmative defenses may not offer the best prospect of minimizing the total costs of contractual failure.

The weaknesses of the expectation damage system are thrown into high relief by comparing it with an alternative regime that gives fixed damages without making any pro-

---

29   See discussion of Evra Corp. v. Swiss Bank Corp., 673 F.2d 951 (7th Cir. 1982), at IVC *infra.*
30   See, for example, George L. Priest & Benjamin Klein, The Selection of Disputes for Litigation, 13 J. Legal Stud. 1 (1984); Donald Wittman, Dispute Resolution, Bargaining, and the Selection of Cases for Trial: A Study of the Generation of Biased and Unbiased Data, 17 J. Legal Stud. 313 (1988).
31   See Susan Rose-Ackerman, Dikes, Dams and Vicious Hogs: Entitlement and Efficiency in Tort Law, 18 J. Legal Stud. 25 (1989), for the importance of mitigation rules in tort law. Her article highlights the difficulty of an explicit doctrinal incorporation of mitigation rules, which are largely unavoidable in the tort context.

vision for separate affirmative defenses. This system of damages could be superior for both parties because of the way in which it reduces the joint costs of litigation while preserving the incentives on both sides to perform as agreed. The plaintiff whose level of recovery is fixed in advance has a powerful incentive to mitigate his loss. Any rule of fixed damages, independent of subsequent events, makes him face the identical incentives of a single owner of all relevant inputs. Every dollar he spends in mitigation now results in a dollar's saving for himself from the reduction in consequential damages. He will therefore behave exactly as he would if he had been the sole and original author of his own harm. While one should not expect perfection in the delicate task of mitigation – the innocent party may be a complex firm with agency-cost problems of its own – clearly there is nothing that the legal rule could do to improve performance once it has eliminated this potential conflict of interest posed by any ad hoc mitigation rule. There is no need to build mitigation doctrines explicitly into legal rules in order to create the correct incentives to mitigate. Any fixed lump-sum damage award has just that effect, regardless of the level at which it is set.

The amount of the fixed damages is critical, however, in influencing the frequency of breach by the plaintiff. If damages were exceedingly high, the level of precautions taken would be low, given the fixed rate of return that the plaintiff could expect to receive. Similarly, the risk of fraudulent or dubious claims of seller's breach would increase as well. Where the seller is suing for the buyer's failure to accept goods or to pay for goods accepted, the question of seller's breach is relatively unimportant, so that all incentives can be directed toward the conduct of the single wrongdoer. Matters are far more complicated with lost profits, personal injury, and property damages, for here the possibility that both sides will be in breach is far more likely. Setting damages below actual loss is far more important in this context precisely because there is frequent need to restrain abuses by defendants and plaintiffs simultaneously.

Any effort to constrain misbehavior by the buyer invites

misbehavior by the seller. But the critical question is the rate of substitution between buyer and seller incentives for breach. Here there are at least two reasons to think that the control of buyer's misconduct will often be the more important issue, pointing to a lower level of fixed damages. First, reputational constraints tend to operate far more powerfully upon institutional defendants than they do upon individual buyers. Major failures are perceived by the market, resulting in a loss of future sales that can best be avoided by maintaining product quality.[32]

Second, it is important to note that even low damage awards can exert a considerable incentive on a defendant to perform his contracts. Consider the standard repair and replacement warranties set out above.[33] Here defendant must lose from any individual transaction if required, say, to refund the consideration received or to make repairs while still having to bear other costs under the contract. In principle, the defendant will have no incentive to supply defective products so long as his breach costs him more than he gains. Even a low level of nonperformance is sufficient to remove all the profits that the defendant derives from other contracts that are performed successfully.[34] The combination of reputational and financial losses helps keep the defendants in check.

The last point concerns administrative costs. Fixing these damages reduces the associated uncertainty and, therefore, the costs of administering the remedial provisions. Nonetheless, if there is any serious question whether the defendant was in breach, the costs of litigation will increase as the size of the damage award increases, even if damages are fixed. These administrative costs will become far larger if the

32 One finding from the event studies is that the stock price of public companies falls far more than the estimated future liabilities that they have to bear. Bad news is bad for business, so the reputational effects are quickly reflected in the financial markets. See generally, Andrew Chalk, Market Forces and Aircraft Safety: The Case of the DC–10, 24 Econ. Inq. 43, 46 (1986).
33 See note 26 *supra*.
34 See discussion of Federal Express Contract, at IIIB3 *infra*.

level of damages is both large and uncertain and subject to reduction for plaintiff's misconduct and failure to mitigate. All in all, the optimal contracting strategy does not appear to call for the high consequential damages, subject to defense rules, that courts have tended to adopt. Less clearly, within the class of fixed damage awards, there is reason to expect these damages to be kept relatively limited, which is what the express contracts have typically provided.

2. Workers' compensation. The same general pattern of limited contract damages was often observed in industrial accident cases in the era prior to mandatory workers' compensation.[35] In this context, the expectation measure of damages suggests that compensation should be provided for lost income, for pain and suffering, and for medical expenses. It also invites the use of contributory negligence and some forms of assumption of risk as affirmative defenses to control plaintiff's misconduct.[36] Yet the voluntary systems often exhibited very

35 For discussion, see Richard A. Epstein, The Historical Origins and Economic Structure of Workers' Compensation Law, 16 Ga. L. Rev. 775 (1982); Price V. Fishback, Liability Rules and Accident Prevention in the Workplace: Empirical Evidence from the Early Twentieth Century, 16 J. Legal Stud. 305 (1987). Fishback notes that there is no reason to believe that a single compensation system will be ideal for all firms within a single industry. Thus, where coal is produced by individual miners working alone, a tort system with a large assumption-of-risk defense may be appropriate, while a workers' compensation scheme might be more desirable where mining is a team operation (*id.* at 314, 324).

36 Alan Schwartz has offered a qualified defense of the similar rules in product liability cases, as best meeting the insurance and compensation objectives of the parties. He concludes first that the full compensation ideal is generally compromised in cases of pain and suffering but works reasonably well without wage losses and medical expenses. The defense of contributory negligence then controls against plaintiff misconduct. Yet even with this system the two goals are in necessary tension, for whenever the defenses are held, the insurance goals cannot be met. Schwartz, *supra* note 1, at 368. His general discussion rightly treats freedom of contract as the preferred regime, but then – incorrectly, in my view – limits the choice of default regimes to negligence and strict liability for defective products, with or without contributory negligence.
    Schwartz relies in part on Fishback's study, *supra* note 35, to dem-

different characteristics. Under the basic structure, the defendant paid less than full damages, but for all harms "arising out of and in the course of employment," not only for those caused by the defendant's negligence. One consequence of the voluntary compensation formula is to preserve incentives on the plaintiff to take care, without having to incorporate an explicit defense of contributory negligence. The plaintiff who does not recover full tort damages always has some incentive to take precautions against loss.

Consistent with this framework, another benefit of the compensation formula is to exert a selection effect so that persons with extra severe injury costs avoid physical labor with a high risk of injury. Fledgling piano players will not work crushing machines in coal mines if they cannot recover a dime for their lost musical opportunities when they smash a finger. So long as the defendant pays damages that are in most cases greater than his own cost of compliance with safety norms, then the compensation rules chosen make each side bear part of the risk so as to ensure, roughly speaking, that each side has some incentive to minimize it. The damage provisions under these systems are geared to specially negotiated formulas and schedules that make no effort to duplicate the numbers that might come from some general expectation, reliance, or restitution measure. The damages provided, while below those of the tort system, are often substantial, especially where the employer is in an effective position to avoid losses. But the need to handle both plaintiff's misconduct and administrative costs still exerts its influence. It is only the modern proposals for comprehensive public insurance that treat full compensation as an ideal,[37]

onstrate the inferiority of workers' compensation solutions. Yet Fishback studied mandatory and not voluntary systems. If the mandatory systems set the level of compensation too high, then workers' compensation may turn out to be inefficient, but the defect could dwell in the price term, not in the basic structure. Schwartz, *supra* note 1, at 395 n.82.

37 See, for example, Jane Stapleton, Disease and the Compensation Debate (1986); Paul C. Weiler, Protecting the Worker from Disability: Challenges for the Eighties 75–76 (1983).

and these programs have been defective precisely because they ignore the moral hazard question associated with plaintiff's precautions.[38]

3. Common carriers. A similar pattern of argument helps explain the contractual provisions governing the liability of common carriers for lost profits attributable to the delayed shipment of goods. The expectation measure of damage calls forth the question of extensive litigation over both plaintiff's and defendant's conduct. In contrast, the use of a fixed tariff regardless of circumstances helps advance the joint interests of the parties. It gives the plaintiff the incentive to mitigate losses, while imposing on the defendant some financial incentives to perform as promised, which are doubtless augmented by the fear of reputational loss. The small level of damages awarded reduces the costs of both litigation and settlement.

In principle, it is possible that expectation-measure damages could dominate over the fixed tariff, but there is evidence from the structure of real contracts that suggests the opposite. The modern Federal Express standard form, for example, calls for a return of the contract price when the package is not delivered – a restitution form of damages.[39] But it also contains a liquidated damage provision for loss or damage to goods that limits recovery to $100 or actual losses, whichever is lower – even when caused by the company's negligence – with opportunity to purchase additional coverage for stated rates.[40] The company then completes its list

38 See M. Trebilcock, The Role of Conduct Variables in the Design of No-Fault Compensation Systems 23, criticizing Weiler, and 33, criticizing Stapleton (unpublished manuscript, J. Legal Stud. office).

39 "Our liability for delays not caused by your negligence shall be limited to a refund of your delivery charges" (Federal Express Terms and Conditions).

40 "Except as otherwise provided in our tariff and our conditions of carriage, our liability for loss or damage (even if caused by our negligence) is limited to the amount of actual loss or U.S. $100, whichever is less, unless you fill in a higher 'declared value' and pay an additional charge. We do not carry cargo liability insurance, but you may pay 30¢ for each additional $100 of declared value. If you declare a higher

of limitations with boldface disclaimers of all liability for incidental, consequential, or special damages, "whether or not we knew that damages might be incurred."[41]

The form contains all the explicit limitations on damages that high-minded judges and academics often deplore, but it is wholly admirable in both its conception and execution. The difference in damages between delay and loss of packages is about eight- or tenfold (if the $100 maximum is awarded), which bears at least rough correlation to the differential levels of losses. Moreover, while that $100 damage figure for loss or damage may look puny, in fact it conveys very powerful information to the consumer about the firm's reliability in making deliveries. If the net profit per standard transaction is, say, 5 percent, then for a $10 transaction, the gain is about fifty cents. A damage award of $100 thus translates into a situation in which a failure rate of half of 1 percent strips the firm of all its profits, even if there were (*a*) no reputational losses to the firm and (*b*) no additional costs to trace lost packages or to process complaints and the like. A rate of failure of less than one in a thousand is probably above the break-even point for the firm and far higher than its actual nondelivery rate.[42] With its sophisticated client base and the competitors snapping at its heels, the limitations on damages found in the Federal Express agreement cannot be attributed to some mysterious contract of adhesion; after all,

value and pay the additional charge, our liability will be the lesser of your declared value or the actual value of your package" (Federal Express Terms and Conditions). Nor does Federal Express conceal its limited warranties. Its money-back guarantee is featured on the outside of its Overnight Letter along with a similar money-back guarantee that it can "tell you the exact status of your package within 30 minutes of your call" (Federal Express Overnight Letter). There is no implied common-law warranty covering this benefit.

41 "In any event, we won't be liable for incidental damages (for example, alternative carrier transportation costs), consequential damages (for example, loss of profits or income), or special damages, whether or not we knew that such damages might be incurred" (Federal Express Terms and Conditions).

42 On-time delivery rate in excess of 99 percent (Federal Express Public Relations office, Memphis, Tenn.).

why stop at disclaiming expectation damages if, as dictator, you could just knock out all liability by dictating contract terms? Instead, the terms limiting liability are best understood as a way to maximize joint benefits to the parties ex ante: they minimize the costs of administration and mitigation that otherwise arise with breach while insuring a certain high level of contract performance by the firm.

IV. DEFAULT RULES

The provisions found in the full range of voluntary contracts in sales, employment, and especially in common carrier contexts provide a framework for evaluating the default rules of contract as they have evolved from that most famous of carrier cases, *Hadley v. Baxendale*. Thus the pattern is explicit that often rejects the expectation measure of damages and its concomitant defenses in favor of far more restrictive measures of recovery. The original *Hadley* decision reached just that result, and for much of the nineteenth century, the cases adhered to that result under the tacit assumption of risk rule. Over time, however, this restrictive interpretation of *Hadley* has given way to a more expansive view of the plaintiff's level of damage recovery. This section traces some high points in that case development, with special reference to consequential damages for late delivery under contracts of carriage.

A. Hadley v. Baxendale

As is well known, *Hadley* involved the defendant carrier, who delayed the shipment of the plaintiff's millshaft for five days. The breach established, the plaintiff claimed recovery for lost profits during the days that the mill was shut down, but these were denied as a proper measure of damage, limiting damages (or so it would appear) to a refund of the money paid to the carrier for shipping the shaft. The familiar rule of decision in that case contained two prongs. "Where two parties have made a contract which one of them has broken,

111

the damages which the other party ought to receive in respect of such breach of contract should be such as may fairly and reasonably be considered either arising naturally, i.e., according to the usual course of things, or such as may reasonably be supposed to have been in the contemplation of both parties at the time they made the contract as the probable result of the breach of it."[43]

Both branches of the rule loosely resonate with the general principle of expectation damages, that a person is responsible for the harm he has caused. But, clearly, more is at stake in the case, for the next sentence indicates that where the plaintiff has "knowledge of special circumstances," the damages that the defendant can contemplate will take into account only those circumstances "so known and communicated."[44] Otherwise, only the damages "generally" flowing from the breach are to be involved. While these rules here look as though they are directed to the measure of damages, in fact they are not. Later on in his opinion, Baron Alderson suggests that one function of the communication of circumstances is to allow the defendant to insist on a variation of the terms of the contract as regards the damage issue. "[H]ad the special circumstances been known, the parties might have specially provided for the breach of contract by special terms as to the damages in that case."[45]

The issue in this case is recurrent across contract law: where does the burden of recontracting lie? In this context the narrower question is, why is the burden of recontracting placed on the defendant, even after he receives communication of special information? It is also possible to hold that the simple communication of notice to a defendant does not increase the recoverable damages unless there is some clear evidence that the defendant had agreed to pay the additional damages associated with that special risk. The explicit disclaimer of all consequential, incidental, and special damages

---

43   9 Ex: at 354, 156 Eng. Rep. at 151.
44   Id.
45   Id. at 355, 156 Eng. Rep. at 151.

on the Federal Express standard form shows how notice often entails the repudiation, not the assumption, of risk. This result comports with the theory of the "tacit assumption of risk" championed by both Judge Willes[46] and Justice Holmes[47] in the nineteenth-century elaboration of the principle.

Theory aside, *Hadley* is a case whose result is at war with its premises. To read the decision, one might think that the liability imposed was very substantial, thus creating a significant cleavage between the standard terms that the law imposes and those found, for example, in the Federal Express standard form. But appearances are deceiving, for *Hadley*, in fact, imposed sharp restrictions on recovery. Baron Alderson's general rule seems to make lost profits from delayed shipment of the crankshaft the "natural consequences" of breach, at least if the only criterion in question were causation in fact. The earlier delivery would have avoided the loss that the later delivery did not. A fortiori the defendant seems hard pressed to take advantage of the special circumstances referred to in the second limb since the opinion (where it applies the principle) treats the case on the assumption that the plaintiffs did communicate to the defendant that the item shipped was a broken crankshaft, and that they were the operators of the mill. Yet the court said that nonetheless the defendants did not have sufficient notice to be on their guard:

> But how do these circumstances show reasonably that the profits of the mill must be stopped by an unreasonable delay in the delivery of the broken shaft by the carrier to the third person? Suppose the plaintiffs had another shaft in their possession put up or putting up at the time, and that they only wished to send back the broken shaft to the engineer who made it; it is clear that this would be quite consistent with the above circumstances, and yet the unreasonable delay in the delivery would have no effect upon the intermediate profits

46 British Columbia Saw-Mill Co. v. Nettleship, 3 C.P. 499, 508–509 (1868).
47 Globe Refining Co. v. Landa Cotton Oil Co., 190 U.S. 540 (1903).

of the mill. Or, again, suppose that, at the time of the delivery to the carrier, the machinery of the mill had been in other respects defective, then, the same results would follow. Here it is true that the shaft was actually sent back to serve as a model for a new one, and that the want of a new one was the only cause of the stoppage of the mill, and that the loss of profits really arose from not sending down the new shaft in proper time, and that this arose from the delay in delivering the broken one to serve as a model. But it is obvious that, in the great multitude of cases of millers sending off broken shafts to third persons by a carrier under ordinary circumstances, such consequences would not,. in all probability, have occurred; and these special circumstances were here never communicated by the plaintiffs to the defendants. It follows, therefore that the loss of profits here cannot reasonably be considered such a consequence of the breach of contract as could have been fairly and reasonably contemplated by both the parties when they made this contract.[48]

Lost profits were disallowed under the special circumstances test. But the result involves a sleight of hand, as Baron Alderson adopts the clever strategy of mentioning two alternative scenarios (the extra crankshaft or the mill that is otherwise run down) which, if true, imply that a delay in shipment yields no lost profits to the firm. He hints that other circumstances might yield the same result. (The government could have put the mill under lock and key to prevent civil disorder.) But at no time does he make anything remotely like a probabilistic assessment of the relative frequency of the various scenarios to determine that the stated probabilities cover the great multitude of cases. In practice, goods are often shipped posthaste long distances precisely

---

48 9 Ex. at 355–56, 156 Eng. Rep. at 151. Note that the reference to "both" parties sounds more restrictive than it is, for the plaintiff will always know those special circumstances. The question is whether they have been communicated to the defendant whose knowledge is decisive, as the modern law now holds. "[I]t is foreseeability only by the party in breach that is determinative. This is now accepted, even though Baron Alderson spoke of the contemplation of 'both parties' " (Farnsworth, *supra* note 21, at 877).

because the want of a single part keeps an entire plant from operation: hence the importance of the air freight business. To call what happened in *Hadley* unforeseeable, or beyond the contemplation of the parties, is to make professional businessmen systematically ignorant of the commonplace. It is more accurate to say that lost profits from delayed shipment of any equipment are the natural and common consequences of the breach, even if the shipper knows nothing about the particulars of any given situation. If anything remotely like the capacious tort standards of foresight are used, then the case is quite trivial – the other way. If a stranger had wrecked the crankshaft as it lay on the carrier's loading dock, lost profits are a required element of damages under any reading of the foreseeability test. Foresight here, like reasonableness in so many quarters of the law, utterly lacks the descriptive content that allows it to be the principled basis for decision.

What is needed is not verbal jousting but functional accounts. The best explanation of *Hadley v. Baxendale* is that the optimum contract structure need not, for the reasons noted above, use expectation damages as the norm in order to maximize the joint gains of the party. The old, restrictive *tacit* assumption of risk test, widely rejected today,[49] could be unsympathetically dismissed as resting on hypothetical and fictional contracts. But that objection can be lodged against *any* test for default provisions: what else can one do except make the best guesses to fit the broad run of cases? The right question to ask is, Which set of rules is more in keeping with the logic of mutual benefit that underlies the law of contract generally, and with the observed limitations in express contractual provisions that can be found today? The idea of "foreseeability" may be widely accepted, but it is "maddeningly vague."[50] More to the point, it is wholly unmotivated by any commercial or business consideration.

---

49 See, for example, Farnsworth, *supra* note 21, at 875, which approves of abandoning the test as "overly restrictive and doctrinally unsound." See U.C.C. 2–715 Comment 2, which rejects this test as well. In neither case are any functional reasons offered for the result.

50 Richard A. Posner, Economic Analysis of Law 115 (3d ed. 1986).

B. Ordinary interest as the expectation measure of damages

The total separation of the legal rule from its social function carries with it substantial costs for legal doctrine. The early nineteenth-century cases read *Hadley* as an assumption-of-risk case but could not explain why the risks assumed were so limited. As the situation emerged, the tension between the overall foreseeability limitations and the restricted recovery allowed under the cases became evident. As the justification for the narrower rules never was forthcoming, the content of the rule itself shifted, leading to the adoption of broader liability in contract for damages that were "not unlikely" to result from the breach. The upshot of this transformation is that damages for the delayed shipment of goods became presumptively the difference between market price at the actual and scheduled time for arrival, even for those cases where the proper use of the standard expectation-measure damages points in favor of a more limited measure of damages – one equal to interest for the period of delay on the capital amount of the shipment. The twists and turns in this unfortunate evolution of legal doctrine are well illustrated by two English contract cases – *The Parana*[51] and *The Heron II*,[52] both of which deal with the liability for late delivery of nonperishable, fungible goods under any ordinary contract for carriage. *The Parana* got the right result, in part for the wrong reasons. *The Heron II*, which mechanically applied *Hadley*, got the wrong result for the wrong reasons. Both cases require some detailed analysis.

In *The Parana*, the defendant had taken for shipment cargoes of sugar and hemp from Ilo Ilo to London. The expected length of time for the journey was between sixty-five and seventy days, but owing to the defective condition of the ship, the journey was 127 days. During the journey, much of the sugar had leaked out of the boat, and the hemp had declined in price. The plaintiff held the hemp for some time

51 2 P. 118 (1877).
52 3 All Eng. Rep. 686 (1967).

after *The Parana* arrived in London and then sold it for a loss of about £289. The registrar and merchants, following standard business practice, allowed the owner to recover for the full value of the sugar but not for the losses associated with the sale of the hemp. The judge of the Admiralty Division restored the award for the hemp, and that determination was reversed on appeal. For the delay in the shipment of the hemp, the proper award was the interest on the principal sum (represented by the value of the hemp) for the period of the delay.

The decision of the registrar and merchants, as affirmed by the court of appeals, is correct. The more troublesome question is the right way to analyze the problem. Here Mellish, L.J., identified some, but not all, of the relevant principles. His opinion began with a dutiful recitation of the two key tests in *Hadley v. Baxendale*, and then argued that the losses sustained by the plaintiff here were in essence speculative because the particular circumstances of the contract were not made known to the carrier. Doctrinally, he held as follows. "In order that damages may be recovered, we must come to two conclusions – first, that it was reasonably certain that the goods would not be sold until they did arrive; and, secondly, that it was reasonably certain that they would be sold immediately after they arrived, and that that was known to the carrier at the time when the bills of lading were signed."[53]

Earlier in his opinion, he had distinguished several cases where such damages for late shipment might have been allowed.

> If goods are sent by a carrier to be sold at a particular market; if, for instance, beasts are sent by railway to be sold at Smithfield, or fish is sent to be sold at Billingsgate, and, by reason of delay on the part of the carrier, they have not arrived in time for the market, no doubt damages for the loss of market may be recovered. So, if goods are sent for the purpose of being sold in a particular season when they are sold at a higher

53 *Supra* note 51, at 123.

price than they are at other times, and if, by reason of breach of contract, they do not arrive in time, damages for loss of market may be recovered. Or if it is known to both parties that the goods will sell at a better price if they arrive at one time than if they arrive at a later time, that may be a ground for giving damages for their arriving too late and selling for their lower sum. But there is in this case no evidence of anything of that kind. As far as I can discover, it is merely said that when goods arrived in November they were likely to sell for less than if they had arrived in October, for the market was lower.[54]

Mellish then observed that nothing constrained the owner of the hemp (in fact, a mortgagee of the cargo with rights of owner) from selling the goods while at sea if he thought that the price was advantageous. The delay, therefore, did not require him to miss a favorable market if one was available. Similarly, the decision not to sell the hemp immediately upon arrival was not mandated by the breach but was an independent decision based on the owner's estimation of the future movement of the market, which he happened to misread. The losses were disallowed because it was too "speculative and uncertain" to calculate when the hemp would have been sold.

The specific institutional arguments made by Mellish contain a good deal more force than the bland proposition that the losses in question were not foreseeable under *Hadley*. It surely counts as a point in favor of the carrier that the cargo owner had complete control over the timing of the sale, but even if that had not been the case, interest on the capital sum is the correct measure of damages, which corresponds with the expectation measure of damages. Revert once again to the model of the "single owner," used to explain why fixed damages give the optimal incentives to reduce loss given the defendant's breach. The key here is to ask the maximum sum of money the owner of the cargo would pay in order to induce the prompt shipment of the hemp to Lon-

54 *Id.* at 121.

don. That sum of money would ordinarily be equal to the amount of money that the single owner of craft and cargo would have spent to avoid the delays in shipment. That sum is, in fact, interest on the principal amount for the late shipment and not more – at least absent the exceptional circumstances noted by Mellish, L.J., above.

The conclusion is dependent on the structure of the relevant market. The London market for hemp was a continuous market where the goods, themselves nondepreciable, could be disposed of at the time of their arrival. The present price in effect contains the best collective estimation of the future price for the goods. The price of hemp could well go down, but, by the same token, it could also go up. Counsel for the seller grasped the relevant point intuitively when he noted the "insuperable" difficulties posed by the loss of market rule for late shipment. He asked, "If sugar had gone up whilst hemp had gown down, it would be impossible to allow the shipper to recover for the hemp and not allow for the sugar, and yet what is to be done if they belong to different shippers? Is the shipowner to lose when the prices fall and not to gain when they rise?"[55] In essence, his argument is that the uncorrelated price variation between two goods provides, ex post, compensation for the loss where there is a single owner – negating his claim for damage payments. Why tolerate the anomaly of having to pay damages for the downward price movement where the hemp and sugar are owned by separate parties?

The argument can be taken a step further because it does not depend on the offsets for two separate quantities being found as a matter of fact ex post. It is quite sufficient to identify the expected price movements for each good ex ante. If the best estimates of future prices for this hemp, itself a durable good, were below the present market price, then the market would be out of equilibrium so that the current price would quickly fall, once again making the value of present and future goods indistinguishable except for the interest

55   2 P. at 119.

component. In this regular world, the owner of hemp knows that the expected price he will get in the future is a function of the actual price that he can get today, even if the hemp could not have been resold while at sea. The only adjustment the owner need make is to take into account the delay in the receipt of the goods or cash, and that itself is represented perfectly by an interest payment. Stated otherwise, the breach by the carrier not only carries with it the prospect of harm but also the likelihood of benefit, which now functions as compensation for the breach. Both the anticipated harm and the anticipated benefit must be taken into account, as they fall, of necessity, to the same person, here the owner. Where the distribution of future prices is normally distributed about the mean figure, then this "in-kind" compensation received in the event of breach exactly offsets the loss that the breach itself has occasioned, save only for the time difference.

The economic measure of efficiency thus corresponds perfectly with the "corrective justice" standard, given that the plaintiff's prospect of gain, when coupled with interest payments, redresses any imbalance that defendant might have created. In addition, risk aversion itself is not an important factor in the analysis because there is a necessary dispersion in future prices, whether the shipment itself takes sixty-five or 120 days. At most, some allowance would have to be made for any increased dispersion of risk owing to the longer time period – a marginal calculation that is just not worth the candle, given the relatively small amounts of money involved. It follows, therefore, that if the cargo owner actually purchased insurance from the shipper for the decline in the market price, he would, in effect, be entering into a separate futures transaction where he purchased a put (that is, an option to sell the goods) for a price equal to that which the market revealed on the expected time of arrival. There is no reason for that futures contract to be embedded in a contract for carriage; it could be as well handled in a separate futures contract or, as Mellish noted, by resale of the goods while at sea. Ex ante the shipper's only anticipated loss in *The Parana* was the interest attributable to the delay in shipment. The prospect of loss was, of course, reasonably foreseeable but so, too, was the equal and opposite prospect for gain.

The situation is, of course, very different in the particular settings mentioned by Mellish, L.J., as exceptions to the general rule. Suppose that a late delivery of goods means that the owner will miss an organized market that does not gather again for another year, and that storage of the goods in the interim is not possible, owing to the substantial risk of spoilage. Now the single owner of both ship and cargo would invest greater sums of money to see that the cargo arrives in good time, for the cost of a later shipment is no longer mere delay but necessarily a loss of market, where no prospect of future gain functions as the appropriate offset. The case of the seasonal market is functionally equivalent to the case of the leaky sugar, and so the customary admiralty rules provided. As there is no compensating benefit from breach, the rules have to be tailored to take into account the increased costs of delay, just as the single owner of ship and cargo would now spend greater sums of money to insure earlier arrivals. Loss of market becomes the proper measure of damages, not interest. Admiralty practice again made the right distinction. The contract/market rule governs whenever (time lag aside) expected future prices do not have a distribution that is symmetrical around the current price – a point that is true in all of Mellish's examples.

The analysis in *The Parana* identified some of the key elements in support of the limited damage rule. The decision also gained strength because it was consistent with the custom of the trade, which moves strongly to the social optimum, even if the parties themselves do not understand fully the economic determinants of a sound decision. *The Heron II*, decided 90 years later, represents a conscious effort to rationalize the contract damage rules in accordance with abstract principle by judges who were wholly ignorant of their internal economic logic. The result was verbal fencing of no possible utility, the repudiation of *The Parana* for aesthetic reasons, and the adoption of the *wrong* default provision for cases of delayed shipment of durable goods.

In *The Heron II*, the plaintiffs chartered the defendants' vessel to carry a cargo of 3,000 tons of sugar from Constanza to Basrah, with the option in the charterer to have the cargo diverted to Jeddah. The option was not exercised, but the owner of the boat was nine days late in arriving at Basrah, having made an illegal diversion of the ship. The sugar on board was immediately sold at a price below what it would have fetched had the ship arrived on time some nine days before. The market for sugar at Basrah was continuous, and just before *The Heron II* reached port, another ship had un-loaded a considerable cargo, which had depressed the price of sugar. If *The Parana* represented good law, then the proper measure of damages was the lost interest on the value of the freight for the nine-day period. But that decision was rejected on the ground that *Hadley*, rightly understood, called for a damage rule that took into account questions of foreseeabil-ity. Even though the remote possibilities of loss were suffi-cient to trigger loss in tort, they could not do the same in contract. Lord Reid tried to identify the right standard in contract cases as follows:

> It appears to me in the ordinary use of language there is a wide gulf between saying that some event is not unlikely or quite likely to happen and saying merely that it is a serious possibility, a real danger, or on the cards. Suppose one takes a well-shuffled pack of cards, it is quite likely or not unlikely that the top card will prove to be a diamond: the odds are only three to one against; but most people would not say that it is quite likely to be the nine of diamonds, for the odds are then fifty-one to one against. On the other hand I think that more people would say that there is a serious possibility or a real danger of its being turned up first, and, of course, it is on the cards.[56]

56 The Heron II, 3 All Eng. Rep. 686, 694–95 (1967).

As a matter of ordinary English, there is every reason to doubt that the probabilities are as Lord Reid would assign them. "Quite likely" might refer to three-to-one odds against, but to speak of a "serious possibility" or a "real danger" is to invoke shorter odds than the long shot (as it would be in racing) odds of fifty-one to one. A serious risk of loss could easily be 10 percent or more in many contexts. But the terminological quibble in the case is not central to the inquiry.[57] What is critical is its economic logic. Once three-to-one against becomes a case of compensation, then it follows that lost profits will be necessarily the routine measure of damages, where the anticipated distribution of prices at the time of delay is identical to that which is found at the agreed-on time of arrival. Given the continuous nature of the Basrah market, the chances are close to 50 percent that the future prices will be lower, far better than the three-to-one stated odds. The same result follows if the question is, Does the shipowner know of the possibility of a decline in market prices? Lord Morris makes the case clear enough. "The appellant shipowner knew that there was a sugar market at Basrah. When he contracted with the charterers to carry their sugar to Basrah, though he did not know what were their actual plans, he had all the information to enable him to appreciate that a delay in arrival might in the ordinary course of things result in their suffering some loss. He must have known that the price in a market may fluctuate. He must have known if a price goes down someone whose goods are late in arrival may be caused loss."[58]

---

57 In this terminological vein, Lord Reid also criticized the test in The Parana, holding that damages were not recoverable so long as it was not "reasonably certain" that the goods would be sold while at sea but would be sold immediately upon arrival. "[S]o strict a test has long been obsolete; and if one substitutes for 'reasonably certain' the words 'not unlikely' or some similar words denoting a much smaller degree of probability, then the whole argument in the judgment collapses" (The Heron II, 3 All Eng. Rep. 696 (1967)). Note that the correctness of The Parana in no way depends on the probability of sale at sea, but on the symmetrical nature of price variations.

58 *Id.* at 701.

Thereafter follows a recitation of the standard expectation measure formula for damage that leads to the inexorable conclusion that the prima facie measure of damage is the difference between the market prices at the scheduled and actual time of arrival.[59] Lord Morris's strategy attributes to the shipowner perfect information over the relevant variables. In fact, both shipowner and cargo owner knew more and could calculate better than he assumes. Morris takes the view of Cassandra and dwells on the downside. He ignores completely what was also common knowledge to both parties, that the price could increase as well. If, for example, the rival trader (whose arrival is both random and unknown) had put into port the week before (instead of the week after) *The Heron II* was scheduled to arrive, then the shipper in *The Heron II* would have benefited from the delayed arrival. The greater gap between the two arrival dates would have increased the price *The Heron II*'s sugar would have fetched on its late arrival. Here the charterer could pocket all the additional profits. The choice of the wrong measure of damages thus places a false incentive on the vessel to arrive on time and limits the opportunity to make diversions that a single owner would otherwise regard it in his interest to make. The inefficient damage rule thereby increases total costs for both sides to the arrangement. The logic of the rule depends on the relationship of the price on the date of scheduled arrival to the full distribution of future prices. Both the cost and the benefit sides of the equation must be taken into account. *The Parana* reached the correct result, even though it did not understand all the dynamics of trade. *The Heron II* misfired because it thought that the first office of the law of contracts was to explicate the language of *Hadley*, not to analyze the recurrent business problem that gave rise to the underlying issue.[60]

---

59 *Id.*
60 Lord Upjohn tried to distinguish The Parana from The Heron II by resorting to an argument of changed conditions. "No doubt in the days of sail pure and simple, when ships might be delayed by head winds for days, loss of market would not be within the contemplation

C. Undercompensating losses from delayed shipment

The Parana and The Heron II are, in my view, relatively easy cases because the implicit in-kind compensation from breach gives a very simple explanation as to why interest for delay gives well-nigh perfect compensation to the buyer. In other cases of delay by common carriers, this condition no longer holds, and now the analysis must revert to the very different paradigm of Hadley, where some systematic undercompensation for consequential losses is needed to induce the proper level of loss minimization. An instructive case is the recent decision of Judge Posner in Evra Corp. v. Swiss Bank Corp.,[61] which adds an overlay of privity problems to the basic question of the proper measure of contract damages.

In Evra, the plaintiff (Hyman-Michaels Co., whose name was changed to Evra Corp.) had made a very profitable charter of a ship, where the contract called for the forfeiture of the charter if the required rental fee was not paid "in advance" to the shipowner's account in a Swiss bank. The money in question had to be paid from Hyman-Michaels in Chicago, via London, to the Swiss bank. Hyman-Michaels used a system of wire transfers that were initiated at most two days before the payments were due. On one previous occasion, the charter payments were late, but an arbitration panel, by divided vote, nonetheless prevented the owner from cancelling the charter party, given that Hyman-Michaels had taken steps to expedite the payments once it

of the parties. In 1877, when The Parana was decided, the steam engine was coming into its own, but it was still the golden age of sail and over half the ships built in this country were sailing ships at this time; these matters may well have influenced Mellish, L.J., when he pointed out the differences between delay in delivery by carriers on land and cases of carriage of goods on long voyages by sea" (id. at 720). But the logic of the expectation measure damages depends on conditions that were identical in both The Parana and The Heron II. The argument from changed conditions is used all too often when the underlying structure of the problem is not understood. See, generally, Richard A. Epstein, The Static Conception of the Common Law, 9 J. Legal Stud. 253 (1980).

61 See note 29 supra.

125

found out about the mix-up. Six months later, Hyman-Michaels again tried to wire its payment from Chicago to London to Switzerland, again less than two days before it was due. But there was a breakdown in the system of crediting by the Swiss bank, so that the deposit was not made in time; this time the owner was able to cancel the charter when arbitrators found that Hyman-Michaels did not try to remedy the defect with all possible dispatch. The question was whether the bank, which had been found negligent, could be held for the increased costs that Hyman-Michaels had to pay to renew its old charter at the far higher current levels.

Under the Swiss law, the bank could not be held liable to Hyman-Michaels because the two parties were not in privity. Judge Posner refused to dismiss the case under Swiss law. Rather than resolve the conflict question, he concluded that Illinois law also denied recovery on the claim, even though it does not adopt the privity rule. In essence, he argued that, while this was a tort case, it was also preeminently a botched commercial transaction, so that the applicable damage principles should be derived from *Hadley v. Baxendale*. Accordingly, much of his opinion is devoted to a dissection of what the bank knew at the time it received the transfer from Hyman-Michaels and when it knew it. He concluded that the bank had no special notice of the urgency for payment, or of the catastrophic consequences of default, and so could not be charged with the loss.

If Posner had stopped here, there would have been little change in the understanding of *Hadley*. But he did not. In addition, he tried to link the remoteness of damage in *Hadley* to the tort doctrine of "avoidable consequences," which comes into play when the plaintiff has the opportunity to take steps to avoid an injury, say, by seeking medical attention after an accident, or by buckling up the seat belt before the accident. Hyman-Michaels's behavior clearly was a monumental high-stakes blunder, for in the effort to save a few days of interest on a $27,000 principal payment, the firm took the substantial risk of losing a favorable charter party worth in excess of $2,000,000. The preferred pattern of cost avoidance was an early transfer of the money to the Swiss account. Posner then identifies the many sources of "imprudence" in Hyman-Michaels's behavior.[62]

It is just here that he misfires. The *Hadley* rule, for all its imperfections, does obviate the need for an in-depth examination of the plaintiff's conduct in this particular transaction. Posner's effort to transform *Hadley* into a contributory negligence rule is wholly inconsistent with the facts of the original case, where the mill owner's conduct was in no way responsible for the delay in shipment. In addition, as Illinois is now itself a comparative negligence state,[63] any use of negligence principles should lead not to a denial of the claim, as happened here, but to an apportionment of loss with the plaintiff recovering perhaps one-half or at least some substantial fraction of its losses. Yet this elaborate system is inconsistent with the economic logic of the transaction, which uses the sharp limitation on damage proper in order to avoid the contributory negligence inquiry, with its Hand-formula baggage. While in *Evra* that claim is easy to establish, other cases can be readily imagined in which it would be more controversial. Some unanticipated emergency might have required a speedy transfer, or earlier payments could have been misplaced by the receiving bank for a longer period of time. In both situations, the contributory negligence defense could raise dogged legal battles and might prove, in the end, unavailable to the defendant. The special knowledge rule avoids all these complications.

One can go further, for here it seems that the Swiss, as is so often the case in financial matters, were correct in adopting the privity limitation. If it is unlikely that the bank would have assumed the risk of enormous losses to a party with

---

62 *Id.* at 955.
63 Alvis v. Ribar, 85 Ill. 2d I, 421 N.E. 2d 886 (1981). The transaction in Evra took place in 1972, and the trial (it appears) in 1981, so the case itself would not appear to be governed by comparative negligence principles. But future cases that followed Evra would be decided under the comparative negligence rules.

whom it was in direct agreement, then there is no reason for the tort law to allow customers to make an end run round the web of contractual understandings solely by using an intermediate bank to implement their transfers. As Posner himself correctly noted, "It seems odd that the absence of a contract would enlarge rather than limit the extent of liability."[64] The advantage of privity is that it uses contractual provisions to govern the full set of liabilities on all the parties. If the Swiss bank must pay limited damages to its London correspondent bank, then the Swiss bank has a (limited) financial incentive to comply, even if the plaintiff himself does not get a refund of the money that he paid out to the continental bank. It therefore follows that the defendant has some incentive to avoid the loss, just as the plaintiff (who does not have specific knowledge of the circumstances) has the powerful incentive to set up some alternative arrangement that guarantees prompt and early payment to the shipowner. Respecting the privity limitation thereby leads to a distribution of gains and losses that is far closer to the contractual ideal than any tort doctrine of judicial invention. The outcome in *Evra* was correct, but its reliance on special circumstances, and especially on contributory negligence, was not.

D. Limitations on expectation damages outside the common carrier case

In closing, it is useful to consider one other class of cases that has caused some difficulty under the damage rule of *Hadley*. Suppose the owner or the plaintiff has entered into some collateral arrangement – for example, a resale at a favorable price – whereby he can obtain supranormal profits should the defendant perform the contract as desired but not otherwise. The typical situation often arises where the plaintiff is fortunate enough to enjoy some quasi-monopolistic situation that offers the prospect of a supercompetitive return

64   673 F.2d at 956.

or a very profitable resale. In *British Columbia Saw-Mills v. Nettleship*,[65] the plaintiff sought to construct a new sawmill in the Pacific Northwest from which the returns might have been very high if it were the first mill in operation in the new location. In *Victoria Laundry (Windsor), Ltd. v. Newman Indus., Ltd.*,[66] the plaintiff enjoyed "especially lucrative" contracts for laundry service in virtue of being of the first to reenter the laundry business at the end of the Second World War when demand was well-nigh insatiable. In each case, the expectation is valuable to the plaintiff, although valuation itself is complicated by its very high variance.

These cases, however, are in their business aspects sharply distinguishable from, and more difficult than, both *The Parana* and *The Heron II*. In *Nettleship* and *Victoria Laundries*, the payment of interest no longer renders the plaintiff indifferent between breach and performance, as the expectation standard itself requires. The net anticipated losses to a single owner would have been greater than interest, so that some additional precautions from prompt arrival would be taken. Given that these are hard cases, the optimal strategy for the plaintiff to protect these gains is to bargain for a higher damage award (coupled with a higher base price) in the event of breach. The difficulty in valuation and the size of the stakes increase the deadweight losses to both sides. It could well be that more sufficient monitoring and cooperation on a day-to-day basis yields a more sensible approach to contract damages. In the alternative, a specific provision for liquidated damages tied to the length of the delay could allow the defendant to calculate its own potential exposure, without having to make a detailed estimate of the plaintiff's future losses – which could well be influenced not only by the defendant's breach, but by many other factors as well, such as the conduct of other independent suppliers. The usual standard of the difference between contract and market, or the cost of replacement, minimizes many of these difficulties and might well be preferred by the parties themselves.

65   3 C.P. 499 (1868).
66   2 K.B. 528, 537 (1949).

The objection, therefore, to awarding special gains from unknown arrangements does not stem from their want of foresight; a problem so recurrent in the academic literature could hardly be unknown to ordinary business firms. The answer is, rather, that it is not clear that a default provision that holds simply that these special damages are recoverable is better than one that studiously refuses to take them into account. The fit between any default rule and the contractual ideal will be worse when extraordinary profits are at issue than it is when they are not. But the only lesson that can be drawn from that melancholy observation is that the gains for contractual individuation are greater for cases that lie at the tail of the distribution than for those located close to its mean. Holding that these losses are not foreseeable, or are beyond the contemplation of both parties or the party in breach, is a tiny part of the complete understanding of the situation.

The point can be briefly shown by looking in detail at one such case involving the lost profits on resale. *In re R. & H. Hall & W. H. Pim (Junior) & Co.'s Arbitration*,[67] the original buyer purchased an unspecified quantity of wheat from the seller at a given price. The buyers then resold the rights under contract to a subbuyer at a higher price, after which the contract right was resold again at a still higher price. Subsequently, the cargo from a certain ship was identified as being the subject matter of the contract, in accordance with standard industry practice. The buyer, once notified, immediately informed his own subbuyer. The market price then fell when the designated ship arrived in port, but the seller still failed to deliver. For its admitted breach of contract, the seller was held liable to its own buyer, but the question was whether it should have to compensate its buyer for its losses in failing to complete its own subcontract and any subsequent losses that the buyer might face in the unlikely event it was sued by that subbuyer. Both elements of damages were allowed because, looked at from the time of the original sale, it was rated an "even chance," hence not unlikely, that the

67 All Eng. Rep. 763 (1928).

wheat would be resold before its delivery in port, and that was enough to bring the buyer's case within the ambit of the second branch of the *Hadley* rule.[68]

The result here may or may not have been right, but the correct answer does not depend solely on the odds of the resale, which must surely have been high, or simply on the movement of the market. The right question to ask is whether the price paid by the buyer included within it compensation at this raised measure, given the breach. It is probably of some interest that the contract was for the sale of a specific cargo, which meant that the buyer could not substitute wheat from any other vessel to perform his own contract obligation. The true winner, therefore, seems to be the subbuyer who is let out from a losing contract. Given, therefore, that the buyer has no other way to lock his subbuyer in, the court's award of the special damages seems to make a good deal of sense. The result looks even stronger since it seems likely that the seller's failure to deliver (while not discussed in the case) may have arisen because he had resold the same cargo to a second purchaser and thereby captured the increase in price that his first buyer should have enjoyed. On this view, it could well be that the seller is only made, roughly speaking, to disgorge the profits from the alternative transaction. The result might have been rendered more precise if the profits from resale had been turned over to the buyer, itself a kind of restitution measure that is generally precluded by cases holding that ideal equivalence demands a uniform expectation measure of damages.[69] The use of the restitution measure necessarily strips the seller of all gains from breach and thus tends to secure compliance and thereby reduce the frequency and importance of suits.[70] Again, the

68 See, for example, *id.* at 767, per Viscount Dunedin, whose language was later approved in The Heron II, 3 All Eng. Rep. 686, 693 (1967), per Lord Reid.
69 See, for example, Acme Mills & Elevator Co. v. Johnson, 141 Ky. 718, 133 S.W. 784 (1911), where, however, the court held that the contract was not for the sale of particular wheat.
70 See Richard A. Epstein, Inducement of Breach of Contract as a Problem

theory of contract damages must address both the defendant's gain and the plaintiff's loss. By leaving out one side of the equation totally, the court *in re Hall* may have come to the right result, but surely for the wrong reason, when it relied on the standard of equal likelihood.

V. CONCLUSION

This article has sought to demonstrate that the question of contract damages can be examined by the same techniques that are ordinarily used to handle other issues of contract interpretation. Where there are express provisions that govern the award of damages, these should normally be followed, unless one can show the same form of fraud, duress, or incompetence sufficient to set aside the basic obligations under the same contract. Where the express provisions of the contract are incomplete or entirely omitted, then the best that can ever be done is to develop those rules which, as a general matter, appear to work to the joint benefit of the parties at the time of contract formation. In working through this analysis, it often occurs that the proper measure of damage is far lower than that which appears to be implied by the now-dominant expectation measure of damages, which provides that the plaintiff is to be left after breach in the same position that he would have enjoyed had the defendant performed in full. In some instances, contract damages are reduced to reflect the need to control plaintiff's misconduct and to economize on litigation and settlement costs. In other cases, these are reduced in order to prevent the cross-subsidization of some plaintiffs by others. In still other instances, damages are lower because the defendant's breach confers on the plaintiff some implicit compensating benefit that reduces the need for cash compensation.

Once these basic patterns are understood, it follows that there will be good reason to reorient basic judicial attitudes

of Ostensible Ownership, 16 J. Legal Stud. I (1987); Daniel Friedmann, The Fallacy of Efficient Breach, 18 J. Legal Stud. 1 (1989).

toward contact damages. First, it seems clear that the verbal formulations of *Hadley v. Baxendale* and its progeny, which emphasize either the likelihood of damage on breach or the defendant's knowledge of special circumstances, should be set aside in favor of the nineteenth-century view that depended on a theory of tacit assumption of risk, which, in fact, can be made far more precise and powerful than has been generally understood. Second, the theory of contract damages has important implications for the techniques of contract construction. The general view today is that limitations on damages ought generally to be narrowly construed, in large measure because they offend the expectation ideal.[71] Yet if these contracts work ex ante to the benefit of both sides, this strategy of interpretation contra proferentem will only favor the few lucky plaintiffs who maintain action for breach while hurting plaintiffs and defendants as a class. The temptation to do justice in the individual case should, therefore, be curbed in order to advance the long-term welfare of contracting parties generally. A simpler rule of ordinary meaning is a more reliable guide to contract construction. Similarly, there should be greater acceptance of freedom of contract as a general principle, as many academics now advocate.[72] In general, the repudiation of explicit contract provisions on grounds of public policy typically follows a detailed judicial examination of the contract provisions. The object of that demonstration is to show that the plaintiff is not perfectly compensated in the event of breach.[73] Yet once it is realized that perfect compensation for damages ex post may yield a systematic increase in overall damages,

71 Farnsworth, *supra* note 21, at § 12.18.
72 See, for example, Schwartz, *supra* note 1. See also Goetz & Scott, *supra* note 10.
73 The most dramatic illustration is still Henningsen v. Bloomfield Motors, Inc., 32 N.J. 358, 161 A. 2d 69 (1960), which ushered in the age of strict liability in tort for product cases by its merciless dissection of the limited warranty provided by Chrysler. The court, however, ignored all the problems with plaintiff's conduct, cross-subsidization of risk, and administrative expense that now haunt so much of modern product liability law.

then this temptation, too, should be avoided. The traditional view of contracts was that custom and common practice were generally sound. Repeat players do not make mistakes on provisions so critical to their personal welfare.

Chapter 5

Rights and remedies in a consent theory of contract

RANDY E. BARNETT

INTRODUCTION

The mere fact that one man promises something to another creates no legal duty and makes no legal remedy available in case of non-performance. To be enforceable, the promise must be accompanied by some other factor. . . . The question now to be discussed is what is this other factor. What fact or facts must accompany a promise to make it enforceable at law?[1]

Which interpersonal commitments are properly enforceable as contracts? When contract theorists and philosophers treat this question, they commonly assume that the institution of contract somehow depends on the institution of promise-keeping. They think that contractual duties are species of the general duty to keep one's promise. I think this approach is wrong, both descriptively and normatively. I think that Arthur Corbin was right to insist that to "be enforceable, the promise must be accompanied by some other factor. . . . " The other factor, by assumption, is extraneous to the promise itself. Moreover, if by a "promise" we mean a commitment to act or refrain from acting at some time in the future, then a contractual duty can exist even where there is no promise – as with an immediate transfer of entitlements.

In this essay, I identify this factor as the "manifested intent to alienate rights" which I shall refer to as "consent."

---

1 A. Corbin, Corbin on Contracts § 110, at 490 (1963).

135

Consequently, I call this a "consent theory of contract."[2] A consent theory posits that contractual obligation cannot be completely understood unless it is viewed as part of a broader system of legal entitlements. Such a system specifies the substance of the rights individuals may acquire and transfer, and the means by which they may do so. Properly understood, contract law is that part of a system of entitlements that identifies those circumstances in which entitlements are validly transferred from person to person by their consent.

In Part I, I explain how a consent theory fits within a broader view of individual entitlements. In Part II, I elaborate the definition of "consent" that is employed in a consent theory. In Part III, I describe the presumptive nature of consent in contract law. In Part IV, I discuss how the distinction between alienable and inalienable rights plays a vital role in determining the appropriate form of remedy for breach of contract.

I. ENTITLEMENT THEORY AND CONTRACT

A. Entitlements as the foundation of contractual obligation

The function of an entitlements theory based on individual rights is to define the boundaries within which individuals may live, act, and pursue happiness free of the forcible interference of others. A theory of entitlements specifies the rights that individuals possess or may possess; it tells us what may be owned and who owns it; it circumscribes the individual boundaries of human freedom. Any coherent theory of justice based on individual rights must therefore contain principles that describe how such rights are ini-

---

2 This chapter is taken with considerable revision from two articles in which I further explained this approach. Parts I–III are based on Barnett, A Consent Theory of Contract, 86 Colum. L. Rev. 269 (1986) [hereinafter A Consent Theory]. Part IV is from Barnett, Contract Remedies and Inalienable Rights, 4 Soc. Phil. & Pol'y, Autumn 1986, at 179 [hereinafter Contract Remedies].

tially acquired, how they are transferred from person to person, what the substance and limits of properly obtained rights are, and how interferences with these entitlements are to be rectified.[3]

These constituent parts of an entitlements theory comport substantially with the traditional categories of private law. The issue of initial acquisition of entitlements in real and chattel resources is dealth with primarily in property law; tort law concerns the protection of and proper limits on resource use; and contract law deals with transfers of rights between rights-holders. Each category contains its own principles of rectification for the breach of legal obligations. Viewing contract law as part of a more general theory of individual entitlements that specifies how resources may be rightly acquired (property law), used (tort law), and transferred (contract law) is not new.[4] And, of course, the actual historical development of these legal categories has not perfectly conformed to the conceptual distinctions that an entitlements approach suggests. But this approach has long been neglected as a way of resolving some of the thorniest issues of contract theory and doctrine.

According to an entitlements approach, rights may be unconditionally granted to another (a gift), or their transfer may be conditioned upon some act or reciprocal transfer by the transferee (an exchange). Contract law concerns the ways by which rights are transferred or alienated. Accordingly, the enforceability of all agreements is limited by the rights people have and by the extent to which these rights are capable of being transferred from one person to another. Whether a purported right is genuine or can be legitimately transferred is not an issue of contract theory only, but is one that may also require reference to the underlying theory of entitlements. The explanation of the

3 *Cf.* R. Nozick, Anarchy, State and Utopia 150–53 (1974).
4 *See, e.g.,* A. Simpson, A History of the Common Law of Contract (1975); P. Atiyah, The Rise and Fall of Freedom of Contract 16 (1979); M. Horwitz, The Transformation of American Law, 1780–1860, at 162 (1977).

binding nature of contractual commitments is derived from more fundamental notions of entitlements and how they are acquired and transferred.

The subjects of most rights-transfer agreements are entitlements that are indisputably alienable. In such cases the rules of contract law are entirely sufficient to explain and justify a judicial decision. However, as will be discussed in Part IV, in rare cases – such as agreements amounting to slavery arrangements or requiring the violation of another's rights – contract law's dependence on rights theory will be of crucial importance in identifying appropriate concerns about the substance of voluntary agreements. For example, agreements to transfer inalienable rights – rights that for some reason cannot be transferred – or to transfer rights that for some reason cannot be obtained, would not, without more, be valid and enforceable contracts.[5] The process of contractual transfer cannot be completely comprehended, therefore, without considering more fundamental issues, namely the nature and sources of individual entitlements and the means by which they come to be acquired.

B. The social function of individual rights

Legal obligations may be enforced by the use or threat of legal force and this dimension of force requires moral justification. The principal task of legal theory, then, is to identify circumstances when legal enforcement is morally justified. Entitlements theories seek to perform this task by determining the individual legal rights of persons – that is, those claims of persons that may be justifiably enforced.

Any concept of individual rights must assume a social context.[6] If the world were inhabited by only one person, it might

---

5 Other bases of obligation are possible besides contractual obligation, however, such as those recognized under the law of tort and restitution.
6 I discuss the subject of entitlements at greater length in Barnett, Pursuing Justice in a Free Society: Part One – Power vs. Liberty, Crim. Just. Ethics, Summer/Fall, 1985, at 50.

make sense to speak of that person's actions as morally good or bad. Such a moral judgment might, for example, look to whether or not that person had chosen to live what might be called a "good life." Yet it makes no sense to speak about this person's rights. The need for rights arises from the moment individuals live in close enough proximity to one another to compete for the use of scarce natural resources. Some scheme of specifying how individuals may acquire, use, and transfer resources must be recognized to handle the conflicts over resource use that will inevitably arise. Certain facts of human existence make certain principles of allocation ineluctable. For example, it is a fundamental human requirement that individuals acquire and consume natural resources, even though such activity is often inconsistent with a similar use of the same resources by others.

"Property rights" is the term used to describe an individual's entitlements to use and consume resources – both the individual's person and her external possessions – free from the physical interference of others. Today, the term "property rights" tends to be limited only to rights to external resources. Traditionally, however, it referred to the moral and legal jurisdiction a person has both over her body and over external resources.[7] The exact contours of a proper theory of rights need not be specified here. We need only recognize that *some* allocation of rights to resource possession and use is an unavoidable prerequisite of human survival and of human fulfillment and that, once allocated, at least some rights must be alienable.

A theory of contractual obligation is the part of an entitlements theory that focuses on liability arising from the wrongful interference with a valid rights transfer. Until such an interference is corrected – by force if necessary – the distribution of resources caused by the interference is unjust. Justice normally requires that this situation be corrected to bring

---

7 *See, e.g.,* J. Locke, An Essay Concerning the True Original Extent and End of Civil Government, in Two Treatises of Civil Government ch. V § 27 (1690) ("every man has a *property* in his own *person*").

resource distribution into conformity with entitlements. In sum, contract law, according to an entitlements approach, is a body of general principles and more specific rules the function of which is to identify the rights of individuals engaged in transferring entitlements. These rights are then used to justify physical or legal force to rectify any unjust interference with the transfer process.

C. Consent as the moral component of contract

To identify the moral component that distinguishes valid from invalid rights transfers, it is first necessary to separate moral principles governing the rightful acquisition and use of resources from those governing their transfer. Rights are the means by which freedom of action and interaction is facilitated and regulated in society, and thus the rights we have to acquire previously unowned resources and to use that which we acquire must not be subject to the expressed assent of others. Although societal acquiescence may be a practical necessity for rights to be legally respected, no individual or group need actually consent to our appropriation of previously unowned resources or their use for our rights to morally vest. Similarly, principles governing rights transfer should be distinguished from principles governing resource use. Tort law concerns obligations arising from interferences with others' rights. A tortfeasor who interferes with another's rights (rather than obtaining a valid transfer of those rights to herself) is liable because of that interference, not because she consented to be held liable for her actions. A tortfeasor can be said to forfeit (as opposed to alienate or transfer) rights to resources in order to provide compensation to the victim of the tort.[8]

In contrast, contract law concerns enforceable obligations arising from the valid transfer of entitlements that are *already vested* in someone, and this difference is what makes consent

8 *See* J. Feinberg, Rights, Justice, and the Bounds of Liberty 238, 239–40 (1980); Kuflik, The Inalienability of Autonomy, 13 Phil. & Pub. Affs. 271, 275 (1984).

a moral prerequisite to contractual obligation. The rules governing the transfer of property rights perform the same function as rules governing their acquisition and those specifying their proper content: facilitating freedom of human action and interaction in a social context. Freedom of action and interaction would be seriously impeded, and possibly destroyed, if legitimate rights-holders who have not acted in a tortious manner could be deprived of their rights by force of law without their consent.

Of course, I can only summarize here the many reasons why viewing consent as the moral basis of contractual obligation – a view that is sometimes called "freedom of contract" – is so important to the operation of the enterprise of entitlements. These reasons cluster around two distinct dimensions of the consent requirement. The first dimension of consent may be called "freedom *to* contract." Viewing the rights-holder's consent as normally sufficient to transfer alienable rights enables persons to exchange entitlements to resources when, on their judgment, they can put the resources they obtain to better use than the resources they transfer. It also permits persons to make gratuitous transfers when they judge that under the circumstances the recipient can put the resource to better use than they can.

The second aspect of consent may be called "freedom *from* contract." Rights to resources may not be taken without obtaining the consent of the rights-holder. By rendering persons' control over resources immune from forced transfers, the requirement of consent permits persons to plan and act in reliance on their future access to their rightfully held resources. Moreover, the requirement of consent mandates that others take the interests of the rights-holder into account when seeking to obtain her rights. Only a requirement of consent can ensure that the welfare of the rights-holder is properly included in another's allocational decision making. And the requirement of consent at the level of individuals is what makes possible the generation of market prices that convey invaluable information about relative scarcity and

141

competing uses for resources in a form that may – indeed must – be taken into account when choices concerning scarce resources are made.

Although it is not altogether novel to suggest that consent is at the heart of contract law,[9] this view did not ultimately prevail among modern contract theorists and philosophers who largely adopted a promissory definition of contract.[10] Perhaps because promising is but a special instance of consent,[11] the prevailing equation of contract with promise[12] is what has blinded the profession to the more fundamental theoretical role of consent. Moreover, that contractual obligation arises from a consent to alienate rights and is thereby dependent on a theory of entitlements or property rights is also largely overlooked.[13] Yet it is certainly a commonly held and plausible conception of ownership that owning resources

---

9 See M. Ferson, The Rational Basis of Contracts and Related Problems in Legal Analysis 60 (1949); id., Fiction vs. Reality, in re Contracts: A Survey, 7 Vand. L. Rev. 325 (1954); Green, Is an Offer Always a Promise? 23 Ill. L. Rev. 95 (1928).

10 See, e.g., Restatement (Second) of Contracts § 1 (1979): "A contract is a promise or a set of promises for the breach of which the law gives a remedy, or the performance of which the law in some way recognizes as a duty." For an example of the typical modern insistence on the promissory nature of contracts, see E. Farnsworth, Contracts § 1.1, at 4 (1982).

Because a consent theory embraces more than the enforcement of promises, the most appropriate terms to describe contracting parties might be "transferor" and "transferee." For convenience, however, the more conventional terms "promisor" and "promisee" will still occasionally be used here.

11 See P. Atiyah, Promises, Morals, and Law 177 (1981) ("Promising may be reducible to a species of consent, for consent is a broader and perhaps more basic source of obligation").

12 See, e.g., C. Fried, Contract as Promise (1981).

13 But see Cheung, Transaction Costs, Risk Aversion, and the Choice of Contractual Arrangements, 12 J.L. & Econ. 23 (1969); Evers, Toward a Reformulation of the Law of Contracts, 1 J. Libertarian Stud. 3 (1977); Friedman, Restitution of Benefits Obtained Through the Appropriation of Property or the Commission of a Wrong, 80 Colum. L. Rev. 504 (1980); Kronman, Contract Law and Distributive Justice, 89 Yale L.J. 472 (1980); Macneil, Relational Contract: What We Do and Do Not Know, 1985 Wis. L. Rev. 483, 523.

gives one the right to possess, use, and consensually transfer the rights to them free from the forcible coercion of others.

II. DEFINING CONSENT

A. Consent and the objective theory of contract

At first blush, a consent theory of contract may appear to some to be a version of a "will theory." A will theory bases contractual obligation on the fact that an obligation was freely assumed. Understanding the fundamental differences between the two approaches, therefore, will assist an appreciation of the comparative virtues of the consent theory. A theory that bases contractual obligation on the existence of a "will to be bound" is hard-pressed to justify contractual obligation in the absence of an actual exercise of the will. It is difficult to see how a theory that bases the enforceability of commitments on their willful quality can justify enforcing objectively manifested agreements when one of the parties did not subjectively intend to be bound. Yet the enforcement of such agreements is, and has always been, widely accepted. In contrast to a will theory, a consent theory's recognition of the dependence of contractual obligation on a rights analysis is able to account for the normal relationship between objective and subjective considerations in contract law.

The concept of rights or entitlements is a social one whose principal function is to specify boundaries within which individuals may operate freely to pursue their respective individual ends and thereby provide the basis for cooperative interpersonal activity. The boundaries of individual discretion that are defined by a system of clear entitlements serve to allocate decision-making authority among individuals. Vital information is thereby conveyed to all those who might wish to avoid disputes and respect the rights of others, provided they know what those rights are. Potential conflicts between persons who might otherwise vie for control of a given resource are thus avoided. Therefore, to fulfill its social function, entitlements theory demands that the boundaries of protected domains be ascertainable, not only by judges who must resolve disputes that have arisen, but, perhaps more importantly, by the affected persons themselves before any dispute occurs.

In contract law, this informational or "boundary-defining" requirement means that an assent to alienate rights must be *manifested* in some manner by one party to the other to serve as a criterion of enforcement. Without a manifestation of assent that is accessible to all affected parties, the aspect of a system of entitlements that governs transfers of rights will fail to achieve its main function. At the time of the transaction, it will have failed to identify clearly and communicate to both parties (and to third parties) the rightful boundaries that must be respected. Without such communication, parties to a transaction (and third parties) cannot accurately ascertain what constitutes rightful conduct and what constitutes a commitment on which they can rely. Disputes that might otherwise have been avoided will occur, and the attendant uncertainties of the transfer process will discourage reliance.

Although requiring the consent of the rights-holder as a condition of a valid transfer of rights is absolutely vital for the reasons discussed in Part I, whether one has consented to a transfer of rights under such a regime, however, generally depends not on one's subjective opinion about the meaning of one's freely chosen words or conduct, but on the ordinary meaning that is attached to them. If the word "yes" ordinarily means *yes*, then a subjective and unrevealed belief that "yes" means *no* is generally immaterial to a regime of entitlements allocation. Only a general reliance on objectively ascertainable assertive conduct will enable a system of entitlements to perform its allotted boundary-defining function.

Given that the function of a rights theory is to facilitate human action and interaction in a social context by defining the boundaries of permitted actions and resolve competing claims, a coherent rights theory should allocate rights largely on the basis of factors that minimize the likelihood of generating conflicting claims. In this regard, objectively manifested conduct, which usually reflects subjective intent, provides a sounder basis for contractual obligation than do subjectively held intentions. Evidence of subjective intent that is extrinsic to the transaction and was unavailable to the other party is relevant, if at all, only insofar as it helps a court to ascertain the objective meaning of certain terms.

What exact meaning must a court conclude was conveyed by a promisor to a promisee to find that a contractual commitment was incurred? If consent is properly thought of as objective or "manifested" assent, what is it that must be assented to for a contractual obligation to arise? It is not enough that one manifests a commitment to perform or refrain from doing some act. Such a manifestation would be nothing more than a promise[14] and contract theory searches for the "extra" factor that, if present, justifies the legal enforcement of a commitment or promise. The entitlements approach sketched above specifies that consent to a transfer of rights is this factor.

The consent that is required is a *manifestation of an intention to alienate rights*. In a system of entitlements where consent to transfer rights is what justifies the legal enforcement of agreements, any such manifestation implies that one intends to be legally bound to adhere to one's commitment. Therefore, the phrase "a manifestation of an intention to be legally bound"[15] neatly captures what a court should seek to find before holding that an enforceable transfer of alienable rights has been effected.

B. The proper limits of the objective approach

A consent theory also explains the limits of the objective approach – why the objective interpretation of a party's acts

14 *See, e.g.*, Restatement (Second) of Contracts § 2 (1979) ("A promise is a manifestation of intention to act or refrain from action in a specified way, so made as to justify a promisee in understanding that a commitment has been made").

15 *Cf.* Green, Is an Offer Always a Promise?, 23 Ill L. Rev. 301, 302 (1928); Lorenzen, Causa and Consideration in the Law of Contracts, 28 Yale L.J. 621, 646 (1919).

will yield, at times, to proof of a different subjective understanding of one or both parties. To find the presence of consent, what matters is the meaning that is generally attached
to some given word or conduct indicating assent – a meaning
to which both parties have access. In contract law, this generalized meaning therefore becomes the presumptive meaning.[16] The presumption can be rebutted, not by reference to
the promisor's subjective intent in performing the consenting
acts, but either by proof of any special meaning that the
parties' behavior reveals they held in common,[17] which
would negate the social function of accepting the generalized
meaning, or by the promisor's proof that the listener did not
actually understand the "reasonable" meaning to be the intended meaning. A promisee is not "justified" in relying on
the ordinary meaning of a promisor's words or deeds where
a special meaning can be proved to have been actually understood by both parties. Similarly, the enforcement of the "reasonable" meaning serves no constructive purpose where it
was not the promisee's actual understanding. The boundary-
determining function of a rights analysis simply does not
require that such reliance be protected or such a meaning
enforced.

Further, permitting a promisor to contest whether a promisee did in fact rely upon the objective meaning does not
jeopardize the boundary-defining function of contract law in
a consent theory. Assuming that a promisor can prove such
an allegation, the reliance that the objective approach is designed to protect is nonexistent, and permitting such proof
would provide few opportunities for fraud. In this regard a
consent theory conforms to the traditionally accepted interpretation of the objective theory.[18]

This analysis also explains why the misuse of a particular
term by party A who was unaware of its ordinary meaning
would not bind A if it could be shown that B, the other party,

16 See Restatement (Second) of Contracts § 201 comment a (1979).
17 See id. § 201 comment a.
18 See, e.g., Embry v. Hargadine, McKittrick Dry Goods Co., 127 Mo.
    App. 383, 392, 105 S.W. 777, 780 (1907).

was made aware of this mistake by the circumstances of the transaction.[19] Proof of this occurrence would show that the normal boundary-defining function of an objective approach designed to protect parties in *B*'s position had been satisfied by *B*'s actual knowledge of *A*'s meaning. A consent theory, therefore, explains both why parties are free to shift away from the ordinary meanings of words or deeds either intentionally or inadvertently, and why, if a shift by both cannot be shown, the ordinary or objective meaning will govern.

Persons generally use conventional words and actions to convey their intentions with a considerable degree of accuracy. Because of this, only in very unusual circumstances will the outcome of an objective approach based upon the ordinary and natural meaning of words and other assertive conduct differ from that of a subjective approach. Most cases would come out the same in either event. But unlike a will theory, a consent theory – because it is based on fundamental notions of entitlements – can explain both why we generally enforce the objective manifestation of consent when it differs from subjective intent and the exceptions where evidence of subjective intent will prevail.

III. DETERMINING CONTRACTUAL OBLIGATION IN A CONSENT THEORY

A. Establishing the prima facie case of consent

Richard Epstein has suggested that legal principles used to determine obligation can best be thought of as presumptive in nature.[20] Any such presumption of obligation, however, may be rebutted if other facts are proved to have existed that undermine the normal significance of the prima facie case. Such responses or "defenses" to the prima facie case are themselves only presumptively compelling. They in turn may be rebutted by still other facts alleged by the person

19 *See* Restatement (Second) of Contracts § 153 (1979).
20 *See* Epstein, Pleadings and Presumptions, 40 U. Chi. L. Rev. 556 (1973).

seeking relief. In this way the principles or elements that determine legal obligation come in "stages."[21]

In a consent theory, absent the assertion of a valid defense, proof of consent to transfer alienable rights is legally sufficient to establish the existence of a contractual obligation. Consent is prima facie binding both because of its usual connection with subjective assent (which protects the autonomy of the promisor) and because people usually have access only to the manifested intentions of others (which protects the reliance of the promisee and others as well as the security of transactions). There are two ways to manifest one's intention to be legally bound.[22] The first is to deliberately "channel" one's behavior through the use of a legal formality in such a way as to convey explicitly a certain meaning – that of having an intention to be legally bound – to another. This is the formal means of consenting. The second and, perhaps, more common method is by indirectly or implicitly conveying this meaning by other types of behavior. This is the informal means of consenting.

1. *Formal consent.* For a considerable part of the history of the common law, the principal way of creating what we now think of as a contractual obligation was to cast one's agreement in the form of a sealed writing.[23] The emergence of assumpsit as the principal action of contractual enforcement required the development of a doctrinal limitation on the enforcement of commitments – that is, the doctrine of consideration.[24] This development eventually resulted in the ascendancy of the bargain theory of consideration, which had the unintended consequence of creating doctrinal problems

---

21 *See* Fletcher, The Right and the Reasonable, 98 Harv. L. Rev. 949 (1985).
22 The analysis presented in this section has been greatly expanded and refined in Barnett & Becker, Beyond Reliance: Promissory Estoppel, Contract Formalities, and Misrepresentations, 15 Hofstra L. Rev. 443 (1987).
23 *See* A. Simpson, *supra* note 4, at 88–90.
24 The Statute of Frauds, passed in 1677, was another such limitation. *See id.*, at 599–600.

for the enforcement of formal commitments where there was no bargained-for consideration. Notwithstanding their ancient history, formal commitments, such as those under seal, came to be thought of as "exceptions" to the 'normal' requirement of consideration. Expressions such as "a seal imports consideration" or is "a substitute for consideration" became commonplace.[25] In a climate of opinion dominated by notions of "bargained-for consideration" and "induced reliance," when there is no bargain and no demonstrable reliance to support enforcement, formal promises have had an uncertain place in the law of contract.

A consent theory of contract, however, provides the missing theoretical foundation of formal contracts and explains their proper place in a well-crafted law of contract. The voluntary use of a recognized formality by a promisor manifests to a promisee an intention to be legally bound in the most unambiguous manner possible. Formal contracts ought to be an "easy" case of contractual enforcement, but prevailing theories that require bargained-for consideration or induced reliance would have a hard time explaining why. For example, when there is no separate bargained-for consideration for making an offer irrevocable for a certain period of time, a bargain theory of consideration would have a difficult time explaining the enforceability of "firm offers" which require neither consideration nor detrimental reliance for enforcement to be obtained.[26] In a consent theory, by contrast, there need be no underlying bargain or demonstrable reliance for such a commitment to be properly enforced.

The same holds true for nominal consideration and for false recitals of consideration. A consent theory acknowledges that, if properly evidenced, the exchange of one dollar or a false recital by the parties that consideration exists may fulfill the channeling function of formalities, whether or not any

---

25 *See, e.g.,* In re Conrad's Estate, 333 Pa. 561, 563, 3 A.2d 697, 699 (1938); Aller v. Aller, 40 N.J.L. 446 (1878); *cf.* Crane, The Magic of the Private Seal, 15 Colum. L. Rev. 24, 25–26 (1915).
26 In sales contracts, firm offers are enforceable without consideration by U.C.C. § 2–205 (1977).

bargained-for consideration for the commitment in fact exists. If it is widely known that the written phrase "in return for good and valuable consideration" means that one intends to make a legally binding commitment, then these words will fulfill a channeling function as well as, and perhaps better than, a seal or other formality. The current rule that the falsity of such a statement permits a court to nullify a transaction because of a lack of consideration[27] is therefore contrary to a consent theory of contract.

2. *Informal consent.* Consent to transfer rights can be express or implied. Formal contracts expressing consent to transfer alienable rights pose no problem for a consent theory. The enforcement of informal commitments where evidence of legally binding intentions is more obscure, however, has plagued contract law for centuries. In such agreements courts must infer assent to be legally bound from the circumstances or the "considerations"[28] or "causa"[29] that induced the parties' actions.

(a) Bargaining as evidence of consent. Within a consent theory, the fact that a person has received something of value in return for a promise may indeed indicate that this promise was an expression of intention to transfer rights. Moreover, in some circumstances where gratuitous transfers are unusual, the receipt of a benefit in return for a promise should serve as objective notice to the promisor that the promise has been interpreted by the other party to be legally binding.[30]

27 *See* Restatement (Second) of Contracts § 71 comment b (1979); *see, e.g.,* Schnell v. Nell, 17 Ind. 29, 32 (1861); Shepard v. Rhodes, 7 R.I. 470, 475 (1863). *But see* Restatement (Second) of Contracts § 87(1)(a) (1979).
28 On this archaic usage of the word "consideration," see A. Simpson, *supra* note 4, at 321.
29 For the possible parallels between consideration and the civilian concept of "causa," *see* Mason, The Utility of Consideration – A Comparative View, 41 Colum. L. Rev. 825, 825–31 (1941).
30 The duties, if any, the receipt of a nongratuitous benefit imposes on the recipient are beyond the scope of this essay, except to note that such receipt may manifest the recipient's intent to be legally bound to a contemporaneous commitment.

Although the existence of a bargain or other motivation for a transaction may be good evidence of the sort of agreement that has been made, in a consent theory the absence of consideration does not preclude the application of legal sanctions if other indicia of consent are present. So if it can be proved, for example, that a party voluntarily consented to be legally bound to keep an offer to transfer rights open, to release a debt, to modify an obligation, or to pay for past favors,[31] the lack of bargained-for consideration will not bar enforcement of these kinds of commitments in a consent theory.

Where bargaining is the norm – as it is in most sales transactions – there is little need for the law to require explicit proof of an intent to be legally bound, such as an additional formality, or even proof of the existence of a bargain. In such circumstances, if an arm's-length agreement to sell can be proved, there presumptively has been a manifestation of intent to be legally bound. For this reason, the Uniform Commercial Code's stricture that "[a] contract for the sale of goods may be made in any manner sufficient to show agreement, including conduct by both parties which recognizes the existence of such a contract,"[32] is entirely consonant with a consent theory.

(b) Reliance as evidence of consent. A consent theory also identifies those circumstances where the presence of reliance provides an adequate substitute for the traditional requirement of consideration. If the primary function of consideration is to serve as one way of manifesting assent to be legally bound, and not as a necessary element of the prima facie case of contractual obligation, then reliance and consideration may sometimes be functionally equivalent. Expenditures made by a promisee in reliance on the words and conduct of the prom-

---

31 These are examples given by Charles Fried as hard cases for traditional consideration theory. *See* C. Fried, *supra* note 12. Note that in real cases of this kind, formalities adequate to indicate consent are often present.

32 U.C.C. § 2–204 (1977).

isor may prove as much about the nature of this transaction as the existence of consideration, especially where the reliance is or should be known to the promisor.

Suppose that A makes a substantial promise to B – for example, a promise to convey land. The promise while clear may be ambiguous as to its intended legal effect. Does A intend to be bound and subject to legal enforcement if she reneges, or is she merely stating her current view of her future intentions? Now suppose that B announces to A his intention to rely on A's promise in a substantial way – for example, by building a house on the land – and that A says nothing. Suppose further that B commences construction and observes A watching in silence. It would seem that under such circumstances A's ambiguous legal intent has been clarified. By remaining silent in the face of reliance so substantial that B would not have undertaken it without a legal commitment from A – A could not reasonably have believed that B intended to make a gift to her of the house – A has manifested an intention to be legally bound.[33]

In this manner, a promisor's silence while observing substantial reliance on the promise by the promisee can manifest the promisor's assent to the promisee. In a consent theory, if consent is proved, then enforcement is warranted even if a bargain or a formality is absent. In sum, bargained-for consideration and nonbargained-for reliance are equivalent to the extent that the existence of either in a transaction may manifest the intentions of one or both of the parties to be legally bound. In any case, the absence of either bargained-for consideration or reliance will not bar the enforcement of a transfer of entitlements that can be proved in some way – for example, by a formal written document or by adequate proof of a sufficiently unambiguous verbal commitment.[34]

---

33   *See, e.g.,* Greiner v. Greiner, 293 P. 759 (Kan. 1930); Seavey v. Drake, 62 N.H. 393 (1882); Roberts-Horsfield v. Gedicks, 94 N.J. Eq. 82, 118 A. 275 (1922). In each of these cases, the promisor remained silent in the face of substantial reliance on a promise to convey land. The courts granted relief despite the lack of bargained-for consideration.

34   It is not being suggested here that such prophylactic measures that

B. Contract defenses: rebutting the prima facie case of consent

Consent, either formal or informal, is required to make out a prima facie case of contractural obligation. This means that, in the absence of an "affirmative" defense to the prima facie case of contractual obligation, the manifested intention of a party to transfer alienable rights will justify the enforcement of such a commitment. Traditional contract defenses can be understood as describing circumstances that, if proved to have existed, deprive the manifestation of assent of its normal moral, and therefore legal, significance. These defenses may be clustered into three groups, each of which undermines the prima facie case of consent in a different way.

The first group of defenses – duress, misrepresentation, and (possibly) unconscionability[35] – describes circumstances where the manifestation of an intention to be legally bound has been obtained improperly by the promisee. The manifestation of assent either was improperly coerced by the promisee or was based on misinformation for which the promisee was responsible. The second group – incapacity, infancy, and intoxication – describes attributes of the promisor that indicate a lack of ability to assert meaningful assent. The third group – mistake, impracticability, and frustration – stem from the inability to fully express in any agreement all possible contingencies that might affect performance. Each describes those types of events (a) whose nonoccurrence was arguably a real, but tacit assumption upon which consent was based, and (b) for which the promisee should bear the risk of occurrence.[36] Each type of defense thus is

serve an evidentiary function - such as a statute of frauds, a parol evidence rule, or certain formal requirements - are inappropriate in a consent theory. This issue is discussed in Barnett & Becker, *supra* note 22, at 470–85.

35 For analyses of unconscionability that would place it in this category of defenses, *see*, *e.g.*, Epstein, Unconscionability: A Critical Reappraisal, 18 J.L. & Econ. 293 (1975); Leff, Unconscionability and the Code – The Emperor's New Clause, 115 U. Pa. L. Rev. 485 (1967).

36 In this third group of defenses, the consent was not improperly induced by the promisee, and the person giving consent was capable

distinguished by the way it undermines the normal, presumed significance of consent. But all valid contract defenses describe general circumstances where the appearance of assent tends to lack its normal moral significance. These traditional contract defenses function in a consent theory, as they do currently, to preserve the actual voluntariness of rights transfer in those comparatively rare cases where consent has been improperly coerced or where we are willing to acknowledge other circumstances, such as misinformation, that vitiate the presence of consent. This refusal to enforce some instances of apparent assent does not, however, reflect a retreat to a subjective will theory. It remains true that an objective manifestation of intent to be legally bound is sufficient to give rise to an enforceable commitment. The only qualification is that this objective manifestation must have been voluntary.

IV. CONTRACT REMEDIES AND INALIENABLE RIGHTS

A. Remedies for breach of contract

Traditionally, the common law has distinguished between legal relief and equitable relief. Legal relief was relief available in "courts of law." Equitable relief was extraordinary relief originally available from the King, then from the King's Chancellor, and finally from the Chancery courts or "courts of equity."[37] Legal relief for breach of contract normally takes the form of money damages. Equitable relief normally consists either of specific performance or an injunction – that is,

of doing so. This, in part, may help explain why courts are quite receptive to arguments by the promisee that the promisor assumed the risk of the mistake, impracticability, or frustration. See E. Farnsworth, *supra* note 10, §§ 9.3–.4, 9.6–.7, at 659–61, 666, 684–86, 692–94.

37 See D. Dobbs, Handbook on the Law of Remedies 24–34 (1973); E. Farnsworth, *supra* note 10, at 818–24. These were not, however, the only court systems that coexisted in England. See H. Berman, Law and Revolution 10 (1984).

the party in breach may be ordered to perform an act or to refrain from performing an act.

The present rule governing legal and equitable remedies for breach of contract can be simply stated: Legal relief – money damages – is available as a matter of right. Equitable relief – specific performance or injunction – is available upon a showing by the party seeking enforcement that legal relief is somehow "inadequate."[38] Put another way, money damages are the presumptive form of remedy for breach of contract. Specific performance orders and injunctions are exceptional forms of contract remedies.[39]

In this section, I explain why a consent theory of contract undercuts the traditional rule favoring money damages and supports a presumption in favor of specific performance – unless the parties have consented to money damages instead. The principal obstacle to such an approach is the reluctance of courts to specifically enforce contracts for personal services. In what follows, I suggest that the philosophical distinction between alienable and inalienable rights bolsters this historical reticence because a right to personal services may be seen as inalienable. If, however, the subject matter of a contract for personal services is properly confined to an alienable right to money damages for failure to perform, specific enforcement of such contracts is no longer problematic. I also consider whether contracts for corporate services are like contracts for personal services in that they may properly be

---

38 The actual historical picture may not be quite this clear-cut. For one thing, medieval English common law courts may not have had as strong a preference for money damages as is commonly assumed. *See* F. Pollock & F. Maitland, The History of English Law 595 (1898). For another, during most of the medieval period, the effective remedy for breach of most contracts in the common law court was enforcement of a penal bond. *See generally* A. Simpson, *supra* note 4, at 88–125. Thus, every sort of obligation could be reduced to a monetary one or a "debt" by the party in breach. Beginning in 1283, a debtor's liability to pay could be enforced by imprisonment; see *id.*, at 87.

39 For a fuller description and excellent assessment of the present law governing this subject, *see* Kronman, Specific Performance, 45 U. Chi. L. Rev. 351 (1978); Schwartz, The Case for Specific Performance, 89 Yale L.J., 271 (1979).

enforced only by money damages, or whether performance of corporate services can be made the subject of a valid rights transfer and judicially compelled in the same manner as contracts for external resources.

B. Inalienable rights

As was discussed in Part I, a property rights conception of entitlements suggests that rights are best construed as enforceable claims to acquire, use, and transfer resources in the world – as claims to control one's person and external resources. As was discussed in Part II, a consent theory of contract specifies that an enforceable transfer of rights requires the satisfaction of at least two conditions: (1) The *subject* of a contract – as opposed to its object (or purpose) – must be a morally justifiable right possessed by the transferor that is interpersonally transferable, or "alienable"; (2) the holder of the right must *consent* to its transfer. Thus, commitments will generally be enforced only if they manifest to the promisee the promisor's assent to transfer alienable rights.

The fact that there must be a consent to transfer *alienable rights* suggests that the issue of contractual enforceability could potentially turn on one of two inquiries into the subject matter of the contract. First, are the rights that are allegedly being transferred to the promisee in fact held by the promisor? Second, are the rights that are the subject of a purported transfer agreement the *kinds* of rights that can be transferred? The second of these inquires involves the distinction between alienable and inalienable rights, a distinction that has been widely discussed in recent years.[40] To characterize a right as inalienable is to claim that the consent of the right-holder is insufficient to extinguish the right or to transfer it to an-

40 Much of the recent legal literature was stimulated by Calabresi & Melamed's seminal article, Property Rules, Liability Rules, and Inalienability: One View of the Cathedral, 85 Harv. L. Rev. 1089–1128 (1972).

other.[41] Such a claim must be distinguished from a claim that a right is forfeitable. As one philosopher has noted, "[a] person who has forfeited a right has lost the right because of some offence or wrongdoing."[42]

Elsewhere I have discussed four reasons why consent might be insufficient to extinguish or transfer certain rights.[43] In this essay I shall confine my discussion to a reason for inalienability that is peculiar to a regime of property rights: namely that, within such a scheme, certain of these rights literally cannot be transferred. If rights are enforceable claims to control resources in the world and contracts are enforceable transfers of these rights, then, when control of a resource cannot in fact be transferred, a right to control the resource also cannot be transferred.

Suppose that *A* consented to transfer partial or complete control of his body to *B*. Absent some physiological change in *A* (caused, perhaps, by voluntarily and knowingly ingesting some special drug or undergoing psychosurgery)[44] there is no way for such a commitment to be carried out. True, *A* could conform his conduct to the orders of *B*, but, his agreement notwithstanding, he would still retain control over his actions and would willfully have to act so as to conform his actions to *B*'s orders. Because *A* cannot in fact transfer the control of his body to *B*, despite the alleged

41 *See* McConnell, The Nature and Basis of Inalienable Rights, 3 Law and Phil. 43 (1984).
42 *Id.*, at 28. *See also* J. Feinberg, *supra* note 8, at 240–42; and D. Meyers, Inalienable Rights: A Defense 13–15 (1985).
43 *See* Barnett, Contract Remedies, *supra* note 2, at 186–94.
44 Arthur Kuflik offers these examples to undercut this type of argument for inalienability. *See* Kuflik, *supra* note 8, at 281 ("This suggests that the impropriety of an autonomy-abdicating agreement has more to do with the impropriety of autonomy-abdication itself than with some general fact that we have no right to make commitments we know we will be unable to keep"). But arguments based on impropriety and one based on the impossibility of such agreements are not mutually exclusive. Kuflik's examples only show that this reason for inalienability is *limited* to those commitments to alienate the future control over one's person which are not made possible by mind-altering drugs, brainwashing techniques, or psychosurgery.

transfer of a right to control from *A* to *B*, *B* would in fact be forced to rely on *A*'s actual control of his body to carry out *B*'s orders.[45] *B*'s "control" of *A*'s body would, then, be metaphorical rather than actual. This is not to say that force is ineffective in getting slaves or servants to obey the orders of their putative masters but, rather, that force would be unnecessary if the actual control of servants' bodies could be transferred to the masters as specified by the terms of the agreement.

This distinction between alienable and inalienable, transferable and nontransferable rights corresponds to the distinction recognized in civil law countries between contracts "to give" and contracts "to do."[46] The former kind of contract transfers a right to control external resources; the latter calls for some future act involving the use of one's person. Surely, the former kind of transfer is possible. What is *my* house or car could equally well be *your* house and car. But bodies are different from other kinds of things. What is *my* body cannot literally be made *your* body. Because there is no obstacle to transferring control of a house or car (of the sort that is unavoidably presented when one attempts to transfer control over one's body), there is no obstacle to transferring the right to control a house or car.[47] But if control cannot be trans-

45 Similarly, a promise to undergo a dependency-inducing procedure would be an unenforceable attempt to transfer an inalienable right: the right to control whether or not to submit to the operation. But third parties might have no right to forcibly interfere with someone who voluntarily undergoes such a procedure. (The claim, for example, that members of religious "cults" may rightfully be kidnapped and "deprogrammed" is properly controversial.) A person who voluntarily submitted to such a procedure (assuming that such a procedure actually worked) might be committing a nonfatal kind of "suicide" (zombicide?) and the "master" or guardian *would* then become legally responsible for his ward.

46 *See* B. Nicholas, French Law of Contract 149 (1982); Treitel, Remedies for Breach of Contract, *in* 7 International Encyclopedia of Comparative Law 13 (A. Mehren, ed., 1976).

47 Transferring ownership in animals may be seen as presenting a special difficulty. Cannot animals refuse the orders of the master? But the problem of control here is less than meets the eye. The second owner gets no more control and hence no more rights than those held by

ferred, then it is hard to see how a right to control can be transferred.

It will not do to argue that such a right to control is transferable because a putative master can obtain legal enforcement of the agreement. Such a claim is a *non sequitur* in an entitlement theory. According to entitlement theories, we do not have rights because our claims are in fact enforced. Rather, our claims are enforced because we can demonstrate that we have rights. Nor would an award of money damages for breach of contract to perform services in the future necessarily entail that a right to the services themselves had been alienated. Rather, as will be discussed below, such a claim could be as well accounted for by saying that it is the right *to the money* – an indisputably alienable right – that has been conditionally transferred; the condition being the nonperformance of the services.

Suppose, now, that the agreement between *A* and *B* was recast to read that *A* transfers to *B* "the right to use force against *A* to compel *A* to conform his conduct to *B*'s commands." It would appear that since it is possible for *B* to use force against *A*, the right to use force can be transferred as well and, therefore, this agreement is not barred by reason of impossibility (though it might be subject to other difficulties). Upon closer inspection, however, such an agreement does not escape the problem of attempting to transfer a right of control which cannot in fact be transferred.

If *B* has the right to use force against *A*, then *A* may not rightfully resist. But *B* has the right to use force against *A*

the original owner. Suppose the promisor attempted to transfer the right to a horse that would cuddle up with you in bed. Unless the first owner actually possessed such a horse, the *right to this kind* of horse could not pass. While the failure to tender this kind of horse would not alone constitute a breach of contract, the possibility of an action for fraud or breach of warranty remains. In contrast, the issue of inalienable human rights concerns the rights an individual *retains* despite the fact that consent to transfer these rights may have been expressed. Therefore, the truly analogous problem with animals is whether or not sentient animals themselves have rights – inalienable or otherwise – in the first place, an issue that is well beyond the scope of this treatment.

only if such force can be justified. Such force may be justified if *A* consented or appeared to consent (and did not change his mind) – for example, if *A* and *B* were prize fighters or stunt men, or if *A* was a masochist. The crucial question, however, is not whether *A*'s consent to the use of force by *B* justifies *B*'s actions, but whether *A*'s prior consent can limit his right to withhold consent in the future when he has a change of heart.

Suppose that, after promising to perform services and granting to *B* the "right" to use force to compel performance, *A* thinks better of it and revokes his consent. When *B* (or a court) attempts to enforce *B*'s commands, may *A* rightfully resist? The argument that *B* may rightfully use force against *A* entails that *A* no longer has a right to resist *B* because, by his agreement, *A* consented to transfer this right to *B*. This is so because, had *A* retained his right to resist B, then *A* would be acting both rightfully and wrongfully should he resist *B* and such a conflict of rights is barred by the com-possibility feature of an entitlements theory.[48] That is, there would be a conflict between *A*'s right to resist and *B*'s right to use force against *A* and the requirement of compossibility requires it be possible for all valid rights to be exercised simultaneously.

Yet *A*'s agreement notwithstanding, *A* retains his ability to resist *B*. Just as *A* cannot alienate his right to the future control of his person because his ability to control his person cannot literally be transferred, *A* cannot have transferred or lost his right to resist when he retains his ability to resist.[49]

---

48 For a discussion of the role of compossibility in property rights theory, *see* R. Nozick, *supra* note 3, at 199; Steiner, The Structure of a Set of Compossible Rights, 74 J. of Phil. 767 (1977); Barnett, *supra* note 6, at 58.

49 True, as above, *A* can voluntarily submit to procedures which would eliminate his ability to resist (although it is very hard to imagine the value to a master of a slave who had lost the power to physically resist violence). The harder question would then be, in the unlikely event that *A*'s ability to resist had been alienated, could others right-fully go to *A*'s defense? This issue would perhaps be best governed by principles of guardianship. *See* Kuflik, *supra* note 8, at 275; Barnett,

Therefore, if *A* may still rightfully resist *B*, then *B* cannot have acquired the right to use force against *A*, since such a right would also impose on *A* a contradictory duty to refrain from resisting.

True, when *A* transfers alienable rights to *external* resources to *B*, *A* loses his right to resist *B*'s use and enjoyment of these resources notwithstanding the fact that *A* retains his ability to resist *B*'s use. But with such an agreement *A* transfers to *B* the "right to use and enjoy the external resources" and it is this right that renders *A*'s subsequent resistance wrongful. *A* loses his right to resist *B*'s use and enjoyment of the resource in question, not because he transferred his right to resist, but because such resistance would interfere with *B*'s right to control the resource. In sum, it is *A*'s consent to transfer an alienable right that renders any subsequent resistance by him wrongful, not his consent to transfer his right to resist. And there is no barrier to transferring the right to control the resource to *B* because *B*, no less than *A*, is capable of exercising such a right.

We can now see why an agreement to transfer *A*'s "right to resist *B*'s use of force" to *B* fails. First, such a rights transfer purports to transfer a right to resist when it is quite impossible for *B* to exercise *A*'s ability to resist; and second, there is no other alienable right to control resources being legitimately transferred that would render *A*'s subsequent resistance wrongful. The only other rights transfer that would render *A*'s resistance wrongful would be the transfer of *A*'s right to control his body and this right, for reasons discussed above, is inalienable. And if *A* retains his right to resist *B*, then, notwithstanding any agreement between *A* and *B*, the requirement of compossibility mandates that *B* may not rightfully use force against *A*. Although this analysis may seem suspiciously complicated, its conclusion should not be surprising, for a "right to resist the force used by another" is simply a specialized instance of the right to control one's person – a right that cannot be alienated.

supra note 6, at 69 (briefly discussing the concept of guardianship in a Liberty Approach).

The implications of this analysis may appear far-reaching.[50] The enforceability of *all* commitments to perform personal services in the future appears to have been undercut. When a promisor who has promised to perform services in the future refuses to perform, because no right to performance has been transferred to the promisee by the promise, no right of the promisee is violated by nonperformance. But, as will be considered below, the actual consequence of such analysis is only to limit the remedy for nonperformance of personal service commitments to money damages.

Anthony Kronman has argued that legal prohibitions of slavery, though permissible, are "paternalist."[51] But, although arguments for inalienable rights may be paternalist, this need not be so. Surely the account just provided is not paternalist. No one may rightfully interfere in the consensual sacrificial conduct of a competent adult – as a parent may interfere with a child – simply because the intermeddler thinks he knows what is best for the individual making the sacrifice. Rather, when a right is viewed as inalienable, the law should not specifically enforce an agreement to transfer such a right when the original rights-holder thinks better of it.

Inalienable rights define a category of decisions about which competent adults may rightfully override *their own* previously expressed preferences. Where *ex ante* consent and *ex post* consent are the same, there would be no breach of contract. Restrictions on alienability, then, are really rules concerning which of two inconsistent expressions of assent by the same party determines the rights of both parties to

50 Note, however, that the analysis just presented neither stems from nor supports a view that the only rights we have are those which we are able to assert – that "might makes right." The analysis of inalienability in the text claims only to describe a feature of those rights which we (arguably) have: some of these rights may be alienated or transferred, others of them may not be alienated because they cannot be. What rights we have and how we come to have them is another story requiring additional analysis. See Barnett, *supra* note 6. I thank Emilio Pacheco for bringing this issue to my attention.

51 *See* Kronman, *supra* note 13, at 774–76.

an agreement. With alienable rights, *ex ante* consent transfers rights to control resources and binds the transferor *ex post;* with inalienable rights, a right to control resources is never transferred by consent, so *ex post* consent takes precedence over *ex ante* consent. In sum, the most salient characteristic of inalienable rights may be that, while a rights-holder may *exercise* her inalienable rights for the benefit of others, a rights-holder may never surrender the privilege of changing her mind about whether to exercise such rights or not.[52]

According to the analysis presented here, which rights are alienable and which are not? The alienability of rights wholly or partially to control the future use of one's person has been called into question. The transfer of even limited rights of bodily control is barred in principle by the literal impossibility of transferring control over one's person. On the other hand, because it is possible to transfer control of external resources, consent to transfer a right to control such resources does not pose the same difficulties as consent to transfer the right to control one's person. Except in the most rare and extreme of circumstances, rights to external resources are alienable.[53]

C. Choosing between damages and specific performance

A consent theory of contract permits us to distinguish between the *subject* of a contract – that is, the particular rights

---

52 *Cf.* J.S. Mill, On Liberty 125 (Lib. of Lib. Arts ed., 1956) ("there are perhaps no contracts or engagements, except those that relate to money or money's worth, of which one can venture to say that there ought to be no liberty whatsoever of retraction"). Extreme situations warranting different treatment can always be hypothesized. For example, may a pilot be forcibly compelled to complete a journey he has contracted to fly and be prevented from parachuting out of a plane? The endangerment involved in the example, however, introduces a tortious element. The better analogy would be to ask whether a pilot who safely lands a plane short of completing a designated route can be compelled to finish the trip.

53 Other reasons for inalienability of otherwise alienable external property have been suggested, but space constraints prevent me from considering them here. *See, e.g.,* Rose-Ackerman, Inalienability and the Theory of Property Rights, 85 Colum. L. Rev. 931 (1985); Epstein, Why Restrain Alienation? 85 Colum. L. Rev. 970, 973–90 (1985).

being transferred from one party to the other – and the *object* (or objective or purpose) of a contract – that is, what the parties are trying to accomplish by transferring the rights that are the subject of the contract. For reasons just discussed, only alienable rights may be the subject of an enforceable rights-transfer agreement. In this section, the problems traditionally associated with specifically enforcing contracts for personal services will be shown to stem from the fact that inalienable rights may improperly be construed as the subject, rather than the object, of such contracts. In contrast, the specific performance of contracts for corporate services gives rise to no such problem.[54]

1. Contracts for external resources. The first kind of contract involves consent to transfer rights to possess, control, and use identifiable external resources, whether land or goods. Because rights to external resources are presumptively alienable, such rights may be made the subject of an enforceable rights transfer.

If *A* contracts to "sell" a piece of land or some good like a car to *B*, most people would expect that when the contract is executed *B* has a right to the specified land or car. Therefore, when this is the normal expectation and intention, the normal or presumptive remedy for breach of contract in such a case should be that *B*'s newly acquired rights to the land or car are respected – he gets the land or car if he still desires to receive it.[55] If not, he may elect to receive money dam-

---

54 This essay does not exhaust the subject of inalienable rights, nor that of the proper choice of contract remedies. Contracts to provide employment, for example, do not easily fit into any of the three categories of contracts discussed in this essay. Determining whether such a contract may permissibly be specifically enforced might turn out to require a more extended discussion of inalienable rights.

55 This category corresponds to the category of contracts to give (*donner*) in French law. *See* text accompanying *supra* note 46. Consistent with the analysis in the text, French law grants specific performance as a matter of right. *See* B. Nicholas, *supra* note 46, at 211; Treitel, *supra* note 46, at 13.

ages.[56] The common law apparently once granted a comparable right of replevin to buyers of goods, but, interestingly, this right appears to have been conceived of as arising from property law, not contract law.[57] A consent theory of contract says that such an agreement would ordinarily be enforced.

Of course, *A* and *B* need not agree to transfer the right to the land or car itself. They might instead include an express provision in their original contract that would rebut the normal meaning of such contracts and limit recovery for breach to money damages. The *object* of such contract might be to secure possession or delivery, but its *subject* would be a conditional transfer of a right to compensation for nonperformance rather than the right to the resource itself.

2. Contracts for personal services. What should happen if *A* breaches a commitment to provide personal services by refusing to perform as agreed? Can a commitment by *A* to *B* that *A* will do something (or refrain from doing something) for *B* constitute a valid contract? If the right to the future control of one's person is inalienable, then the personal services in question cannot be the subject of a valid rights-transfer agreement. Therefore, if a promise to provide personal services is only a commitment to exercise an inalienable right, then it is unenforceable. By breaching his promise to *B*, *A* may commit a morally bad act. He has not, however, committed a legally cognizable wrong.

---

56 *See* Dawson, Specific Performance in France and Germany, 57 Mich. L. Rev. 532 (1959). It is arguable that, in some cases, sellers might be permitted to show why buyers should not get the thing contracted for. For example, if a fungible replacement good is easily available to the buyer on the market, but performance would be an extreme hardship on the seller, then where the contract is silent on the form of relief, the seller might be liable only for money damages. Where these circumstances can be shown to exist, and in the absence of an express clause, it may no longer be safe to presume that sellers would have consented to specific relief. In contrast with the traditional rule, however, the burden of proof is placed on the appropriate party: the party in breach. For arguments against this defense *see* Schwartz, *supra* note 39, at 289 n.

57 *See* F. Kessler & G. Gilmore, Contracts: Cases and Materials 1000 (2d ed. 1970).

Alternatively, a contract "to provide personal services" might accurately be construed as a commitment to transfer alienable rights to money damages (or other alienable resources) on the condition that specified personal services are not performed as promised. Such an agreement would not purport to transfer the inalienable right to a person's services. Rather, such an agreement would (conditionally) transfer alienable rights to the money that would satisfy the judgment; it would be enforceable in the event that the condition was satisfied – that is, in the event that services were not performed as agreed. In essence, the actual commitment in an enforceable agreement to provide personal services would be: "I'll do X for you and, if I fail to perform, you will have the right to money damages from me."

While the *object* or purpose of such a contract for personal services would be to assure that one party will exercise his inalienable rights in a certain way some time in the future, the actual *subject* of such a contract would be the transfer of alienable right to the money. "Every obligation to do or not to do (*de faire ou de ne pas faire*) resolves itself into damages in the case of non-performance by the debtor."[58] Thus, if A consents to a legally binding commitment to personally paint B's picture, then no matter what the contract specifies, B's only right is to money damages (specific enforcement of the transfer of the money)[59] – even if A's performance is unique or monetary damages are inadequate for some other reason. When construed in this manner, enforcing contracts for personal services would not constitute an exception to a presumption in favor of specific performance for the breach of any contract. In the event of a failure to perform a personal services contract, the conditional transfer of the right to the

---

58 French Civil Code, art. 1142, as it appears in B. Nicholas, *supra* note 46, at 210.
59 What the contract specifies might influence which *measure* of money damages is used. For an explanation of the various possible measures of contract damages, *see* Cooter & Eisenberg, Damages for Breach of Contract, 73 Cal. L. Rev. 1432 (1985); Fuller & Perdue, The Reliance Interest in Contract Damages, 46 Yale L.J. 52 (1936).

money is the subject of the contract and it is this alienable right that is specifically enforced.

Limiting the proper subject of contract for personal services to money damages (which will be specifically enforced) produces legal results which are entirely consonant with the common law's traditional reluctance to grant specific relief for breach of personal services contracts. A consent theory of contract and a proper distinction between alienable and inalienable rights both explains and justifies what now appears to be an *ad hoc* "public policy" exception.

3. Contracts for corporate services. At first blush, it may appear that if Firm *A* legally commits itself to provide corporate services involving individual labor to a consumer or another firm, such a contract should be governed by the same rule that applies to contracts for personal services. There is, however, an important difference. If Firm *A* breaches its contract to provide services, it need not be the case – and, in fact, it is quite unlikely – that the reason for the breach is the unwillingness of the employees of the firm who are personally to provide the services to perform. Rather, what has likely happened is that, for one reason or another, the owners or managers of Firm *A* have found it inexpedient to honor their commitment. They might, for example, have found a more profitable opportunity elsewhere, or something may have occurred to make performance more costly to them than they had anticipated.

If the undesirability of performance to the owners or management of a firm, not the reluctance of the workers supplying their labor, accounts for the decision to breach, a court may still be faced with practical problems of administering a decree of specific performance. It will not, however, confront the issue of involuntary servitude that plagues the specific performance of personal services contracts. True, as with personal service contracts, the services of the employees cannot be the subject of a valid contract because such services consist of the employees' exercise of their inalienable rights. And if an employee breaches his contract to perform services

167

for the firm, he would only be liable to the firm for money damages. Unlike contracts for personal services, however, the subject of a valid contract for corporate services need not be limited to the payment of money damages for failure to perform as agreed. The following series of examples illustrates that another morally permissible construction exists as well.

First, suppose that *A* wishes to have his house painted and is unable or unwilling to paint it himself. *A* can contract with individual *B* that *B* will paint the house – that is, *B* commits herself to compensate *A* if she fails to paint the house. If *B* breaches this contract to provide personal services, she is liable only for money damages. Suppose, instead, that *A* decides to buy Firm *C*, which is a house painting company. As the owner of Firm *C*, *A* may then order its painters to paint his house. (If any painter refuses to do so, then that painter may have breached whatever employment contract she has with Firm *C* and, if so, she is liable to the firm for money damages.) This may mean that Firm *C* might have to pass up the opportunity to contract with *D* to paint *D*'s house. As the new owner of the company, the right to make this decision now belongs to *A*.

Now, suppose *A* thinks that it is both too much trouble and too expensive to buy a painting company merely because he wishes to have his house painted. The only right of ownership that *A* really wants is the right to order the employees of Firm *C* to paint his house. To secure this and only this right, instead of buying Firm *C*, *A* contracts with it to paint his house. The principal difference between the two transactions is that a direct purchase of Firm *C* gives *A* many more rights (and risks) in addition to the right to direct the firm's painters to paint his house – rights which he neither desires nor can afford to purchase. A contract for corporate services, on the other hand, may transfer only the narrow right to direct the employees to paint his house, which *A* desires, and nothing more. A court order that Firm *C*'s employees paint *B*'s house is no different from *A* issuing this order as the owner of the firm. While one person cannot own another person, a person can own a share of a firm. This suggests that where *A* contracts to buy corporate services from Firm *C*, *A* might have acquired a (very limited) kind of ownership right to the resources *of the firm*.

Whether *A* has in fact acquired such a right depends entirely on the construction given the terms of the contract. The agreement might have given *A* only a right to money damages for breach; or it might instead have specified that *A* gets the same right to have Firm *C*'s employees directed to paint his house that he would have acquired by buying the company and becoming its owner. No matter which form of relief the parties agree to, however, there is no moral problem of the sort that exists with specifically enforcing personal services contracts.

Suppose, now, that the contract is silent on the issue and there exists no trade custom governing this issue.[60] An important reason exists for favoring specific performance of a contract for corporate services, provided that the victim of the breach is an individual (as opposed to another firm). Purchasers who are legally unsophisticated – that is, unfamiliar with the legal background rules governing the choice of remedy – most likely assume when they contract for performance from a firm that, because performance is what they bargained for, performance is what they get if there is a breach. If the legal background rule governing the choice of remedies awarded only money damages, then such persons – who are by assumption ignorant of this legal background – would be most unlikely to insist on an express clause to the contrary. Their silence would not, then, reliably indicate assent to the terms provided by the legal background rule. By interpreting this silence as assent, courts in such cases

60 Determining the appropriate gap-filling technique in a consent theory when the parties are silent on an issue merits further consideration. The analysis of this issue that follows in the text should be considered as tentatively offered. For an insightful exploration of this important problem from a "bargaining theory" perspective, *see* the following essay in this book. See also Ayres & Gertner, Filling Gaps in Incomplete Contracts: An Economic Theory of Default Rules, 99 Yale L.J. 87 (1989).

169

would likely be giving firms a beneficial term they had not paid for.

In contrast, a firm in the business of regularly providing corporate services is, by virtue of its past experience (or legal counsel), very likely to be aware of the prevailing background legal rule and, should it wish not to be bound by this rule, it can try to insert in the contract an expressed provision to the contrary – that is, a term that mandates money damages only. This suggests that when a contract to provide corporate services that is silent on the issue of remedy is breached by the service provider,[61] and the victim is an individual (not another firm), a court should, at the request of the victim of the breach, order specific performance. Service providers might arguably be permitted to oppose a request for specific performance by showing that the services they provide are readily available elsewhere and performance is for some reason an extreme hardship. But, as with contracts for external resources, the recognition of such a defense would be controversial.[62]

In sum, when the purchaser of corporate services is an individual consumer, the reverse of the traditional rule governing contract damages should apply and specific performance should be favored. Providers of corporate services who wish to limit their liability to monetary damages would have to attempt to insert a clause to this effect in their contracts. A presumption of specific performance when the recipient of corporate services is an individual forces the party with better access to the background rule (the firm) to educate the less knowledgeable party by its bargaining behavior.

D. Summary of remedies in a consent theory

The traditional approach to remedies for breach of contract is that only money damages are available to the victim as of

---

61 The provider of "corporate services" is by definition a firm. When the service provider is an individual, rather than a firm, this is a contract for *personal* services for which only money damages for breach of contract should be obtained.

62 See *supra* note 56.

right. Specific performance is an exceptional form of relief available only when money damages are inadequate. Even when damages are inadequate, however, a contract for personal services will not be specifically enforced. A consent theory of contract suggests the following rule to govern the choice of remedies for breach of contract: The only enforceable agreements are those which consensually transfer alienable rights; all such agreements should presumptively be specifically enforced.

Where a contract transfers the right to *external resources,* then a transfer of these resources should be ordered by a court. If parties do not wish this result, they may agree – or, if they are silent, trade custom might establish – that only monetary damages will be due for failure to deliver a promised resource. Since a right to *personal services* is inalienable, persons wishing to enhance the reliability of a promise to perform personal services by means of a contract may accomplish this object by making a transfer of alienable rights (to money or other property) conditional on nonperformance. Upon failure to perform the desired services, the rights transfer could be specifically enforced. Where a contract calls for the provision of *corporate services,* the subject of the contract may either be a right to money damages or a limited right to control the firm. Since both of these rights are potentially alienable, when either right is transferred, a court may order a firm to specifically perform the obligation incurred. Where the purchaser of corporate services is an individual, a court should (at least) presumptively award specific performance.

CONCLUSION

My purpose in developing a consent theory of contract is not to end discussion of contract theory or doctrine, but rather to permit the ongoing discussion of contractual obligation to emerge from its longstanding intellectual cul-de-sac and begin traveling a more productive course. If the "death of contract" movement is a product of a disillusionment with and abandonment of both the will theory of contract as a distinct source of contractual obligation and the bargain theory of consideration as the means of formally distinguishing between enforceable and unenforceable exercises of the will, the "resurrection of contract" is a recognition of contract law's proper function as a transfer mechanism that is conceptually dependent on more fundamental notions of individual entitlements.

A consent theory of contractual obligation views certain agreements as legally binding because the parties bring to the transaction certain rights and they manifest their assent to the transfer of these rights. This approach accurately captures what is at stake when individuals seek to exchange or bestow entitlements that they have acquired or will acquire; it explains the most fundamental aspects of contract law; and it solves previously vexatious theoretical problems. A better theoretical understanding of contractual obligation should ultimately result in rules and principles of contract that better facilitate the important social need to make and rely upon enforceable commitments.[63] These and other promises of the consent theory await future performance.

63 For other implications of a consent theory for contract doctrine, *see* Barnett & Becker, *supra* note 22; Barnett, Squaring Undisclosed Agency Law with Contract Theory, 75 Cal. L. Rev. 1969 (1987).

Chapter 6

A bargaining theory approach to default provisions and disclosure rules in contract law

JULES L. COLEMAN,
DOUGLAS D. HECKATHORN,
AND STEVEN M. MASER

I. THE PROBLEM

Legal rules facilitate as well as constrain human freedom.
H.L.A. Hart captures the difference between these two functions of law by distinguishing between primary and secondary rules.[1] Primary rules impose obligations and thereby
constrain behavior. Secondary rules empower individuals to
create relations that confer rights and impose duties.[2] Thus,
the criminal law constrains individual liberty; the law of contracts enhances it.

The earlier versions of this article were presented at the University of
Virginia and at conferences on Norms (in Delaware), Legal Liability (at
Bowling Green State University), and the Calculus of Consent (at Santa
Cruz). The article benefited from comments made on every such occasion.
The authors are especially indebted to Alan Schwartz and Randy Barnett
for comments, criticisms and suggestions on earlier drafts. The authors
would also like to acknowledge support provided by the following grants:
Guggenheim Foundation Fellowship (Coleman); George A. and Eliza
Gardner Howard Foundation (Heckathorn); Atkinson Fund of Willamette
University (Maser).
    This essay first appeared in the *Harvard Journal of Law and Public Policy*,
vol. 12, no. 3 (Summer 1989). It is reprinted here with the kind permission
of the journal.
1 H.L.A. HART, CONCEPT OF LAW (1961).
2 Hart is not always consistent in drawing the distinction. He charac-
    terizes secondary rules as power conferring. Some confer power on
    private individuals, others authorize officials. Unfortunately, the rule
    of recognition, which for Hart is the signature of a legal system, is a
    secondary rule, but it confers power on no one.

Within this framework, the foundation of contracting is mutual agreement. Contractual duties are self-imposed. They are consequences of individuals authoritatively exercising their autonomy under private enabling rules. Coercive civil authority is justifiably employed to enforce contractual obligations because the parties have agreed so to constrain themselves. Of course, even if the parties to a contract agree to bind themselves to one another, it does not follow that they have agreed thereby to have their obligations to one another enforced by the state (or by any other third party).[3]

A. The default rule

On the assumption that contracting parties are narrowly rational and fully informed, a contract between them that foresees and responds to all possible contingencies would be efficient, or Pareto optimal. That is the definition of a fully specified contract. Because a fully specified contract is efficient, it puts the parties to it in a position where neither can improve his or her lot except at the other's expense. A fully specified contract is also an equilibrium, that is, it is self-enforcing in the sense that no party has an incentive unilaterally to defect from its terms.

3 Randy Barnett (and much black letter law) holds a different view. For him, to contract is to commit oneself to an enforcement mechanism. This view presupposes a conception of contract embedded within legal or other institutions, including those with the authority and power to enforce contractual terms. *See* Barnett, *The Consent Theory of Contract*, 86 Colum. L. Rev. 269 (1986). We can distinguish between two senses of "contract." The first is the legal one in which to contract is to commit oneself to a coercively enforceable set of rights and responsibilities. The other is the ordinary langage or nontechnical sense in which legal enforcement is not presupposed. Our goal here is to understand the legal practice of contracting. To do so, we believe it is helpful to explain the roles of courts in enforcing agreements by asking under what conditions, if any, rational parties would call upon third parties, including courts, to facilitate or to enforce agreements between them. This approach presupposes that we can imagine circumstances of contracting without law. Thus we take the ordinary sense of contracting as basic and the legal or juridical one as derivative. We explain the latter in terms of failures of private contracting, as we define that term later in this article.

Although imagining problems in contract design and execution and devising adequate safeguards against all possible sources of contract failure is a logical possibility, it remains (for everyone but the Gods) a practical impossibility. Even were it practically possible, fully specifying a contract might be irrational in that the expected costs of a more complete specification may exceed the expected gains from nailing down a particular solution to an imaginable, but unlikely, possibility.

Unlikely events are not impossible, however. Contingencies arise with which the contractors have not explicitly dealt. Such is the stuff of contracts casebooks. When contingencies arise for which no adequate provisions have been made ex ante, the parties may disagree about their respective rights and duties ex post. Sometimes they are able to resolve the conflict privately. If they are unable to resolve the conflict privately, however, the parties may find themselves in court. What rights and responsibilities can a judge, legitimately exercising his or her authority, impose upon them ex post?

It is often suggested that a judge should apply the following general rule: confer those rights and impose those duties to which the parties would have agreed ex ante.[4] Thus, when transaction costs make an explicit agreement too costly ex ante, the court should apply a *default* rule that "mimics" the outcome of a hypothetical contract between them.[5] The hypothetical contract is the one the parties would have made had transaction costs not made their doing so irrational.

As a default rule, the ex ante contract raises two distinct kinds of issues. The first concerns the content of the rule. How are we to model or to understand the ex ante contract? The second concerns the justification a court might have for

4 *See* Schwartz, *Proposals for Products Liability Reform: A Theoretical Synthesis*, 97 YALE L.J. 353 (1988), in which the tort problem of specifying the conditions of liability for defective product is recast as a contracts problem: that is, the terms of liability should be those the parties would have agreed to ex ante.
5 This is, of course, not the only default rule a judge can apply. In the alternative, a court might assign rights and responsibilities according to a principle of social justice, wealth redistribution or insurance.

imposing upon litigating parties the rights and responsibilities implied by the ex ante contract. The problem of justification is complicated by the fact that the parties are being held in contract to terms to which they did not explicitly agree. Given the ex post nature of the obligations and rights it distributes, is there any reason to think that one default rule is any more justifiable than another? Is there, in particular, a case to be made for the ex ante contract as the default rule?

B. Consent and the default rule

One approach to the problem of justifying a default rule is to connect it to a general theory of contractual obligation. What kind of argument might the theory of contractual obligation suggested by Hart's notion of a private empowering rule – that is, a consent theory – offer? What, in other words, is the relevant connection between explicit consent and hypothetical ex ante contracting?

We can distinguish between at least two kinds of arguments a consent theorist might advance to support the claim that an ex ante hypothetical contract is a uniquely appropriate way to establish ex post the terms of incompletely specified contracts. The first argument relies on the justificatory force of hypothetical consent. Roughly, the argument is as follows: the claims the parties have explicitly imposed upon one another are legitimately enforced against the parties because they have actually consented to those terms. The default rule imposes rights and responsibilities to which the parties would have consented. To the same extent and in the same way that consent justifies a court imposing the rights and responsibilities made explicit in a contract, hypothetical consent justifies imposing the rights and responsibilities that are implied by the application of the default rule. Is the argument persuasive?

In the case of explicit consent, we recognize a difference between *unfree* acts and *irrational* ones. A person may consent to conduct detrimental to his interests (irrational, but free), or he may be compelled against his will to promote his interests (rational, but unfree – as in some forms of paternalism). The distinction between consent and rational self-interest becomes murkier in arguments attempting to establish the terms to which a particular person conceived of in a particular way *would* have consented. An example drawn from the economic analysis of law nicely illustrates this problem in arguments from hypothetical consent and the additional, more fundamental problem of justifying the imposition of duties ex post on the grounds that they would have been agreed to ex ante.

Economists evaluate allocations of resources and states of the world by the criterion of efficiency. From the moral point of view, is the efficiency of an allocation or of a social state a desirable property of it? In effect, this question is an invitation to consider the normative underpinnings of economic analysis. Moral arguments in favor of efficiency are of two sorts: utilitarian and consensual.[6] Only the latter concerns us here.

Economists distinguish among three criteria of economic efficiency: Pareto superiority, Pareto optimality and Kaldor-Hicks efficiency. S^1 is *Pareto superior* to S^0 if and only if no one prefers S^0 to S^1 and at least one person prefers S^1 to S^0. S is *Pareto optimal* if and only if there exists no S^i Pareto superior to it. S^1 is *Kaldor-Hicks efficient* to S^0 if and only if S^1 is potentially Pareto superior to S^0. S^1 is potentially Pareto superior to S^0 if in going from S^0 to S^1 resources could be arranged so that no one prefers S^0 to S^1 and at least one person prefers S^1 to S^0. Because the other efficiency concepts are defined in terms of Pareto superiority, we might ask what the relationship between it and consent could be. The consensual defense of Pareto superiority is very simple, and although it has been employed primarily by Richard Posner in his defense of efficiency, the argument has its roots in Nicholas Kaldor's work some fifty years earlier.[7] The argument is as follows:

6 See J. COLEMAN, MARKETS, MORALS AND THE LAW 95–132 (1988).
7 For a discussion of the argument, see *id.* at 115–29.

(1) S^1 is Pareto superior to S^0 if and only if no one prefers S^0 to S^1 and at least one prefers S^1 over S^0.
(2) Therefore, each person would consent to S^1, that is, would choose S^1 over S^0.

Some Pareto improvements like rational, voluntary market transactions are in fact consented to, though it remains a further question whether typical market transactions are morally defensible because they are Pareto improving or because they have been voluntarily consummated. In any case, many Pareto improvements are not consented to by every person affected. Take the famous case of *Vincent v. Lake Erie Transportation Co.*[8] In this case, a dock owner refused to allow a ship to remain docked beyond the period of time set forth by the terms of a contract between the dock owner and the ship's captain, and ordered it to leave. The captain refused to set his ship free because it would very likely have been lost at sea, a victim of an impending storm. The ship remained docked, the storm came, and the ship repeatedly smashed the dock, resulting in $500 damages to the dock. The court held that even though the ship's captain acted correctly in firmly tying the boat to the dock, he was required to compensate the dock owner. If the ship's captain acted rationally, he was better off taking the risk and compensating the dock owner ex post than he would have been had he set the ship to sea. Provided the dock owner was fully compensated for whatever damages resulted from the ship captain's decision, the dockowner should be indifferent between what actually occurred and what would have occurred had the captain set his ship afloat. Thus, the outcome of the case constitutes a Pareto improvement, but not one to which all the relevant parties consented. In fact, the dock owner made every effort to express his unwillingness to agree to the captain's decision. Here we have a Pareto improvement that could not be justified on the grounds of consent.[9]

8 100 Minn. 456, 124 N.W. 221 (1910).
9 Posner has argued that by accepting compensation ex post, one gives consent, *see* Posner, *The Ethical and Political Basis of the Efficiency Norm*

So the consent argument for the legal rule must be that ex ante the parties seeking to maximize overall wealth or utility *would have consented* to it, not that they actually *did* consent. The premise in that argument is simply the one stated above: all the relevant parties are made better off by the Pareto improving state (or at least are made no worse off by it). Thus, they prefer the Pareto improving state to the Pareto inferior one (Premise One). To say that they prefer one state to the other is to say that under normal conditions they *would choose* the former to the latter (Conclusion): thus we have the connection of Pareto superiority to hypothetical consent. The premise in the argument expresses the individual rationality of the proposed change; the conclusion expresses the parties' hypothetical consent to it. From the fact that a social state makes someone no worse off (that is, it is not irrational for him), we are to infer that the agent would have consented to it. Consent follows as a matter of *logic* from considerations of rationality.

Consequently, the concept of hypothetical consent expresses nothing that is not already captured in the idea of rational self-interest. The distinction between consent and rationality central to moral theory apparently evaporates. The claim that imposing obligations ex post is justified because the parties would have consented to them ex ante adds nothing to a defense of such a proposal that is not already expressed by the argument that imposing obligations ex post is justified whenever such obligations would have been *rational* for the parties ex ante. Thus, the reliance on ex ante rational bargaining provides a rationality or welfarist defense of the default rule, not a consensualist one.

in Common Law Adjudication, 8 HOFSTRA L. REV. 487, 491 (1980), which in this case means that in spite of his protestations to the contrary, the dock owner consented to the captain's decision by accepting compensation. Surely this is seriously confused; first, because often people demand compensation not to give their consent to being harmed, but as *redress* for a wrong done to them; second, because if to accept compensation is to give consent, then the only way not to consent is to refuse compensation, which, of course, would ordinarily count as *giving consent*. The argument that compensation constitutes consent has things absolutely backwards.

179

A consent theorist needs another way of connecting hypothetical rational bargaining to hypothetical consent, a way that maintains both the analytic distinction between the two and the significance of both to a full consensual defense of contractual obligation. One approach could rely on the claim that the relationship between hypothetical rational bargaining and hypothetical consent is *epistemic*, not analytic. What it would have been rational for the parties to bargain for ex ante is not *equivalent* to what they would have agreed to, nor does it formally imply their agreement. It is, nevertheless, *evidence*, perhaps the best evidence, of what the parties would have agreed to ex ante. Rather than trying to derive hypothetical consent from rationality, the suggestion is that the former provides presumptive evidence of the latter. In the absence of contradictory evidence, that is, evidence contrary to that derived from the hypothetical rational bargain, it is legitimate to infer that the parties would have consented to that which would have been the outcome of a rational bargain between them.

The consent theorist's first strategy for defending the ex ante contract as a default rule, then, ultimately rests on the fact that what would have been rational for the parties ex ante is extremely strong evidence of the terms to which they would have agreed. What the parties would have agreed to ex ante in turn provides some justification for holding them to the terms ex post. This line of defense is, of course, incomplete pending an account of why it is that something to which individuals would have agreed (though they did not in fact) provides a civil authority with grounds for imposing those conditions upon them now (when they quite explicitly do not agree to those conditions).

The second line of defense open to the consent theorist is designed to obviate this last problem. In this view, by the very act of contracting the parties consent not only to a framework of explicitly created rights and duties, but to a jurisdiction for resolving conflicts that might arise in construing those rights and duties. Should the occasion arise, the jurisdiction to which the parties consent is authorized to impose rights and duties ex post that were not made explicit ex ante. To contract is, among other things, to consent to the relevant default provisions of the law. Thus, the rights and responsibilities allocated by a default rule ex post are, in a suitable sense, consented to ex ante. This line of argument eliminates the need to demonstrate either that the terms imposed by the default rule would have been consented to by the parties, or that what the parties would have consented to ex ante provides a reason for imposing those terms upon them now. The importance of hypothetical consent simply disappears, and with it the need to establish an evidentiary or analytic connection between it and the ex ante rational bargain.

This approach appears to obviate two problems – specifying the relationship (analytic or epistemic) between rational bargaining and hypothetical consent, and arguing for the normative punch of the latter – but at the expense of creating others. The problem is that if this line of argument constitutes a sound consensual defense of the ex ante contract default rule, it also constitutes an equivalently good defense of all default rules. For if by consenting to a contract, one consents to a jurisdiction's default rule, then one consents to whatever rule the court applies – from those rules aimed at reconstructing a hypothetical bargain to those imposing fair terms, to others imposing efficient terms, to those imposing obnoxious terms, and so on. This reconstruction of the consent theory of contractual obligation, in other words, provides no sense in which the ex ante rational contract is special. If the ex ante rational bargain as a default rule has a special attraction for this sort of consent theorist, it cannot be, strictly speaking, a matter of consent.

If this argument works at all, it works too well. The next question is whether it works at all. It makes sense to say that two contracting parties consent to the obligations and rights their contract specifies to the extent each has alternative opportunities, or at least provided that none of the contractual terms are imposed unwillingly upon either of them. It follows, then, that the parties could be said to consent to a relevant authority's default rule only if they willingly, that

181

is, noncoercively, choose it. This is not typically the case, however. The default rule of any jurisdiction is generally a non-negotiable part of their bargain. For that reason, it is questionable whether by consenting to a framework of contractual rights and responsibilities, the parties consent to the application of the operative default rule.

It is no counterargument that the parties could reduce the extent to which they rely upon the default rule. Although it is true that the parties could more fully specify their contract and thereby reduce the scope of the rule's application, this shows only that the parties can agree to reduce or to minimize the rule's impact, not that in doing so they consent to the rule's use in the areas they do not contract around.

To feel comfortable with the claim that by contracting parties consent to the relevant default rule, we would have to assume something like a competitive market in authoritative jurisdictions. Then, the parties would choose jurisdictions based, among other things, on the default rule in effect.

If the consent theorist's claim is that a default rule is justified to the extent that it would be freely chosen in a competitive market for authoritative jurisdictions, then he too ends up relying upon arguments from hypothetical, not explicit consent. Moreover, the argument the consent theorist would very likely employ to defend the ex ante contract as a default rule would be that among all the possible rules, it is the one that is rational for the parties ex ante. In other words, the ex ante contract is individually and collectively rational and, for those reasons, would have been chosen by rational parties free to pick among alternative default rules. The rationality of the default rule follows from the fact that it reduces the costs of contracting. It enables each party to avoid the costs under other rules of contracting out, of ever more fully specifying their contract. Once again, the argument for the ex ante contract ultimately relies on hypothetical consent and a relationship, analytic or epistemic, between what is rational for someone ex ante and what that person would have consented to ex ante. The effort to replace hypothetical with explicit consent does not, in the end, avoid these problems.

In effect we can characterize a kind of research program for a consent theorist bent on defending the ex ante contract as a uniquely appropriate default rule. The program has three components. The first is to specify rigorously the content of the hypothetical rational bargain between the parties. The second is to determine what sort of evidence, if any, exists about what the parties would have agreed to that could ever contradict the evidence supplied by the hypothetical rational bargain. The third problem we have already mentioned. Even if we can specify rigorously the content of hypothetical rational bargains envisaged by the default rule, and can determine successfully in individual cases (or in general) the reliability of this information for demonstrating what the parties would in fact have agreed to, it is a further question whether what they would have consented to provides a court with sufficient justification for imposing those terms upon them, let alone whether it provides the same sort of justification their actual consent would.

C. Rationality and the default rule

One problem that keeps emerging when we try to develop a hypothetical consent defense of the default rule is that the best evidence we have of what the parties would have agreed to is that to which it would have been rational for them to agree. We are left then to draw inferences from the latter to the former on the apparent assumption that, as between the two, only the former – what the parties would have consented to – provides a justification for allocating rights and responsibilities. Perhaps that assumption is unwarranted; perhaps considerations of rationality have justificatory force on their own. In that case, one could more straightforwardly defend the ex ante contract not on the grounds that parties in fact agree to it or would have agreed to the allocation of rights and responsibilities it sets out, but on the grounds that it or the rights and responsibilities it imposes are *rational*.

In this approach *rationality*, not consent, is the basis of contractual obligation and the foundation of legitimate third party enforcement. Thus, the justification for applying the default rule is not that it constitutes or is presumptive evidence of the parties' consent, but that, when made rigorous, it specifies rights and obligations that are rational for the parties. Such rights and responsibilities, because they are rational, are justifiably imposed on the parties.

This approach, which can also be characterized as a research program, also raises three kinds of problems. First, like the consent theory, the rationality theory must specify rigorously the content of the hypothetical rational bargain between the parties. Second, while the consent theory has an intuitively plausible theory of enforceable claims made explicit in contracts, it lacks a plausible theory of the default rule. That is, it takes consent as justificationally basic and is left to explain the relevance of rationality to consent. In contrast, the rationality theory has a plausible interpretation of the default rule: that is, the default rule provides a specification of the terms to which it would be rational for the parties to have agreed. It must now give a plausible account of the role of actual consent, when such consent is present. In other words, because the rationality theory takes principles of rationality as justificationally basic, it gives an immediate explanation of the relevance of the default rule. It is left, however, with the task of explaining the significance of explicit consent in contract. If rationality carries the moral weight, what significance does consent have? Third, the rationality theory must show why rationality binds. We take it for granted that a state of affairs to which individuals voluntarily agree is, ceteris paribus, morally unobjectionable. But it is not obvious how the moral defensibility of a state of the world can be said to follow from its rationality.

In the rationality view, the relationship between rationality and actual consent cannot be one of entailment. Just as it does not follow logically that people agree to what is in their interests, it cannot follow logically that what they agree to is rational for them. Thus, in the rationality theory, actual consent, when present, does not justify; rather it provides *evidence*, again perhaps the best evidence, of what is rational for the parties. There is an interesting analogy in the relationship of consent to rational bargaining in the consent and rationality theories of contractual obligation. In the consent theory, rationality provides evidence of consent. In the rationality theory, consent provides evidence of rationality. Both theories also face justificatory obstacles. The consent theory may explain how consent justifies, but its adherence to the default rule requires it to explain how hypothetical consent justifies. Similarly, the rationality theory explains the relevance of the default rule, but it needs to explain the moral relevance of rationality.

Common to both strategies, moreover, is the problem of specifying the content of the default rule. The difference between them is the normative use to which the model is put. In the consent theory, the model of the "ex ante bargain" provides evidence of the terms to which the parties would have consented. In the rationality theory, it specifies what, in a particular case, is rational, and, given appropriate premises connecting rationality to morality, what morally can be required of the parties.

What we have done so far is sketch out two research programs. Both rely on the ex ante bargain as a default rule, but which gives a better justification of the legitimacy of a court's applying that rule? In this article we do not intend to adjudicate this dispute in the normative theory of contract. Our aims here are in a sense both more modest and more ambitious. We intend to take seriously the concept of the ex ante bargain and give it some flesh. We want to take appeals to the rational bargain that until now have been more abstract than concrete and give them some structure and rigor. It is not our concern here whether in doing so we advance the cause of any particular theory of contractual obligation. Our goal is to make a contribution to contract theory more generally: for without a specification of the parameters and struc-

185

ture of the rational bargain, appeals to it, however attractive in theory, will be empty in practice. Thus, we intend to give a full and rigorous characterization of rational bargaining in a way that will shed considerable light on both the analytic and the normative questions of contractual obligation. In the course of our presentation of this analytic structure, we attempt to explain how a central doctrine of contract law – disclosure – can be usefully illuminated by conceiving of the process of contracting as a scheme of rational bargaining.

If the idea of the contract as a rational bargain is ultimately unpersuasive, or if our efforts to illuminate some contract doctrines in rational choice terms are unconvincing, we nevertheless will have provided a way of giving content to the default rule: a way that is both rigorous and rich. For the idea of a rational bargain is a complex one, far more complex and difficult to apply than either contract theorists or judges have until now grasped.

II. THE RATIONAL CONTRACT

A. Bargaining and contract: introduction

We begin by looking at how two parties engage in a contractual transaction, how they secure a rational bargain, *without law*. Our analysis benefits from recent formal literature on bargaining under both complete and imperfect information, part of the theory of cooperative games. It looks at how people resolve disputes involving elements of both conflict and cooperation. We depict contracting as a divisible prisoner's dilemma game. Here, the parties secure no contract unless they agree on a way of enforcing their agreement and of distributing any potential gains. The conditions under which they invoke third-party participation, including judicial or legislative intervention, and the form of that participation, depend on the costs of consummating the deal. Those costs derive from the inherent risks associated with imperfect information concerning the parties' transaction and the resources they devote to minimizing those risks. In sum, we

186

look at contract law in light of what we know about bargaining, rather than vice versa. That is, although we think analytic study of bargaining "in the shadow of the law"[10] is important and useful, the theory of rational bargaining in the absence of law has a claim to analytic priority. It is that claim we mean to stake.

Anyone familiar with the literature on rational bargaining knows that there are different solutions to the bargaining problem, different ways of spelling out the distribution to which rational parties will agree. We employ a form of the theory that relies on the idea of bargaining as consisting of making claims and rational concessions from those claims. We call this concession theory.[11] Our purpose in doing so is not to establish that the specific distributions the concession theory predicts are superior to the distributions predicted by competing theories. Rather, concession theory captures important features of the way people go about bargaining, synthesizes unique features in the other theories, and adopts assumptions common to all. Therefore, it has a lot to say about the rules people would adopt ex ante to encourage contracting.

A bargaining theoretic approach to contract law has four features that recommend it over competing approaches. First, the bargaining approach admits reward-triggering norms as a basis for social control. Typically, economic and sociological theories, especially those based solely on the prisoner's dilemma logic, depend on negative reinforcements to induce compliance with norms.[12] But according to bargaining theory, although one might sanction someone for failing to offer concessions or for violating an agreed upon division, the idea is to reward and to encourage concession-making so as to secure cooperation. We can ask whether legal doctrines do that, and if so, in what ways.

10 *See* Mnookin & Kornhauser, *Bargaining in the Shadow of the Law: The Case of Divorce*, 88 YALE L.J. 950 (1979).

11 *See* D. GAUTHIER, MORALS BY AGREEMENT (1986): Heckathorn, *A Unified Model for Bargaining and Conflict*, 25 BEHAVIORAL SCI. 261 (1980).

12 *See* Ellickson, *Of Coase and Cattle: Dispute Resolution Among Neighbors in Shasta County*, 38 STAN. L. REV. 623 (1986).

Second, a bargaining theoretic approach takes explicit account of fairness as a part of contractual exchange. If people worry about fairness and if in every theory of rational contracting the parties ineluctably confront fairness concerns, then when and how do the courts take account of it? In fact and in theory, fairness matters. Under what conditions, then, will rational contractors require courts to act on that concern – and in what capacities?

Our approach shares with law-and-economics the importance of efficiency. It differs from many forms of economic analysis in virtue of bargaining theory's emphasis upon the division or fairness problem. Our approach shares with the law-and-society tradition, the importance of *context*. Rational decision-making is necessarily sensitive to the context of the decision. The status quo is relevant; contracting always occurs within a pre-existing web of continuing, contractual relationships. The resources parties bring into bargaining are relevant. And the uncertainties peculiar to different contexts are relevant.

Our approach shares with moral theories the importance of fairness and justice to the legitimacy of civil authority. However, unlike other theories, it appeals to criteria of fairness or justice endogenous to transaction relationships. It does not view contracting as necessarily constrained by external standards of fairness; rather it views the process of rational contracting as, in part, specifying the relevant conception of fairness.

Third, bargaining theory takes a unified view of contracting. It dispels the illusion that contract law doctrines are independent of one another. For example, legal scholarship and judicial decisions present damage measures, disclosure rules, and unconscionability as if they have nothing to do with each other. That is wrong. People will have difficulty reaching an agreement not only if they fear it may become uneconomic, which is relevant to establishing damage measures, but also if they fear it might become unfair, which is relevant to recision because of unconscionability. Their estimates of these fears depend in part on their investments in information, including the representations they make to each other, which in turn bear on the appropriateness of disclosure rules.

Fourth, analyzing the process of rational bargaining in the absence of law yields insight into the varying role of the court in contracts, specifically, into the conditions under which people turn to courts, and the defensibility of various contract law doctrines that have emerged in response. Like any other device to safeguard bargains, the court mitigates some of the risks of contracting better than others, but it is imperfect and costly. It can be more efficacious than alternative devices. People choosing among devices aim to minimize the sum of the costs of uncertainty and of safeguarding against it. Specialized doctrines in law emerge when rational bargainers charge the courts with effecting that policy.

B. Three problems in contracting

The terms of an agreement to cooperate among two or more people, their *contract*, stipulates (1) specific actions by each to be carried out at some time in the future, and (2) rewards and penalties to be meted out following compliance or defection. These terms constitute safeguards crafted to minimize and allocate risk, but in doing so the terms create risks of their own. What are the conditions under which rational actors will agree to cooperate if charged explicitly with designing a policy to cope with risk and uncertainty in their environment?

The decision-making calculus that rational actors use in crafting a contract is relatively complex because it requires resolving three distinct but intertwined problems: (1) coordination, (2) division, and (3) defection. These problems are captured in a type of game termed the divisible prisoner's dilemma. While other types of games (for example, pure coordination or division games, prisoner's dilemmas) typically isolate one feature of rational decision that can come into play in contracting,[13] this game describes *three* such fea-

13 *See* Landa & Grofman, *Games of Breach and the Role of Contract Law in*

		Player B Performance		
		Contract 1	Contract 2	Non Performance
Player A	Contract 1	Contract $_1$ 19, 7 C_1	Status quo 9, 2 D	B free rides 3, 11 NP_b
	Contract 2	Status quo 9, 2 D	Contract $_2$ 16, 10 C_2	B free rides 3, 11 NP_b
	Non Performance	A free rides 22, 1 NP_a	A free rides 22, 1 NP_a	Status quo 9, 2 D

Figure 1. Divisible prisoner's dilemma

tures, the interaction between those features, and their informational requirements.

The divisible prisoner's dilemma involves three principles of rationality: (1) rational cooperation, (2) rational division, and (3) rational compliance. Failure to satisfy any one of the three demands of rationality leads to contract failure; satisfying all three is necessary and sufficient for agreement and performance on a contract.

An example of the divisible prisoner's dilemma is depicted in matrix (normal) form in Figure One. For the moment, assume that each player knows both payoffs in all of the cells. Player A (row) and player B (column) each make a three-

Protecting the Expectation Interest, in 3 RESEARCH IN LAW AND ECONOMICS 67 (R. Zerbe ed. 1981).

190

dimensional choice. Each must decide whether to contract or not; and if the choice is to contract, whether to seek and honor contract one or contract two. In making this decision each of three problems of rational contracting emerges.

The *coordination problem* is resolved by whether or not the parties share a common interest in contracting over acting individually. To motivate acting in concert, they must identify feasible gains that would otherwise be unobtainable. In our example, the two contracts represented by cells one and five represent higher payoffs for both parties than do the noncontract alternatives. Thus, we would expect the players to solve their coordination problem. Doing so is not sufficient for contracting, however, for two problems remain. A *division problem* arises if player *A* prefers contract one to contract two whereas player *B* has the opposite preference. Consequently, opposed preferences regarding how to contract complicate the common preference for a contract over no contract. A *defection problem* arises if a player gains from unilaterally defecting from a contract once agreement is secured.

The defection problem is illustrated powerfully in the nondivisible or standard prisoner's dilemma in which the dominant strategy for each player is to defect from whatever agreements he or she has made. In our example, *A* gains by defecting to cell seven or eight, and *B* gains by defecting to cell three or six.

C. Phases in contracting

Each problem in the contractual relationship corresponds to a distinct phase of the contracting process and involves a distinct principle of rationality.[14] First, in the *pre-phase* the decision whether to coordinate, that is, whether to seek a

---

14 For the sake of the exposition, we treat each phase in temporal progression and as distinct from the others. In fact, a rational bargainer may treat concerns arising in different phases of the process at the same time or in the reverse order we suggest. Ours is an analytic device, in which the phases of contracting progress in logical space-time.

contract, is made. If the parties are rational, each predicates an affirmative decision on expectations that joint gains will be attainable under the contract. Second, in the *negotiation phase* the decision of how to contract is made. That is, the parties agree upon the terms of the contract, specifying the manner in which the gains resulting from the contract and the burdens of enforcing it are to be allocated. Finally, in the *post-phase* each party makes the decision to fulfill or to violate the contract and monitors the compliance of others.

Each phase contains a potential pitfall. That is, individuals may fail to contract because (1) one or more of the essential parties prefers to act independently rather than to seek a contract, (2) the parties fail to agree upon the terms of the contract, or (3) the contract collapses owing to a violation of its terms. Each phase is distinct not only in the sense of carrying its own pitfalls to contracting; to succeed at each phase, a contract must meet the demands of distinct but ultimately related rationality conditions. The phases of contracting and their respective rationality conditions are developed below.

1. Pre-phase: joint rationality. No one can expect another person to engage in contracting unless *each* perceives an opportunity for *mutual* gain. That surely is the operating assumption when a buyer responds to a seller's "for sale" notice and when labor negotiates with management. Indeed, it is such a commonplace that we tend to take it for granted, overlooking its analytical importance.

We can put this obvious fact about contracting in an analytically precise way. A necessary condition for agreeing to a contract is that its expected outcome satisfies what may be termed the *joint rationality* condition. If U_i is the utility that individual i expects to secure in contracting; D_i is i's utility from disagreement (that is, the status quo); $U = (U_a, U_b)$ is a given agreement's utility vector; and $U' = (U'_a, U'_b)$ is any other feasible agreement's utility vector, U is jointly rational if for each feasible outcome U',

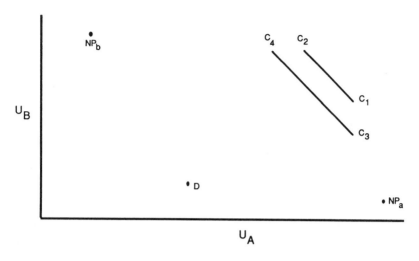

Figure 2. Divisible prisoner's dilemma in utility space

$$U_a > U'_a, \text{ or } U_b > U'_b. \quad (1)$$

The joint rationality condition can be clarified by analyzing Figure Two.

C_1, C_2 represents the contract curve, that is, the set of Pareto optimal outcomes to the northeast of D. D, in turn, represents the disagreement point, the outcome that results if the parties fail to reach agreement. NP_a and NP_b are the non-performance outcomes. NP_a results when A and B reach agreement with which B complies and from which A defects. NP_b represents the outcome that results when A complies and B defects. These are the free-rider outcomes. Both are Pareto optimal in the sense that no points lie to their northeast in the utility-space representation of the game. Though Pareto optimal, they are not Pareto superior to D, and thus, they do not lie on the contract curve C_1, C_2. NP_a, NP_b, and all the points on the contract curve C_1, C_2 are jointly rational or Pareto optimal. Only points on the contract curve, however, are Pareto optimal and Pareto superior to D.

If information is imperfect or incomplete, each party has an incentive to expend resources to inquire whether a bargain with someone else promises to be advantageous. These resources are *transaction resources*. At the coordination or prephase, parties may expend transaction resources to identify and secure D at the outset. Everyone wants a referent from which he can evaluate feasible outcomes. Contracting will break down and may not even begin without it (as is the case in labor-management negotiations with newly certified unions whose legitimacy is uncertain). Similarly, individuals cannot take for granted the existence of the contract curve, even though opportunities for more efficient cooperation tend to exist in every relationship. If people must expend resources to determine the location of the disagreement point or the contract curve, some or all of the gains from contracting are consumed, that is, in terms of Figure Two, C_1, C_2 moves toward C_3, C_4.

The magnitude of the coordination problem measures the social gains forgone by failing to coordinate.[15] We define the *magnitude of the coordination problem*, M_C, as the *maximum proportion of the gains attainable from contracting that a rational contractor in the system could be motivated to expend on transaction resources to resolve the coordination problem*. This is the ratio of the gain resulting from coordination to the maximum gain attainable from contracting over not contracting. The former is the difference between the individual's best hope payoff, B_i, defined as the highest payoff awarded on the contract curve, and the individual's payoff from the noncooperative outcome, N_i, that is, the utility awarded individual i by the outcome (or mix of outcomes) resulting if the potential contractors act independently rather than jointly. For example, in Figure One's game if the players sought to contract but failed to correlate their choices between the two alternative contracts (that is, each would choose contract one or two with equal probability), they would contract only fifty percent of the time (cells one or five), and end up at the status quo (cells two or four) the rest of the time. That mixture of out-

---

15 For an analysis of coordination games, see T. Schelling, The Strategy of Conflict 83–118 (1960).

comes would, on average, award a utility of $N_A = 13.25$ and $N_B = 5.25$.[16] The difference between the best-hope outcome and the noncooperative outcome, $B_i - N_i$, is the gain attributable to coordination. This is the maximum amount that a rational contractor could be motivated to expend to resolve the coordination problem.

Similarly, the maximum gain awarded to the individual as a result of contracting is the difference between the best-hope payoff, B_i, and the disagreement payoff, D_i, that is, $B_i - D_i$. In consequence, the magnitude of the coordination problem for individual i, M_{Ci}, is given by the following expression:

$$M_{Ci} = (B_i - N_i)/(B_i - D_i). \qquad (2)$$

For example, in Figure One's system, player A's coordination problem is $M_{Ca} = (19 - 13.25)/(19 - 9) = 0.575$, and player B's problem is $M_{Cb} = (10 - 5.25)/(10 - 2) = 0.59$.

The magnitude of the coordination problem faced by a group of individuals can be defined as the maximum problem faced by any of its members, that is,

$$M_C = \text{Max}[M_{Ci}]. \qquad (3)$$

For example, in Figure One's system, $M_C = 0.59$. This expression indicates the maximum proportion of contractual gains that any rational group member could be motivated to expend on resolving the coordination problem. This figure is not identical to actual expenditures to resolve the coordination problem. According to the principles of transactions-cost economics, individuals have incentives to minimize their expenditure of transaction resources, so actual expenditures will tend to fall below that theoretic maximum. Other things

16 Alternatively, if the focus of analysis is the problem of coordination in general, rather than the problem of implementing given a prior decision to contract, the noncooperative outcome can be defined as the Nash noncooperative equilibrium. *See* Nash, *Non-cooperative Games*, 54 ANNALS OF MATHEMATICS 286–95 (1951).

equal, actual expenditures on transaction resources will be positively related to the magnitude of the coordination problem.

Contracting to secure mutual gains consumes transaction resources that are scarce and costly to obtain. In the old law-and-economics tradition, transaction costs are assumed to be low in contracting situations, so that parties are able to gather all pertinent information and to assign all relevant risks.[17] Because the old law-and-economics tradition assumes individuals have perfect information, are completely rational, and face no impediments to entering transactions, "[i]t would be surprising if such superhumans were *not able* to manage their own affairs without the intervention of government."[18] As it happens, however, sometimes they are not.

The newer law-and-economics tradition emphasizes transaction costs even in contract (as opposed to "tort" or "stranger") situations. Because this tradition assumes individuals have imperfect information and limited rationality, and encounter substantial impediments in contracting, it would be surprising if such patently imperfect individuals were *able* to manage their affairs without the intervention of government. As it happens, in some cases, they do.

This discontinuity between "prohibitive" and "non-prohibitive" transaction costs is, of course, an analytic artifice begging for elaboration. The private and governmental controls that people craft depend on the relative size of the transaction costs involved. Because each of the three decision-making problems in any relationship involves unique hazards from imperfect information, the undifferentiated, generic treatment of transaction costs is analytically untenable as well.

17 Just think of the Coase Theorem and the long line of Chicago-style law-and-economics that sees itself as driven by Coase's insight that when transaction costs are low, individuals contract around inefficiencies. Thus, we have the identification of contract with low transaction costs. Coase himself did not commit the mistake of identifying contracting with low transaction costs.

18 Farber, *Contract Law and Modern Economic Theory*, 78 Nw. U.L. Rev. 303, 305 (1983).

2. The negotiation phase: concession rationality. Recognizing that contracting would increase efficiency, that it would generate benefits in excess of costs, is not a sufficient condition for contracting to occur.[19] Contracting requires that parties to the negotiations resolve the division problem, either directly by agreeing upon allocations of benefits and costs, or indirectly by agreeing upon a set of procedures by which these allocations are to be determined. The problem is not just the cost of establishing a set of feasible and acceptable outcomes. Even if that cost is nil, the *strategic* nature of the choice may induce a noncooperative outcome.[20] Strategy may require players to disguise their true intentions in pursuit of an agreement, moderating or exaggerating their demands based on their view of how each will respond to the other. Thus, failure to resolve the division problem can complicate the process of contracting even to the point of defeating it.

Returning to Figure Two, the division problem arises because the players have opposite preferences regarding where along the contract curve agreement should occur.[21] Expressed in bargaining theoretic terms, C_1, contract one, is player A's *best-hope outcome* because it is the outcome that is (i) most preferred by A, (ii) no worse than disagreement for B, (iii) feasible, and (iv) enforceable. Similarly, C_2, contract two, represents B's best hope. The players' best hopes correspond to opposite endpoints of the contract curve. When a *concession* is defined as agreeing to an outcome less preferred than one's own best hope, it is obvious that agreement requires concessions. Either one player makes all the concessions required for agreement by assenting to the other's best-hope outcome,

19   See McClelland & Rohrbaugh, *Who Accepts the Pareto Axiom? The Role of Utility and Equity in Arbitration Decisions,* 23 BEHAVIORAL SCI. 446 (1978).
20   *See* Coleman, *Market Contractarianism and the Unanimity Rule,* Soc. PHIL. & POL'Y, Spring 1985, at 69; Cooter, *The Cost of Coase,* 11 J. LEGAL STUD. 1 (1982).
21   Whereas mixtures between contracts one and two are assumed to be feasible in this game (hence, the C^1C^2 line), mixtures between other outcomes of this game are assumed not to be feasible. We adopt this convention to simplify the analysis.

or both players make concessions resulting in agreement at an intermediate point on the contract curve. If bargaining over the allocation of concessions fails, so too does contracting.

Intuitively, we recognize the problem of settling on a division of cooperative gains as endemic in human behavior and know that people resolve it when the conditions are right. Empirical studies confirm that standards of "fair division" sometimes guide rational agreement even in the absence of third-party enforcement. In particular, Kahneman, Knetsch and Thaler have shown that when unanticipated events induce unanticipated divisions, they do not necessarily threaten the economic viability of an arrangement.[22] In other words, individuals sometimes appeal to a sense of fairness to solve division problems when failure to reach agreement in division may jeopardize an opportunity for mutual gain. Laboratory experiments testing the Coase Theorem demonstrate as well that parties are able to secure jointly maximizing outcomes, though different methods of assigning property entitlements influence the division of the gains.[23] Other studies confirm (1) the importance of the status quo in choices over division rules, and (2) the heavier weight ascribed to losses than equivalent gains in evaluating outcomes.[24] In short, empirical studies suggest that players are often able to solve their division problem and point to some of the relevant factors in settling on particular divisions: namely, the allocation of initial entitlements, a sense of fairness, the relative disparity in weighting equivalent gains and losses, and so on.

Under a broad range of conditions, then, contracting par-

22 See Kahneman, Knetsch, & Thaler, *Fairness and the Assumptions of Economics*, 59 J. Bus. 285 (1986).

23 See Hoffman & Spitzer, *Entitlements, Rights, and Fairness: An Experimental Examination of Subjects' Concepts of Distributive Justice*, 14 J. Legal Stud. 259 (1985).

24 See Frohlich, Oppenheimer, & Eavey, *Choices of Principles of Distributive Justice in Experimental Groups*, 31 Am. J. Pol. Sci. 606 (1986); Kahneman, Knetsch, & Thaler, *Fairness as a Constraint on Profit Seeking: Entitlements in the Market*, 76 Am. Econ. Rev. 728 (1986).

ties settle on distributions of the gains from trade, which simply means that they allocate concessions. They also have in mind which among the available points on the contract curve they intend to *safeguard* by the terms of any contract. Put analytically, a necessary condition for agreeing to a contract is that its expected outcomes satisfy what may be termed the principle of *concession rationality*.[25]

Each of the formal models in the literature provides a distinct meaning to the concept of concession rationality. No single point-specific solution to the bargaining problem has gained universal acceptance. But we are less concerned with predicting a specific distribution than with identifying the parameters that influence the choice of rules for making it. We want a model that applies to a broad range of contractual settings and incorporates fundamental principles universally accepted as affecting the relative bargaining power of parties.

The problem with many bargaining theories is that while they take account of the parties' relative bargaining strengths, they assume away many of the other problems that lead to bargaining failure, for example, uncertainty. Thus, they typically yield the result that bargainers will secure a cooperative division of the gains that reflects their initial relative bargaining strengths. This outcome is not surprising, but because of all the evidence of noncooperation (wars, strikes, etc.), these models are neither predictive nor descriptive.[26] Again, though all bargaining models view the relative costliness of conflict as affecting relative bargaining power, many do not take into account the parties' best hopes or aspiration levels, which influence the bargainers' willingness to incur costs in reaching agreement. That is inconsistent with a siz-

25 Formal theoretic accounts of bargaining have been proposed by economists, game theorists, social psychologists, and strategic analysts. *See* J. Harsanyi, Rational Behavior and Bargaining Equilibrium in Games and Social Situations (1977); A. Roth, Game-Theoretic Models of Bargaining (1985); O. Young, Bargaining: Formal Theories of Negotiation (1975); Binmore, Rubinstein, & Wolinsky, *The Nash Bargaining Solution in Economic Modeling*, 17 Rand J. Econ 176 (1986).
26 *See* Cooter, *supra* note 18.

J. COLEMAN, D. HECKATHORN, S. MASER

able body of experimental evidence indicating that aspiration level is positively related to bargaining power.[27]

In contrast, what we call *resistance theory* renders an explicit account of the conditions under which negotiations break down, treats aspirations as part of the decision making calculus, and describes the information rational contractors require to reach agreement. Thereby, it illuminates the conditions under which people will expend resources to contract.[28] As conceived in resistance theory, bargainers assess the relative strengths of their strategic positions based on the utility structure of the game, for example, based on the location of the disagreement point, on the location and shape of the contract curve, and on their risk and time preferences. The strength with which a bargainer strives to avoid concessions, termed his resistance, depends on (1) the costliness to the individual of the concessions required by the agreement (the greater the concession cost, the greater will be the resistance to the agreement); (2) the costliness of conflict (an increase in conflict's cost increases the willingness to make concessions and diminishes resistance); and (3) the aspiration level (higher aspirations enhance resistance). The very existence of opposing proposals reveals conflicting aspirations. They establish concession limits and distributional expectations based on those assessments. Only outcomes in which those limits and expectations overlap satisfy concession rationality.

Formally, if D_i is any bargainer i's utility from disagreement (conflict); B_i is i's aspiration level or best hope – the enforceable outcome on the contract curve that he most prefers, or equivalently, the outcome he most prefers which is enforceable, feasible, and no worse than conflict for any other bargainer; and U_i is i's utility from a given outcome U, i's resistance to outcome U, $R_i(U)$ is defined as

27 *See* S. BACHARACH & E. LAWLER, BARGAINING POWER, TACTICS AND OUTCOMES (1981).

28 *See* Heckathorn, *A Formal Theory of Social Exchange: Process and Outcome,* in 5 CURRENT PERSPECTIVES IN SOCIAL THEORY 145 (S. McNall ed. 1984) [hereinafter Heckathorn, *A Formal Theory*]; Heckathorn, *supra* note 11.

$$R_i = (B_i - U_i)/(B_i - D_i). \tag{4}$$

During negotiations, each bargainer assesses his own resistance against that of others, which takes into account everyone's strategic position. Under conditions of complete information, each will agree to an outcome only if the concessions it requires are at least matched by the relative concessions of others. On the assumption of equal rationality, each party will make equal relative concessions.[29] It is not rational to be exploited. Expressed in terms of resistances, this means that the bargainer will agree to an outcome if his own resistance to it would equal or fall below the resistances of others. Formally, where $R_i(U)$ is any bargainer i's resistance to outcome U, and $R_j(U)$ is another bargainer's resistance to outcome U, then that outcome lies in the agreement set of i, A_i, if

$$R_i(U) < R_j(U). \tag{5}$$

Concession rationality requires that an actor's concession behavior fulfill this requirement. Resistance theory posits that in the presence of complete information, people exhibit concession rationality. Under conditions of complete information, rational individuals make equal relative concessions. When information is incomplete, a bargainer will agree to an outcome if he judges it to be rational in that sense, that is, if his own resistance is matched or exceeded by the expected resistance of everyone else. That is, if i's resistance to U is $R_i(U)$, and i's expectation concerning j's resistance to U is $E_i(R_j(U))$, then the set of outcomes to which i would agree, his agreement set A_j, includes outcomes fulfilling the requirement

$$R_i(U) < E_i(R_j(U)). \tag{6}$$

Of course, for an outcome to be agreed upon, it must lie in the agreement sets of each individual with the ability to block

29   This is also David Gauthier's view. *See* D. Gauthier, *supra* note 11.

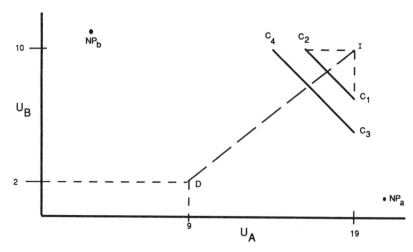

Figure 3. Equal resistance line

an agreement. For example, in a system of bargainers A and B, the outcome must lie in the intersection of sets A_a and A_b.

The implications of concession rationality for the outcome of bargaining can be illustrated graphically. Consider Figure Three. The outcomes when players' resistances are equal lie on the line connecting the disagreement point D (9,2), where each resistance equals one, to the *ideal point* I (19,10), a nonfeasible outcome where players simultaneously attain their best hope payoffs and resistances are consequently equal to zero. If person A exhibits concession rationality as defined in Equation Three, his agreement set lies on or to the right of the line ID; and if person B is similarly rational, his agreement lies on or above the line ID. Hence, if both exhibit concession rationality and they possess complete information, their point of agreement must lie on the line ID.

Resistance theory is one way of specifying the content of concession rationality. Concession rationality in turn expresses a condition of rational cooperation or rational contracting. Its domain is the division of the gains from cooperation or the parties' joint stakes in contracting.

The division problem can be more or less troublesome. The magnitude of the division problem in a particular case is a function of the discrepancy between the players' best hopes. If the individuals' best hopes exactly coincide, as in the *nondivisible* prisoner's dilemma game, the contract curve shrinks to a point, and agreement requires no concessions. As the contract curve lengthens, the required concessions increase. That in turn makes divisional bargaining an enterprise with higher stakes. Consequently, expending resources to enhance the strength of one's bargaining position becomes more rational, as do any measures to minimize one's own concessions and to maximize those secured from others.

The *magnitude of the bargaining problem*, M_B, can be formally defined in terms of potential expenditures of transaction resources, as the *maximum proportion of the gains attainable from contracting that any rational contractor in the system could be motivated to expend on transaction resources to enhance bargaining power*. As thus defined, the magnitude of the bargaining problem is the ratio of the gain attainable from bargaining to the gain attainable from contracting. The former is the difference between the payoff from the individual's best-hope outcome, B_i, that is, the most preferred point on the contract curve, and the individual's *worst hope*, W_i, that is, the *least* preferred point on the contract curve, which is $B_i - W_i$. This is the maximum amount the individual could be rationally motivated to expend in an endeavor to augment bargaining power. Furthermore, recall that $B_i - D_i$ is the maximum gain attainable from contracting, so the maximum proportion of the gains from contracting that the individual could be motivated to expend on enhancing bargaining power is

$$M_{Bi} = (B_i - W_i)/(B_i - C_i). \qquad (7)$$

For example, in Figure One's system, the magnitude of player A's bargaining problem is $M_{Ba} = (19 - 16)/(19 - 9) = 0.3$, and player B's problem is $M_{Bb} = (10 - 7)/(10 - 2) = 0.375$.

The magnitude of the bargaining problem, M_B, faced by a *group* of actors is defined as the maximum problem faced by any member of that group, that is,

$$M_B = Max[M_{Bi}]. \qquad (8)$$

For example, in Figure One's system, $M_B = M_{Bb} = 0.375$. This expression describes the maximum proportion of the gains attainable from contracting that any rational bargainer in the system could be motivated to expend on transaction resources.

3. *Post-phase: individual rationality.* We noted above that in the non-divisible prisoner's dilemma, there is no bargaining over the gains from cooperation. The parties' best hopes coincide, and no concessions are required. That is why the prisoner's dilemma is best thought of as illustrating the problem of rational defection, not the problem of rational agreement. The payoffs from cooperation are set; no concessions are required. Once agreement is secured, however, the question remains whether it is in the interest of either or both parties to comply with it.

The defection problem reflects the problematic nature of mutual trust, owing to the presence in most contracts of burdensome provisions and potential loopholes. Frequently, an individual can gain by defaulting upon a contract, often at the expense of those who perform according to its terms. A prerequisite for contracting, then, is a system of enforcement with which to preclude or to deter noncompliance, or to compensate parties injured by others' noncompliance. Not surprisingly, debating whether negotiations are undertaken in "good faith" and carefully scrutinizing contracts for hidden loopholes are prominent features of virtually all contracting.

The compliance or defection problem can be expressed in terms of a third condition of rationality. A necessary condition for rational agreement to a contract is that its expected outcome satisfies *individual rationality.* Neither player will permit himself to be left worse off than the status quo, or disagreement point. That is, when U_i is individual i's expected utility from participating in a contract, and D_i is i's utility from disagreement, i is *individually rational* if

$$U_i \geq D_i. \tag{9}$$

With reference to Figure Three, player A prefers defection if point NP_a is to the right of the point on the contract curve at which agreement occurs, and player B prefers defection if NP_b is above the contract point. Player A would not agree to an outcome lying to the left of point D, such as point NP_b in which B free rides, even though NP_b is jointly rational. Such an agreement would make A worse off than he would be were no agreement made, thus violating the individual rationality condition. Nor would player B accept any outcome below point D, such as NP_a, for analogous reasons. Hence, if both players are individually rational, neither will tolerate the other's free-riding. The outcomes of Figure Two's game that satisfy each player's requirement of individual rationality include the status quo point, D, and all of the points on the contract curve C_1, C_2. Rational parties will not agree to contracts they expect to make them worse off; thus, they must find a way to eliminate or to minimize the risk of defection. This is no easy task.

A defection problem arises if either player can gain from free-riding. The strength of the incentive to free ride depends on the relationship between each player's unilateral defection payoff and the payoff from points on the contract curve. In general, that incentive is strongest when the utility awarded by contracting is lowest. Thus, driving a hard bargain increases the incentives for others to defect from that contract's terms, and in consequence may be self-defeating. Notice, however, that in Figure One's system a contractor has some incentive for defection even if the agreement represents his best hope or most preferred contract. Every unilateral defection outcome gives him a payoff in excess of *any* cooperative outcome.

Described quantitatively, the *magnitude of the defection problem*, M_D, can be defined as the *maximum proportion of the gains attainable from contracting that a rational individual could be motivated to expend to secure the gains potentially available by defecting*. Recall that the defection problem arises because defection is more rewarding than cooperation. Let NP_i be individual i's *payoff from free-riding*, the payoff awarded a unilateral defector. An actor's incentive to defect is then measured by the difference between that payoff (NP_i), and the payoff from contracting, a payoff that is minimal when the individual attains his worst hope, W_i. Thus, the individual's maximum possible defection incentive is $NP_i - W_i$, indicating that he could be motivated to expend *up to* $NP_i - W_i$ for the privilege of free-riding with impunity rather than contracting. When the gain from defection ($NP_i - W_i$) is divided by the gains attainable from contracting ($B_i - D_i$), that yields the expression for the magnitude of the individual defection incentive M_{Di}. For any individual i, M_{Di} is

$$M_{Di} = (NP_i - W_i)/(B_i - D_i). \tag{10}$$

For example, in Figure One's system, the magnitude of player A's defection problem is $M_{Ba} = (22 - 16)/(19 - 9) = 0.6$, and player B's problem is $M_{Bb} = (11 - 7)/(10 - 2) = 0.5$.

The magnitude of the defection problem faced by a group of actors is defined as the maximum problem faced by any member of the group, that is,

$$M_D = \text{Max}[M_{Di}]. \tag{11}$$

For example, in Figure One's system, $M_D = M_{Da} = 0.6$. In sum, the magnitude of the defection problem[30] refers to the strength of the incentive to defect from contracts relative to the gains attainable from contracting.

To resolve the defection problem, each party must reduce the other party's incentive to defect. The power of the incentive to defect can be mitigated in several analytically distinguishable ways. Compliance can be made more rewarding, defection less rewarding, or opportunities to defect

---

30 Heckathorn & Maser, *Bargaining and the Sources of Transaction Costs: The Case of Government Regulation*, 3 J.L. Econ. & Org. 69, 80 n.4 (1987).

reduced or blocked. Of these, the second is the most common because the first tends to be more costly and the third tends to be impractical given the near impossibility of removing all opportunities for nonperformance. In short, no party will rationally agree to comply and to let the other party free ride. But since both parties have at least some incentive to free ride, each party has an incentive to deploy resources to insure the compliance of the other.

Individual rationality, then, requires that an agreement be *enforceable*, not just that an individual be protected against an outcome worse than the status quo.[31] For an agreement to be enforceable, the parties must expect that each estimates a cost of violation exceeding the gain from unilaterally defecting. That is, no agreement on C_1, C_2 is enforceable without penalties sufficient to deter defection, termed the *force of agreement*.[32]

Viewed graphically, an enforcement system that penalizes defection displaces the defection points NP_a and NP_b toward the origin, making compliance more rewarding relative to defection. In Figure Three, for example, if each player faces a violation cost that makes him indifferent between defecting and his best-hope outcome, then no points on the contract curve will be enforceable. But if each faces a violation cost that makes him indifferent between defecting and the other party's best-hope outcome, then the entire contract curve constitutes a domain of enforceable agreements.

In general, the greater an individual's defection incentive, the stronger must be the penalties that would succeed in making compliance rational. Further, the greater the incentive to defect, the stronger are the incentives for the individ-

---

31 At least in the case of cooperating to produce a public good, which can be studied as a prisoner's dilemma game, experimental evidence reveals cooperation rates significantly better when people expect an agreement to be enforceable as compared to when they receive money-back guarantees that they will be no worse off than when they started if the group effort fails. See Dawes, Orbell, Simmons, & Van de Kragt, *Organizing Groups for Collective Action*, 80 Am. Pol. Sci. Rev. 1171, 1183 (1986).
32 *See* Heckathorn, *A Formal Theory, supra* note 28, at 153.

ual to seek to evade or undermine an enforcement system. Put simply, the more a person wants to defect, the harder and more costly it will be to prevent him from doing so. Although it is not rational to accept a contract that is unenforceable, or one that gives others the opportunity to defect, making a contract enforceable requires expenditure of considerable resources. The greater the incentive to defect, the greater the resources required to prevent it.

D. Summary of rational contracting

The resistance solution to a bargaining game of complete information can be described in terms of the rationality conditions. Individual and joint rationality, which together comprise the classical notion of economic rationality,[33] together suffice to motivate contracting but not agreement on any unique contract. With reference to Figure Two, they restrict the outcomes of agreement to the portion of the welfare frontier called the contract curve, C_1, C_2. This contains, of course, many feasible outcomes. In classical economic theory, no choice among them can be said to be more or less rational than any other. The choice among them cannot be a matter of rationality! Thus, in the usual forms of economic analysis, the choice among Pareto optimal (collectively or jointly) outcomes is said to be a matter of distributive fairness, not a matter of economics (or rationality).

The additional requirement of concession rationality, the signature of the bargaining theory approach we adopt, restricts that outcome to a point on the equal resistance line, ID in Figure Three, so the cumulative effect of these requirements is to specify the intersection of the contract curve and the equal resistance line. For bargainers A and B with complete information, the outcome of the bargaining U satisfies the expression

$$\min[R_a(U) = R_b(U)]. \tag{12}$$

33 See J. Harsanyi, supra note 25, at 141–42.

Agreement and performance on a contract occur, then, if and only if it satisfies all three requirements for each party to the transaction. Taken together, then, these conditions are necessary and sufficient; they define a party's interests in a contractual relationship.[34]

Bargaining theory differs from the more common forms of economic analysis precisely by its commitment to a principle of concession rationality. This principle is aimed at explaining and defending some outcomes along the frontier as more rational than others. Concession or bargaining theory thus makes the division of the gains from contracting, that is, the distribution of the game's stakes, a matter of rationality. Unlike forms of economic analysis that set aside questions of distribution, rational bargaining theory takes the division problem to be a part of the problem of rational choice. As a consequence, concession theory not only can explain and defend outcomes of contracting as more or less rational depending on the way in which the gains are distributed; it can explain safeguards in contracting aimed at securing certain divisions, and failures in contracting as often resulting from failures to solve the bargaining or concession problem, or as owing to the high costs of safeguarding agreed upon divisions.

III. SAFEGUARDING THE RATIONAL CONTRACT

In the model we have just explicated, bargaining takes place sequentially (at least in logical space-time). First individuals search for potentially advantageous opportunities to cooperate, then they seek agreement on the gains, and finally they monitor compliance with the contract's terms. Each phase leaves plenty of room for contract failure. Thus, guarding against failure is rational – up to a point. That is, one does not want to spend more on preventing failure than failure costs in terms of forgone benefit. The important an-

---

34 The conclusions reached here also hold in the n-person cases and in the dynamic context. We use the static one to simplify the analysis. *See* Heckathorn, *A Formal Theory, supra* note 28.

alytic point is that at least some expenditure of resources to guard against contract failure is rational for all players. We call this process of expending resources to prevent contract failure "rational safeguarding."

The order in which actors safeguard their interests in contracting reverses the order in which they contract (again in logical space-time). In the divisible prisoner's dilemma, both parties have incentives to defect from unprotected agreements. If it is rational for player A to defect from an agreement, then it cannot be rational for player B to bargain with player A over the gains from trade, and *vice versa*. Bargaining without compliance is simply a waste of resources and is, therefore, irrational. If bargaining over the gains from trade is to be rational, the parties must be reasonably confident of one another's subsequent compliance. Thus, the defection problem must be resolved prior to pursuing a division of contract gains.[35] Similar considerations apply regarding the other phases of bargaining. Crafting safeguards to satisfy joint rationality is pointless unless the parties expect both the division and defection problems to be soluble. Early phase decisions are dependent upon expectations regarding decisions in a later phase; anticipating breakdown at a later phase may block affirmative decisions at a prior one.

Each party would prefer that the other bear the full costs of safeguarding. The parties in general cannot insist upon this preference. Concessions are rational, and parties can secure an agreement about distributing the costs of safeguarding. This "contract," that is, the contract over safeguards, has all the same conditions and pitfalls of bargaining over the gains from trade. So in the complete rational contract, the parties bargain both over the costs of safeguarding and over the gains from trade.

Negotiations over safeguards in a contract comprise a series of nested subgames, corresponding to a type of sequential decision making that Shubik terms "backward

---

35 *See* Kraus & Coleman, *Morality and the Theory of Rational Choice*, 97 Ethics 715 (1987).

induction.''[36] Here, the outcome of one game affects the potential payoffs of the next and issues are analyzed in the reverse of their ultimate behavioral order. Treating the divisible prisoner's dilemma in this way transforms it from a single game in which the defection incentive dominates, so contracting never gets under way, into two cooperative games.

The two cooperative games are then analyzed as follows. The first game involves negotiating over enforcement costs. In this game, we once again assume that the players command resources adequate to enforce an agreement, so that they need not call upon third-party enforcement mechanisms. (This assumption is crucial; otherwise, the account cannot proceed. For otherwise we will generate an infinite regress of nonenforceable contracts.) The only question at this stage – in this game – is, who shall bear which costs in solving the defection problem? If *this* bargaining problem is solved, then the second cooperative game is played. The players' mutual interest is to bargain over points on the contract curve only. The enforceable solutions to the second game therefore lie on the contract curve. Thus, the second bargaining game is over points on the curve.

The first, or enforcement, game is connected to the second, or division-of-the-gains, game in three ways. First, solving the enforcement game is a necessary condition for playing the division game; second, any particular solution to the enforcement game will affect solutions to the division game. How much one is willing to concede in bargaining over the gains from trade may well depend on how much one has had to expend in creating safeguards against defection. Third, because they are both bargaining games, the theory of rational bargaining developed above applies to both. In principle there should be equilibrium solutions to the conjunction of these two games that satisfy the rationality conditions.

---

36 *See* M. Shubick, Game Theory in the Social Sciences: Concepts and Solutions (1982); *see also* T. Schelling, *supra* note 15; Heckathorn, *A Formal Theory, supra* note 28.

J. COLEMAN, D. HECKATHORN, S. MASER

In general, party A will create a safeguard so long as the potential burden imposed on B to overcome it exceeds the cost to A of creating it; party A expects B to have a comparable incentive.[37] The equilibrium effect of following these strategies gives rise to an optimizing effect. When parties contract with one another, they bargain so as to minimize the sum of the costs players impose on each other and the costs they must bear to safeguard themselves. Under conditions of *complete information* both cooperative games are solved so that the following is true: a rational contract minimizes the sum of the costs the players impose on one another and the costs they bear to protect themselves.

A. Safeguarding against uncertainty

Problems in contracting arise when information is not complete, when instead actors are required to behave under conditions of uncertainty. Almost every contract dispute that winds up in litigation turns on a point about an incomplete contract; the traditional reasons for incomplete contracts are matters of information cost: 1) a contingency may be unforeseeable; 2) planning for every foreseeable contingency can be expensive; and 3) some contingencies may involve private information. Indeed, because a complete contract must specify a suitable mechanism for transmitting information to deal with contingencies, it can be particularly costly to devise. Therefore, actual contracts tend to be incomplete and subject to renegotiation.[38]

When bargainers possess less than complete information,

---

37   The comparisons here, as with those involved in making concessions, entail no invalid interpersonal comparisons of utility. The calculus for creating safeguards follows the calculus of resistance theory. In resistance theory, people are comparing concessions normalized with respect to each individual's stake in the game. Because the mathematical expressions take the form of the ratio of two utility differences, resistances are validly comparable across individuals. In this way, resistance theory captures a prominent feature of actual bargaining and actual equity judgments.

38   Tirole, *Procurement and Renegotiation*, 94 J. Pol. Econ. 235, 239 (1986).

failure to identify opportunities for gain or fear of outcomes worse than the status quo can prevent contracting from even getting off the ground. Once it does, agreement can still be blocked or the point of agreement may diverge from the contract curve's equal resistance outcome.[39] For example, if bargainers underestimate one another's resistances, they demand more concessions than the other will grant, and the result is conflict. Unresolved conflict does not entail that the rationality conditions are violated. Rather, divergences from the outcome predictable under complete information are predictable consequences of rational actors facing imperfect information. Bargaining with incomplete information can be both rational and unsuccessful.

If uncertainty exists, each party may benefit by manipulating information to create the appearance that conflict has become less costly to him or more costly to others. That makes his threats credible and signals an unwillingness to give in. Similarly, every bargainer possesses incentives to oversell his own preferred contract while denigrating the other's preferred contract. And each possesses incentives to invest in safeguards against precisely this sort of behavior because it threatens the divisions to which they would otherwise agree.

One consequence of this analysis is that the main reason for expending resources in contracting is to overcome some sort of uncertainty, uncertainty that threatens the equilibrium solution to which rational actors would otherwise agree. Because the possible sources of uncertainty differ in each phase of contracting, the logical character of the costs rational bargainers are willing to incur to reduce uncertainty differs as well.

People incur *search costs* because they are uncertain about the feasibility of alternative outcomes. Each bargainer wants information about the group's prospects. To resolve the coordination problem, information about group gains, or the opportunities to secure a Pareto improvement, is necessary.

39   *See* Heckathorn, *A Formal Theory, supra* note 28, at 161–68.

It helps to motivate contracting that satisfies the *joint rationality* condition.

People incur *bargaining and decision costs* because they are uncertain about the acceptability of alternative divisions. Each bargainer wants information about the agreement set. Securing adequate information about one another's resistances is necessary to create an agreement that satisfies the *concession rationality* condition.

People incur *monitoring costs* because they are uncertain about the enforceability of alternative outcomes. Each bargainer wants information about the consequences of the other party's defecting. In that sense, information about the force of the agreement is relevant to creating an enforceable contract that satisfies the *individual rationality* condition.

If an individual need only estimate *his* expected utility for the outcomes *possible* under a proposed contract against that of the status quo to ensure that its terms are no worse than not contracting, then the information required to judge outcomes by this test is the least stringent of all. But because each party needs to estimate the defection incentive and the force of agreement, then, in addition to the information needed to estimate joint and concession rationality, each must estimate NP_a and NP_b.

Significantly, each phase of contracting entails greater risks than the preceding one because, as an inspection of equations (1)–(12) reveals, more terms come into play at each step, so more information is required by succeeding calculations. That means more potential sources of uncertainty exist, more estimates must be made, each with a risk of error. In other words, the mathematics suggests that gathering information sufficient to fashion safeguards against defection is more difficult than securing information sufficient to safeguard against exploitive divisions, and so on. The more general point is that by incurring search, bargaining, and decision costs, individual contractors are able to mitigate *ex ante* risks; by incurring monitoring costs they hope to mitigate *ex post* risks. Thus, one can understand the object of contracting as the joint attempt to minimize the sum of the costs of uncer-

tainty and of its avoidance, when uncertainty afflicts all three
dimensions of rationality.[40]

B. *Factors affecting uncertainty*

Different but often related contextual features influence the
ability of decision makers to estimate the terms comprising
the calculus of contracting; that is, they affect the amount
and accuracy of the information that must be acquired, ver-
ified, communicated, or processed during the course of
contracting.

First, as the *number of principal parties* to the potential contract increases, the number of lines of communication and
the amount of information that must be processed during
negotiation increase. Opportunities for joint gain can be ob-
scured simply by the noise. Group size affects the defection
problem because in larger groups an individual's defection
tends to be less noticeable, weakening incentives for individuals to participate in sanctioning defectors.[41] Monitoring

40 This generalizes a formulation found in G. CALABRESI, THE COST OF
ACCIDENTS 26–31 (1970), and implied in Cooter's analysis of Coasian
versus Hobbesian perspectives on assigning liability, a seminal application of bargaining theory to legal issues, *see* Cooter, *supra* note
18. The Coasian perspective supposes the obstacle to cooperation is
the cost of communicating, so courts need only enforce private agreements; Cooter recognizes that the strategic nature of the situation and
the absence of a division rule may preclude cooperation, even when
communication costs are zero, evoking a more intrusive court. However, Cooter's perspective does not count the cost of concessions as
part of the strategic problem to which a court might attend. The
Hobbesian perspective supposes that bargainers increase their demands on each other at every opportunity, defeating cooperation
unless a third party exists to dictate the terms of a contract. Cooter
recognizes that people may adapt their strategies to achieve an agreement, evoking a less intrusive court. He concludes that institutions
such as markets serve efficiency without an extraordinarily intrusive
state because a market eliminates the power of parties to threaten
each other. But the proper standard of efficiency is generating optimal
threats, not eliminating threats. Our analysis joins the Coasian and
Hobbesian treatments of law, making the court's role contingent on
contextual features of social relationships that defeat cooperation.
41 *See* M. OLSON, THE LOGIC OF COLLECTIVE ACTION 45 (1965).

compliance in a large group is generally more difficult and more demanding of given resources than in a smaller group. Hence, contracting is riskier.

Second, as *heterogeneity among the principal parties* increases, the bargaining range – if one exists – and defection incentives increase. To be sure, differences of preference are required to provide a basis for exchange and contract, but the less interchangeable the actors, the more difficult the transaction. For example, the commonality among workers at particular job sites facilitates collective bargaining with management. Only minor adjustments are required to adjust for individual differences in seniority, skill level, and work classification. By contrast, when each party to a contract possesses a wholly unique set of attributes and relations to each other participant, bargaining may prove impossible even in a quite small group. Any bargain ultimately struck will inevitably leave more people disgruntled and, therefore, will create higher, more disparate defection incentives than would an agreement among a more homogeneous assembly.

Third, as the *spatial dispersion* of the group increases, communication costs increase. Bargaining and enforcement systems both require communication. In geographically concentrated groups, oral communication and incidental observations of behavior may suffice, but linking a dispersed group with equally adequate communication between each pair of individuals is technically more difficult. Conversely, improvements in the technology of communication, holding dispersion constant, reduce communication costs, so transaction resources go further.

Fourth, as the *temporal distribution* of the costs or benefits at issue in the transaction increases, they become more difficult to detect and control. For example, delayed defection costs impede monitoring because the adverse consequences become apparent only long after the fact. Similarly, delayed benefits hamper divisional bargaining because bargaining to allocate anticipated gains may appear to be an exercise in wishful thinking.

Fifth, and closely related, as the *level of acceptable risk* decreases, monitoring problems increase. If people engaged in contracting for the sheer thrill of it, then even expending resources in search of opportunities for gain might appear counterproductive. But in classical economics and game theory, the expected utility of a prospect is the product of its probability and utility. An actor who is rational in that sense is indifferent, for example, between the certainty of losing $10, a $\frac{1}{10}$ chance of losing $100, and a $\frac{1}{100}$ chance of losing $1,000. Yet such outcomes are not equivalent in their implications for contracting. In contrast to defection that imposes a certain cost, "defection" that merely creates a risk of damage can remain undetected unless actual harm occurs. Monitoring is especially difficult when defection results in a very small risk of grave damage (analogous to the $\frac{1}{100}$ chance of losing $1,000), because only a tiny portion of defections actually impose damage. Just as the absence of damage does not imply that no defection occurred, the presence of a damage does not necessarily prove defection. Risk is simply endemic. That is why so much contract litigation involves assigning liability in the case of an unforeseen contingency that affects the ability of one party to perform.

Sixth, as the *nontransferability of costs and benefits* increases, negotiating becomes more intractable. Bargaining determines how benefits and costs will be allocated, so it requires that at least some benefits or costs be transferable. The problems of quantifying and intersubjectively verifying nontransferable benefits and costs underlie the distinction between fungible and unique goods that has been used, for example, to justify the choice between damages and specific performance in contract disputes.

Seventh, as *instability* increases within a relationship, more transaction resources are required to secure rational outcomes. The best way of understanding how instability increases costs is to understand how stability reduces them. Because decisions themselves convey information about the risks of interacting, frequent and consistent decisions reduce the incentives to expend transaction re-

217

sources on searching and bargaining over acceptable divisions. Moreover, stability facilitates developing internal systems of enforcement with which to deter defection. For egoists in repeated plays of the same prisoner's dilemma game, cooperation rather than defection can become optimal because defection would disrupt a mutually rewarding pattern of cooperation.[42] If the short-term gains from defection are consistently offset by larger long-term losses, a stable pattern of cooperation emerges.

C. The rational expenditure of transaction resources

This is a good time to recap the analysis to this point. (1) Rational contractors seek to create mutually advantageous, enforceable agreement. (2) Doing so requires that they satisfy three independent rationality conditions: joint, concession and individual rationality. (3) These rationality conditions correspond to three phases in the contract process and enable the parties to solve three problems of rational choice: (a) the pre-phase coordination problem (joint rationality), (b) the negotiation-phase division problem (concession rationality), (c) the post-phase compliance problem (individual rationality). (4) A process of rational bargaining can satisfy these conditions but still fail to reach fruition in virtue of uncertainty deriving either from incomplete or imperfect information, or from potential defection. (5) Consequently, it will be rational for parties to create safeguards against contract failure. (6) Creating safeguards requires parties to incur three distinct kinds of cost corresponding to the phases in contracting: (a) search costs (pre-phase), (b) decision costs (negotiation phase), (c) monitoring costs (post-phase). (7) The magnitude of these costs will depend on contextual factors shaping the extent of uncertainty under particular circumstances. (8) In general, the magnitude of uncertainty is greatest in guarding against defection, less great in securing a division and least pressing in safeguarding against coordi-

---

42 See R. Axelrod, The Evolution of Cooperation 174 (1984).

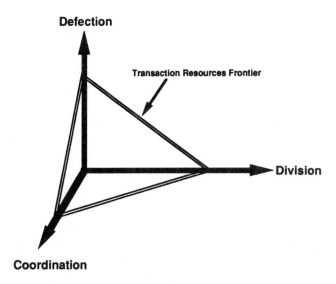

Defection

Transaction Resources Frontier

Division

Coordination

Figure 4. Transaction space diagram

nation failure. (9) Rationality requires that crafting safeguards proceed in the opposite temporal direction from contracting corresponding to the general magnitude of risk of failure. Because the risk of defection dominates in the nondivisible prisoner's dilemma, uncertainty about compliance is greatest and, consequently, crafting safeguards against defection is most pressing. (10) The process of creating safeguards can itself be modeled as a rational bargain over the costs of safeguards. The costs of safeguarding deplete transaction resources.

The capacity of the contractors to employ their own resources to reduce uncertainty and create safeguards can be represented graphically. Figure Four describes the types of interactions to which contractual arrangements may be matched in the form of a *transaction space diagram*. The vertical axis represents the magnitude of the defection problem. The horizontal axis represents the magnitude of the division problem. And the axis perpendicular to both of these represents the magnitude of the coordination problem.

When a transaction lies near the origin in Figure Four,

so that the problems are quite minor, the burden placed upon transaction resources is minimal. In transactions at increasing distances from the origin, indicating that the problems of identifying prospects, of bargaining or of defection are more major, the availability of transaction resources becomes more problematic; the farther any transaction lies from the origin, the greater the transaction costs required for contracting.

In contexts in which the seven factors affecting uncertainty are *favorable* to contracting, only modest resources are required to make contracting possible. For example, small residential groups such as nuclear families possess sufficient endogenous transaction resources with which to develop exceedingly complex systems of mutual understandings. Similarly, conditions in the most hospitable region of transaction space (that is, the area close to the origin) correspond rather well to those identified in any introductory economics text as conducive to private exchange in perfect or near perfect markets. Even in the (otherwise) most inhospitable regions of transaction space, that is, far upward and to the right of the origin but still within the frontier, ingenious safeguards evolve, such as "exchanging hostages" and giving collateral,[43] where people arrive at and enforce contracts independently.

In contexts where the factors affecting uncertainty are unfavorable to contracting, the parties' transaction resources quickly become exhausted. The worst case arises when members of a large, geographically dispersed group with diverse interests consider negotiating an arrangement in which the benefits and costs are delayed, nontransferable, and laden with risk. Locating a national nuclear waste storage facility is an example. Here, the transaction resource frontier will lie close to the origin, indicating that even slight concern over the feasibility of the alternatives or modest division or defection problems exceed the group's ability to contract independently.

43 *See* Kronman, *Contract Law and the State of Nature*, 1 J.L. ECON. & ORG. 5 (1985).

Bargaining theory

IV. THIRD-PARTY INTERVENTION

A. The preference for endogenous transaction resources

We need not presume that a forum external to the original setting of a contract – notably, authoritative experts like judges operating under the auspices of the state – will be more efficacious than private ordering in resolving disputes. This presumption, termed "legal centralism," informs much of the law and economics tradition.[44] That courts or other jurisdictional bodies are necessary to the very idea of contract and are thereby presupposed by the concept itself may simply be an unwarranted theoretical assumption. It does not follow from anything in the analysis presented to this point. To be sure, by assuming that courts exist and stand prepared to enforce whatever agreements private parties make, such a view isolates the problem of breach from those of cooperation and division. In doing so, however, it misleads. For tradeoffs are inevitable among all three problems in contracting. Moreover, judges attempting to make decisions in accord with the theory are denied insights about the constraints rational actors would want on the judges as third-party interveners. Private parties – including social scientists – may find judicial decisions less coherent. Indeed, the resource efficiency of decisions motivated by the paradigm is put in doubt. On grounds of theory, prediction, and policy, the presumption should be struck down in favor of a more realistic one.

Third-party intervention must be explained, not assumed. And it is more plausibly assumed if we start out presuming that people are never without some endogenous transaction resources with which to contract. That means they do not always rely upon or even want a third party to secure agreements.

44 *See* O. Williamson, The Economic Institutions of Capitalism (1985); Galanter, *Justice in Many Rooms: Courts, Private Ordering, and Indigenous Law*, 19 J. Legal Pluralism 1 (1981); Llewellyn, *What Price Contract? An Essay in Perspective*, 40 Yale L.J. 704 (1931).

Endogenous resources, however, are finite. The points in transaction space at which private parties exhaust these resources define what we term the *transaction-resource frontier*. The frontier is simply a way of visualizing the limits to private settlement and the reasons for involving a third party. Attainable gains are lost when contextual features place transactions beyond the frontier and block contracting. That provides an incentive for parties to the transaction to seek third-party intervention. When transactions lie outside the transaction-resources frontier, principal parties tend to seek third-party support.

A third party can facilitate contracting in any of three analytically distinct ways. First, it can help to resolve the coordination problem by providing *exogenous transaction resources* to augment the endogenous transaction resources already present in the relationship. If, for example, communication channels are poor, owing to the large number of parties or their geographic dispersion, the centralized channels and *information-processing services* provided by a *mediating* third party may well prove more efficient. Sometimes a mediator recognizes opportunities for mutual gain or audits the status quo more effectively than the principals. Described graphically, this type of intervention moves transactions inside the transaction-resources frontier, or in effect increases the region within which contracting among the principal parties becomes possible. It need not entail granting discretion to the mediator to allocate the gains by defining the terms of an agreement or to enforce one by punishing breach.

Second, third parties can help to resolve the division problem by providing *division services;* for example, a *coalition-building* or *arbitrating* third party may be granted discretion to allocate the gains under the contract, or merely to narrow the range of divisions possible under the contract. Described graphically, this moves the transaction leftward in transaction space, closer to the origin where conditions for contracting are more favorable. It need not entail granting discretion to the arbiter to enforce an agreement, but arbiters, like mediators, need to be a central agent in processing information.

Third, third parties can help to resolve the defection problem by providing *enforcement services*: for example, a *policing* third party may be granted discretion to punish defectors so as to increase the force of contractual agreements. Described graphically, this moves the transaction downward in transaction space, again closer to the origin. It may not entail granting the enforcer discretion to design the terms of an agreement, but to monitor behavior an enforcer needs centralized communication channels like a mediator, and in applying the force of agreement across disputants, the enforcer's judgments may well involve arbiter-like divisioned responsibility.

The existence of finite resources and the need sometimes to expend more than what the parties have available to them creates an incentive for both parties to seek outside help in making and securing contracts. Intervention by a third party, however, may be as problematic as it is promising. First, intervention by a third party complicates the transaction by creating a new contracting problem between it and the principal parties. An n-person game becomes an n + 1 person game. The more extensive the intervention, the more powerful the third party can become vis-à-vis the principals.

The third party creates a new coordination problem. The process of searching for a suitable third party and negotiating the terms of its performance is costly. Improperly crafted third-party services may prove redundant or unnecessarily intrusive. The greater the intervenor's role in processing information and forging communication channels, the greater too becomes the potential asymmetry between the intervenor and the principals. That can impede the principals' efforts to monitor it as well as each other. In short, the principals may not find it worthwhile to involve a third party even when it is a prerequisite to contracting.

Intervention is likely to create a new division problem. How are the residual gains from intervention to be allocated among the principal and third parties? Again, the answer depends on their relative bargaining power. The power of the principals depends on how well they can effect divisions

223

before the intervenor becomes involved. But the more extensive the intervenor's role in determining how contractual gains will be divided, the greater its potential to seize a larger than anticipated share. Greater too is the potential for the intervenor to become embroiled in partisan disputes among the principals and to empower some at the expense of others.

Intervention also creates a new defection problem. The outside party may fear that the principal parties will default on payments after services have been rendered. Alternatively, the more extensive the intervenor's role in establishing enforcement, the greater its potential to punish exploitatively. Indeed, a third party's special access to and control over information makes more difficult the principal parties' problem of preventing its defection by fraud or misrepresentation.

For these reasons, third-party intervention will always strike the principal parties as potentially more threatening than relying on *equivalent* endogenous resources. The implication is that people will prefer using endogenous resources not only because they tend to be less costly, more accessible spatially and temporally, and more readily mobilized than functionally equivalent resources that might be provided by a third party, but also because these resources are less burdened by risk. Moreover, having maximum involvement in shaping the contract helps ensure the principals that it takes efficient account of their preferences and so strengthens their incentives to honor its terms. Studies of arbitration, for example, show that bargainers who succeed in reaching agreement are more likely to honor it than are those who fail and have one imposed by an arbitrator. Finally, even under the simplest conditions, contracting with a third party is asymmetric because the original parties, being more numerous, must bargain among themselves first.

Many of the problems of third-party intervention can be mitigated by competition among providers of the service. Competition gives principals an alternative and, thereby, a safeguard. Thus, it can reduce their bargaining problem and their fear of exploitive mistreatment. This is an important point, because it gives analytic plausibility to suggestions that under conditions in which it is otherwise particularly difficult to constrain a third party, competition among mediators, arbiters, and enforcers may be preferable to a state monopoly on power.[45]

Still, establishing and maintaining a mechanism for third-party intervention is no mere technical exercise by which deficiencies in endogenous transaction resources are corrected. Rather it can be at least as conflictive and politically charged as private contracting. It, too, can fail. Thus, parties have incentives to avoid third-party orderings, such as courts provide, and instead to devise private orderings.[46]

B. When only intervention will do

The existence of uncertainty sufficient to threaten contract failure does not provide a sufficient reason for the parties to call upon third-party intervention. Only when endogenous transaction resources are depleted do the parties have sufficient reason to pursue outside intervention. As we demonstrated above, third-party intervention can create costs in excess of gains. Only if the endogenous resources of the parties are inadequate *and* the expected costs of third-party intervention do not exceed expected gains, would it be rational for contractors to require third-party intervention.

Figure Four depicts the range of cases in which safeguarding against contract failure requires the parties to consume transaction resources.[47] Type I cases fall within the frontier

45 *See* Barnett, *Pursuing Justice in a Free Society: Part One – Power vs. Liberty,* CRIM. JUST. ETHICS 50 (Summer–Fall 1985).
46 *See* Galanter, *supra* note 44.
47 The axes and frontier correspond in part to a classification system described in Ellickson, *A Critique of Economic and Sociological Theories of Social Control,* 16 J. LEGAL STUD. 67, 69–71 (1987). Ellickson sees administering positive and negative sanctions as involving rules that divide human behavior into three categories: (1) good behavior triggers rewards; that can have something to do with doctrines encouraging concession-making as well as trust; (2) bad behavior triggers punishment; his concern here is clearly with doctrines discouraging defection; and (3) ordinary behavior warrants no judicial response; this corresponds to our type 1 situation where parties have sufficient

where between them the parties possess adequate resources to resolve whatever problems they face. Moving outward along each axis, endogenous resources prove to be increasingly inadequate. In type II cases, the parties possess internal resources sufficient to solve division and defection problems, but lack resources to identify opportunities for coordination. In type III cases, the parties possess internal resources adequate to identify feasible contracts and to solve the division problem, but are unable by using their own resources to solve the defection problem. In type IV cases, the parties possess internal resources sufficient to solve their defection problem, but are incapable on their own of identifying or solving the division issues. Off the axes, we find a universe of other cases in which the principals in varying degrees lack the resources to resolve combinations of these problems.

This model suggests that we should find that several different types of institutional arrangements emerge in contracting. First, there will exist cases in which private parties are able to solve their problems without recourse to the intervention of third parties. In fact we find such institutions. The best example is the competitive market. In the market parties are engaged in bilateral agreements, discrete in time and place. A governmental enforcement mechanism is not necessarily a precondition for exchange; self-enforcing convention – sometimes called customary business practices – can work just as well. Markets provide ready sources of alternative exchange opportunities that can be sufficient to safeguard against one party's defecting *before* either performs on an agreement. Without resorting to violence or invoking third-party intervention, private parties can depend on reputational effects and devices like hostage-giving to safeguard against the risks of defection *after* one party acts in reliance on a promised performance.

Transactions along the coordination axis beyond the

endogenous resources. As he put it, "The prevalence of tripartite systems is a clue that rulemakers are attuned to an overarching goal of minimizing costs, including administrative costs." *Id*. at 71.

transaction-resource frontier pose a risk of joint failure sufficient to exhaust the parties' resources for identifying opportunities for mutual gain; that discourages exchange. The simplest convention, like drivers slowing down on approaching an intersection and stopping to wave a crossing vehicle through, break down. More densely settled areas and a more heterogeneous population of drivers will strain the convention, pushing the risks of motorized travel to the point where people begin to forgo its benefits or endure increasing costs. Someone can reduce the strain simply by setting a rule, almost any rule: when two vehicles approach an intersection simultaneously, the vehicle on the *right* proceeds first; where traffic density makes simultaneity increasingly expensive and variable to judge, install a traffic signal.

Contract law has, for example, the mailbox rule: an offeree has power to accept and close a contract by mailing a letter of acceptance, properly stamped and addressed.[48] Little economic justification can be found to support dating the contract from the mailing of the acceptance rather than from its receipt. Its economic justification can be found in the market-expanding properties of having a rule.[49] Like trade associations in various industries that develop consensus standards for product attributes so as to expand the total market for their products, the court expands the resource frontier so that private parties will engage in more transactions.

Beyond the frontier along the division axis, the participants primarily lack resources with which to solve the division problem. The parties would not get to the division problem without having identified an opportunity for productive exchange. Solving the defection problem is less significant,

48 *See* A. CORBIN, CORBIN ON CONTRACTS 124 (1952).
49 "One of the parties must carry the risk of loss and inconvenience. We need a definite rule; but we must choose one. We can put the risk on either party; but we must not leave it in doubt. The party not carrying the risk can then act promptly and with confidence in reliance on the contract; the party carrying the risk can insure against it if he so desires. The business rule throwing the risk on the offeror has the merit of closing the deal more quickly and enabling the performance more promptly." *Id.* at 126.

either because of ample internal enforcement resources or because incentives to defect are comparatively weak.

Some scholars have noticed the significance of the division problem in contract doctrine. But almost all of these scholars have confused the rational division problem as a matter of private law with a social or public theory of "fair distribution." For example, Farber suggests that contract law has a mandatory risk sharing system, a social safety net, and it is difficult for parties to bargain around it.[50] Thus, although freedom of contract means the power of parties to allocate risks between themselves, some contract rules reveal a countermanding principle of loss spreading, for example, rules against penalty clauses and warranty disclosure for personal injury to prevent catastrophic losses to one party. Similarly, Dalton has claimed that doctrines such as quasi-contract, duress, and unconscionability police the limits of acceptable bargains by private parties in the name of social (public) norms of fairness.[51] And Cohen claims that court adjudication supplements an original contract as a means of distributing gains and losses from unanticipated events. In this view, contract law consists of rules by which the courts accomplish this according to the equities of such cases. That follows not from the agreement between individuals but as a way of enforcing some kind of distributive justice within the legal system.[52]

These characterizations of the distributive dimensions of contract law may go too far. Our model implies that when courts impose distributive schemes on the parties, their doing so is compatible with the interests of the parties in the contract. No appeal to a global concern for distributive fairness, therefore, is necessary to understand or to justify a court's willingness to impose a distribution of risk among the parties. The legitimate exercise of that authority is restricted to the domain of outcomes the parties would have bargained

---

50 See Farber, *supra* note 18, at 336.
51 See Dalton, *An Essay in the Deconstruction of Contract Doctrine*, 94 YALE L.J. 999, 1001 (1985).
52 See M. COHEN, LAW AND THE SOCIAL ORDER 101–02 (1967).

within, and not to the set of outcomes that would be preferable from the point of view of a principle of social justice or social insurance. However, to the extent that the court, acting as an arbiter, seeks to implement a doctrine likely to resolve a wide range of division disputes efficiently, it may turn to widely accepted principles of social justice for guidance on the grounds that those principles themselves represent an evolved, rational or efficient solution to a wide range of division problems.

Transactions beyond the frontier along the defection axis indicate the defection problem is intractable internally but the cooperation and division problems are soluble. Parties here have relatively abundant internal bargaining resources but deficient internal enforcement resources. Intervention therefore takes the form of an externally applied enforcement system that moves the transactions downward, inside the frontier. Within the constraints of that system, individuals retain control over the terms of the contracts they enter.

The features that make a market such an attractive governance system – anonymity, spontaneity, disaggregated decisions adaptive to local circumstances – exacerbate the endemic risks of defection. Classical economists at least since Adam Smith have foreseen a productive role for a centralized enforcing agent. If third-party intervention diminishes ex post risks, people are freer to expend resources ex ante on searching for and reaching agreements that satisfy joint and concession rationality. Hence, common-law, judicially crafted safeguards that penalize contract breach are widely regarded as promoting economic efficiency.

Of course third-party safeguards designed primarily to reduce the probability of defection can influence the concession rationality of private decisions. That is because the remedies available under contract cannot escape dividing the residual risks of social intercourse and imposing different burdens of proof on the affected parties when one defaults.[53]

---

53 For examples, see the essays in THE ECONOMICS OF CONTRACT LAW (A. Kronman & R. Posner eds. 1979).

In areas of transaction space away from an axis and outside the frontier, the internal deficit of transaction resources is more profound. Here, assistance is required in solving a combination of problems that afflict contractual relationships. Indeed, even if in absolute terms a relationship is richly endowed with transaction resources, it is virtually assured of falling farthest from the three axes when all of the contextual features we identified impose large obstacles to contracting. Consequently, the degree of third-party intervention is greater because the third party must not only enforce contracts but also specify their terms and bring contractors to the bargaining table.

V. IMPLICATIONS FOR CONTRACT LAW

Our theory implies the following about contractual relationships: (1) not every effort to contract in the absence of law will succeed; (2) contract failure can result from a failure to solve problems of either (a) coordination, (b) division or (c) defection (compliance); (3) these problems are in principle solvable by rational parties negotiating with complete information; (4) contract failure is, therefore, best thought of as owing to some form of uncertainty; (5) parties to an agreement seek to reduce uncertainty by expending endogenous resources; (6) contract failure in the absence of law results when these efforts at safeguarding are inadequate.

That implies the following about law: (1) Law as a means of safeguarding can not, therefore, be assumed by a theory of contract, but must be explained instead. (2) The best explanation of it is that law is rational for contractors only if (a) it provides exogenous transaction resources that are necessary to insure a successful contract, and (b) the benefits of appealing to law to enable contracting exceed its costs. (3) Once law is in place, however, it is less costly for individuals to appeal to it to help resolve their contractual disputes than it would have been for them to *create* law for these purposes. (4) In reviewing cases in contract to understand or to criticize developing legal rules, we should inquire into whether uncertainty in coordination, division or compliance is the source of contract failure. We want to know whether the parties are in court because they lack sufficient search, negotiation or monitoring transaction resources. Then we can determine what kind of legal role the court is being asked to play: mediation, arbitration, policing, or all three. A full rational-choice theory of contract law will demonstrate how different cases can be analyzed as falling into all three categories and the conditions under which rational default rules will call for intervention by courts. (5) The rationality of legal rules, from the point of view of this theory, will not depend on their abstract rationality or efficiency, but on their rationality in the context in which they are to apply.

To this point we have identified the phases of contracting; three associated conditions of rationality that must be satisfied if contracting is to be rational; three related problems rational actors may face in securing a rational contract; the safeguards – endogenous and exogenous – available to protect against contract failure; and the factors that affect the nature and scope of the transaction cost problem. If we are correct, many cases or doctrines in contract law can be assessed as rational responses to problems of coordination, division and defection, corresponding to the three axes defining the transaction resource space. Our long range ambition is to demonstrate the power of the theory in each of these areas where courts have been asked to serve the function of providing exogenous resources.

In this essay, having set forth the general theory for the first time, we attempt a more modest illustration of its relevance. Thus, we take up the role a court might be asked to play in solving coordination problems by playing what we have called a mediating role. In doing so, we analyze in detail a famous case in contract law, *Laidlaw v. Organ*,[54] which in most other accounts is seen primarily as a case creating a property right in information unencumbered by a duty to disclose – a right lauded by proponents of economic effi-

54   15 U.S. (2 Wheat.) 178 (1817).

ciency. Contrary to prevailing wisdom, we argue that the court's decision is best understood as serving a coordination function. The decision promotes efficiency, not because a property right in information is efficient, but because the court's authoritative pronouncement reduces uncertainty and provides salience. Thus, we choose the disclosure issue as it arises in *Laidlaw v. Organ* to illustrate both how our theory leads one to think about cases *and* how it may lead to answers different from those suggested by traditional economic analysis.

A. Coordination, search, and disclosure

Nothing could be more fundamental to the notion of a rational bargain than the behavioral presumption that decision makers calculate the relative benefits and costs of alternative contracts predicated upon available information. Because information is costly, it follows that decision makers invest in information to refine their expectations, or in other words, to safeguard themselves. The efficiency of these investments in mitigating risk is always a private and a social concern. It can become a legal concern when one party knows or has reason to know that another is in error about information material to the calculation. When does a contracting party have a duty to disclose, failing which the other party will be excused from performance?

According to Kronman,[55] the nondisclosure doctrine the courts have crafted encourages socially efficient contracting by creating a property right in information. People may retain the benefits of their efforts to secure information relevant to productive exchange opportunities, except in circumstances in which they would have come by the information without effort. When they can come by the information without effort, a disclosure requirement would not reduce the incentive to produce it, and so might not be inefficient. In cases of

---

55 Kronman, *Mistake, Disclosure, Information, and the Law of Contracts*, II J. LEGAL STUD. I (1978).

mistake and disclosure, this argument holds, the court has been called upon as a third-party enforcement agent and it has done so in a way that is at least consistent with the principle of economic efficiency.

Kronman is surely right about the incentives that this doctrine can give individuals to invest in information: "One effective way of insuring that an individual will benefit from the possession of information (or anything else for that matter) is to assign him a property right in the information itself – a right or entitlement to invoke the coercive machinery of the state in order to exclude others from its use and enjoyment. The benefits of possession become secure only when the state transforms the possessor of information into an owner by investing him with a legally enforceable property right of some sort or other."[56]

The more secure the right to information, the more an individual will be inclined to invest in producing it. The *social* as opposed to the *individual* benefits of such a property right, however, are not as obvious, nor is the distinction between information that results from deliberate search and that which has been casually acquired necessarily decisive in establishing the economic efficiency of the appropriate legal doctrine.

To see where Kronman's argument goes awry, consider the case that is central to his analysis: *Laidlaw v. Organ*. Kronman's recitation of the pertinent facts is illuminating. Organ, a New Orleans commission merchant, had been bargaining with Francis Girault of Laidlaw & Co., also commission merchants, to purchase 111 hogsheads of tobacco. Early in the morning of February 19, 1815, Organ received news that the Treaty of Ghent had been signed, formally ending the War of 1812. Organ obtained the news from a Mr. Shepard, who had a financial interest in the transaction with Laidlaw and whose brother was one of three gentlemen who brought the news from the British fleet. Before 8 A.M., when the news would be made public in a handbill, Organ called on Girault

56 *Id.* at 14.

to consummate the purchase. Girault asked "if there was any news which was calculated to enhance the price or value of the article about to be purchased"; the record is not clear on Organ's response other than Laidlaw's attorney alleging "the vendee was silent." Nevertheless Girault and Organ entered into a contract.

The price of tobacco quickly rose by thirty to fifty percent as news of the treaty circulated, signalling an end to the naval blockade of New Orleans and the resumption of exporting. Kronman reports that Laidlaw retained possession of the tobacco, but the court record indicates that he first transferred it to Organ, then recaptured it by force. In any case, Organ then brought suit for damages and to block Laidlaw from otherwise disposing of the tobacco. The trial judge evidently directed a verdict in Organ's favor, deciding from the testimony that no fraud occurred. On appeal before the Supreme Court, Laidlaw's attorney argued, among other points, that fraud was a matter for the jury to decide.

The Court agreed, reversed the judgment, and remanded with directions for a new trial. Other than noting that Organ's silence may have been fraudulent, Kronman puts aside questions of fraud. He focuses on the *dictum* rather than the holding in the Court's opinion, delivered by Chief Justice Marshall. Generally regarded as an accurate statement of the law, it reads as follows:

> The question in this case is, whether the intelligence of extrinsic circumstances, which might influence the price of the commodity, and which was exclusively within the knowledge of the vendee, ought to have been communicated by him to the vendor? The court is of opinion that he was not bound to communicate it. It would be difficult to circumscribe the contrary doctrine within proper limits, where the means of intelligence are equally accessible to both parties. But at the same time, each party must take care not to say or do anything tending to impose upon the other.[57]

57 *Laidlaw*, 15 U.S. (2 Wheat) at 195.

The attractiveness and subsequent longevity of Marshall's opinion derives, in Kronman's view, from its consistency with the principles of economic efficiency. It gives contracting parties incentives to get valuable information to the market as quickly as efficient investment in producing knowledge permits. Indeed, "[t]he greater the likelihood that... information will be deliberately produced [acquired at a cost that would not have been incurred but for the likelihood that the information in question would actually be produced,] rather than casually discovered [by chance], the more plausible the assumption becomes that a blanket rule permitting nondisclosure will have benefits that outweigh its costs."[58] In addition, the administrative costs facing the courts in crafting exceptions are lower compared to the costs of imposing limits on a blanket rule creating a duty to disclose. In sum, a rule of nondisclosure is productively efficient, and a rule of disclosure is too costly to administer.

It is not obvious, however, that a property right in information is productively efficient. Moreover, what is relevant in determining the efficiency of the rule is not the manner in which the information is obtained (casually or deliberately), but its incentive effects (productive or redistributive). Consider, in this regard, an argument by the economist Hirshleifer.[59] Central to Hirshleifer's account is the distinction between foreknowledge – predicting events that nature will autonomously make known to all – from discovery – recognizing something that possibly already exists, though hidden from view until human action extracts it. Information of either sort has value only if it can affect action. From an individual's perspective, the value of new information and hence of investing in generating it, derives from *technology*, gains from allocating resources more efficiently, and *distribution*, wealth transfers that follow from price changes. In the case of technology, information makes the "pie" larger

58 Kronman, *supra* note 55, at 18.
59 Hirshleifer, *The Private and Social Value of Information and the Reward to Inventive Activity*, 61 AM. ECON REV. 561 (1977).

and thus increases ex ante each person's potential share. In the case of distribution, information does not increase the pie's size, only the shares of those who have the relevant information.

From society's perspective, the consequences of technological information are largely salutary, while those of redistributive information are not. As Hirshleifer puts it, "The distributive advantage of private information provides an incentive for information generating activity that may quite possibly be in excess of the social value of the information."[60] The argument is this: all information has a technological as well as a redistributive dimension. In many cases, investment in information will be socially efficient because the technological gains will outweigh the costs of investment. However, in some cases, the technological effects will be less significant than the redistributive ones. In these cases, private investment can exceed social return.

Consider two cases. In one case, Jones and Smith each invest $1 to gather information, the technological effect of which is $10, while the redistributive effect is $1.50. Two dollars are spent to secure $10; $1.50 goes to the discoverer, say Jones, with the net gain of $8 shared among the group (including Jones). In the other case, Jones and Smith again invest $1 to uncover information whose social value is only $.25, but whose redistributive value is $1.50. Jones and Smith each act rationally, spending $1 to seek $1.50, but the net effect is inefficient. Two dollars are spent to create $.25. Thus, giving individuals the full benefit of the information they obtain may lead them to act in socially inefficient ways whenever the redistributive aspect of information dominates its technological dimension.

Kronman recognizes that a rule in favor of nondisclosure can create perverse incentives and, therefore, that the decision to permit nondisclosure of certain information forces a practical choice between over- and underinvestment. His considered judgment is that because it is "certain" that elim-

60 *Id.* at 570.

inating property rights will result in underproduction, and "merely a danger" that recognizing them will result in overproduction, the economic case for recognizing them is strong ("but not conclusive"), especially when information is deliberately acquired.[61] Neither alternative is optimal, he notes, but assuming legal rules cannot be more finely tuned, the latter one is better.

Though Kronman relies upon considerations of the sort Hirshleifer summons, his conclusion – that a property right to information that does not require disclosure is, on balance, efficient – is, if Hirshleifer is right, unwarranted. As Hirshleifer sees it, the incentives to secure a distributive advantage "eliminate any *a priori* anticipation of underinvestment in the generation of new technological knowledge."[62] That is, investment in information that is likely to be primarily redistributive with little apparent gain in efficiency may be so great under a rule of nondisclosure that the costs of such a rule in terms of inefficient rent-seeking behavior may outweigh its benefits in terms of the production of net social gains. Thus, Kronman ought not confidently claim, as he does, that "allocative efficiency is best served by permitting one who possesses deliberately acquired information to enter and enforce favorable bargains without disclosing what he knows."[63] Whether the social gains created by a property right in information unencumbered by a requirement of disclosure will outweigh the social costs of investment depends on the relative effect – technological or redistributive – of the information.

Kronman's argument can be read as supporting a property right in information unencumbered by a disclosure rule on the grounds that any more finely-tuned rule will be too costly to administer. Administrative, rather than allocative, efficiency becomes the core of the argument. In order to create an adequate incentive to invest in information, a legal right

61 Kronman, *supra* note 55, at 17 n.46.
62 Hirshleifer, *supra* note 59, at 573.
63 Kronman, *supra* note 55, at 17.

to the information must be created, and the shape of that right, whether it requires disclosure or not, depends on considerations of administrative cost avoidance. The latter point is emphasized by Chief Justice Marshall.

The foregoing argument rests on three assumptions: first, of course, that a legal property right in information unencumbered by a disclosure rule is *necessary* to secure the benefits of information; second, that such an approach produces benefits in excess of costs; and third, that the property rule in information cannot cost-effectively be more finely-tuned. The truth of none of these assumptions is obvious. First, creating a legally enforceable right is not the *only* means to security. Indeed, people may be able to make the benefits of possession relatively more secure by resorting first to their endogenous transaction resources rather than depending upon legal rules. That was our point much emphasized in Part IV, and, as we shall show, *Laidlaw* in particular was a case in which the parties, commission merchants dealing in a competitive commodities market, were particularly well-suited to secure the gains from information in the absence of legal safeguards. Property rights were neither necessary nor rational. Second, given the risks of third-party intervention we identified in Part IV, action by the state cannot be assumed to secure benefits in excess of costs. Finally, while circumscribing a duty to disclose might be difficult, as Chief Justice Marshall opined, we cannot *a priori* rule out its feasibility in all circumstances.[64]

---

64 *See Laidlaw*, 15 U.S. (2 Wheat.) at 195. Chamberlin and Scheppele argue that Kronman's approach is wrong because the risk is deeply strategic, a risk that secrets may be employed to influence the actions or feelings of others. The question before the court is how to allocate knowledge between two parties given that one party has it already; the answer turns on the advantage people may be allowed to take of each other. This is something of a distributive risk rather than one of allocative efficiency. Chamberlin and Scheppele effect a Rawlsian solution, analyzing the legal rules as the product of a hypothetical agreement reached among rational actors in advance of knowing whether one or another will be in possession of a deep or shallow secret. *See* J. Chamberlin & K. Scheppele, Fairness and Symmetry in Information

Even if Kronman's analysis of the problem in terms of the efficiency of a rule of nondisclosure is unpersuasive, he correctly sees the general problem: if the parties to a contract fail to allocate risks and turn to the court for remedy, what default rule makes sense? The answer depends on the risks that will be of concern to rational actors. Kronman takes it that rational actors are primarily concerned with what Hirshleifer called technological risks; in allocating the risk of a mistake, for example, a nondisclosure rule imposes that risk on the mistaken party. The question before the court in applying that default rule is whether the information required to avoid the mistake is more likely to be generated by chance or by deliberate searching. But what of the redistributive risk that Hirshleifer identified, that is, the risk that private information can be used for redistributive ends? In *Laidlaw*, do technological or redistributive risks dominate?

In bargaining theoretic terms, the default rule embraces both risks: the rule minimize the sum of the costs of uncertainty and of its avoidance. The question before the court is who is in the best position to accomplish that? In some contexts, in which the risks are primarily technological, the court should act in accord with Kronman's formulation of the default rule. When other risks, especially distributive ones, predominate, focusing on whether the information to be disclosed is more likely to be revealed by chance or by deliberate search will not be an appropriate test. In sum, Kronman may be right that the rule is efficient, but for the wrong reasons. Thus, his formula for applying the default rule is misguided.

Examining more closely the context, as well as the holding, in *Laidlaw v. Organ* provides a good illustration of a more rigorous formula consistent with the theory outlined in Sections II through IV. First, the end of the naval blockade, like a drought or a blight, describes a state of nature inevitably to be revealed to the public; information about them is less

Games, Paper Presented at the Meetings of the American Political Science Association (Aug. 1986).

technological than distributive. So this is *not* the sort of case that, on either Kronman's or Hirshleifer's account, suggests a nondisclosure rule.

Second, the context reveals a network of pre-existing contractual agreements within which the dispute arose. That sheds light on the demand for third-party intervention and sets the stage for Chief Justice Marshall's dictum. The case concerned a contract for a commodity. Conditions in commodity markets represent a close real-world approximation to those found in a theoretical model of a pure exchange economy. Goods are exchanged on the spot, so contracts are well defined in time, place, and purpose. Allowing for readily observable differences in grades, tobacco is a relatively homogeneous and divisible good. Although merchants in a given city who specialize in one commodity might be a relatively small fraternity of members who come to know each other over time, they tend to be sufficiently numerous – or potentially so with relatively low entry costs – so no one sets prices. So long as many exchanges occur, the primary safeguard afforded a tobacco merchant lies in the alternative merchants waiting to deal.

If tobacco merchants buy on their own accounts, as did Organ and Laidlaw, they take on an economic function more than that of sales agents. Commission merchants facilitate market exchange in two ways, both characterized by specializing in *search* activities. First, they collect a transaction fee for bringing buyers and sellers together, narrowing the spread between price bid and price asked. Second, they speculate on extrinsic circumstances, as Chief Justice Marshall phrased it, hedging their exposure to risk by adjusting their inventories. Given the uncertainties, varying initial conditions, and costs of exchange faced by their principals, commission merchants become "market makers," specialists who increase the liquidity and reduce the costs of participating in the commodity trade.[65]

---

65 "[S]peculation in grain, for example by setting aside a certain class of persons to assume the risks of trade, has the effect of reducing these

We might expect these merchants to have ample endogenous resources for private contracting. Long before *Laidlaw v. Organ*, they invested in information, making deals and allowing producers to specialize in production. They need no third party to *mediate;* indeed, the merchants are mediators. Moreover, these merchants regularly negotiate over quantity, quality, and price. The risks of unfair divisions are mitigated by transforming the decisions into a sequence solvable within the constraints of available bargaining resources held by private parties. As a consequence these merchants do not normally need a third party to *arbitrate.* Finally, alternative exchange opportunities and reputation effects typically mitigate defection incentives without unduly straining enforcement resources. Thus, the merchants need not risk creating a third-party *enforcer,* except to deal with those categories of defections that are unusually costly to safeguard.

In short, given the theory presented here in which the principal parties are viewed as rational actors embedded in particular contexts, it would appear to follow that neither Laidlaw nor Organ had sufficient reason to seek any form of third-party intervention. The context, which is so important to our analysis, is one that suggests that the parties in this case possessed easy access to ample endogenous transaction resources.

Two aspects of the case need to be explained. The first is the holding in the case; the second is the dicta. To explain the Supreme Court's holding in the case, we need first to understand how the case came to court, and the question of law the Court was asked to resolve. Recall that we distinguish among three sorts of risks parties will seek to safeguard against, first by deploying endogenous transaction resources, and then by pursuing third-party intervention in the event their resources are inadequate to the task. These

risks by putting them in the hands of those who have most knowledge, for, as we have seen, risk varies inversely with knowledge." I. Fisher, The Theory of Interest 221 (1930); *see also* S. Khoury, Speculative Markets 169–70 (1984); Williams, *Futures Markets: A Consequence of Risk Aversion or Transaction Costs,* 95 J. Pol. Econ. 1000 (1987).

are risks of failed coordination, division and defection. When courts are sought to safeguard, we say that they play mediation, arbitration or enforcement roles respectively.

The case comes to court framed as a defection problem in which the principal parties are requesting the court to play an enforcement or policing role. Organ brought the case to court claiming Laidlaw's breach. Laidlaw's defense to the charge of breach rested on Organ's alleged fraudulent misrepresentation of the facts. For his part, Organ sued for possession of the tobacco and for his damages, in effect seeking to employ the power of the state to enforce the contract and, thereby, to punish Laidlaw's breach. The trial judge refused to submit the question of fraud to the jury. The jury refused to award damages, preferring instead to award possession of the tobacco. To be sure, Laidlaw's counsel raised the division problem on appeal: "Though [Laidlaw], after they heard the news of peace, still went on, in ignorance of their legal rights, to complete the contract, equity will protect them."[66]

Because the issue as presented on appeal was that of fraud, the Supreme Court could not avoid addressing the question of defection. It agreed with Laidlaw that the trial judge erred in refusing to submit the question of fraud to the jury and accordingly remanded for a new trial. On the other hand the court did not allow itself to be dragged into protecting against unfair divisions under precisely the conditions where the parties could safeguard privately at much lower transaction cost. Division problems are more cheaply solved in a competitive market, as was the context here, than in a court. That accounts in part for Chief Justice Marshall's concern about the administrative costs of judicial intervention: "It would be difficult to circumscribe the contrary doctrine [disclosure] within proper limits, where the means of intelligence are equally accessible to both parties."[67]

Following Kronman's lead, economic analysis ignores the

---

66 *Laidlaw*, 15 U.S. (2 Wheat) at 190.
67 *Id*. at 195.

Court's holding, focusing entirely on Chief Justice Marshall's dictum. Our analysis offers a plausible reconstruction of both. Part III shows that safeguarding against defection is the most information-intensive of the three dimensions in rational contracting. The calculus of safeguarding against breach is the most complex. The probability of mistake is greatest and, accordingly, so are the costs of guarding against it.

To see this, consider the difference between errors made in safeguarding divisions and those made in safeguarding against potential defections. If the principals or a court errs in safeguarding against unfair division, the error simply moves the parties from one point along the contract curve to another. The parties remain on the contract curve and, therefore, are better off than both would have been had no contract been made.

In contrast, a mistake in discerning or correcting for an alleged breach can make either party worse off than he would have been in the absence of agreement. Mistakenly determining that no breach has occurred enforces the breaching party's nonperformance payoff. That necessarily makes the other party worse off than he was at the point of no agreement, that is, the status quo. On the other hand, because the force of agreement is aimed at displacing the defection payoff towards the point of no agreement, imposing a penalty when no breach has occurred forces both parties off the contract curve.

Further, when a court as third party determines that a breach has occurred, it sends a message of potential unreliability to other potential cooperators. It thus chills cooperative endeavors. It reminds the parties of the need to expend transaction resources to reduce the probability of nonperformance, and it reminds everyone that sometimes even the optimal expenditure of resources will not foreclose entirely the chance of being victimized by one's partners.

Given this, it is that much more important that courts reduce the probability of error. Court decisions regarding divisions of the gains from trade have no comparable effects on markets. In this sense, mutual trust is more important than is fairness to a scheme of cooperation by contract. In sum, the greatest probability and cost of making a mistake in rational contracting occur in discerning or protecting against defection.

As between a judge and a jury, the jury is better positioned to determine whether a fraudulent "imposition was practiced," that is, whether a defection occurred. The reason is rather straight-forward. A finding of fraud typically turns heavily on findings of fact, such as the prevailing practices in the business community (because that delimits what each party can be assumed to have known) and who communicated what, to whom and when. For accuracy, reliability, and community representation in fact finding, a multi-member decision-making body operating under unanimity rule is preferable to a single decision maker, perhaps even an experienced one.[68] Given that the principal parties could no longer resolve the issue privately, remanding for a new jury trial places discretion where the sum of the costs of uncertainty and of safeguarding against it is likely to be least. Thus, our theory provides an extremely plausible account of the case's holding. Now to Chief Justice Marshall's famous dictum.

One supposes that part of what makes commodities markets valuable is their ability to process information – even information about extraordinary events – without recourse to either violent or legal action. However extraordinary an event the signing of a treaty is, it is not more so than is a blight or drought, all of which create opportunities for merchants to use for their personal benefit information not yet available to others.

After having turned over the tobacco, on the day following circulation of the handbill announcing the Treaty, Laidlaw, "by force" retook possession of the tobacco and withheld it

---

68 *See* R. HASTIE, S. PENROD, & N. PENNINGTON, INSIDE THE JURY (1983); Kaye, *And Then There Were Twelve: Statistical Reasoning, the Supreme Court, and the Size of the Jury*, 68 CALIF. L. REV. 1004 (1980).

from Organ. That action, should it prevail as a practice, would threaten the network of communication channels that makes possible market exchange, the specialized normative infrastructure that permits commission merchants to extract payment for their services. The decision to seek to sequester only highlights the extent of the risk, for doing so put at risk whatever gains had been captured by the initial contractual scheme of cooperation.[69]

Think of the problem this way: Laidlaw and Organ are potential cooperators. They disagree about whether individuals who have private information affecting prices should make full disclosure to their contracting partners. That they disagree about disclosure may be unknown to both of them, and in the bulk of the transactions between them their disagreement has no impact. In the circumstances presented by the facts of the case, however, the difference of opinion obviously makes a difference. The important difference between the parties, however, is *not* that one of them is right from either a moral or an economic point of view about the duty to disclose. Rather, what is important is the existence of a *difference*, period. The existence of a difference makes coordination difficult. Bargaining is always easier when property rights are well defined, and it is most difficult when genuine disagreement about them exists.

This disagreement about the norm regarding disclosure or

---

69 Although two parties always invest in crafting contractual safeguards when allocating risk, it is particularly difficult to craft a force of agreement that will ensure compliance when, as here, the contract entails the small risk of a large loss. Laidlaw lost big. The facts ex post created a circumstance in which reclaiming the tobacco made sense even accounting for possible legal action by Organ and approbation from the community. Whatever privately enforced norms existed among commodity brokers in New Orleans, Laidlaw, who appeared to be performing in accord with the contract long after news of the Treaty circulated, no doubt had to confront his client, a New York merchant who might not have had a stake in those norms. Indeed, whether in the absence of legal action reputation effects would have ultimately punished Laidlaw or Organ for violating a norm could well have been unclear. Given the immediate stakes, each party had ample incentive to seek authoritative affirmation of his view.

its applicability in the circumstances surrounding the sale is played out in Laidlaw's recapture of the tobacco (or his failing to deliver it – depending on one's reading of the record). This action ultimately invites the Supreme Court to provide an authoritative pronouncement regarding disclosure or misrepresentation. In doing so the Court will play a *mediating* role, specifying authoritatively the norms governing market transactions, thereby reducing the risks and costs of cooperation. To see this, we should consider both the context of the case and the longevity of the Court's dictum.

We can distinguish between the coordination and welfare effects of a rule. In circumstances of the sort commission merchants faced, any authoritative rule would have solved their coordination problem. This was, as we noted, a highly competitive market in which the principal parties were repeat players. What Laidlaw and Organ needed was an authoritative characterization of the rule – whatever its content. In that sense, either ruling on disclosure would have sufficed. Thus, from a coordination point of view, the rule expressed in Chief Justice Marshall's opinion has no special efficacy with respect to people investing efficiently in information. Once the rule is in place, negotiations between the parties are easier because the threat of noncoordination is reduced.

If it happens that all negotiating parties discover that they could do better under the alternative rule, then the rule the court announces will be unstable. No party will diverge from it unilaterally but all may be inclined to do so jointly. In the case under discussion, as we already noted, the private information concerned *price changes* and was fundamentally distributive, not productive, in its impact. Thus, there is no reason to think that a norm requiring disclosure would be any less efficient from a welfare point of view than would the rule the court actually advanced. So in the instant case and in competitive or repeat play circumstances generally, either ruling would be efficient in both the coordination and welfare sense.

The point of the Court's opinion, then, is to facilitate communication by providing salience in the form of a nearby arbitrary choice. With respect to all other matters relating to coordination, the Court put the burden of deciding how much to expend on safeguarding squarely on the shoulders of those in the best position to exercise that judgment – the principal parties. That is just as it should be. As Michael Taylor has argued in other contexts, by serving an authoritative coordination role unnecessarily, the state decreases the incentives for parties to devise creative solutions of their own.[70] By substituting legal pronouncements for endogenously devised ones, the state weakens the bonds of community, or, in this case, weakens the market structure. In short, however disinclined they may become to rely upon or to exhaust their transaction resources in favor of a third-party solution, when the principal parties remain in the best position to contract efficiently, courts should place the burdens of safeguarding on them. That is precisely what this case does.

We say that the Court's choice of a rule that does not require disclosure is *nearly*, but not fully arbitrary, for the following reason. Sometimes principal parties will lack endogenous transaction resources sufficient to resolve all conflicts on the terms of cooperation. Perhaps the market in which they transact is inadequately competitive and therefore too few alternatives exist; or the players are contracting on a one-time basis, in which reputational effects are minimized. In these circumstances the parties may rationally call upon the court to mediate. In that event, the rule that does not impose a duty to disclose may be easier to administer than likely alternatives to it. Moreover, if the Court retained discretion to allocate the search and distributive risks involved here, it might incur high direct costs as well as frequently abuse the notions of fair division held by private parties and communities, thereby calling into question the legitimacy of its value as a third-party intervenor.

This is a case about coordination and mediation. As such, either legal rule would have sufficed. Moreover, from the

70 *See* M. TAYLOR, ANARCHY, COMMUNITY AND LIBERTY (1982).

point of view of wealth or welfare maximization, the circumstances of this case provide no argument for nondisclosure as a default rule ex ante. In short, the choice of the nondisclosure rule rests ultimately on considerations of administrative efficiency.

To sum up, Kronman, like much of the law and economics literature that follows his article, reads *Laidlaw* as creating a property right in information, one that can be squared with efficiency. We have argued first that a property right in information may not be generally efficient, and second that a more compelling characterization of *Laidlaw*, one that follows from the theory developed here, sees it primarily as a court resolving a coordination problem by providing salience via authoritative ruling. A court thus mediates rather than arbitrates or polices and, in that way, protects against the transaction-resource frontier shrinking.

Though our analysis of *Laidlaw* is at odds with traditional economic analysis, there are bound to be many areas of overlap. After all, nothing we have said diminishes the incentives associated with protecting the right of one party to realize the gains associated from specialized investments in information. However, it may not be necessary or appropriate to reach the distinction emphasized by Kronman between casual and deliberately acquired information in order to explain the case law. A more plausible explanation, we believe, has the Court distinguishing among the relative efficacy of alternative safeguards – including judicial intervention – given the risks of contract failure involved, and placing responsibility and discretion with the party or parties who are in the best position to safeguard. Perhaps we can further illustrate the force of our theory by comparing the analysis of other cases it suggests with the analysis Kronman offers.

Two lines of cases Kronman explores involve real estate, either the existence of subsurface oil or mineral deposits known by the buyer but not the seller, or the anticipation of a development of some sort that will make the property in question more valuable.[71] In both cases we have speculative, commodity-like markets. Courts would avoid intervening without more compelling reason because the disputants are the most efficient allocators of the risks.[72]

The third line of cases involves distinguishing patent from latent defects. The logic of the standard economic argument merits attention. Suppose the seller can come by the information about a defect without deliberate investigation. If the argument against a disclosure rule applies to information available only through investment in discovery, why do the courts not impose a duty to disclose on the seller as the party able to avoid a mistake at least cost? In fact, the court imposes no such duty. Kronman resolves the inconsistency by saying the "rule that a seller of real property has no duty to disclose *patent* defects makes economic sense where – as is often the case – the seller has no reason to know that the buyer is

---

71 In the case of Neill v. Shamburg, 158 Pa. 263, 27 A. 992 (1893), a cotenant on an oil lease, Shamburg, discovered a particularly valuable well in the course of developing an adjacent parcel. He did not disclose this when he purchased the interest of his cotenant, Neill. The court rejected Neill's request to set aside the sale. Curiously, Shamburg's information might have been casually acquired in the sense Kronman means; Shamburg was incurring costs to develop the adjacent parcel for oil production anyway.

72 Kronman notes that the courts find a compelling reason in many of these cases because the problem involves breach of a confidential or fiduciary relation between parties to the contract. In these instances, failure to disclose is constructively fraudulent – defection. In other instances, the problem involves discriminating between nondisclosure and positive misrepresentation (fraud). Because these cases center on difficult questions of fact "about which it is difficult to generalize in a way that is theoretically interesting," he elects not to discuss these problems. *See* Kronman, *supra* note 55, at 19. From the perspective of bargaining and transaction costs, interesting generalizations become possible. We should be able to discriminate among these sorts of relationships, that is, guardian and ward, partner and copartners, principal and agent, where market safeguards will be less readily available to mitigate heightened risks, especially ex post risks of defection. In addition, discriminating who is in the best position to ascertain facts and act efficiently with respect to them should prove more tractable than ascertaining the facts themselves.

mistaken."[73] Kronman's resolution does not reach the question whether the seller would come by the information through deliberate investigation for defects, and therefore does not invoke the distinction between casual and deliberate means of obtaining information. Rather, his solution invokes considerations much more amenable to our analysis, for it turns on the question of who should allocate risk when information is public and, hence, has no economic value; that is, information as a safeguard is cheap. And markets provide the most efficient safeguards when no party need invest heavily in information about other parties' knowledge (doing that makes more sense in contexts where the division or defection incentives are particularly high and alternative safeguards are few). So the issue Kronman finds decisive is the same one we find decisive. A court would not intervene so long as market safeguards are available.

On the other hand, courts tend to impose a duty to disclose *latent* defects in products, such as termites in a house for sale. As Kronman says, a disclosure requirement would not be likely to reduce the production of such information.[74] But distinguishing on this score between information about attributes of goods held for sale, as in this case, and information about markets such as demand or supply shifts, as in *Laidlaw*, is not so helpful. For example, availability of product and support services may be attributes affecting price. Most importantly, with latent defects the distributive risks overwhelm the technological risks; ex post costs of remedy for unfair divisions are high, if contractual remedy exists at all.

A reputation for fair dealing helps, but in a fragmented industry such as housing, especially existing housing, reputation is a scarce commodity. Perhaps one motivation for state courts permitting nondisclosure about termites through the mid 1950s and requiring disclosure more frequently thereafter was an explosion in owner-occupied housing likely to

73   *Id.* at 23.
74   *See id.* at 25.

generate numerous occasions of defection by failing to disclose latent defects. Indeed, only recently have real estate brokers begun to offer inspection services and guarantees (sometimes because mortgagors require it), in effect acting as a centralized bonding agency.

B. The default rule revisited

We close with a brief reconsideration of the default rule. The most powerful implication of our analysis of rational bargaining for contract law concerns the legitimacy of applying the so-called default rule. Courts are often required to fill in the blanks of incomplete contracts by answering the question of what the parties would have agreed to ex ante. Hopefully, one thing we have made perfectly clear is that answering that question is no trivial undertaking – even under the best of circumstances.

Economists of law cite the "ex ante contract" as part of the argument for applying an efficiency interpretation of contract doctrine. Their reason for doing so is clear. The ex ante contract is to be modeled as a rational bargain between the parties and Pareto optimality (joint rationality) is a condition of rational bargaining. Indeed it is.

But so are the conditions of individual and concession rationality. And in all cases, satisfying the demands of rationality in a contract is considerably more complex than the hand-waving response of the legal economist – namely, to find an allocation of rights and responsibilities that is jointly wealth maximizing – would suggest. In fact, any number of distributions of rights and responsibilities between the parties would be jointly profit maximizing. These distributions differ from one another in how they divide the gains from contracting. Thus, to impose any jointly maximizing allocation of rights and responsibilities is incompatible with the lessons of the rational bargaining model developed here. For rational bargainers are as concerned with problems of rational division as they are with joint rationality. It is, therefore, as inappropriate for courts

251

to impose jointly maximizing outcomes on them in the name of efficiency without regard to concession rationality as it would be to impose a distribution of rights and responsibilities that satisfies the concession rationality condition without regard to whether that distribution is jointly rational (or profit maximizing).

More importantly, empty appeals to abstract efficiency or justice ignore the importance of context to rational contractors. What rational parties are prepared ex ante to leave for a court to resolve depends on the transaction resources available endogenously. Attending to those factors enables us to see *Laidlaw* as a case in which the court is being asked to solve a coordination problem by providing an authoritative statement of the norm regarding disclosure. Failing to attend to specific contextual features of disputes in the name of reconstruction in the light of the abstract norms of efficiency and justice makes a mockery of the idea of the ex ante contract as a default rule. For in abstracting from the context, a court is disabled from asking "What would *these* parties have agreed to ex ante?" and asks instead "What would be efficient or just from a global point of view?" We have no doubt that it is an interesting question to ask what is either just or efficient, but it is simply not the question the ex ante contract as a default rule necessarily asks.[75]

75 The approach we are developing here takes seriously the idea that in filling out incomplete contracts, courts ought to impose on the parties ex post that to which they would have agreed ex ante. To do that, courts must reconstruct a hypothetical rational bargain between (or among) the parties. What rational individuals in fact agree to under certain conditions need be neither fair nor efficient. Thus, that to which they would have agreed under those conditions may also be neither fair nor efficient. Do we really mean to suggest that courts should impose a division of rights, responsibilities and risks that merely transmits inequities in the parties' relative bargaining positions, thereby exacerbating, rather than alleviating, whatever injustices between them already exist?

This is a difficult question. Our tentative answer is a qualified "yes." One central aspect of the rational bargaining approach is the importance of conserving transaction resources. To see this, imagine any

Whatever one's theory of contractual obligation, whether based on consent, promising or rationality, a minimum condition for justifiably applying the default rule is that it imposes obligations on the parties – including the use of third-party interveners – that reflect what would have been rational for them in the circumstances of their contract. But on any such account, to impose jointly rational outcomes without regard to context is, at the least, to incompletely understand the default rule, and, at worst, to encumber in-

default rule that sought to rectify pre-existing inequalities by imposing rights and responsibilities ex post in a way that nullified or minimized pre-existing advantages. Because any default rule would be in effect only to the extent that the parties did not contract around it, its net effect would be to encourage as little reliance upon it as would be rational for the parties. In order to protect pre-existing advantages, parties will simply seek more completely to specify their contracts, thus reducing the rule's impact. By doing so, both parties will further deplete their resources, reducing the extent to which those resources can be employed to reduce uncertainty regarding other aspects of negotiations.

Secondly, we should draw a distinction between two concepts of fairness, one endogenous to the transactional framework, the other external to it. We would not want to dispute the possibility of a standard of justice in distribution according to which both pre-existing holding and entitlements that result from the contractual process can be evaluated or criticized. By such a standard, it may well be that a default rule of the sort we are discussing encourages rather than reduces unfairness. Notice, however, that the default rule merely transmits the unfairness of the initial holdings. The unfairness, if there is one, resides in the conditions that comprise the parties' relative bargaining positions. To rectify that problem, we should want to preclude *explicit* agreements that take advantage of those inequities, not just those that are imposed in the absence of explicit agreement. There is, in other words, nothing especially objectionable about the default rule itself. Moreover, it is a further question whether these sorts of inequalities are best rectified by courts on a case-by-case basis.

Let us consider the concept of transactional fairness. Any default rule that sought to annul ex post a pre-existing advantage would confer upon the advantaged party less than he could have or would have secured by making the terms of the agreement explicit. In doing so, the rule may treat that party unfairly relative to his trading partners. Not only would such a rule fail the test of rationality by encouraging the use of transaction resources, thereby increasing uncertainty, it may treat the parties, at least from a transactional point of view, unfairly.

dividuals by unjustifiably exercising the coercive authority of the state.[76]

76 To examine the role of the court when it is asked to solve division problems by playing what we have called an arbitrating role, one could look to a line of cases and scholarship associated with doctrines such as *laesio enormis* (under Roman law, a standard of equivalence in exchange that, despite its apparent rejection in modern times, arguably has been smuggled into current doctrines under other guises) or unconscionability (a test evaluating one-sided clauses that oppress or unfairly surprise a party). This examination would uncover the guidelines or principles of fairness that may be covert, and should be overt, in common law; and it would assess these in view of the theory of rational bargaining proposed here. *See* Eisenberg, *The Bargain Principle and its Limits*, 95 HARV. L. REV. 741 (1982); Trebilcock, *The Doctrine of Inequality of Bargaining Power: Post-Benthamite Economics in the House of Lords*, 26 TORONTO L.J. 359 (1976).

To examine the role of the court when it is asked to solve defection problems by playing what we have called an enforcing role, one could look at doctrines associated with damage measures or specific performance. For example, the model of behavior posited in the divisible prisoner's dilemma has parallels in the analysis of expectation, reliance, and restitution measures in Fuller & Purdue, *The Reliance Interest in Contract Damages*, 46 YALE L.J. 52 (1936); *see also* Bishop, *The Choice of Remedy for Breach of Contract*, 14 J. LEGAL STUD. 299 (1985); Goetz & Scott, *Liquidated Damages, Penalties, and the Just Compensation Principle: Some Notes on an Enforcement Model and a Theory of Efficient Breach*, 77 COLUM. L. REV. 554 (1977); Goetz & Scott, *The Mitigation Principle: Toward a General Theory of Contractual Obligation*, 69 VA. L. REV. 967 1983); Rubin, *Unenforceable Contracts: Penalty Clauses and Specific Performance*, 10 J. LEGAL STUD. 237 (1981).

Extensions of the analysis could apply to statutory law as well, accounting for conditions under which judicial intervention will tend to prove less satisfactory than legislative action. For example, in the context of administrative processes, see Heckathorn & Maser, *supra* note 30. In the context of constitutional choice, *see* Heckathorn & Maser, *Bargaining and Constitutional Contracts*, 31 AM J. POL. SCI. 142 (1987).

Part III

Risk, compensation, and torts

Chapter 7

Theories of compensation

ROBERT E. GOODIN

From a moral point of view, the function of compensation is
straightforward. Compensation serves to right what would
otherwise count as wrongful injuries to persons or their property. That is the role of 'compensatory damages' in the law
of torts.[1] That is the role of 'just compensation' paid in return
for the public taking of private property, pursuant to the
state's power of eminent domain.[2] That is what the New
Welfare Economists are relying upon when making the possibility of gainers compensating losers the proper measure
of permissible policies.[3]

It would, however, be wrong to presume that we as a
society can do anything we like to people, just so long as we
compensate them for their losses.[4] Such a proposition would

Earlier versions of this paper were presented at the Universities of Arizona,
Chicago, Georgetown, Göteborg, Maryland, Pennsylvania, Stockholm,
Uppsala and York. I am particularly grateful for the comments, then and
later, of John Broome, John Dryzek, Jim Griffin, Russell Hardin, Sheldon
Leader, Julian Le Grand, Keith Lehrer, Howard Margolis, Bob Sugden
and Gordon Tullock.

This essay is reprinted from the *Oxford Journal of Legal Studies*, vol. 9,
no. 1 (Spring 1989), by permission of Oxford University Press. © Oxford
University Press 1989.

1   W. L. Prosser and J. W. Wade, *Restatement (Second) of the Law of Torts*
(ALI 1979) secs 903 ff.
2   F. I. Michelman, 80 *Harvard LR* 1165 (1967); B. A. Ackerman, *Private
Property and the Constitution* (Yale Univ Press 1977).
3   N. Kaldor, 49 *Economic J* 549 (1939); J. R. Hicks, 49 *Economic J* 696 (1939).
4   Or, in the hypothetical formulation of the Kaldor-Hicks principle, could
compensate them for their losses.

mistake part of the policy universe for the whole. The set of policies to which it points – policies that are 'permissible, but only with compensation' – is bounded on the one side by a set of policies that are 'permissible, even without compensation' and on the other side by a set of policies that are 'impermissible, even with compensation'.[5]

There clearly are some things that we as a society can do to people without compensating them in any way for their ensuing losses. This is familiar to American constitutional lawyers through, eg, the distinction between actions arising under the state's 'police power' and those arising under the state's 'takings power'.[6] The state, or its officials, need not compensate those who are stopped from endangering public health, safety or welfare. No one expects state inspectors to compensate owners of insanitary restaurants or unsafe factories which they close down. No one supposes that the legitimacy of public health authorities putting victims of smallpox into quarantine is in any way contingent upon compensation being paid to them for lost wages. No one expects the police or courts to compensate the murderers or thieves they incarcerate.[7] No one expects the legislature to compensate tax accountants when passing new legislation to close a lucrative loophole in the present code, or owners of gas-

5   My focus here is on what public officials may legitimately do to individuals. Analogous issues arise in deciding what individuals may legitimately do to other individuals; see R. Nozick, *Anarchy, State and Utopia* (Blackwell 1974) 59.

6   See Michelman, above n 2; Ackerman, above n 2; J. L. Sax, 81 *Yale LJ* 149 (1971); and more generally E. S. Corwin, *The Constitution and What It Means Today*, 14th edn (Princeton Univ Press 1978) and L. H. Tribe, *American Constitutional Law* (Foundation Press 1978) 461 ff. Cf R. A. Epstein, *Takings* (Harvard Univ Press 1985).

7   True, those who are quarantined or imprisoned are ordinarily paid a small *per diem*, collectable upon discharge. But this is ordinarily a modest sum, rarely constituting anything approaching *full* compensation, even just for earnings (even legal ones!) that the individuals have lost while they have been detained. As evidence of this, notice for example that those who successfully sue for false imprisonment get far more, even in purely 'compensatory damages', than they would have received as the *per diem* due to any prisoner whether rightly or wrongly imprisoned.

guzzling cars when increasing the petrol tax, or taxpayers generally when levying a new tax.[8] Nor, for that matter, do American courts suppose that the owners of Grand Central Station need be compensated when its being declared a Historical Landmark precludes them from building an office block on top of it.[9] Such actions as these, taken under the state's police or taxing powers, are perfectly permissible, even without compensation being paid to those who lose as a result.[10]

The converse is also true. There are some things that we as a society cannot do to people, even if they are compensated

8   At least under certain conditions, one or another of which almost always obtains: if the tax affects everyone in general (Epstein, above n 6, chap 18); or if the tax does not alter people's relative economic standing (M. Feldstein, 6 *J Public Economics* 77 at 95–6 (1976)); or if the tax was explicitly intended to be redistributive (H. Sidgwick, *The Elements of Politics* (Macmillan 1891) 188).

9   Nor do we expect people to be compensated by one another, or by the public at large, for losses inflicted in the ordinary operation of economic markets. Indeed, to do so would fundamentally undercut the market, removing any incentive for people to reallocate their resources to more productive uses. See R. H. Haveman, V. Halberstadt and R. V. Burkhauser, *Public Policy Toward Disabled Workers* (Cornell Univ Press 1984) 32; cf T. Blough, 3 *Bulletin of the Oxford Institute of Statistics* 99 (1941).

10 How to distinguish these two classes of cases lies beyond the scope of this article. It is not just a matter of compensation being due when rights have been violated and wrongs done, for compensation is sometimes required (eg, in cases of voluntary sale) even though no one's rights were violated; J. J. Thomson, *Rights, Restitution and Risk* (Harvard Univ Press 1986) 77. The converse may well be true, however: one of the reasons we do not provide compensation, when we do not, is to make it more insecure and hence less attractive for people to engage in 'socially mischievous' activities (Sidgwick, above n 8, 187). Allied to that is an explanation couched in terms of 'legitimate expectations': we need not compensate people when depriving them of things that they had no reason to expect they would be able to keep; we do need to compensate them when depriving them of things they had no reason to expect would be taken away. Yet another analysis, owing to Epstein (above n 6, chap 14), is that those public activities not requiring explicit compensation are ones forming part of a larger social contract from which everyone in society derives 'implicit in-kind compensation'; those for which explicit compensation is due are those carrying no such 'implicit in-kind compensation'.

for their resulting losses. This class of cases provides the principal focus for the present article.

When trying to carve out a case for absolute prohibitions, earlier writers have usually tended to argue that some policies are impermissible because it would be impossible to compensate people fully for their resulting losses.[11] One tack is to say that the losses would be infinite, and impossible to compensate for that reason; another is to regard the losses and compensation as incommensurable, so we could never know whether compensation was adequate to cover losses.[12]

Both these approaches have run into serious difficulties. As a purely practical matter, it is difficult to adjudicate conflicts between two things each of which has infinite value – unless we care to talk in terms of 'different sized infinities'.[13] More fundamentally, infinite values imply lexicographical priority rules, which are wildly implausible: there are few (if

11 This is Nozick's (above n 5, 66 ff) approach. He tries to disguise this fact, however, by running his argument for prohibitions through the notion of 'fear'. He argues that some things should be prohibited because there are 'some things we would fear, even knowing we shall be compensated fully for their happening' – for example, someone intentionally breaking your arm. But if the compensation that would be paid really is *full* compensation, then you would have nothing to fear. As I conclude elsewhere, 'The only way to make sense of [Nozick's] intuitions . . . is to say that those are occurrences for which one can never be fully compensated'; R. E. Goodin, *The Politics of Rational Man* (Wiley 1976) 81. Alternatively, we might try to found the case for prohibitions on considerations of efficiency or distributive justice, rather than on the impossibility of compensation, as do G. Calabresi and A. D. Melamed, 85 *Harvard LR* 1089 (1972).

12 R. Zeckhauser and E. Shaefer, in R. A. Bauer and K. J. Gergen, (eds), *The Study of Policy Formation* (Free Press 1968) 38 ff; L. H. Tribe, 2 *Philosophy and Public Affairs* 66, 87 ff (1972); J. Feinberg, *Social Philosophy* (Prentice-Hall 1973) 92; B. Williams, *Moral Luck* (Cambridge Univ Press 1981) chap 5.

13 E. J. Mishan, in R. Layard, (ed), *Cost-Benefit Analysis* rev edn (Penguin 1974) 462, noticing that some replies to surveys undertaken by the Roskill Commission imply that people would suffer 'infinite' losses from being forced to move, remarks 'this would obviously wreck any cost-benefit criterion'. Feinberg (above n 12, 92 n 8), however, claims that this is a virtue of describing particularly important values as 'infinite': it would prevent one person's loss of that value (eg, freedom) being made up by any number of other persons' gains of that value.

any) pairs of goods such that we would refuse to sacrifice any quantity, however small, of the more valuable to secure any gain, however large, in the less valuable.[14]

The 'incommensurability' approach has more superficial appeal.[15] But in the end, it too must be rejected. Its great flaw is that it misrepresents hard choices as easy ones.[16] We may find it hard to say whether Sartre's student should abandon his aged mother to fight with the Resistance or abandon his country to stay and comfort his mother; but whatever else we say about this choice, we are confident that it is rightly to be regarded as a *hard* choice. Representing the competing claims of kin and country as incommensurable would carry the opposite implication. Since no one solution would then be demonstrably any better than any other, the student might as well just flip a coin rather than agonizing over the choice. That, however, is surely *too* easy.[17] Wherever we are tempted to say that the values at stake in some choice are incommensurable, we are likely to be similarly uncomfortable with such a trivialization of a choice that we think should rightly be regarded as tragic.

Here I shall take a different tack altogether. I shall not be saying that policies are impermissible because compensation is impossible in either of these ways. I shall concede that compensation in some sense can be paid. But that is compensation in a *different* sense from that which renders permissible

---

14 A. Sen, 4 *Theory and Decision* 301 (1974); J. C. Harsanyi, 69 *American Political Science Rev* 594 (1975). See more generally R. Nozick, 13 *Natural L Forum* 1 (1968).

15 See, eg, S. Williston, *Restatement of the Law of Contracts* (ALI 1932) sec 361 comment e, saying that the reason specific performance is sometimes ordered is that 'there are interests . . . recognized by the law . . . [that] are not commensurable with money. . . . '

16 Similar objections were lodged against the 'anything goes' implication that seemed to follow from Kuhn's arguments about the 'incommensurability' of scientific paradigms; see, eg, I. Lakatos and A. Musgrave, (eds), *Criticism and the Growth of Knowledge* (Cambridge Univ Press 1970).

17 C. Taylor, in A. O. Rorty, (ed), *The Identities of Persons* (Univ of California Press 1976) 281, 290–1. See more generally J. Griffith, 7 *Philosophy and Public Affairs* 38 (1977) and Williams, above n 12, 76 ff.

otherwise impermissible policies. For that transformation, compensation of a *strong* sort is required. In the class of cases here in view, only compensation of a different and much weaker sort is available.

Of course, some other right-making characteristic might always intervene to render a policy permissible even if the right form of compensation is unavailable to do so. It is no part of my thesis that all policies not admitting of this strong form of compensation are necessarily illegitimate *tout court*. My thesis is merely that arguments couched in terms of compensation cannot, in these cases, provide the needed legitimation.

I. THE NOTION OF 'COMPENSATION'

Compensation in general

The general idea of 'compensation' is straightforward enough. To compensate someone for something is, in the words of the landmark decision of the US Supreme Court in this area, to provide that person with 'a full and perfect equivalent' for that thing.[18] If he is given more than that, we would say he has been 'over-compensated'; if less, 'under-compensated'. Being bracketed as it is between these other two notions, the notion of compensation *per se* clearly implies the providing of the *exact* equivalent – neither more nor less.

To compensate someone is to provide him with something that is good, ie, with things that are desired (or at least are

---

18 *Monongahela Navigation Co v US* 148 US 312, 326 (1893). In Britain, too, 'the lawyer generally thinks of compensation as a method of making good a "loss", of replacing something of which a person has been deprived'; P. Cane, *Atiyah's Accidents, Compensation and the Law* 4th edn (Weidenfeld and Nicolson 1987) 5. As Atiyah continued, in an earlier edition: 'It is the simple principle that the plaintiff is entitled to a full indemnity for his losses; that he is to be made "whole" so far as money can do this'; P. S. Atiyah, *Accidents, Compensation and the Law* 3rd edn (Weidenfeld and Nicolson 1980) 5. See also J. P. Day, 56 *Philosophy* 55 (1981).

desirable).[19] The aim is to bring him up to some baseline of well-being. That baseline to be used for reckoning the adequacy of compensation will typically be identified by reference to some *status quo ante*, ie, some position that the individual himself actually enjoyed at some previous time. Thus, in the law of torts, the baseline for compensatory damage calculations is the position that the injured party was in before the tort was committed against him; when property is taken under the government's power of eminent domain, the compensation due is reckoned as the amount of the property-owner's loss, understood as the difference between his position in the baseline situation prior to the seizure and his position afterwards; and so on.[20]

Finally, notice one further general point. Compensation is not the same as restitution. It is one thing to restore the object itself to its proper owner. That is what we (and the *Oxford English Dictionary*) call 'restitution'. It is quite another thing to compensate the person for its loss. Such compensation is characteristically a matter of providing something which will, in the words of the *Oxford English Dictionary*, 'counterbalance,

19   Some commentators talk of 'revenge' – inflicting harm upon (or removing goods from) people who are above the baseline, in order to bring them down to it – as a kind of 'negative compensation'; see G. MacCormack, 21 *American J of Comparative L* 69 (1973). But that cannot constitute 'compensation', strictly speaking, unless we suppose that other people who are themselves below the baseline will benefit from people above it being made worse off. Sometimes, of course, that will be true; A. Sen, 35 *Oxford Economic Papers* 153 (1983).

20   Prosser and Wade, above n 1, secs 903 ff; Cane, above n 18, chap 7; Corwin, above n 6, 402. Occasionally the baseline used is some independent norm or ideal which, although perhaps standard among some reference group in the population at large, was never previously enjoyed by the individual being compensated. This is an attenuated sense of 'compensation', no doubt. But this is in the sense in which we claim to 'compensate' the congenitally handicapped for vision that they never had by providing seeing-eye dogs, or the educationally disadvantaged for stimuli that they never enjoyed at home by providing pre-school education. See A. J. Culyer, in D. Lees and S. Shaw, (eds), *Impairment, Disability and Handicap* (Heinemann, for the SSRC 1974) 17 at 22–3; and Haveman, Halberstadt and Burkhauser, above n 9, 30.

neutralize or offset' the loss.[21] What all those terms suggest, in turn, is not the restoration of the object itself, but rather the provision of something else altogether.

Two kinds of equivalence

The central claim of this article is that there are two kinds of compensation. These correspond to the two fundamentally different ways in which one object can constitute an 'equivalent' for another object which the person has lost.

The first kind of compensation might be called *means-replacing compensation*. The idea here is to provide people with equivalent means for pursuing the *same* ends (the same as before they suffered the loss, or as they would have pursued had they not suffered the disadvantage).[22] Giving someone who has been blinded a sighted amanuensis or someone who has lost a leg an artificial limb are attempts at this kind of compensation, which I shall hereafter call compensation$_1$.

The second kind of compensation might be called *ends-displacing compensation*. The idea here is to compensate people, not by helping them pursue the same ends in some other ways, but rather by helping them to pursue some other ends in a way that leaves them subjectively as well off overall as they would have been had they not suffered the loss at all. Giving someone who has suffered a bereavement an all-expenses-paid Mediterranean cruise might be an example of this sort of compensation, which I shall hereafter call compensation$_2$.

The distinction between these two kinds of compensation might be summarized thus. The first kind of compensation attempts to provide people with equivalent means to the same ends. The second kind of compensation attempts to

---

21 See similarly Sidgwick, above n 8, 180.
22 Those who suppose that the means-ends distinction is illusory, on the grounds that every end is in turn a means to some deeper end, are referred to the discussion of the structure of preferences in Section III below.

provide them with equivalent satisfactions through different ends.[23]

Both standards of compensation insist that people must be made as well off as they would have been, had it not been for the loss for which they are being compensated. With compensation$_2$, however, they will be as well off as they would have been, but *differently* off than they would have been. To achieve compensation$_1$, it is not enough that they somehow or another be made as well off. They must be left *identically* situated with respect to exactly the same set of ends.

II. COMPENSATION IN PRACTICE

In due course, I shall argue for the moral superiority of compensation$_1$ over compensation$_2$. In attempting to motivate that argument, however, it might be useful first to reflect upon compensation as it is currently practiced in public policy. Contemporary societies have developed a wide variety

23 The closest I have come to finding this distinction in the extant literature is in Atiyah's distinction between 'equivalence compensation' and 'substitute (or solace) compensation'; Cane, above n 18, 474–6. The former aims to 'give the victim back what he "lost" '; the latter aims to 'provide some other pleasures to the victim, in lieu of those he can no longer enjoy, . . . substituting . . . a new pleasure for the lost one'. In the examples he gives, however, Atiyah blurs this valuable distinction. Among his examples of 'substitute compensation' are these: 'The man who is blinded and can no longer watch television may be enabled to buy a gramophone and a collection of records, to give him an alternative form of pleasure. The man who loses a leg and can no longer go for a country walk may be enabled to buy a car, and savour the pleasures of the countryside in a different way.' But whether those count as compensations$_1$ or compensations$_2$ – as 'equivalents' or 'substitutes', in Atiyah's terms – surely depends upon how the injured man conceptualizes his pleasures. If the original pleasure was conceptualized as 'walking in the country', then a drive in the country truly is only a substitute (compensation$_2$) for that. If, however, the original pleasure was conceptualized as 'seeing the country' or even 'getting out into the country', then a car would indeed be an alternative means for attaining the same end – and hence constitutes what I call compensation$_1$, and what Atiyah himself would seem to call an 'equivalent'.

of ways for compensating people for all manner of accidents, injuries, illnesses, disabilities, losses, etc. In surveying them all, it is striking how many of our public policies aim at what I have here called compensation$_1$, and how few aim at compensation$_2$.

The distinction is never phrased in precisely those terms, of course. Instead, lawyers typically distinguish between compensation for pecuniary harms and for non-pecuniary ones. Pecuniary harms include damage to one's property or earning capacity or the creation of legal liabilities; non-pecuniary harms include bodily harm, emotional distress, humiliation, fear and anxiety, loss of companionship, loss of freedom, distress caused by mistreatment of a third person or a corpse, and so on.[24]

Now, compensation of the sort lawyers have in view will come in a pecuniary form, as monetary damage awards or other cash payments. Hence, pecuniary compensation for pecuniary losses would constitute what I have called compensation$_1$: the replacement of like with like. Compensation of a pecuniary sort for losses which themselves were non-pecuniary seems to constitute compensation$_2$: the substitution of one sort of pleasure for another.[25]

One good indicator of the balance of compensation$_1$ to compensation$_2$ in our existing compensation policies, then, is the extent to which they attempt to compensate for pecuniary versus non-pecuniary losses.[26] In practice, the former

24 Prosser and Wade, above n 1, secs 905 and 906.
25 This is not a necessary truth. A large cash payment may be seen as a mark of social esteem, thus overcoming one's sense of humiliation; a large bankroll may directly contribute to making one less anxious and fearful; etc. But it is presumably only rarely that a pecuniary compensation will be expected to work in some such way to restore the identical non-pecuniary good that was lost.
26 Another indicator is the way in which courts order 'specific performance' of contractual duties where 'the remedy in [monetary] damages would not be adequate' because, inter alia, of 'the existence of sentimental associations and esthetic interests, not measurable in money, that would be affected by breach' or 'the difficulty, inconvenience, or impossibility of obtaining a duplicate or substantial equivalent of the promised performance by means of money awarded as damages'; Williston, above n 15, secs 358(1) and 361(b–c).

typically involves payments to replace lost earnings or to cover extra expenses associated with injuries or disabilities, whereas the latter typically involves payments compensating for 'pain and suffering' or the 'loss of faculties or amenities'.[27] Perhaps the most comprehensive survey of compensation policies is the one carried out by the Oxford Socio-Legal Studies Centre in the late 1970s. Eighteen categories of financial support available to UK victims of illness or injury are studied.[28] Of these, only four (or perhaps five) offer any provision at all for pain-and-suffering or loss-of-faculties payments.[29] Summarizing these findings, the Oxford team writes,

> Most benefits . . . give priority to meeting either the loss of income or the reimbursement of the extra expenses incurred

27 Atiyah's distinction between 'equivalence compensation' and 'substitute (or solace) compensation' (Cane, above n 18, 473–6) is best understood in these terms: the former is a matter of giving pecuniary compensation for pecuniary losses, the latter of giving pecuniary compensation for non-pecuniary losses. D. R. Harris, in Lees and Shaw, above n 21, 30, 48, similarly observes that, 'since it is impossible to quantify in money terms the value of a lost limb, or the "loss" involved in pain and suffering, the question should be asked why the attempt need be made'. The reply Harris offers makes it clear that compensation$_2$ is what he has in mind. Prosser and Wade (above n 1, sec 903, comment a) similarly remark that 'when . . . the tort causes bodily harm or emotional distress, the law cannot restore the injured person to his previous position. . . . Nevertheless, damages given for pain and humiliation are called compensatory', presumably in the second of my senses.

28 These include two types of damages (damage at common law, as modified by statute; criminal injuries compensation), ten types of social security income support (industrial injury benefit; disablement benefit, and special hardship allowances and unemployability supplements thereto; war pensions and associated special allowances; sickness benefit; invalidity benefit; non-contributory invalidity pension; invalid care allowance; supplementary benefit); four types of social security expense payment (attendance allowance; constant attendance allowance; mobility allowance; the family fund), and two types of private provision (sick pay from employers; private insurance). See D. R. Harris et al, *Compensation and Support for Illness and Injury* (Clarendon Press 1984) 4–12.

29 These are: criminal injuries compensation; disablement benefit; war pensions; and (often) private personal accident insurance. Ibid.

by disabled people. A few – damages, criminal injuries compensation, the disablement benefit for industrial injuries, and war pensions – do provide some money to assuage suffering or to give an alternative pleasure where the . . . victim can no longer enjoy a particular activity. But this type of loss is covered by social security only in exceptional cases, and few people take advantage of the opportunities to buy private insurance to cover against it.[30]

Furthermore, among those programmes offering pecuniary compensation for non-pecuniary losses, only one (tort law) provides substantial sums to large numbers of people in many jurisdictions. 'Personal accident insurance policies (rare enough in themselves) are usually limited to medical expenses or income losses; and though small disability pensions are often made under comprehensive road traffic insurance policies, they rarely exceed £500 for severe disablement, with lesser sums for other cases.'[31] Compensation for pain-and-suffering or loss-of-faculties associated with war injuries, industrial injuries or criminal injuries is obviously available to only very limited numbers of people injured in very particular circumstances; and even then, the pain-and-suffering or loss-of-faculties component in the award (as compared with the loss-of-earnings component) is typically quite small.[32] Tort law, although notionally gener-

30　Ibid, 15.
31　Cane, above n 18, 475.
32　Note, for example, the experience under New Zealand's Accident Compensation Act 1972, which merged all major public programmes for compensating people for accidental injury (including workmen's compensation, criminal injuries compensation, and compensation for road accidents): '80 per cent of awards under section 120 [which covers 'loss of amenity' and 'pain and suffering'] are for less than $1000'; see T. G. Ison, *Accident Compensation* (Croom Helm 1980) 65. Notice, furthermore, that many of these compensation schemes did not originally (and in many places, still do not) make provision for pain-and-suffering or loss-of-amenity payments at all. See, on the early California experience with workmen's compensation, P. Nonet, *Administrative Justice* (Russell Sage 1969) 20–5. Indeed, circa 1971, criminal injury compensation schemes covered pain-and-suffering only in England, Hawaii and New Zealand, in the last case being limited to

ous, in practice often offers little more: in one study of out-of-court settlements, 'the mean sum for non-pecuniary losses such as pain and suffering, was £973, which . . . is a relatively low sum, especially since in just under 40 per cent of the cases the . . . amount agreed for damages took account of some permanent disability.'[33]

Sums like these can hardly pretend to 'make up' for serious bodily harm. They are instead token payments. As with 'nominal damages' in tort law, the sums involved are not 'utterly derisory'; but pretty clearly, the principal value of the awards is meant to be symbolic.[34] The aim, in Atiyah's terms, is surely to provide 'solace' rather than 'substitutes'.[35]

Thus it would seem that monetary payments principally serve to replace monetary losses. The vast majority of compensation programmes doling out pecuniary awards do not even try to compensate for non-pecuniary losses at all.[36]

$500; A. N. Enker, in I. Drapkin and E. Viano, (eds), *Victimology* (Lexington Books 1974) vol 2, 121, 131 and R. Elias, *Victims of the System* (Transaction 1983) 33, 151–7.

33 Harris et al, above n 28, 90.
34 G. Williams and B. A. Hepple, *Foundations of the Law of Torts* 2nd edn (Butterworth 1984), 57–8. The same is true of the $20,000 compensation being paid almost half a century later to Japanese Americans unjustifiably interned during World War II. As one advocate of their cause put it in Congressional testimony: 'Nothing can ever adequately compensate the Japanese Americans for the wrongs done them. . . . But what this bill can do is make it possible for this nation once again to hold its head high in remorse and thus in decency . . . and thus give new vitality to its commitment to civil freedom'; J. L. Rauh Jr, *Washington Post (National Weekly Edition)*, 12 May 1986, 28.
35 Atiyah, in Cane, above n 18, 474. Enker, above n 32, 131, remarks similarly that the $500 limit formerly imposed by the New Zealand criminal injuries compensation scheme on pain-and-suffering awards suggested that the real function of such awards was merely as a 'concrete expression of public sympathy for those victims'.
36 In some (but surely not all) of the social security programmes, the explanation might be that they do not aim at compensation at all but are intended instead to serve other social functions. Nonet, above n 32, 20, quotes one early administrator of the California workmen's compensation scheme as saying the aim of his programme 'is not compensation. . . . What it is, is insurance . . . necessary to tide the injured person and those dependent upon him over their periods of adversity until they can again become self-sustaining. That is all that

Those few that do tend, in practice, to make only token gestures along such lines. That strong preference for replacing like with like, money with money, would seem to betray a preference for compensation$_1$ over compensation$_2$.

The same pattern reappears when we look more deeply at the way in which compensation schemes characteristically function. We provide the blind with talking books, readers and audible street-crossing signals. We provide the wheelchair-bound with access ramps to public buildings. We provide invalids with home help (or an Invalid Care Allowance, to allow them to hire it), and the lame with transport (or a Mobility Allowance, to allow them to acquire it), and the disabled with rehabilitation and retraining.[37]

All those things are by way of compensation$_1$ – improving people's lives in broadly the same respects as some accident, injury or disability has worsened them. What we typically do *not* do is offer compensation$_2$, compensating people in one realm for losses suffered in some other realm entirely. Monogamous societies do not, typically, make an exception to allow a blind man to take two wives. That might make him better off in some global sense. But it would be deemed inappropriate, having nothing to do with his blindness.

III. THE STRUCTURE OF PREFERENCES AND THE POSSIBILITY OF COMPENSATION

Modern welfare economists no doubt would, on the face of things, find this preoccupation with compensation$_1$ baffling.[38] From their perspective, the point of compensation is merely to leave people as well off as we found them. If

it is. We have got the right thing but we have got the wrong name for it'.

37 Haveman, Halberstadt and Burkhauser, above n 9, 45–6; both what they term 'ameliorative responses' and what they term 'corrective responses' would fall within my larger category of compensation$_1$. See more generally details of programmes in Harris et al, above n 28, chap 1 and Cane, above n 18, chap 16.

38 'On the face of things', in deference to the possibility discussed in note 68 below.

indifference curves are conceptualized as connecting points representing different bundles of goods that a person regards as as good as each other, then being compensated must surely be a matter of ending up on the *same indifference curve* afterwards as before. There is no need to restore someone to the *same point* on that indifference curve (ie, to restore exactly the same bundle of goods to them) since, *ex hypothesi*, he is indifferent between all alternative points on the same curve.[39] For the welfare economist, the choice between compensation$_1$ and compensation$_2$ all comes down to cost; and if in practice it proves cheaper to make losses up to people in some way other than restoring things like those they have lost (as typically it will)[40] then compensation$_2$ is from the welfare economist's perspective decisively to be preferred.

What underlies welfare economists' insensitivity to the distinction between compensation$_1$ and compensation$_2$ is their studied indifference to the deeper structure of people's preferences.[41] With conventional consumer theory, everything is presumed to substitute for everything else at the margin.[42]

39 In introducing his Compensation Principle, for example, Kaldor (above n 3, 551 n 1) acknowledged that 'individuals might, as a result of a certain political action, sustain losses of a non-pecuniary kind'. But all he infers from that fact is that 'something more than their previous level of money income will be necessary to secure their previous level of enjoyment'. Apparently he proposes to make up this shortfall merely by providing people with a larger money income. Culyer (above n 21, 22) has recently reaffirmed the economist's faith that 'non-pecuniary costs are in no way conceptually distinct from any other costs'.

40 Getting him back to the same indifference curve (compensation$_2$) can never cost *more* than getting him back to some particular point on that indifference curve (compensation$_1$) obviously. Often, it will cost less.

41 In his influential essay, 'Rational Fools', A. Sen, 6 *Philosophy and Public Affairs* 317, 335 (1977) rails similarly against traditional utility theory for having 'too little structure'. A similarly complicated structure among a person's moral values is also suggested by Nozick's (above n 14, 33 ff) discussion of the various different ways in which values might 'override', 'outweigh', 'neutralize', 'weaken', 'dissolve', 'destroy', 'invalidate', 'preclude' or 'nullify' one another.

42 Earlier political economists, though firm in this conclusion, tended to offer rather more subtle arguments for it than their modern succes-

Now, even within economics there is a growing band challenging this presumption. Georgescu-Roegen wryly observes that 'bread cannot save someone from dying of thirst, . . . living in a luxurious palace does not constitute a substitute for food, etc.'[43] Or as Lancaster says, there must be something about margarine that makes it a good substitute for butter but a bad substitute for a Chevrolet. Building on such observations, Lancaster goes on to offer his New Consumer Theory,

> breaking away from the traditional approach that goods are the direct objects of utility, and instead supposing that it is the [objective] properties or characteristics of the goods from which utility is derived. . . . Utility or preference orderings . . . rank collections of characteristics and only rank collections of goods indirectly through the characteristics that they possess.[44]

In Sen's terms, 'commodities' are valued not only in their own right but rather by virtue of the 'capabilities' that they bestow.[45] In short, goods have certain objectively-defined capacities to serve our subjectively-defined ends. The particular importance of this model for the present argument lies in its analysis of the way in which goods can substitute for one another. One thing is a good substitute for another if, however different it might otherwise be, it has the same objective capacity to promote exactly the same end as does the other. In Lancaster's terms, two goods are 'perfect substitutes' if they present exactly the same 'characteristics' in exactly the same proportions; they constitute 'close substitutes' if the associated characteristics-bundles are substantially similar.[46] In Sen's terms, they are good substitutes in

sors. See V. Pareto, *Manual of Political Economy*, trans A. S. Schwier (Kelley 1971) 182–6 and P. H. Wicksteed, *The Common Sense of Political Economy* (Routledge 1933) 152–3, 360–1.

43 N. Georgescu-Roegen, 68 *Quarterly J of Economics* 503, 516 (1954).
44 K. J. Lancaster, 74 *J of Political Economy* 132, 133 (1966). See further K. J. Lancaster, *Consumer Demand* (Columbia Univ Press 1971).
45 A. Sen, *Commodities and Capabilities* (North Holland 1985).
46 Lancaster, 74 *J of Political Economy* 132, 144 (1966).

so far as they promote the same capacities.[47] Thus, objects that are otherwise very different – as are trains and cars (ask any engineer) or butter and margarine (ask any chemist) – might nonetheless constitute close substitutes for one another, in so far as they present the same deeper Lancastrian 'characteristic' or promote the same 'capabilities' or, in layman's terms that connote almost the same thing, serve the same ends.

For many things, there *are* close substitutes. Production-line manufacture being what it is, one Ford Fiesta is to all intents and purposes just like another. So, unless you happen to form sentimental attachments to your automobiles, you can be fully compensated in the first sense as well as the second for the loss of one Ford Fiesta by being given another. One five pound note is much like another. So, unless you attach particular importance to how you came by it (eg, it was the first you ever earned, or it was given to you by your grandmother before she died), you can be fully compensated in the first sense as well as the second for the loss of one five pound note by being given another. And so on.

There are many things, however, for which there are *no* close substitutes. One rich source of examples concerns personal integrity: both bodily integrity and moral integrity are the sorts of things that, once lost, are largely irreplaceable. Other examples concern goods which are valued on account of their histories. Works of art, keepsakes, historical landmarks and natural wonders are all irreplaceable in so far as what we value about them is intrinsically bound up with the history of their creation. That is what makes facsimiles, which are otherwise identical to their originals, mere 'fakes'.[48]

There being no close substitutes for objects that are irreplaceable, it is impossible to compensate people in the first

---

47 Sen, above n 45.
48 For a fuller account of 'irreplaceable assets', see R. E. Goodin, 21 *International J of Environmental Studies* 55 (1983); R. E. Goodin, *J of Public Policy* 53 (1982); and R. E. Goodin, *Political Theory and Public Policy* (Univ of Chicago Press 1982) 120–1, 157–8, 181–3. On 'fakes', see M. Sagoff, 75 *J of Philosophy* 453 (1978) and R. Elliot, 25 *Inquiry* 81 (1982).

sense should those things be lost. All we can do is to compensate them in the second sense, offering them goods with different characteristics, speaking to altogether different desires, and yielding altogether different satisfactions.

The welfare economist's case for ignoring any distinction between the two kinds of compensation, sketched in the opening paragraph of this section, was that 'indifference is indifference; it does not matter where compensation puts you on an indifference curve, just so long as you are restored to the *same* curve'. Recasting the argument of this section into those terms, we have seen that indifference is not all of a cloth. There are, in fact, two kinds of indifference, corresponding to the two kinds of compensation.

In the form of indifference that parallels compensation$_1$, we might be indifferent$_1$ between two options because they are equivalent ways of achieving the same goal. We might be indifferent$_1$ between the high road and the low road because they both get us to the same destination in the same time and with the same effort. In the form that parallels compensation$_2$, we might be indifferent$_2$ between options because they are ways of achieving equivalently-good goals. We might, for example, be indifferent$_2$ between the Glasgow road and the Edinburgh road because both cities offer amusements which, however different, are equally amusing. Economists, in their continuing quest to 'extract the minimum of results from the minimum of assumptions',[49] use the same curve to represent both fundamentally different phenomena.

IV. THE SUPERIORITY OF COMPENSATION$_1$

With this apparatus in hand, we can now return to address the question of how it can be wrong for the state to do certain things to people, even if it compensates them for their losses. The short answer, foreshadowed in the introduction, is that the compensation in view is inadequate to legitimize the policy because it is of the wrong kind. The cases where com-

49 Lancaster, 74 *J of Political Economy* 132 (1966).

pensation is adequate to legitimize policies, I submit, are cases where there is something irreplaceable at stake. Since there are no close substitutes for the things people would lose, the state could compensate them only in the weaker, second sense; and that is just not good enough.[50]

Why is that not good enough? After all, something might be irreplaceable without being of infinite value. Each oil painting is, in some sense or another, an utterly irreplaceable 'one of a kind'. That, however, does not stop artists (even rich ones, who are not in any sense acting under duress) from selling their works. The same seems to be true for a wide variety of other things that we would regard as irreplaceable. There is usually *some* price such that people would be induced to part with them.

But it is one thing for someone, in exchange for something else altogether, voluntarily to part with some thing that is irreplaceable.[51] It is quite another for the state compulsorily to force that trade.

The way compensation works to legitimize public policies is by removing any distributional objections to the consequences of those policies. That is clearly the role economists

50 'Not good enough', because it does not do what compensation is particularly supposed to do, viz, restore the *status quo ante*. That compensation$_2$ makes people better off in other ways, and might leave them better off in terms of overall utility, is therefore irrelevant. The point of compensation is not just to make people better off, but to bring them back to where they were. Of course, perfect compensation$_1$ is often impossible; and when it is, it is an open question whether imperfect compensation$_1$ is or is not better than whatever form of compensation$_2$ is on offer. This follows from 'the general theory of second best', R. G. Lipsey and K. J. Lancaster, 24 *R of Economic Studies* 11 (1956).
51 This slides over the question of what constitutes a 'coercive offer'. Certainly it is true that if people have no choice but to accept the putative offer (eg, otherwise they would die) the exchange can be said to have been coercive, whatever its outward form. The same may perhaps be said of cases where the price is extraordinarily high, compared to the sort of capital that a person could otherwise expect to accumulate. If for example some perfectly well-paid clerk were offered £10 million for his left thumb, that might be thought to constitute a 'coercive offer', even though the clerk's option of continuing life as before is a perfectly viable one.

275

see it playing. If gainers actually compensate losers and still have some gains left over, then the policy constitutes a paretian improvement: someone wins, no one loses. If gainers hypothetically could compensate losers and still have some gains left over, then at least that shows we could have neutralized the distributional effects of the policy and still have shown a profit; that we refuse to do so is itself a distributional decision.[52]

There is nothing peculiarly economistic in viewing compensation in this way. Lawyers and courts of law have long taken a similar view of it.[53] What *is* peculiarly economistic is the way of putting the point. In explaining how compensation removes distributional objections, the economist would typically say something along these lines: 'If everyone is as well off as he was before the policy was instituted, then no one has any grounds for complaint.'

That way of putting the point, however, focuses on *interpersonal* redistributions while ignoring *intrapersonal* ones. As shown in Section III above, people's preferences and goals are not one undifferentiated mass. Rather, they fall into several distinct, subjectively-defined categories. To guarantee the distributive-neutrality of our policies under those circumstances, it is not enough that people be left globally *as well off* as we found them. We must furthermore make sure they are left exactly *as* we found them. The former consideration speaks to interpersonal distributions, the latter to intrapersonal ones. It would be wrong, to the same extent and for the same reasons, for the state peremptorily to redistribute priorities between goals and projects that constitute one person's own life as it would be to redistribute resources be-

---

52 This is its role both in the theoretical welfare economics (Kaldor, above n 3; Hicks, above n 3) and in applied economics. On the latter, see: J. L. Cordes, 55 *Land Economics* 486 (1979); J. L. Cordes and R. S. Goldfarb, 41 *Public Choice* 351 (1983); H. M. Hochman, in H. M. Hochman and G. E. Peterson, (eds), *Redistribution Through Public Choice* (Columbia Univ Press 1974) 320; G. Tullock, 2 *Regulation* 50 (Nov/Dec 1978).

53 Michelman, above n 2, 1168; see similarly Ackerman, above n 2, and Tribe, above n 6, chap 9.

tween the goals and projects that constitute different people's lives.[54]

Compensation$_1$, where it is possible, successfully avoids both sorts of distributional objection. Where they are given close substitutes (as defined above) for what they have lost, people are not only as well off as before but also in exactly the same position with respect to exactly the same goals as before. All that has changed is the means by which those goals are to be pursued.[55] Where no close substitutes are available for what has been lost – where compensation$_2$ alone is possible – some amount of intrapersonal redistribution is inevitable. People might be as well off as before, but they will be differently off. They will have been forced to shift their goals, and not just their means of achieving their goals. Thus, compensation$_1$ erases all distributional objections to policies, whereas compensation$_2$ erases only half of them. Therein lies the superiority of the first sort of compensation over the second. That explains why compensation$_2$ is just not good enough to legitimize certain sorts of policies.

(Again, I should emphasize that distributive neutrality is neither a necessary nor a sufficient criterion of a legitimate policy, from a broader perspective. As I said at the outset, all kinds of state action are perfectly permissible without any compensation whatsoever. My point here is a much narrower one: the only way compensation can do anything at all to render legitimate otherwise illegitimate policies is by removing distributional objections to them; and compensation$_2$, by itself, can do only half that job.)

54 At this point economists protest that the two are not analogous: in the interpersonal case, the distributional objection is that someone has been harmed; but in the intrapersonal case, no one has been harmed. But that latter proposition is true only if 'having been harmed' is completely analysable in terms of 'having been shifted to a lower indifference curve' (which of course they have not); and it is precisely that proposition that is here in dispute. Economists making this reply are thus merely asserting what they are being asked to prove.

55 Perhaps people have chosen their means, just as surely as they have chosen their ends. But presumably people's 'moral personalities' are more heavily invested in the latter sorts of choices than the former.

There are two independent ways of explaining what, exactly, is wrong with imposing on people such intrapersonal redistributions, forcibly shifting them from one set of plans and projects to another. The first has to do with the value of 'coherence and unity' in a person's life.[56] Critics of classical utilitarianism have made much of the objection that it requires us to lead an incoherent life: fifteen minutes collecting for Oxfam, three hours as a nurse, twenty minutes as an investment banker, two hours shearing sheep, etc. Such a life, maximize social utility though it may, in some deeper sense adds up to nothing in the end.[57] One way of capturing this thought is to say that you can be either a saint or a sinner, but that there is no point in being a saint and sinner on alternate days.

As it stands, this is a perfectionist objection to forced intrapersonal redistributions between a person's plans and projects. That is to say, a life characterized by more coherence at any moment in time and by more stability across time is a 'better' life, by some *external* criterion.[58] Of course, it is also a more satisfying life by the internal criteria that most people use in deciding what makes their own lives satisfying. But some people might happen to prefer a less coherent life to a more coherent one – regarding 'coherence' as a straitjacket constraining creativity, or whatever. Given this potential divergence, perfectionist arguments based on the objective

56 Indeed, one of the more important arguments for compensation itself has long pointed to its role in providing stability, and hence coherence, in people's lives — removing 'insecurities', shoring up 'legitimate expectations' and easing 'psychological traumas' of those who fear (perhaps groundlessly) that they will be harmed (Sidgwick, above n 8, 179–80; Tullock, above n 52, 54). As one modern writer puts it, 'Individuals have as a matter of principle a right to reasonable security in their persons and possessions, and accordingly a right to be compensated when that reasonable security is infringed'; N. MacCormick, *Legal Right and Social Democracy* (Clarendon Press 1982), 214.

57 B. Williams, in J. J. C. Smart and B. Williams, *Utilitarianism, For and Against* (Cambridge Univ Press 1973) 75, 108–18 and Williams, above n 12, especially chap 1.

58 R. Nozick, *Philosophical Explanations* (Harvard Univ Press 1981) 403–51; R. Wollheim, *The Thread of Life* (Cambridge Univ Press 1984).

goodness of a more coherent and unified life are potentially open to powerful anti-paternalist rejoinders.

Remember, though, that the objection here in view is to *forced* shifts between a person's plans and projects. If someone freely chooses to adopt and abandon projects willy-nilly, that would be one thing. Even if we suppose that would be a less good life, by some external standard, we might nonetheless suppose that he should be allowed to lead his own life as he pleases. But for someone to be forced, by some external agency, to drop one project and take up another (even one that he would himself regard as an equally good project) is something else altogether. Far from endorsing that policy, the anti-paternalist argument firmly condemns it.

Second is the logically quite separate argument, from 'autonomy', against forced intrapersonal redistributions between a person's plans and projects. It is, after all, a central tenet of the liberal ethos that 'respecting' people means taking them as we find them.[59] It is important, in those terms, that people should be free to choose their own life plans for themselves; and it is equally important, in those terms, that once those choices have been made other people should respect them.[60]

Modern welfare economics grasps this point, albeit imperfectly. There, 'the criterion used for [specifying] an increase in an individual's welfare . . . [is] that he is in a chosen position'.[61] But surely taking people as we found them means

59   O. O'Neill, 14 *Philosophy and Public Affairs* 252 (1985).
60   We are obliged to respect those choices, not necessarily for their own sake, but rather for the sake of the dignity of those making them; Goodin, *Political Theory and Public Policy* (above n 48) chap 5. By that standard, too, compensation$_2$ would constitute an inadequate substitute for compensation$_1$, and for much the same reason. Mucking about with a person's life plans, forcibly shifting him from one goal set to another (even if it is, from his own point of view, an equally good set of goals) is hardly the way to preserve the person's self-image or sense of dignity.
61   I. M. D. Little, *A Critique of Welfare Economics* (Clarendon Press 1957) 37. Sometimes welfare economists phrase this test in terms of preferences or well-being, of course. But, operationally, they find themselves incapable of analysing these in any way except in terms of people's choices.

respecting people's *actual* choices – ones that they *really made*, rather than ones they might have made in some counterfactual world that never has (and perhaps never will have) existed.[62] What we are supposed to be respecting is people's choices, not their disembodied preference orderings.[63] It would be flatly contrary to the fundamental ethos of liberal welfare economics to force people to consummate pareto-optimal deals, or to make such trades on their behalf without their permission.[64] Suppose someone has contrived to sell my house out from under me, without my consent. Surely it would not suffice for him to reply to my protests that he got an exceptionally good price for it and that, despite the fact it was not for sale, I certainly would have agreed to sell it for that price if only he had been able to contact me. Whether or not I would have agreed, the point remains that I did not. By virtue of that fact alone, my autonomy has been violated.[65]

Means-replacing compensation$_1$ respects both of these val-

---

62 R. M. Dworkin, *Taking Rights Seriously* (Duckworth 1977) chap 6; R. M. Dworkin, in M. Kuperberg and C. Beitz, (eds), *Law, Economics and Philosophy* (Rowman and Allanheld 1983) 123, 124–9.

63 Nor is it their *reasons for choosing* that we are supposed to be respecting. It is true that there were various arbitrary forces shaping choices (prices, market conditions, opportunity sets and budget constraints), of course. But that does not make the choices, once made, any less *their* choices: A. Lerner, 62 *American Economic Review (Papers and Proceedings)* 258 (1972).

64 B. Barry, in J. Elster and A. Hylland, (eds), *The Foundations of Social Choice Theory* (Cambridge Univ Press 1986) 11, 41. The same point is made in Sen's (above n 41, 93) parable of 'two boys who find two apples, one large, one small. Boy A tells boy B, "You choose". B immediately picks the larger apple. A is upset and permits himself the remark that this was grossly unfair. "Why?" asks B. "Which one would *you* have chosen, if you were to choose rather than me?" "The smaller one, of course," A replies. B is now triumphant: "Then what are you complaining about? That's the one you've got." '

65 For the liberal, 'the conclusion that A should come about rather than B cannot shake itself clear from the requirement about the manner of its coming about, namely that [the person involved] should have chosen it'; J. Broome, 30 *Oxford Economic Papers* 313, 316 (1978). See similarly J. Kleinig, 8 *Canadian J of Philosophy (Supplement)* 91, 98 (1982), and Calabresi and Melamed (above n 11, 1126).

ues, whereas ends-displacing compensation$_2$ respects neither. Providing people with alternative means to the same
ends (compensation$_1$) allows them to pursue the same, self-
selected goals as before. That they are the 'same' ensures
unity and coherence; that they are 'self-selected' ensures autonomy.[66] Compensation$_2$, in contrast, might leave people
'as well off as before', in some sense or another, but it forces
them to pursue different goals than before. That they are
different compromises unity and coherence; that they are
forced compromises autonomy.

Compensation$_2$, in effect, forcibly pushes people along
their indifference curves. The fact that a person remains on
the same indifference curve means that, *ab initio*, he would
have been equally prepared to accept either option, either
his previous bundle of goods or his new bundle.[67] He *would*
have been: but as a matter of personal history, he did not
(his life has gone down a different track, now); and as a
matter of public morality, no one ever asked (he did not
consent to the change). Morally, both those facts are vital.[68]

66 Respecting autonomy obviously means giving the person what he has
    selected, instead of giving him yet another choice between multiple
    ways of getting something else – in part because maximizing auton-
    omy is not a matter of maximizing options, and in part because we
    reasonably doubt whether any of his subsequent selections will be
    honoured, either. A programme of strong, means-replacing compen-
    sation$_1$ may, in all sorts of ways, involve more interference with or
    intervention in a person's life than would a programme of weak
    compensation$_2$. (Rehabilitation is more intrusive than cash compen-
    sation, for example.) But, again, autonomy is not a simple matter of
    non-intrusiveness, either.
67 Thomson, above n 10, chap 10, puts it in terms of your being willing,
    ex ante of your rights being violated, to sell their violator the right in
    exchange for that price being now paid as compensation.
68 If people themselves happen to value 'unity and coherence' or 'au-
    tonomy' in their lives, then a more sophisticated welfare economist
    can easily accommodate these points by saying that to be 'as good'
    the new bundle of goods foisted upon people must compensate for
    those losses as well. A corollary to that proposition, though, would
    be that we are free to neglect these considerations altogether if the
    person himself is not concerned by them – with the paradoxical con-
    sequences for liberalism noted in J. S. Mill's discussion, in *On Liberty*
    (Parker 1859) chap 5, of allowing people to sell themselves into slavery.

For those reasons, when a new bundle of goods is simply foisted upon people in compensation$_2$, whether or not it is an equally good bundle is simply irrelevant.

V. POLICY IMPLICATIONS

In so far as we are counting on compensation to right what would otherwise constitute wrongful inflicting of harms upon people, we must respect the following precepts that follow from the arguments developed above.

(1) Prevention is better than compensation, where it is an irreplaceable object that would be lost.

The logic of this proposition is simple. If something irreplaceable is lost, only the weaker form of compensation$_2$ would be possible. People would be as well off but differently off than before. If the loss is prevented, however, that would leave them in exactly the same position as before, still in possession of the irreplaceable object itself.[69]

This explains the differential, noted by several economists, between how much people are prepared to spend to protect certain things and how much they are prepared to insure them for. Zeckhauser offers the compelling example of a woman facing the risk of breast cancer. Imagine she is willing to spend £5,000 for medical treatment to reduce the risk of cancer from 10% to 5%. That implies that the value of a

---

69 Introducing his discussion of public policy with respect to accidental injuries, Atiyah comments that 'compensation is nearly always second best; prevention is usually the first aim' (Cane, above n 18, 7). But he never explains why. The primacy of prevention might be overdetermined. Irreplaceability apart, psychometric evidence shows that people attach much more value to avoiding the loss of what they already have than to securing what would appear to be symmetrically large gains. See D. Kahneman and A. Tversky, 47 *Econometrica* 263 (1979); J. L. Knetsch and J. A. Sinden, 99 *Quarterly J of Economics* 507 (1984); and R. Gregory and T. McDaniels, 20 *Policy Sciences* 11 (1987); on the implications for the welfare economic analysis of law, see E. J. Mishan, 19 *Oxford Economic Papers* 255 (1967) and 9 *J of Economic Literature* 1 at 19 ff (1971).

healthy breast to her is £100,000. Suppose now she is offered insurance at the rate of £20 of coverage per pound's premium. Does it necessarily follow that she will pay £5,000 more to cover the full £100,000 that the breast is worth to her? Zeckhauser concludes that it does not: since the insurance money would not restore the breast, 'it would be quite rational for her to insure no more than the medical expenses' of the mastectomy. Similarly, when a Constable painting valued at £100,000 turned out, after having been stolen, to have been insured for only £2,000, the vicar explained: 'We never had any intention of selling it and we could never replace it so there wasn't any point in insuring it for its full value'.[70]

This principle is also reflected in certain practices of the courts. Ordinarily, the courts let people do as they will; and they order tort damages *after* the fact if people have, in the end, caused others some harm. Sometimes, however, the 'nature of the interests' that stand to be harmed is such that damages would be a 'relatively inadequate remedy'. Where the interests that would be 'harmed by tortious conduct are so remote from the marketplace that . . . it is idle to speak of their compensation in terms of money', courts will not wait until after a tort has been committed. Instead, they will issue an injunction designed to prevent the tort from ever occurring.[71]

---

70 R. Zeckhauser, 23 *Public Policy* 419, 454 (1975); S. Reeve, *Colchester Evening Gazette*, 23 Oct 1985, 3; see more generally P. J. Cook and D. A. Graham, 91 *Quarterly J of Economics* 143 (1977). Another example of much the same form – offered by Culyer, above n 21, 23 and reproduced almost verbatim but without attribution by Haveman, Halberstadt and Burkhauser, above n 9, 30 – leads Culyer (above n 21, 25) to conclude that 'in the preventive area, where we are considering measures to reduce the number of disabling events', the smaller *ex post* sum would be the proper measure of the cost of the loss. Surely the only reason the sum is smaller, however, is that the compensation is inadequate to cover the full loss, which is properly represented by the other, larger sum; it is that larger sum that thus represents the true social worth of a successful policy of prevention.

71 Prosser and Wade, above n 1, secs 936, 944, 944 comment b. See similarly Williams and Hepple, above n 34, 68–73. Among the examples Prosser and Wade (above n 1, sec 944 comment b) give of such interests that qualify for protection by injunction are 'interests in pri-

Finally, notice that much that presents itself as compensation policy might just be an oblique form of prevention policy. This is so because, in many realms of compensation policy, the compensation would have to be paid (in whole or in part, directly or indirectly) by the persons responsible for causing the damage. Tort law is the clearest example of this; a weaker one might be workmen's compensation, where the employer's contributions are uninsurable or where the premium paid for such insurance varies according to the number of claims the insured has lodged. Since the risk of incurring such expenses would presumably serve to deter people from actions likely to harm others, compensation policies in this way might double as prevention policies. It is hard to discern what the balance might be as between these two very different aims in present compensation schemes. But the prevention rationale clearly does explain what otherwise appear as anomalies in present policies, such as the awarding of compensation for 'loss of amenities' to a person who, through severe brain damage, has been rendered 'totally insensitive to his loss'. Here the deterrent/prevention rationale is clearly controlling. The principle at work is simply that 'it should not be cheaper to kill than to maim, and, further, it should not be cheaper to injure a person so severely that he is incapable of obtaining any enjoyment from a sum awarded to him as compensation than to injure him less severely'.[72] That argument has nothing to do with the adequacy of compensation for the victim, and everything to do with the adequacy of the deterrent for the tortfeasor.

(2) Where a lost object is replaceable, the compensation offered should include the closest possible substitute for that which has been lost.

vacy, personal reputation, domestic relations, and personal property that is especially valuable to the owner because of the sentiment he attaches to it'.

72 Williams and Hepple, above n 34, 83; see also Cane, above n 18, 187–8. On deterrence and accident prevention more generally, see Cane, above n 18, chap 24 and G. Calabresi, *The Costs of Accidents* (Yale Univ Press 1970).

The aim of that form of compensation which can legitimize otherwise illegitimate state action – compensation$_1$ – is to allow people to remain in exactly the same position with respect to exactly the same ends as before the damage occurred. The goal is to make sure that means can be replaced without ends being displaced. The more nearly perfect the replacement (the better the substitute) that is being offered, the more nearly this goal of compensation$_1$ has been accomplished.[73]

This principle goes some way toward explaining why we are relatively comfortable in compensating people for losses that can be truly said to have some 'fair market value'. The advantage usually claimed for this class of cases is that here we can unambiguously fix a fair (ie, market) price on the losses.[74] But that, I think, is the smaller part of the story. The real advantage in such cases lies, I think, not in the fact that there is a *market price* for those things which are marketed. It lies instead in the fact that there is a *market* in those things which are marketed. That is to say, people can take the money they receive in compensation, go out into the marketplace, and buy another object just like the one they have lost.

73 In so far as 'autonomy' is the value underlying our preference for compensation$_1$, we should wherever feasible give people a choice between the most perfect substitute or something else, if they preferred. (The argument in Section IV above is for the most perfect possible substitute to be *among* those compensations offered, merely.) That might argue for cash rather than in-kind compensation, at least in so far as 'the most perfect substitute' could itself be obtained in the market for cash. Often, of course, it could not.

74 Corwin (above n 6, 402) and Calabresi and Melamed (above n 11, 1108) discuss this in connection with exercise of powers of eminent domain, Prosser and Wade (above n 1, sec 903 comment a) in connection with tort damages. Some go so far as to argue that the only reason we prohibit certain acts under the criminal law, rather than letting criminals 'buy out' their victims with compensation, lies in the difficulty of pricing what has been lost in a criminal assault: court-assessed damages 'represent only an approximation of the value of the object to its original owner and willingness to pay such an approximate value is no indication that it is worth more to the thief than to the owner'; Calabresi and Melamed, above n 11 (see similarly Nozick, above n 5, 64–5).

Robert E. Goodin

This principle also explains the emphasis upon *rehabilitation* in so many of our actual compensation policies, detailed in Section II. Rehabilitation, understood literally, consists in restoring lost functioning of that which has been damaged; understood metaphorically, it consists in substituting for that which has been damaged something that will perform much the same function. Occupational therapy is an example of the former, prosthetic devices of the latter.[75]

This emphasis upon rehabilitation also goes some way toward explaining why public policy should so often strive to aid the injured (and disabled, in particular) as a group rather than as individuals. As Donald Harris observes,

> Handicapped people are usually dependent on governmental or community projects to provide them with specially-adapted housing or transport, parking and recreational facilities, access to buildings open to the public such as museums, theatres, cinemas, etc. The common law notion of giving the individual his own sum of money to find his own facilities on an individual basis is not realistic in the modern world. . . . [76]

Giving someone who has been crippled monetary damages does not help him up the stairs to the City Council chambers, whose meetings he used regularly to attend. Building him a wheelchair ramp does. 'The importance of these facts is that they suggest that public expenditure of money to overcome difficulties of this kind may be a higher priority than more private compensation for disabilities as such.'[77]

(3) People should be compensated as best they can for irreplaceable objects once lost; but that does nothing to legitimize policies deliberately inflicting those losses.

Sometimes people suffer irreparable losses, despite our best efforts at preventing them. Or sometimes we find ourselves

75 Haveman, Halberstadt and Burkhauser, above n 9, chap 4.
76 Harris, above n 27, 48.
77 Atiyah, in Cane, above n 18, 379 ff.

286

inflicting irreparable losses as part and parcel of some policy that is independently legitimized whether or not compensation is paid. Once irreplaceable objects have been lost, compensation$_2$ is the only possible remedy. It is a very inadequate remedy, to be sure: *ex hypothesi*, there are no close substitutes available. Still, inadequate though it may be, compensation$_2$ is surely better than nothing. There can be little doubt that it should be paid.[78]

We must, however, be very clear as to what its payment might accomplish. Payment of compensation in the strong sense – compensation$_1$ – can right wrongs fully and completely legitimize our loss-inflicting course of conduct. Payment of compensation in the weak sense – compensation$_2$ – cannot. In so far as losses are irreparable, compensation is necessarily inadequate. And in so far as compensation$_2$ is thus inadequate, so too is the plea that 'compensation has been (will be, could be) provided' inadequate to excuse a loss-inflicting course of action that would otherwise be illegitimate.

The distinction I have in mind here can best be evoked by examples from criminal injuries compensation policies. It is one thing to pay the widow of a soldier killed by IRA snipers £100,000 in compensation after the fact; it is quite another to use that sum in deciding ahead of time whether or not to buy soldiers flak jackets that would save their lives.[79] Or, for another example, it is one thing to decide that we should pay rape victims £1,000 in compensation; but it would be quite another to decide that it would be cheaper to pay off the two victims that will predictably get raped in some particularly dark street than to install a £3,000 lighting system.

78 Calabresi and Melamed, above n 11.
79 So, for example, if the flak jackets cost £100 each, they would be provided only if more than 1,000 soldiers will be shot in ways that would prove fatal without the jackets but would not prove fatal with the jackets; cf Tullock, above n 52, 53–4. This leaves open the question of whether it is permissible to impose or incur mere risks of such losses. For diverse views on this, compare: Nozick (above n 5, 82 ff); Goodin, *Political Theory and Public Policy* (above n 48) 157–8; and Thomson, above n 10, chap 11.

That compensation of this sort is inadequate does not mean that it should not be paid at all. But it does mean that it should not be counted upon to right all the wrong. Prevention is still the best policy.

VI. CONCLUSION

For our conclusion, let us return to that classic cautionary tale concerning economism and public policy, the Roskill Commission. Among the things that needed to be calculated in reckoning the costs and benefits of a third London airport were the losses to homeowners who would be displaced. Just reckoning the value of a house at its market price obviously understates the true value of the house to the householder. After all, he declines to sell his house on the free market at the market price: what right do we then have to assume that he would be fully compensated for its loss by the same price he has already rejected when it is compulsorily purchased by the government?[80] So the Roskill Commission set about surveying residents, asking, 'What price would be just high enough to compensate you for leaving this house (flat) and moving to another area?'

The striking thing about this survey was that 8 per cent of respondents said that they would not move at any price. Now, as Mishan says, 'it may be that a good interviewer would have elicited a finite sum ... – perhaps £50,000? or £5 million?' But, as he goes on to say, 'it is not altogether inconceivable that for some older, or unworldly, people all that [money] could buy for them would not suffice as compensation for having to live elsewhere'.[81]

Presumably few people would be so silly as to deny that with £5 million in compensation they would, in some sense, be better off moving out of their £5,000 house and living

---

80 Of course, one of the reasons homeowners do not sell privately but might be fully compensated publicly is that the public would also compensate them for the costs of moving, which private purchasers would not.

81 Mishan, above n 13, 462–3.

elsewhere. What these respondents would surely have said is not that they are better off, but rather that no amount of money can replace lost friends, etc. In my terms, it is the impossibility of compensation$_1$, not the inadequacy of compensation$_2$, that was at issue here.

This, I dare say, is a common pattern. Most policies will probably run up against at least 8 per cent of losers who feel hard done by in some such way. That is not to say that we should not carry forth with the policy. There are all sorts of reasons for and against building a third London airport; the uncompensatable$_1$ loss of displaced residents is just one among many, and on balance we may well decide that it is best to go ahead with the policy. What we cannot say, however, is that since losers will (or could) be compensated, they have no grounds for complaint.

Chapter 8

Liberty, community, and corrective justice

ERNEST J. WEINRIB

I

In a well-known article, Duncan Kennedy has stated that the central problem for law is its treatment of the fundamental contradiction of our condition.[1] On the one hand we are dependent on others for protection against destruction and for the fullest realization of our sense of ourselves; on the other hand we recognize in others a threat to our own well-being. Kennedy regarded the dilemma "that relations with others are both necessary to and incompatible with our freedom"[2] as the essence of every legal problem, and he ascribed to the liberal conception of law the historical function of dressing up as rational or natural the structures of bondage that emerged as its particular resolutions. Kennedy's contradiction invokes the recurrent tension between the notions of liberty and community that supply traditional vantage points for the analysis of social and political relations. The reconciliation of these notions poses an enduring philosophical problem, and one need not agree with Kennedy's

I am grateful to Peter Benson, David Copp, Peter Schuck, and Roger Shiner for comments on earlier drafts of this paper.

1 Kennedy, The Structure of Blackstone's Commentaries (1979) 28 *Buffalo L.R.* 205, 211–13. See also Gabel and Kennedy, Roll Over Beethoven (1984) 36 *Stanford L.R.* 1, 15 (renouncing the fundamental contradiction). The issue is discussed in Hunt, The Theory of Critical Legal Studies (1986) 6 *Oxford J. of Legal Studies* 1, 24–28.
2 Kennedy supra n. 1, at 28 *Buffalo L.R.* 213.

unflattering assessment of the law's function to realize that it is a problem in which law too has been centrally implicated. My concern in this essay will be the way in which private law,[3] especially tort law, deals with this dilemma. Several considerations justify attention to the theory of private law. First, no-one can read the great classics of Western political and moral philosophy without being impressed by the hold that private law has had on such writing. Second, during the last decades the enterprise of theorizing about private law has taken on a new life, similar to (and no doubt influenced by) the general revival of interest in political and moral philosophy. Tort law especially has occasioned a rich corpus of theoretical writing that has recognizably libertarian, economic and Kantian strands.[4] Third and most important, there is the nature of private law itself. Private law is an ordering of a pervasive and fundamental set of juridical relations.[5] Not typically the product of a single legislative will, private law is a decentralized and collective wisdom, an elaboration and refinement by different jurists of the norms that are regarded as justified in their legal culture.[6] A dispute in private law is, of course, always pressing to at least one of the parties,

3 Throughout this essay "private law" is used as a conventional term that includes tort law, contract law, and the law of restitution. As will be seen, however, my focus is not on the content of this conventional term but on the ordering of corrective justice that underlies the most significant features of private law. Legal doctrines that are not intelligible on this basis (e.g. contribution among tortfeasors) are beyond the purview of this essay, although they might conventionally be included in private law.

4 For critical surveys of the leading approaches in contemporary tort theory, see Steiner, Economics, Morality and the Law of Torts (1976) 26 *University of Toronto L.J.* 227; England, The System Builders: A Critical Appraisal of Modern American Tort Theory (1980) 9 *J. of Legal Studies* 27; Coleman, Moral Theories of Torts: Their Scope and Limits (1982) 1 *Law and Philosophy* 371, (1983) 2 *Law and Philosophy* 5.

5 On the fundamental nature of private law, see *Pashukanis: Selected Writings* (1979), Beirne and Sharlet (eds.) 72 ff.; Kojève, *Esquisse d'une Phénoménologie du Droit* (1981).

6 Cf. Hobbes, *A Dialogue Between a Philosopher and a Student of the Common Laws of England* (Cropsey ed. 1971) 55: "The Law of England . . . hath been fined and refined by an infinite number of Grave and Learned Men."

291

and its resolution cannot await a definitive philosophical treatment. Nonetheless, because it holds itself out as being not merely an aggregation of disconnected decisions but a *body* of law that is internally coherent and systematically articulated under the discipline of reason, private law purports to be inchoately philosophical.

The themes of community and liberty suggest differing conceptions of human interaction, the former pointing to the interactors' commonality, the latter to their disjunction. Human interaction is also the domain of private law. Accordingly, the aspirations of private law to coherence and rationality require private law either to resolve or to avoid the tension between liberty and community.

Now private law is not a distant ideal but a supposedly intelligible reality. One understands private law by taking seriously the claim of intelligibility implicit in it and spelling out the terms under which this claim can be sustained, if it can at all. This requires attention to the elements within law that supply the pervasive features of discourse, the fixed points around which legal reasoning turns, and the institutions and the concepts that such reasoning invokes or presupposes. In other words, one proceeds from within private law to the specification of the ensemble of characteristics that makes private law understandable on its own terms and that, consequently, contains the principle of its intelligibility.

In the common law, for example, the following features can be discerned as central to our understanding of tort law: the normative determination of the rights of the parties through adjudication; the issuing of a reasoned judgment after the presentation of reasoned arguments by the parties; the singling out of two parties, a plaintiff and a defendant, for standing to present these arguments; the irrelevance to the litigation of particular characteristics of the parties, such as wealth or overall moral virtue; the distinction between non-feasance and misfeasance, and the insistence upon a causal relationship between the defendant's behaviour and the plaintiff's injury.

I have argued elsewhere[7] that the intelligibility of this ensemble of features is captured by what Aristotle termed corrective justice.[8] This form of justice discloses the nature of rationality in a transaction, i.e., where the interaction is conceived as being immediate to the parties as doer and sufferer of a single wrong. The immediacy of interaction in corrective justice can be contrasted with distributive justice, where interactions are understood as mediated by a criterion of distribution according to which benefits or burdens are divided among a pool of recipients. These two forms of justice are categorically different: the ordering of corrective justice can be represented arithmetically as the transfer of a quantity from defendant to plaintiff, and it can therefore be distinguished from distributive justice's representation as a proportion that divides things among persons in accordance with a distributive criterion. In corrective justice the parties to a transaction are considered to be notional equals, whatever their actual differences in virtue or in resources. Wrongfulness consists in the violation of this notional equality and rectification in its restoration through the transfer of a quantity from the defendant to the plaintiff. The rectification thus operationalizes the equality applicable to the notion of a transaction. Inasmuch as it realizes corrective justice, private law is an elaborate and collective reflection, in the context of particular instances, on the nature of transactions and their ordering.

It is important to notice that corrective justice requires two parties and only two parties. With less than two parties there is no transaction at all, but only a single person putting forth

7 Weinrib, Toward a Moral Theory of Negligence Law (1983) 2 *J. of Law and Philosophy* 37; Weinrib, The Intelligibility of the Rule of Law, in Hutchinson and Monahan (eds.), *The Rule of Law: Ideal or Ideology* (1987) 59–84; Weinrib, The Insurance Justification and Private Law (1985) 14 *J. of Legal Studies* 681; Weinrib, Causation and Wrongdoing, in Symposium on Causation in Tort Law (1987) 63 *Chicago-Kent L.R.* 407; Weinrib, Legal Formalism (1988) 97 *Yale L.J.* 949.
8 Aristotle, *Nicomachean Ethics* V, 2–4, discussed by Weinrib, Aristotle's Forms of Justice (1988) 1 *Ratio Juris.* 80.

effects into a desert island environment. With more than two parties there also is no transaction, because the immediacy of interaction characteristic of transactions is lacking and the ordering of this multiplicity of parties has to be patterned according to some distributive criterion. The representation of corrective justice in arithmetic terms as the restoration of an antecedent equality through the transference of a specified quantity makes this clear, since only between two can equalization be accomplished by the transfer of a quantity. In private law a plaintiff sues a defendant for the reparation of a wrong or the restoration of a benefit; the category of corrective justice exhibits the structure of the ordering that inheres in this bilateral situation.

The indissoluble linkage of two parties in private law is not easily reducible either to liberty construed in individualistic Hobbesian terms as the absence of external impediments of motion or to the more expansive concept of community. The significance of Aristotle's category of corrective justice is that it presents this feature of private law as part of an integrated conception of interaction and not as an uneasy compromise between the many who constitute the community and the individual for whom unrestricted action is freedom. In this essay I wish to deal with the implications of this first for community and then for liberty.

II

Community is an amorphous ideal, more easily proclaimed than articulated. It summons up an image of mutual accommodation, moderation in pressing one's claims, a ready and spontaneous expression of the benevolence of human nature, the blurring of the distinctness of mine and thine. None of this, however, bears on the intelligibility of private law.

Two related but not equivalent conceptions of community can be discerned.[9] In its more radical form, community bespeaks the denial of the separateness of individuals, so that

9   Cf. Arendt, *Men in Dark Times* (1968) 31 f.

all are regarded as constituents in a single more comprehensive whole. Its most uncompromising expression is found in Plato's *Republic*, where everyone participates in everyone's joy or pain as if it were his own, just as a single person – or as Plato puts it, "the community tying body and soul together in a single arrangement"[10] – is affected by pain or pleasure in any of his parts. The more moderate version, which underlies Aristotle's conception of friendship,[11] posits the separateness of the individuals forming the community but connects them by the reciprocal wishing by each of the good of the others. Here participation in community is characterized by the combination of interpersonal externality and an internal attitude that is directed toward the particular welfare of other participants. The reciprocity of community thus both presupposes and passes beyond the discrete existence of the constituent units. In the mutual valuing of each person's well-being, "the reciprocity of love does not come to rest at either pole".[12]

The more extreme conception of community allows no scope to the private, and is accordingly incompatible with private law. The claim is sometimes made, however, especially by exponents of the natural law tradition,[13] that the Aristotelian conception of friendship grounds the notion of the common good that renders all juridical relationships intelligible. On this view perfect friendship, i.e., the friendship that is completely characterized by the friends' mutual wishing of each other's true well-being, is taken to have the explanatory primacy of a central case, of which the multifarious relationships of civil friendship are variants and dilutions. The illumination of law generally, including private law, is thus rooted in a grasp of the dialectics of love.

---

10 Plato, *Republic* 462C.
11 Cooper, Aristotle on Friendship, in Rorty (ed.), *Essays on Aristotle's Ethics* (1980) 301; Kronman, Aristotle's Idea of Political Fraternity (1979) 24 *American J. of Jurisprudence* 114.
12 Finnis, *Natural Law and Natural Right* (1980) 143.
13 Most recently by ibid., chapter VI (on community) and pages 9–11 (on central cases).

The distance between this notion of community and the ideas that animate private law is illustrated in the old Massachusetts case of *Rodgers* v. *Elliot*,[14] in which the plaintiff, who was convalescing in his home from a severe case of sunstroke, was thrown into convulsions by the daily ringing of the neighbouring church bell. The custodian of the church had been apprised of the effect of the ringing of the bell upon the plaintiff, and the court expressed no incredulity at the bizarre causal connection between the church's behaviour and the plaintiff's suffering. However, the plaintiff's action for nuisance, i.e., his allegation that the defendant was unreasonably interfering with the use and enjoyment of his property, was dismissed. The church's indifference to the suffering it was inflicting on the plaintiff had no legal significance, because it revealed a lack of humanity on the defendant's part rather than a transgression of the plaintiff's legal right. The existence of a regime of right to which considerations of humanity are irrelevant indicates that the litigation cannot be understood in terms of the mutual willing of each other's good that is the mark of association among friends.

Even the weaker notion of community is, accordingly, an inappropriate vehicle for understanding private law. What it ignores is the parties' entitlement in private law to regard themselves as completely external to – and thus indifferent to the good of – each other. This mutual externality is expressed in the difference between misfeasance and nonfeasance that lies at the heart of private law and that precludes the existence of a general obligation to respond to another's need or promote another's good. In its central cases private law is a regime of right in which the willing of the good of another – or the failure to do so – has no indigenous significance. We may celebrate the relationships of love and friendship in literature and mark the richness of our personal lives by their presence, but the intelligibility of private law is not informed by any acknowledgement of their primacy.

14   (1888) 146 Mass. 349.

The conception of interaction in terms of the mutual externality of the agents is, accordingly, of decisive significance for the intelligibility of private law. A systematic elucidation of this fundamental point is not to be found until Kant's legal philosophy, where it is grounded in the nature of agency itself. In the introduction to his *Rechtslehre*, Kant locates the conceptual origin of law in the notion of juridical honour, which, as an expression of the right of humanity in our own person, "consists in asserting one's worth as a human being *in relation to others* and this duty is expressed in the proposition 'Do not make yourself into a mere means *for others*, but be at the same time an end *for them*' ".[15] Kant regards juridical honour as the capacity for self-determination that lies at the root of an intelligible system of juridical relationships. Kant's account highlights the fundamentally external orientation of this capacity. His view is that if we work back from law to its ultimate conceptual preconditions we come to a conception of the person as a locus of self-determining activity who can be conscious of the rest of the world as something that is other than himself. This otherness allows the world to stand available to his activity and for his appropriation and so renders possession according to law a possibility. It also entitles him to resist the encroachment of the alien world upon him, because his nature as a locus of self-determining activity is incompatible with his being merely passively subject to the action upon him of the domain of otherness. Because what matters is the status of the actor as actor, rather than the particular objects of his specific activity, juridical honour can be regarded as the formal aspect of just conduct.[16]

Corrective justice arises from juridical honour when the possibility of possessing and resisting the external world actualizes itself in interaction with other persons, i.e., with elements of this otherness that are also loci of self-

15 Kant, *The Metaphysical Elements of Justice* (Ladd tr. 1965) 42 (emphasis added), discussed in Weinrib, Law as a Kantian Idea of Reason (1987) 87 *Columbia L.R.* 472, 491–500.
16 Kant, supra n. 15, 70.

determining activity. This interaction in turn requires both a body of legal doctrine that will be adequate to the formal rights of those endowed with juridical honour and an apparatus of positive law that can transcend the initially particular viewpoints of the parties and publicly proclaim the reciprocal duties with which these rights are necessarily instinct. Throughout this series of conceptual transformations, however, private law remains intelligible in terms of the mutual externality of agents: the progress is merely from the person as an assertor of juridical honour, who can be conscious of the externality of the world upon which he acts, to the person as legal subject, who must recognize and be recognized by elements of this external world who also are self-determining and therefore can also make claims upon it. Juridical honour, when embedded in a regime of positive law that expresses corrective justice, becomes an obligatory object of recognition by others. The actor may, accordingly, insist upon it even though – as perhaps in the case of the Massachusetts church – he falls short of fulfilling the moral requirements he sets or ought to set for himself. No matter how ignoble his behaviour, juridical honour entitles the actor to resist subordination to the purposes of others. The actor is an end *in* himself, and his failure to act in an ethically worthy manner and thus to treat himself as an end *for* himself does not affect his status as an end *for* others. The less appealing implication of this is revealed in Hegel's dictum that juridical honour is often accompanied by a cold heart and restricted sympathies.[17]

The significance of the restriction of the sympathies in private law emerges from the structure of corrective justice. It is a striking characteristic of private law that the particular aspects of a litigant's character or overall situation are ignored. The wealth or need in a party's material situation, the goodness or evil of his character, and the nobility or mean-

---

17 Hegel, *The Philosophy of Right* (Knox tr. 1952) s. 37A. Cf. Aristotle, *Nicomachean Ethics* VIII 1155a 26 and Cooper's comment on this passage in Aristotle on the Forms of Friendship (1977) 30 *Review of Metaphysics* 619, at 646.

ness of his social status are all regarded as irrelevant to the norms incumbent upon him. Some have attempted to account for this remarkable feature as an entailment of the moral requirement of generalization.[18] This explanation, however, elides the formal qualities that make a legal rule a rule and the content of a specific proposition that has this status. Rules can generalize the most particular qualities, as is evident from taxing statutes. The significant point about private law's abstraction from particularity is not that it is an aspect of the generalization of private law, but that it is part of the nature of private law as a realization of corrective justice.

It will be recalled that corrective justice brings into relief the structural features of a transaction as an immediate interaction between two parties. In interaction the parties remain distinct from each other but related as two mutually extrinsic entities. Now equality is the term of relationship appropriate to the ordering of distinct entities, and inasmuch as corrective justice is an ordering of an external relationship it can make use of this concept. Accordingly, corrective justice posits for immediate interaction an initial notional equality between the parties that serves as the point against which the transaction is judged and to which it is restored through adjudication. Whatever their material or dispositional inequalities the parties are regarded as notionally equal, and this equality is either preserved through the transaction if it is lawful or restored through a rectifying transfer of holdings from defendant to plaintiff if it is not. The exclusive focus is on the transaction itself, and all the background circumstances not part of this immediate interaction are an irrelevant residuum. Because the transaction is a relationship between two and because equality is the term through which the ordering of such a relationship is conceived, the indifference of this residuum is expressible as an equality.

The equality of corrective justice that is the indifference to so many inequalities has been criticized as a construct of

18   E.g., Hume, *A Treatise of Human Nature* (Selby-Bigge ed. 1978) 497.

ideology,[19] and it unquestionably abstracts from the totality of the person's situation. If they are equal, the parties must be equal in some respect, and what respect is that? Since corrective justice looks only to the interaction in its immediacy, the sole aspect available for the ascription of equality is the bare capacity for imputable action that is exercised in the transaction. In other words, the equality of the parties in corrective justice is the equality of what Kant, and Rawls following him, have termed moral personality and is characterized by the capacity to form and promote a conception of one's own good.[20] Moral personality is a way of referring to the capacity for self-determining purposiveness that stands prior to any of the agent's particular purposes. The latter are the outcropping of particular desires, opportunities, needs and dispositional qualities; in abstracting from these, corrective justice regards the parties as interacting moral persons. The abstraction from the differences and inequalities of their particular situations signals the equality of each moral person as a locus of self-determining activity. And although the bare capacity for self-determining purposiveness is realized in the world in the execution of particular purposes, corrective justice is not concerned with and does not pass judgment upon the value of these particular projects as such or with the particular conceptions of the good which one has formed and is pursuing through these projects.[21] It looks only to whether the effecting of these projects is consistent with the anterior equality that holds between the parties to the transaction as moral persons. Accordingly, the Aristotelian category of corrective justice is intimately tied to the Kantian notion of moral personality, with corrective justice bringing out the structure of immediate interaction and moral personality indicating the conception of agency presupposed in this structure. Corrective justice requires moral personality

19 Marx, *Grundrisse* (Nicolaus tr. 1973) 239 ff.
20 Kant, supra n. 15, 24; Rawls, Kantian Constructivism and Moral Theory (1980) 77 *J. of Philosophy* 515, 525 ff.
21 Kant, supra n. 15, 34.

as the equal substratum of its equal treatment of plaintiff and defendant.

Juridical honour is moral personality viewed externally, i.e., from the standpoint of possible interaction with others, rather than internally from the standpoint of the actor's virtue. The imperative of juridical honour, that one not make oneself into a mere means for others, reflects the requirement indigenous to self-determining activity, that the actor assert himself against – rather than be passive toward – the world outside him. Corrective justice is the ordering of interaction that is adequate to the assertion of juridical honour by moral persons. In its concern with the external relationships of moral persons, corrective justice is intelligible independently of factors (such as need and benevolence) that are internal to the interacting agents.

The understanding of private law as the realization of corrective justice points to the infelicity of applying to private law any substantial notion of community. As corrective justice, private law is a mode of ordering the external relations of persons regarded as separate entities, each of whom is entitled to vindicate his own juridical honour. Their relationship cannot be understood as a version of the coalescence of separateness or the promotion of good which occurs in love or friendship. In corrective justice, two parties are linked in immediate interaction, but in the immediacy of this link the only relevant commonality between them is that both interactors evince the capacity for self-determining purposiveness that constitutes moral personality. Moral personality stands back from every determinate need, characteristic, and virtue, and is thus too thin to sustain the full-blooded richness of community.

What is relevant is not community but the bare recognition by one actor of the equal standing of the other. Those components of the world that lack the purposiveness of self-determining activity can in private law have no standing other than as things passively available for use by persons. However, inasmuch as one person's activity affects another person, each must recognize in that other an equal status. An actor cannot regard as the passive receptacle of the effects of his action an entity whose nature is not passive and whose capacity for self-determining action is identical with his own. Juridical honour, which is the vehicle of each moral person's assertion that he not be merely a means to another but an end also, precludes the relegation of the wronged victim to the status of passive component of the actor's world. Private law, understood as the realization of corrective justice, makes explicit the recognition as an equal that one moral person can demand of another in the immediacy of interaction.

Recognition is a normative reflex of the interaction of purposive beings and is, therefore, necessarily social. It does not, however, require community. The recognition is of each party as an ego abstracted from his particular determinations. These egos are conceptually identical, in that purposiveness as an abstracted capacity does not differ from one to the other. However, they remain individualized because they stand for the capacity of each person to act for whatever ends he or she chooses. The egos neither fuse into each other nor undergo a metamorphosis into a collective entity. Each remains an "I", indifferent to the communal dimensions of the "we."[22]

The fundamental principle of contemporary negligence law, the "neighbour principle", is to be understood in the light of this notion of recognition. In the great case of *Donoghue* v. *Stevenson*, Lord Atkin expressed the basic approach as follows:

> ...in English law there must be, and is, some general conception of relations giving rise to a duty of care, of which the particular cases found in the books are but instances. ... The rule that you are to love your neighbour becomes in law, you must not injure your neighbour; and the lawyer's question, who is my neighbour? receives a restricted reply. You must take reasonable care to avoid acts or omissions which you can reasonably foresee would be likely to injure your neighbour.

22 Cf. Goldmann, *Immanuel Kant* (Black tr. 1971) 170.

Who, then, in law is my neighbour? The answer seems to be
– persons who are so closely and directly affected by my act
that I ought reasonably to have them in contemplation as being
so affected when I am directing my mind to the acts or omissions which are called in question.[23]

There is no trace of community in this passage. The transformation of the Biblical injunction that one should love one's
neighbour into the legal norm that one is not to injure one's
neighbour implies that the phenomenon of love as a medium
of interpersonal relations is not available for assimilation into
private law. The neighbour is specified not in terms of the
warmth and reach of community but in terms of the reasonably foreseeable effects of one's action. This more modest
formulation is consistent with the interpretation of private
law as demanding the mutual recognition of moral persons
in the immediacy of interaction. The purposiveness of agency
has a bearing on others only when the agent gives effect to
his purposiveness by acting in the world, by extending the
manifestations of his purposiveness outwards. This externalization not only stamps the actor's environment with his
inwardly determined purposes, but it inevitably mingles
those purposes with a natural world beyond him and his
control. Purposiveness, in projecting itself outward, produces effects in a realm that is alien to it, and these effects
may therefore take a form other than that expected or intended by the actor.[24] But since this possibility of untoward
consequences is a necessary concomitant of the outward exercise of purposiveness, these consequences cannot be regarded as no business of the actor's. He cannot both claim
an entitlement to act and abjure the effects into which his
capacity for action materializes. When realization of his purposes affects other moral persons, victims of action can demand of the actor that he recognize their violated equality
as moral persons and can demand of the court that the equality be made explicit and concrete in an award of damages.

23 [1932] A.C. 562, at 580 (H.L.).
24 Hegel, supra n. 17, s. 118.

ERNEST J. WEINRIB

The neighbour test gives voice to the recognition of actor and victim as equals by insisting that the effects of one's action on others ought to be within the actor's contemplation when he directs his mind to the particular projects that are expressions of his purposiveness.

III

I wish now to make some remarks on the connection between private law, especially tort law, and liberty. Here we might expect private law, with its purportedly individualistic orientation, to be on more familiar ground than it was with community. Indeed one of the foremost contemporary tort theorists, Professor Richard Epstein, has suggested that the first task of the law of torts is to define the boundaries of individual liberty, and he has accordingly proposed a reformulation of tort law which would shift it from its present basis of liability in the defendant's fault to strict liability.[25] Epstein's proposal is elaborately worked out, but one can say, at the risk of considerable over-simplification, that its fundamental idea is that the defendant should be liable even in the absence of any negligence on his part for any harm that he causes the plaintiff. This reformulation is libertarian in its spirit; it is similar to Nozick's conception that the sphere of an individual's natural rights can be viewed as a line or hyperplane circumscribing an area in moral space around him.[26] In Epstein's view any penetration by another into this area of moral space is in principle grounds for liability.

There is an element of paradox in this as a libertarian proposal.[27] One would have thought that a libertarian would be concerned to minimize the role of government. But strict liability is a broader liability rule than the negligence standard that it would replace, and its adoption would signal a dra-

25 Epstein, *A Theory of Strict Liability: Toward a Reformation of Tort Law* (1980).
26 Nozick, *Anarchy, State, and Utopia* (1974) 57.
27 Cf. Fletcher, The Search for Synthesis in Tort Theory (1983) 2 *Law and Philosophy* 63, at 69 f.

304

matic increase in the incidence of judicial intervention. Strict liability maximizes the protection of the victims of others' action and therefore maximizes the role of state officials in the provision of this protection. The libertarian point of view would be better served, one would have thought, by narrowing the ambit of liability. This could be accomplished by restricting liability to harms resulting from actions known to the actor to be wrongful.

The possibility of holding the defendant to what might be called a subjective standard was broached and rejected by the common law a century and a half ago. In the 1837 case of *Vaughan* v. *Menlove*[28] the defendant had placed his rick of hay close to his neighbour's barn, ignoring warnings that spontaneous combustion in the rick might set the barn afire. When the barn subsequently burned down after fire spread to it from the rick, the defendant's lawyer argued that his client should be absolved because he meant no harm: he was a stupid man, and "he ought not to be responsible for the misfortune of not possessing the highest order of intelligence".[29] The court, however, ruled that whether he was subjectively blameworthy or not was legally irrelevant: his failure to act as a person of reasonable and ordinary prudence was sufficient for his liability, even though this standard, the objective standard of negligence, might be beyond the range of compliance on the part of persons such as the defendant.

The negligence standard affirmed in *Vaughan* v. *Menlove* is exposed to a libertarian attack from either direction. It requires of a person that he act reasonably and holds him liable for a failure to do so. On the one hand there is no liability for harm resulting from the defendant's reasonable action; negligence law thus appears to countenance an invasion of the area in moral space which makes up the sphere of the plaintiff's natural right. On the other hand it requires that the defendant's action conform to a norm with which it is impossible for him, through no fault of his own, to comply;

28 (1837) 3 Bing. N.C. 467 (C.P.).
29 Ibid., at 471.

it therefore authorizes liability for failure to come up to a standard that the defendant is incapable of meeting.[30] The objection on the side of strict liability is that negligence law allows boundary crossings into the victim's sacrosanct area of freedom; the objection on the side of the subjective standard is that the defendant may be coerced into compensating for harms that materialized from no moral failing on his part.

Now I want to point out that the very fact that the libertarian can attack the prevailing common law standard from both of these directions reveals the inadequacy to private law of his conception of liberty. The abundance of the possible avenues of attack confronts him with a dilemma as to which is he to choose. Strict liability protects the liberty of the plaintiff by ignoring that of the defendant; under this liability regime defendants will be liable for the contingency that their reasonable actions resulted in harm. The subjective standard vindicates the freedom of the defendant by allowing him to act up to the limit of his moral innocence, but subjects the plaintiff to an increased number of uncompensated-for boundary crossings. The two libertarian alternatives are mirror images of each other, and the choice of either will turn the other against it with redoubled fury.

Epstein himself opts for strict liability, because he conceives tort law as an embodiment of corrective justice. Strict liability works the necessary correction by restoring the plaintiff to the position which the defendant's action disturbed. What he does not notice is that the dilemma confronting the libertarian derives its force precisely from corrective justice.

It will be recalled that corrective justice renders private law intelligible by disclosing the internal structure of a transaction as an immediate interaction between persons. The central feature of this structure is the link between the parties to the transaction, which emerges in law as the plaintiff's claim against the defendant. This claim integrates through some legally cognizable event in their relationship the plaintiff's entitlement to receive compensation and the defendant's ob-

30 Epstein makes this criticism of negligence supra n. 25, at 6.

ligation to be the source of this compensation. The nexus between the parties is conceptually necessary because without it there would be no transaction, but rather a merely coincident juxtaposition of a disadvantage affecting the plaintiff and a demand for money lodged against the defendant. What entitles *this* plaintiff to claim against *this* defendant is not the former's status as a sufferer of disadvantage and the latter's status as a potential source of funds (for in these capacities there would be no reason to single *these* two out from the respective classes of persons sharing these features) but the impingement of the one party upon the other in a transaction. In the award of damages corrective justice makes explicit the immediate nexus between the parties implicit in a transaction. The parties so related are notional equals who must interact on terms of the equality of Kantian moral persons.

The difficulty with the possible libertarian suggestions for tort law is that both of them fail to respect and embody the equality embedded in corrective justice. Each is one-sided in its attention to the plaintiff's injury or the subjective moral capacity of the defendant. Whereas corrective justice discloses the intelligibility of the relationship between parties who are equal in their interaction, the libertarian alternatives, in their preoccupation with one or the other of the poles of this relationship, fail to understand it as a *relationship* between *equals*. Each is inconsistent with the structure of intelligibility that underlies in private law, and their mutual contradictoriness is an aspect of the inadequacy which they share. The one-sidedness which each alternative wields against the other shows that they are both wrong and for the same reason.

Here we must recall that moral personality in law takes juridical honour as its external aspect, and juridical honour enjoins each actor to be not merely a means for another but an end also. The concept of juridical honour entitles each person to assert his worth as a locus of self-determining activity and to resist reduction by others to a passive element in their environment. Juridical honour is the basis of the recognition that one actor can demand of another, and it considers moral personality from the standpoint of external relations, i.e., as relevant to justice and not to virtue. Its focus is on the operation of moral personality outward into the surrounding world rather than on the inward consciousness of the ethical quality of one's conduct. The plea of the defendant in *Vaughan v. Menlove* not to be blamed for the misfortune of his own stupidity cannot be an assertion of juridical honour. His own stupidity is a factor internal to him and therefore an element in the very particularity from which private law abstracts. The successful invocation of this stupidity would subordinate the plaintiff to the defendant's purposes by allowing the subjective limitations of the defendant to set the terms upon which the plaintiff must tolerate his neighbour's impingements. The defendant's argument asserts the defendant's right unilaterally to determine the contours of a bilateral relationship of equals. The self-preference of this argument prevents the assertion of this right from being validated by the law as right's reality.

The incoherence in the defendant's position can be seen if we attend to the nature of the judgment concerning his action that he is inviting the court to make. Such an incoherence would be especially significant, because it would confirm the incompatibility of the subjective standard with the Kantian grounding of corrective justice. As we have seen, this grounding is itself tied to the nature of action in a self-determining, purposive being. Just as Kantian legal philosophy shows how the concepts and institutions of corrective justice emerge out of a coherent notion of self-determining activity,[31] so one would expect a liability standard inconsistent with corrective justice to incorporate an incoherence with respect to action.

The incoherent judgment about his action that the defendant's plea involves can be formulated as follows. An action is the actualization of the capacity for purposiveness in the external world. The initial stage of this actualization,

31 Weinrib, supra n. 15, 478–91.

in which a person's purposive capacity is directed to a specific purpose, is on the Kantian view completely within the range of the actor's self-determination: I can decide to put my rick of hay here or there. But in extending this capacity into the external world, I must step out of the area of self-determination into a realm of nature, contingency and the cross-purposes of others. Only thus can I complete my action. The exercise of my own freedom requires entry into a domain beyond my freedom. In placing my rick here, I render it contiguous to my neighbour's barn, and I expose both rick and barn to natural forces through which both may be destroyed. The defendant's argument that his purity of heart ought to constitute the standard of liability is an argument appropriate to the evaluation of action at the stage of potentiality, when the actor's self-determination has not yet issued into the world beyond him and when an internal standpoint of judgment corresponds to the internal locus of the inchoate action. The judgment that he is now inviting about his action, however, is inconsistent with the stage to which the maturation of his purpose has progressed. In pleading that he is too stupid to have taken account of the external effects of his action, the defendant is claiming an entitlement to realize his projects in the world while retaining the exclusively internal standpoint applicable to projects as mere possibilities. He wishes to have the actuality of his projects treated from the standpoint of a now superseded potentiality.

Now one might suppose that this criticism of the defendant's argument in *Vaughan* v. *Menlove*, whatever its correctness, proves too much. I earlier stated that the subjective standard proposed by the defendant was the mirror image of Epstein's libertarian proposal of a tort regime of strict liability. In saying that the judgment upon action which the defendant is inviting the court to make is incoherent in that it ignores the actualized state of the action being judged, I may seem to be criticizing the subjective standard on a ground utterly inapplicable to strict liability. For what is strict liability but the treating of the external effects of the defendant's action as sovereign?

309

I wish to argue, however, that the parallelism holds and that strict liability presupposes a view of judgment upon action as incoherent as that of the subjective standard. The point was noticed a century ago by Oliver Wendell Holmes in his masterful survey of the available tort regimes.[32] Holmes argued that a standard which held a person answerable for all the consequences of his acts was inconsistent with the well-established doctrine that there is no liability in tort in the absence of an act, i.e., of a voluntary muscular contraction, by the defendant. The point of this doctrine is to allow an opportunity of choice with reference to the consequence complained of, and "a choice which entails a concealed consequence is as to that consequence no choice".[33] "Unless my act is of a nature to threaten others," Holmes continued, "unless under the circumstances a prudent man would have foreseen the possibility of harm, it is no more justifiable to make me indemnify my neighbour against the consequences than to make me do the same thing if I had fallen upon him in a fit, or to compel me to insure him against lightning."[34]

Let me restate Holmes' argument against strict liability in terms consistent with corrective justice and the Kantian notion of moral personality that grounds it. Inasmuch as my action flows from the capacity for purposiveness that certifies my status of a moral person, the action is an implied assertion that I am not merely an object, not a merely a passive recipient of effects from other sources. The right of humanity in my own person, which for Kant was the essence of juridical honour, is simply the right which inheres in self-determining activity. It would be inconsistent with this right for me to treat others who, as moral persons, are not essentially different from me as the merely passive recipients of my effects. My right to act implies their right to complain about the consequences of my act; my standing as an actor implies their standing as complainants.

32 Holmes, *The Common Law* (1881) 88 ff.
33 Ibid., at 94.
34 Ibid., at 96.

Now since the standing of the plaintiff is a reflection of the agency that both litigants embody, the complaint cannot demand a judgment on action that renders action illegitimate. Liability implies that what the defendant did was inconsistent with the equal status of the plaintiff as a moral person. The point of an award of damages is to vindicate juridical honour by undoing those instances of it that cannot coexist with the juridical honour of others. Because juridical honour is an imperative that flows from a purposive being's capacity for self-determining activity, the vindication of juridical honour ought not to imply the illegitimacy of the exercise of this capacity. Just as the wrongfulness of a tortious act consists in the act's violating the abstract equality of actors, so the correction of this wrongfulness must restore this antecedent equality without impliedly making action impermissible. In Hegelian terminology, the award of damages can be only the negation of a negation of action,[35] not a negation of action itself.

Strict liability, however, makes action illegitimate by implying that the assertion of juridical honour can itself be a violation of the equality of moral persons. Juridical honour is the external aspect of moral personality, and its assertion therefore produces effects in the external world. As was noted earlier in connection with the subjective standard, these effects can be contingent inasmuch as they are not the intended consequences of the actor's purpose. Precisely because action has effects, the plaintiff's case cannot be constituted by the mere pointing to those effects. Strict liability makes the contingent consequences of my action decisive for judgment upon it, although those consequences are, as contingent, beyond the scope of my purposiveness and, as consequences, required for its completion. Effects are the fruition of activity, and to ascribe liability to my action, regardless of culpability, for whatever harmful effects it has had simply because they *are* my effects, is to hold me liable for being active. For the plaintiff to say that I can act provided that

35 Hegel, supra n. 17, ss. 96–101.

311

contingent effects do not occur is to subordinate my purposiveness to the contingency of nature's effects and thus simultaneously to affirm and to deny my status as an actor. This condemnation of my action for its effects implies the severing of my capacity for action from its realization. By thus conceding to me a potentiality whose actualization is deemed wrongful, the plaintiff would be denying my moral personality under the guise of vindicating his own. I would be allowed the enjoyment of a potentiality that was incapable of actualization and was therefore no potentiality at all. Moreover, in so arguing for the negation of my moral personality, the plaintiff would be negating his own as well, since his status as a complainant is based on the equality which we share as actors. He cannot sterilize my capacity to act without undermining his standing to complain.

This account highlights the parallelism between strict liability and the subjective standard. Both liability regimes implicitly treat the defendant's completed action as merely potential. The defendant's argument in *Vaughan* v. *Menlove* was that despite the materialization of his projects into effects harmful to the plaintiff, he should be entitled to invoke his moral innocence and so to limit his liability to the stage appropriate to an unrealized capacity. The argument for strict liability passes adverse judgment on the effects to which any completed action may give rise and so exposes to liability any action that has progressed beyond the stage of mere potentiality. The subjective standard confines action to potentiality by ignoring its completion and adopting a standard appropriate to a capacity; strict liability confines action to potentiality by assessing liability with reference to contingencies inherent in its completion and thus implying that its completion is beyond the limit of the actor's entitlement. Both standards accordingly presuppose a conception of action which is incoherent, in that it cannot carry the action through from its origination in the actor to the materialization of its effects in the victim. Since corrective justice considers the parties solely as actors in immediate interaction and requires that judgment upon action embrace the moral personality of both parties on equal terms, this incoherence disqualifies these libertarian liability regimes as adequate expressions of corrective justice.

Now it might be argued that strict liability does not make action incoherent but rather imposes a cost upon it, and some legal commentators have analyzed strict liability as a judicially imposed activity tax that forwards the purpose of compensation or loss spreading or cheapest cost avoidance.[36] Since the incidence of a tax can fall on any feature of the actor or any segment or effect of his conduct as specified by positive law, the connection between liability and the integrated construal of the maturation of action is broken. Inasmuch as the language of costs and taxes is the mark of distributive and not corrective justice, however, this interpretation is both unsatisfactory for the libertarian and inconsistent with the structure of intelligibility that private law attempts to realize. Liability under corrective justice is not a tax but a judgment. The role of the judge in the working of corrective justice is to make explicit the ordering immanent in the transaction, and he has no standing to add considerations of public welfare that would make that transaction subordinate to some wider purpose of his choosing. An activity tax would take the interaction outside corrective justice by depriving it of its immediacy, because the relation between the parties would now be mediated by the purpose of the tax. The tort plaintiff's status in corrective justice is not that of a lobbyist approaching a taxing authority for a private bounty equal to the tax to be imposed on the defendant. His claim, rather, is that he is the victim of a wrong at the defendant's hand, and that he is entitled to have this wrong corrected.

The difficulty with strict liability is that the incoherent view of action that it implies gives us no reason to regard the plaintiff's injury as anything but a mere fact of history. Ep-

---

36 E.g. Calabresi and Hirschoff, Toward a Test of Strict Liability in Tort (1972) 81 *Yale L.J.* 1055. The term "activity tax" is taken from Henderson, Process Constraints in Tort (1982) 67 *Cornell L.R.* 901, at 915.

stein's argument rightly pointed to the centrality of causation to our moral consciousness,[37] but he failed to notice that unless causation is linked to a viable conception of action its moral force is drained, and the injury is transformed into an occurrent datum of nature beyond the scope of judgments of liability. This was the point of Holmes' comparison of strict liability to compulsory insurance against lightning: once the injury is divorced from human action it ranks as a misfortune rather than as a justiciable wrong.

IV

This essay has outlined the relationship between corrective justice, especially as manifested in tort law, and certain notions of community and liberty. Its contentions have been that

i) corrective justice is the structure of immediate interaction for Kantian moral persons;

ii) in this interaction, the abstraction of moral personality from particularity renders bare recognition and not community the appropriate characterization of what this interaction presupposes; and

iii) the interpretation of private law, especially tort law, as a one-sided vindication of liberty is inconsistent both with the bilateral nature of corrective justice and with the conception of action underlying moral personality.

These considerations do not, of course, exhaust the intelligibility of private law. Academic lawyers frequently – and if the views expressed in this essay are correct, mistakenly – understand private law as promoting the collective goals of distributive justice. Such interpretations are nurtured by many roots: a residual utilitarianism; an attitude among legal academics that any study of law that is not "black-letter" must be instrumentalist; the consideration of distributive justice to be the only framework for exploring the rationality of

37   Supra n. 25, at 15 ff.

interaction, and the consequent depreciation of the autonomous conceptual status of corrective justice; a positivism which denies that the content of law, as opposed to its form, can be intelligible from within, and thus regards the law's content as available for any extrinsically imposed reform; the assumption that everything is to be understood in terms of something else, so that private law can be grasped only as an aspect of a different, if related, discipline, such as ethical or political or economic theory. These views, and their effects on the analysis of private law, raise issues which go to the heart of legal philosophy. I mention them, not in order to discuss them now, but only to signal the fecundity of private law as an area of philosophic reflection.

I should not be taken as claiming that there is no construal of liberty or community appropriate to private law. My invocation of the Kantian conceptions of moral personality and juridical honour indicates that there is at least one view of liberty that is applicable: Kant's. Kant regarded freedom as the only innate right and saw justice as the coexistence of the freedom of all in accordance with a universal law. The relationship between freedom and universal law was for Kant one of mutual entailment: moral personality in freely abstracting from particularity is itself a universal, and to require action in accordance with universal law is to require moral personality to realize its own nature. Kant's project in his legal philosophy was to explore the structure of freedom in the external relationship of free beings and thus to generate the legitimacy of positive law and its attendant coercion out of the inherent requirements of freedom itself. This naturalization of positive law required a shift in natural law from its traditional preoccupation with the nature of man to a new attention to the nature of law.[38] What is of interest to the

---

38 In Notion et Portée de la "Volonté Generale" chez Jean-Jacques Rousseau (1912) 20 *Révue de Métaphysique et de Morale* 383, at 384, Rudolf Stammler formulates Rousseau's decisive conceptual innovation in terms of this shift. Hegel describes a similar transformation in his Prefatory Lectures on the Philosophy of Law (1978) 8 *Clio* 49, at 57–61 (Brudner tr.). Cf. Habermas' account of what he terms "the posi-

lawyer in this exercise is that for Kant the initial configuration of the laws of freedom is private law, which is a domain of right conceptually anterior to political and ethical good.[39]

I think that it is worth recovering Kant's perspective on these matters. Much contemporary theorizing in a Kantian vein either ignores private law[40] or interprets private law as an enforceable subset of personal morality[41] or treats rights as a limitation of, and therefore as essentially a negative relation to, certain types of political justification.[42] What Kant affirmed was the intelligibility of private law as conceptually prior to politics or personal morality, with the consequence that private law is resistant to notions of community and to unilateral conceptions of liberty. In so affirming, Kant articulated what is already understood, if only imperfectly, by lawyers who work through and take seriously the rationality exhibited by any sophisticated system of private law.

tivization of Natural Law" in *Theory and Practice* (Viertel tr. 1973) 82 ff.

39 For an outline of the significance of the Kantian priority of the right, see Weinrib, supra n. 15, 501–3. The matter is dealt with at length in a forthcoming article, Benson and Weinrib, The Right and the Good.
40 Rawls, *A Theory of Justice* (1971) 8; Gewirth, *Reason and Morality* (1978).
41 Fried, *Contract as Promise* (1981).
42 Dworkin, *Taking Rights Seriously* (1977).

Chapter 9

Risk, causation, and harm

GLEN O. ROBINSON

I. PROBABILITIES AND LIABILITIES

Tort law is deterministic in its view of causal relationships. The basic paradigm is A causes harm to B, with "causes" denoting some fixed, and fully determined (at least ex post), relationship between act and injury. Variants of the model deal with direct and indirect causal connections, the latter sometimes taking bizarre forms as every first year law student learns to his discomfiture upon encountering the subject of proximate cause. But in most cases the underlying assumption is one of determinism: in whole or in part A did or did not cause the harm. Uncertainty is acknowledged, but relegated to issues of proof; probabilities are seen as "evidence" questions, not as part of the fabric of liability rules.

A change in this perspective can be detected, albeit dimly, with the recent emergence of "toxic torts" – including environmental and various products-related harms.[1] The Agent

1 As I use it the term "toxic torts" is rather loose nomenclature for tortious activities that involve (assumedly unreasonable) risks of harm to a large group of persons and are typically manifested years after the germinating cause. Another common term for large scale accidents, "mass torts," covers similar ground. However, for my purpose the latter is too broad insofar as it includes mass disasters – such as explosions, fires, the collapse of a dam, the release of a deadly gas, etc. – which do not typically create the kind of causal ambiguities that are the subject of this essay. Typical of the kind of cases that are relevant to my discussion are the asbestos cases (*e.g.*, Borel v. Fiberboard Paper Products Corp., 493 F.2d 1076 (5th Cir. 1973)), the DES and Bendectin drug cases (*e.g.*, Sindell v. Abbott Labs., 26 Cal. 3d 588, 607 P.2d 924, cert.

317

GLEN O. ROBINSON

Orange, DES, asbestos cases, to mention only a few prominent disasters of recent years, have made students of tort law more aware of the indeterminacy of causal relationships for many types of modern torts and a growing scholarly literature recognizes the need for tort law to accommodate the probabilistic character of many injuries.[2] The courts for their part have resisted the idea of such an accommodation. A few decisions like *Sindell v. Abbott Labs*[3] and more recently *Jackson v. Johns-Manville Sales Corp.*[4] have shown a greater disposition to recognize this indeterminacy and to try to come to terms with it in making liability judgments. But it would be a mistake to regard these cases as typical. The *most* one can say is they are straws in the wind of change.

Of the two cases, *Sindell*, it seems to me, is the least exceptional. In *Sindell* plaintiff was injured by DES taken by her mother but she could not establish the identity of the manufacturers that made the particular pills that caused the injury. The court held that liability should be apportioned among DES manufacturers in proportion to their share of the market. In effect it is not much more than a new rule of apportionment of liability among multiple tortfeasors. As an apportionment (or contribution) rule it is not really more

denied, 449 U.S. 912 (1980); In re Bendectin Product Liability Litigation, 749 F.2d 300 (6th Cir. 1984)) and Agent Orange cases (In re Agent Orange Product Liability Litigation, 534 F. Supp. 1046 (E.D.N.Y. 1982)). On the problems of mass/toxic injury torts generally see Kenneth S. Abraham, "Individual Action and Collective Responsibility: The Dilemma of Mass Tort Reform," *Virginia Law Review* 73 (1987): 845.

2 See, *e.g.*, Glen O. Robinson, "Probabilistic Causation and Compensation for Tortious Risk," *Journal of Legal Studies* 24 (1985): 779. For earlier discussions see, *e.g.*, Mario J. Rizzo & Frank S. Arnold, "Causal Apportionment in the Law of Torts: An Economic Theory," *Columbia Law Review* 80 (1980): 1399; Glen O. Robinson, "Multiple Causation in Tort Law: Reflections on the DES Cases," *Virginia Law Review* 68 (1982): 713, 759–69; David Rosenberg, "The Causal Connection in Mass Exposure Cases: A 'Public Law' Vision of the Tort System," *Harvard Law Review* 97 (1984): 851, 869–74; William M. Landes & Richard A. Posner, "Tort Law as a Regulatory Regime for Catastrophic Personal Injuries," *Journal of Legal Studies* 13 (1984): 417.

3 See, *supra* note 1.

4 781 F.2d 394 (5th Cir. 1986).

radical than the venerable *Summers v. Tice*,[5] which has long been regarded, in the classroom at least, as a conventional, pragmatic response to an unusual problem of indeterminate causal responsibility. However, *Sindell* was pregnant with revolution insofar as its market-share allocation rule could be translated into a more generalizable principle of liability proportional to a relative weighing of the probabilities of different causal agents – market share being a rough surrogate for the probability that each of the respective defendants made the pills responsible for the injury. Mario Rizzo and Frank Arnold have argued for such a causal apportionment based on what they call "probabilistic marginal product."[6] Rizzo and Arnold's proposal calls for strict liability, following an argument of Richard Epstein for strict liability grounded in causal factors.[7] Strict liability based solely, or even predominantly, on causation seems to me unattractive either on grounds of public policy or moral principle,[8] but the notion

5 33 Cal. 2d 80, 199 P.2d 1 (1948). In *Summers* plaintiff was injured by gunshot fired by one of two negligent hunters, but he could not prove which one fired the particular shot. The court held that he could recover against either or both hunters.

6 See Rizzo and Arnold, *supra* note 2.

7 See Richard A. Epstein, *A Theory of Strict Liability* (San Francisco: Cato Institute, 1973). Epstein's notion of causation is, however, not a probabilistic one; quite the contrary it is essentially a mechanistic conception based on very stylized descriptions of interacting forces. As an aside it might be noted that Epstein himself is not fully committed to liability based solely on causation inasmuch as his proposed liability rules introduce noncausal elements in the form of affirmative defenses and excuses. Causation simply establishes a *prima facie* case for liability. *Id.* at 25. However, to the extent that causal factors dominate his argument for liability we can follow Epstein's own characterization of his liability criteria as strict.

8 There has been no lack of critical commentary on Epstein's theory of strict liability, from a variety of perspectives. See, *e.g.*, John Borgo, "Causal Paradigms in Tort Law," *Journal of Legal Studies* 8 (1979): 419; Richard A. Posner, "Epstein's Tort Theory: A Critique," *Journal of Legal Studies* 8 (1979): 457; Ernest Weinrib, "Causation and Wrongdoing," *Chicago-Kent Law Review* 63 (1987): 407. While an extended treatment would be out of place here, a couple of brief observations may be in order.

In his original development of the theory Epstein's sole justification for making causation the foundation of liability is a quoted assertion

of probabilistic causation is compatible with other liability rules based on traditional fault or other defined requirements of public policy.[9] From this notion of probabilistic causation as a basis for apportioning liability one can derive a broader (and more controversial) principle of liability based on the tortious creation of probabilistic injury (risk) alone. Essentially that is what the court in the *Jackson* case did in allowing recovery for the risk of future cancer from inhalation of asbestos fibers. In *Jackson* plaintiff had contracted asbestosis from inhalation of asbestos fibers; the same inhalation also created a risk of future cancer. The court held that plaintiff could pursue

of Leon Green that " 'a deep sense of common law morality [requires] that one who hurts another should compensate him.' " Epstein, *supra* note 7 at 25 n.25. As mere rhetoric about the moral force of requiring injurers to compensate victims (which is all that Green intended: he was not arguing for a theory of causation-based liability) the statement is unexceptionable, but as an articulation of moral theory it is breathtakingly insufficient. To say the least its appeal to common law judgment is misleading: for at least one hundred years the central foundation of common law liability has been fault not simple causation, and in those limited areas – for instance product-related accidents – where the common law has developed strict liability it has not done so on the basis of causation alone but on the basis of public policy factors that are wholly at odds with Epstein's philosophical premises.

In later elaborations of his theory Epstein has attempted to draw on a property rights conception as a justification: strict liability is required to give proper recognition to individual property rights. See, *e.g.*, Richard A. Epstein, *Takings: Private Power and the Power of Eminent Domain* (Cambridge, Mass.: Harvard University Press, 1985), pp. 97–98. The basic infirmity of this argument can be quite simply stated: substituting property right notions for tort principles is a semantic evasion of the core question of how the rights should be defined. No rights are absolute; at the very least they are limited by reciprocal rights of others. Property law no less than tort law must recognize this reciprocity; if A has a "property right" to be free of any and all intrusions by B, then B's liberty (which may also entail a property right) is to that extent constrained. No principle of property rights – or of "common law morality" – requires that A's right automatically trump B's, as by means of a strict liability regime.

9 By "other defined requirements" I mean to include the various existing forms of strict liability such as that which is imposed for defective products. By no stretch of the legal imagination could such existing strict liability rules be explained or justified in terms of causation alone.

claims for the present injury from asbestosis and the risk of future injury from cancer. The case is somewhat special in that the plaintiff already had contracted asbestosis from the same incidents and the court rationalized recovery for cancer risk in terms of avoiding claims splitting and possibly avoiding the running of the statute of limitations. Still, inasmuch as asbestosis and cancer are different injuries imposing liability for the latter necessarily meant basing liability on risk alone.

I think it important at this point to emphasize that liability based on risk, that is, on the probability of harm, does not require one to accept probability as a statement of causation. Some have criticized the concept of "probabilistic causation" as a confusion, and have insisted that causes are deterministic, only our knowledge is probabilistic.[10] It may be. I think it could be debated on a philosophical level whether the deterministic view gives a better account of reality, but such a debate would entail nothing less than an inquiry into reality itself. Happily, it is not necessary to pursue the nature of reality in order to decide whether probability of harm – risk – is a proper basis for apportioning or establishing liability. Risk is an intelligible concept, one that has social and legal significance. The pertinent question is whether, in some circumstances, it makes sense to measure legal liability according to risk. This is not an ontological question; it is a question of public policy.

To this point I have not distinguished cases where probability (risk) is used as a basis for assessing causal responsibility for injuries already manifest from those where it is used as a basis for assessing damages in advance of injury. Probably most people would intuit these to be quite different cases, and I concede they may present somewhat different practical problems. However, in terms of the theoretical arguments involved, surprisingly little turns on the question whether all harms have materialized. Indeed, even as a mat-

10 See Richard W. Wright, "Causation in Tort Law," *California Law Review* 73 (1985): 1741, 1821–26.

ter of practical administration I am not sure one can make very much of the distinction. For most of the tortious events with which we are concerned – "toxic torts" – the claims are likely to be brought in class actions and the classes will include those who have suffered the injury and those who have suffered an increased probability of its occurring. If the information base for such claims remains relatively unchanged over the period of exposure, there will be little to distinguish the probabilistic injury in the first case from that of the second. The probabilistic evaluations will be based on aggregate statistics that will not differentiate between manifested harms that probably *were* the product of a particular risk exposure and anticipated harms that probably *will* ensue from it. Nevertheless, to test the strength of the idea of risk-based liability, I want to address the case for "probabilistic causation" in terms of imposing liability for *expected* harm alone.

II. PRECEDENTS

Basing liability simply on the tortious creation of risk is revolutionary. Or is it? On first acquaintance the idea seems radically at odds with contemporary tort law doctrine. On a closer look, however, it will be seen that tort liability has many elements that are probabilistic in character, whether or not they are explicitly recognized as such.

Consider first the standard of care. Courts have yet to create a rule of absolute liability for all injury-producing risk. Even the so-called strict liability standard in products cases presupposes some "defect" in manufacture or design that in turn implies a discrimination between mere risk and risk that is unreasonable when viewed against community norms. Those norms have usually been articulated in terms of benefit–cost analysis or a public expectation standard or both.[11] On either standard the appropriate reference point is

11 In the case of unintended manufacturing flaws the standard of product quality is determined by reference to the norms of the firm or industry

the information and the norms prevailing at the time the risk was created.[12] In other words the creation of risk is the basis on which fault liability "fault" is premised. The trier of fact may, of course, be aided by an ex post perspective. That perspective, however, ought not to be used to distort the nature of the risk as it (should have) appeared to the parties, and to the community, at the time of its creation (or at such subsequent times as the parties could be expected to respond to the risk). If this argument is sound – it is widely accepted – it follows that application of the relevant standard of care requires an ex ante assessment of the risk that is not different from that required under a risk-based liability system.

Second, consider the question of damages. In wrongful death cases, and in virtually all cases involving significant losses occurring over an extended future, the court must make numerous probabilistic estimates of both the occurrence and the amount of injury. These probabilistic estimates may be formal, as in the common use of statistical tables to determine the victim's expected lifetime or to estimate future

itself; liability is "strict" in the sense that no inquiry is allowed into whether the flaw was the result of a particular act of negligence. In the case of design defects where there is no set firm or industry norm by which to measure the individual product or product line, determining the requisite standard of product quality for liability purposes is hence more problematic. Although courts frequently use the same strict liability labels for these cases, most of them apply a reasonableness test that is more akin to negligence than strict liability. See Barker v. Lull Eng'g Co., 20 Cal. 3d 413, 573 P.2d 443 (1978). See generally Louis R. Frumer & Melvin I. Friedman, *Products Liability* (Albany: Matthew Bender, 1981), vol. 2 § 16A(4)(f)(iv). Exceptions exist. Some courts have refused to accept, or at least acknowledge, that reasonableness is relevant to the standard even in design cases. A New Jersey decision involving liability for asbestos-related injury is probably the best known example. See Beshada v. Johns Manville Prods. Corp., 90 N.J. 191, 447 A.2d 539 (1982). However, it is noteworthy that the same court later confined this case "to its facts." (It did not, unfortunately, specify precisely the relevant set of facts.) See Feldman v. Lederle Laboratories, 97 N.J. 429, 479 A.2d 374 (1984) (liability for failure to warn of product risks depends on manufacturer's having reason to know of such risks).

12 See, *e.g.*, Wilson v. Piper Aircraft Corp., 282 Or. 61, 577 P.2d 1322 (1978). But see *Beshada, supra* note 11.

earnings (or future costs), or they may be intuitive. But in all cases the process of making such determinations is virtually identical to that required for risk-based liability.

Closely related to the damage issue is the causation issue. The *Sindell* case allowed recovery based on what is essentially a notion of probabilistic causation; but more conventional precedent can be found in a line of cases usually called the "lost chance" cases where courts have allowed recovery for negligent destruction of a chance of some future benefit.[13] The typical case involves medical negligence that deprives plaintiff of a chance of survival or restoration to good health. Viewing the question as one of causation, courts have typically followed a conventional all-or-nothing approach using a more-likely-than-not standard to determine whether plaintiff would have survived or been restored to good health but for defendant's negligence. However, a few cases have more sensibly allowed recovery for the value of chance to plaintiffs showing less than a 50 percent chance of survival.[14] Tortious exposure to risk is in fact really the obverse of these lost chance cases, and the problems of causal determination and valuation are virtually identical. To the extent courts now

13 For a general analysis of the lost chance cases see Joseph H. King, Jr., "Causation, Valuation and Chance in Personal Injury Torts Involving Preexisting Conditions and Future Consequences," *Yale Law Journal* 90 (1981): 1353.

14 See, *e.g.*, Herskovits v. Group Health Co-op., 99 Wash. 2d 609, 664 P.2d 474 (1983) (36 percent reduction in chance of survival sufficient to show proximate cause); Jeanes v. Milner, 428 F.2d 598 (8th Cir. 1970) (35 percent probability sufficient to show proximate cause); James v. United States, 483 F. Supp. 581 (N.D. Cal. 1980). Even some of the less-than-even-chance cases are ambiguous on the question of valuation, that is, whether plaintiff's damages are the full cost of his injury or the value of the chance – injury costs discounted by the probability that they would have occurred anyway. However, in recent years several courts have explicitly recognized that the award is for the value of the lost chance. See, *e.g.*, the *James* and *Herskovits* cases, *supra*. See also Schwegel v. Goldberg, 209 Pa. Sup. 280, 228 A.2d 405 (1967) (challenge to expert testimony of a "one chance in twenty" estimate of future loss should be addressed not to the testimony but to the damage).

recognize compensation for the value of the loss of a chance, they could equally recognize tortious risk exposure. I do not want to overstate the degree to which traditional tort law doctrine recognizes probabilistic determinations. My point is merely to show that in several fundamental respects present doctrine either recognizes or implicitly rests on such determinations more than is commonly supposed.

It does not follow, of course, that because something is being done, it is the right thing to do. That courts can and do make probabilistic judgments within the framework of existing liability rules, which are still articulated in deterministic terms, does not necessarily imply they should accept probabilities – risks – as sufficient bases of recovery. Nevertheless, I shall argue, cautiously, that at least in toxic injury type cases[15] the tortious creation of risk is an appropriate basis of liability, with damages being assessed according to the value of that risk, as an alternative to forcing risk victims to abide the outcome of the event and seek damages only if and when harm materializes. My argument is twofold, following the familiar pattern of examining liability rules from the twin perspectives of utility and corrective justice.

15 The class of cases for which risk-based liability would be a useful concept is a limited one. There is little reason to change the present focus of enforcement in the mine-run automobile accident case. Indeed, it is difficult to conceive as a practical matter how one could have an action for the *risk* of an automobile accident. Either plaintiff has been in an accident or he has not; if he has not it seems queer to think of bringing suit against a negligent driver for a harm that might have occurred but did not. (One might, I suppose, permit private enforcement of public fines against negligent driving, but this approach would take us outside the realm of tort law, for the action would be based not on any risk to the individual but on a more diffuse risk to the community at large.)

How one defines the class of cases appropriate for risk-based liability may be less important than how claims are aggregated. I draw back from a recent suggestion to *force* all toxic injury cases into class actions, see Rosenberg, *supra* note 2, but class actions doubtless would be, and should be, the prevailing format for risk-based claims for they are ideally suited to dealing with the kind of epidemiological and other statistical evidence needed to support such claims.

III. UTILITY

Arguments from utility start with a view of the tort system as a system of efficient risk management in which the central object is to reduce the net social costs of accidents, that is, the excess of accident-related costs over activity-related benefits.[16] This involves two quite distinctive cost reduction strategies: deterring accidents and insurance – spreading accident losses to minimize their impact on individuals.

The focus of deterrence policy is properly on the avoidance of unreasonable risks, not simply on the avoidance of injury. Normally, of course, we hope to avoid both. When liability is imposed for actual injury arising out of unreasonable risk, the supposed effect is to deter the creation of the risk itself. However, the present all-or-nothing character of injury-based liability rules can distort deterrence. On the one hand it can produce overdeterrence: where an unreasonable risk is deemed a "substantial factor" it will bear the entire liability burden – putting to one side comparative apportionment or contribution among multiple tortfeasors.

Probably more serious, however, is the risk of underde-

---

16 Generalizing the utilitarian argument in this manner suppresses a considerable variety among utilitarian/efficiency claims. Part of the variety is accounted for by differences in the way that existing tort law is described and explained, specifically the extent to which it can be explained in efficiency terms (typically expressed in terms of efficient behavioral incentives). See, *e.g.*, William M. Landes & Richard A. Posner, *The Economic Structure of Tort Law* (Cambridge, Mass.: Harvard University Press, 1987). Within the framework of purely normative theories (which are unfortunately often intermixed with positive, descriptive claims) the variety among efficiency arguments largely reduces to differences in the amount of emphasis given to categorical rules fixing liability for general classes of actors and situations versus the individualized, ad hoc approach of the common law. See, *e.g.*, Guido Calabresi, *The Costs of Accidents* (New Haven: Yale University Press, 1970) (categorical approach); Richard A. Posner, "A Theory of Negligence," *Journal of Legal Studies* 1 (1972): 29 (ad hoc approach, based on positive claims of the inherent efficiency of common law adjudication). For a general guide to, and critique of, efficiency theories, see Lewis A. Kornhauser, "A Guide to the Perplexed Claims of Efficiency in the Law," *Hofstra Law Review* 8 (1980): 591.

terrence where significant but not "substantial" risks go un-penalized. Imagine, for example, an activity that creates a set of risks deemed unreasonable because the expected injury costs exceed the costs of care, where the expected "injury" costs take the form of diffused risks of increased predisposition to injury. Suppose a contaminant in the workplace exposes workers to a greater probability of an illness that is associated with multiple agents. We may know enough about the incremental risk (and the costs of avoiding it) to make a judgment that the risk was unreasonable and therefore warrants deterrence. Yet we may have great difficulty in proving that it was associated with a particular victim's injury because of the incremental, probabilistic character of the causal association.

The focus of present legal rules governing causation, with their emphasis on deterministic, all-or-nothing causation, can lead to the underdeterrence of some significant risks. In effect the risks are masked by the confusion of multiple causal factors, all of which can be measured only in probabilistic terms. Needless to say, this problem is compounded for risks that do not manifest identifiable injury for long periods after exposure – as with carcinogenic risks. Assuming the risk victim is not hermetically sealed following exposure to a particular risk, a plausible (if not scientifically precise) generalization is that the complexity of assigning causal responsibility is proportional to the elapsed time between the exposure and its causal determination.

Long-lagged effects also escape deterrence because the errors are not detected and corrected until long after they are made. It is a common criticism of modern corporations that their managerial incentives skew decision making toward short-term gains.[17] If, as I believe, this bias is not overcome

---

17   See, *e.g.*, Richard M. Cyert & James G. March, *A Behavioral Theory of the Firm* (Englewood Cliffs: Prentice-Hall, 1963), p. 119. On the relevance of such short-term perspective to products design, see James A. Henderson, Jr., "Product Liability and the Passage of Time: The Imprisonment of Corporate Rationality," *New York University Law Review* 58 (1983): 765, 780–82.

by the market for managerial services,[18] then the deterrent value of legal penalties for managerial error depends heavily on the proximity of the penalties to the actions for which they are assessed. One of the vexing problems of the traditional liability rules is that the imposition of liability occurs outside the time horizons of the corporate decision makers; thus the deterrent effect of liability is blunted.[19]

Deterrence is not the only utilitarian function of tort liability. The efficiency model of cost reduction takes into account loss spreading, which for present purposes we may equate to finding some means of compensating victims. How would recognition of risk without injury serve that function? The inquiry asks us to isolate the compensation function from the deterrence function (or, in the corrective justice model, fairness considerations) in order to seek a legal rule that facilitates efficient insurance arrangements for expected injuries.

Under present legal arrangements, payments for most torts are covered by liability insurance. Where they are not the loss must be borne by the victim and/or his own insurer. Notice that in the first instance the victim is not compensated for bearing the risk itself, but only for the injury. The risk itself is not treated as a real loss or in any sense regarded as an item for which compensation is appropriate. For short-

18 On the market for managerial services as a monitor of managerial behavior see generally Eugene Fama, "Agency Problems and the Theory of the Firm," *Journal of Political Economy* 88 (1980): 288. Doubts about the ability of that market to discipline managerial performance rest largely on information problems and the inability to link firm performance to the behavior of individual executives. See Saul Levmore, "Monitors and Freeriders in Commercial and Corporate Settings," *Yale Law Journal* 92 (1982): 49, 60–61.

19 A similar argument is made in Mark Roe, "Bankruptcy and Mass Tort," *Columbia Law Review* 84 (1984): 846, 909, but in the quite different context of arguing for early bankruptcy adjudication based on liability exposure. The problem here is not simply that corporate managers will purposefully ignore long-term consequences in favor of the short term – as argued by Henderson, *supra* note 17. It is also that even conscientious managers will have difficulty accounting for distant future outcomes unless some present event (such as liability) gives these outcomes operational salience.

lived risks this simplification may be appropriate, as it is not any great burden for the person exposed to the risk to abide the event. But what of the person exposed to a long-lived risk that may not manifest an identifiable injury for a decade or more? Possible complications of the statute of limitations to one side, the right of action that accrues when risk materializes into injury still leaves risk itself uncompensated as an element of damage.

In a few instances courts have recognized emotional distress arising from fear and anxiety about the risk,[20] and some courts have allowed recovery for medical costs incurred to monitor the risk.[21] One could argue that recovery for present emotional injury and medical costs is sufficient to take care of the risk problem. But adjudicating the issues necessary to determine the liability for these damages would also settle many of the basic issues necessary to determine full liability for probabilistic harm. Assuming that the risk is one that would give rise to liability when the actual loss is suffered, why not adjudicate the entire case by awarding the victim the present value of the risk at the point at which the risk can be identified and given some measurable value? That value is equal to the present value of the future losses multiplied by the estimated probability of their occurrence.

One objection to recovery for risk is that it both over- and undercompensates real loss. If the future risk does not materialize, then the victim's present recovery would be a windfall. However, it is one that accurately reflects the burden of risk, and in any event the windfall so created must be set against the windfall to risk creators under the present system from escaping all liability for tortiously creating risks that did not result in injury. (While it seems clearly correct that those persons who recover probabilistic harms early on should not recover full damages once injury occurs, it does not follow

---

20 Compare Hagerty v. L & L Marine Services, 788 (5th Cir. 1986) (recovery for "cancerphobia") with Payton v. Abbott Labs, 386 Mass. 540, 437 N.E.2d 171 (1982) (denying recovery).
21 See *Hagerty, supra* note 20, allowing recovery for medical monitoring costs.

that no damages should be given to all parties for the uncertainty they must bear for the defendant's wrongful conduct.)

The flip side of overcompensation is undercompensation. If the risk does materialize, then the victim's recovery would be insufficient to meet the actual losses, given the differences in valuation ex ante and ex post. Here compensation for probabilistic harm divides the responsibility for risk bearing between the "injurer" (risk creator) and the "victim," such that the former must provide immediate compensation for probabilistic injury, while the latter must either bear or insure against any residual loss. This implicit allocation of risk rests on the assumption that plaintiffs have access to private insurance markets or substitute investment opportunities for those who want to be self-insurers. Although this assumption has been challenged,[22] there is no reason to think that these arrangements would be any less available for this residual risk than for any other. One could simply use the funds recovered in tort to purchase additional protection, under some standard disability or death policy if there is no insurance for the toxic risk in question.

Allowing risk-based liability imposes a division of loss-bearing responsibility. The tortious creator of risk is made to bear the burden of the expected losses; yet once that risk has been identified with sufficient clarity to permit evaluation, the victim may choose to bear it because he is best able to monitor the risk and take appropriate steps to reduce its scope. My proposal would allow risk victims to institute suit at any time after exposure, including the time of actual injury (the statute of limitations would run from manifestation of injury). Presumably actions by at-risk plaintiffs would be brought only by victims who perceive significant advantage from the early adjudication of liability and who are content with the reduced compensation that this entails.

The situation under risk-based liability would not differ, except in degree, from that which now confronts persons

22 See Roe, *supra* note 19 at 866 n.57, 883–84 n.114.

who recover lump sum awards for future (probable) injury. The practice of lump sum awards, as opposed to periodic payments as future losses are incurred, is rationalized on efficiency grounds primarily as creating incentives for victim mitigation of future losses. Lump sum payments avoid the moral hazard that would be created by making future payments contingent on losses being incurred. This implies, quite sensibly I think, that the victim is in a better position than the injurer to reduce future costs once the initial accident costs have been assessed. Similar considerations are relevant to the argument for risk-based liability.

IV. CORRECTIVE JUSTICE

The argument from corrective justice parallels the argument from utility.[23] The wrong to be corrected is the *creation* of tortious risk. This is true whether one frames the ethical issue in deontological or consequentialist terms. This is virtually definitional for deontological reasoning where the moral character of an act is judged wholly independent of its effects. For consequentialism effects are critical, of course, but even here moral judgment does not turn on *particular* outcomes.

23 As I use it the term "corrective justice" is not a term of art, at least not artful precision. I use the phrase only to denote a concept of justice as moral fairness more or less independent of instrumentalist aims of public policy. The variety of substantive content in corrective justice theories of tort law confounds any attempt at simple summary. For a sample of perspectives prominent in the literature of tort law see, *e.g.*, Epstein, *supra* notes 7 and 8 (corrective justice requires strict liability as a matter of basic fairness and protection of entitlements); George P. Fletcher, "Fairness and Utility in Tort Theory," *Harvard Law Review* 85 (1972): 537 (corrective justice supports both strict liability and negligence based on the principle of protecting persons from "nonreciprocal risks"); Jules L. Coleman, "Corrective Justice and Wrongful Gain," *Journal of Legal Studies* 11 (1982) 421 (corrective justice requires that wrongful losses be rectified and wrongful gains be cancelled but does not require that the two be linked); Weinrib, *supra* note 8 (criticizing both Epstein and Coleman; corrective justice requires symmetry between victim and injurer: wrongfully inflicted losses must be redressed by the injurer who "gained" from the wrong).

From a consequentialist perspective an act is wrong by reason of its normal tendencies, that is, its *expected* consequences. If the creation of particular risk is wrong, then it is so by reason of the intrinsic character of the act, or its general effects; no part of the judgment should depend on the chance set-up of events beyond the actor's influence.

There is a school of thought to the contrary, which argues that moral culpability is somehow contingent on outcomes. On this theory creation of risk, even "unreasonable" risk, is not wrong unless the risk materializes. Thomas Nagel[24] and Judith Jarvis Thomson[25] have advanced such a notion of "moral luck" (Nagel's phrase)[26] based on their perception of the ethical intuitions and judgments of ordinary persons. Their discussions unfortunately do not offer the kind of systematic exploration of the subject that would support confident applications to the problem of legal responsibility for risk. Thomson's discussion comes closest to the question of legal responsibility. Though she never quite reaches the problem of what to do about risky behavior, there is implicit in her discussion a notion that legal responsibility for risk stands on a shaky moral foundation, at least a foundation much less

24 See Thomas Nagel, *Mortal Questions* (Cambridge: Cambridge University Press, 1979), pp. 24–38.
25 See Judith Jarvis Thomson, "The Decline of Cause," *Georgetown Law Journal* 76 (1987): 137.
26 The term "moral luck" is taken by Nagel from Bernard Williams, *Moral Luck* (Cambridge: Cambridge University Press, 1981), pp. 20–39. However, Williams' treatment of "luck" appears quite differently oriented from that of Nagel. For Williams the luck consists not in avoidance of actual injury to others but in achieving a higher goal that, in a sense, redeems the harm caused to others. His essential message seems to be that man does not live by Kant alone: the demands of the good life sometimes trump the moral demands of a particular situation. Nagel explores this problem – the conflict between "living well and living right," as he puts it – in *The View from Nowhere* (Oxford: Oxford University Press, 1986), pp. 189–207. Of course, at this level of discourse the question of the moral significance of "luck" is not one of evaluating discrete actions but one of evaluating moral reasoning generally. That level of moral discourse is not very meaningful in the present context where the law demands some kind of judgment in order to respond to the injured victim's claim for justice.

firm than that which supports responsibility for actual harm. It is that notion I want to challenge.

Thomson begins by imagining this simple scenario. A and B carelessly back out of their respective driveways without looking behind. A is lucky; there is no one behind the car. B is unlucky; there is a child whom B hits. Echoing an intuition of Adam Smith,[27] Thomson believes that common sentiment would regard B's conduct as worse than A's because of the actual harm, despite the insistence of "Kantian moral sophisticates"[28] that there is no moral distinction between the two. Thomson finds this perceived common sentiment puzzling, but she nevertheless thinks it is a relevant and important element of moral judgment all the same. Indeed, she implies the common sentiment is more important than the abstract moral conception of philosophers who have, she suggests, spent too much time in the study and not enough in the "open air" among "men and women in the street."[29]

I don't doubt that open air can be a good tonic for moral philosophers – or for that matter theorists of any stripe – though I do doubt that the solution to this "puzzle" is to stroll the streets, casually interrogating passers-by as to their feelings about the morality of accident law. I am by no means certain how they would respond in any event if the question were carefully put to them. I know of no empirical study of

27 Adam Smith, *The Theory of Moral Sentiments* 176 (Indianapolis: Liberty Press, 1976, 1st ed., 1776). Smith defends legal rules that are directed only at outcomes on the ground that it would be oppressive to attempt to punish mere state of mind or sentiment. *Id.* at 195–96. Obviously what Smith had in mind was quite different from the situation addressed here, which does not involve punishing mere state of mind but conduct – albeit conduct the particular consequences of which are only known probabilistically.
28 Thomson, *supra* note 25 at 145.
29 *Id.* at 143, 148. Thomson's plea brings to mind Hume's wish that philosophers had "a share of the gross earthy mixture" possessed by those persons who are wholly "employed in their domestic affairs, or amusing themselves in common recreations." David Hume, *A Treatise of Human Nature*, L. A. Selby-Bigge, ed. (Oxford: Clarendon Press, 1955, 1st ed., 1888), p. 272.

popular moral attribution that would confirm or disconfirm Thomson's perception that ordinary folks feel differently about risk-creating behavior depending on whether it happens to result in harm. In an early study of the moral judgments of children Jean Piaget found that very young children seem to attribute blame predominantly or entirely on the basis of outcomes, but emphasis must be placed on "very young" for he found no trace of this view in children over the age of 10.[30] I have been unable to discover any relevant evidence of blame attribution by adults that would tell us how far Thomson's "men and women in the street" differ from "Kantian moral sophisticates."

For want of better evidence of public attitudes we necessarily fall back on personal intuition and experience. It is common, and up to a point reasonable, to generalize from introspective examination of our own attitudes, aided by what we think we know of others from observation. We need to be clear about what attitudes are being examined, however, and here I think Thomson's discussion becomes confused. Returning to the driveway scenario she puts us in the driver's seat, so to speak, and invites us to reflect on how we would feel about (a) carelessly backing out the driveway and (b) carelessly backing out and nearly striking a child.

In case (a) she suggests we may feel guilty, but only fleetingly, while in the latter case we will feel "awful." (For some reason she does not ask us to imagine how we would feel if we actually hit the child, but presumably we would feel much worse.) But what does this tell us about moral evaluation? People *feel* guilty about all manner of things that have, on any reflective judgment, no moral significance.[31] For instance, parents feel guilty when their children die from nat-

---

30 Jean Piaget, *The Moral Judgment of the Child* (New York: Free Press, 1965, 1st ed., 1932), pp. 121–24.
31 See Michael Ross & Garth J. O. Fletcher, "Attribution and Social Perception" *in* Gardner Lindzey & Elliot Aronson, eds., *Handbook of Social Psychology*, 3d ed. (New York: Random House, 1985), vol. 2, pp. 73, 106–10 (reviewing studies on the "irrationality" of blame attribution).

ural diseases and victims of wholly chance accidents often blame themselves.[32] I would be surprised to hear it suggested that we should take such feelings of guilt as a basis for moral evaluation. Ascribing moral significance to feelings is a tricky business. At the very least we need to be sure that the feelings to which we accord such significance can be appropriately translated into general rules of ethical behavior.

If it is necessary to be discriminating about the kinds of psychological feelings which count in the formation of a moral code, it is also necessary to be cautious about reliance on everyday expressions and attitudes. Underlying Thomson's argument is a repudiation of abstract Kantian formalism as the basis for moral judgment;[33] instead, reliance is based on cultural norms, as evidenced, *inter alia*, by how we express ourselves. I do not quarrel with the anti-Kantian notion that moral values are more a reflection of shared community norms than of abstract, a priori imperatives. And how we express ourselves, how we talk in everyday discourse, is relevant evidence of those shared norms. Still, moral reasoning surely consists of more than recording every vagrant sentiment that expresses itself in moral vernacular. No doubt, as Thomson indicates, we sometimes intuit that the behavior is morally wrong – punishable – only if it results in actual harm. We often talk this way in ordinary discourse. However, the appropriate reference is not to casual conversation but to deliberative reflection, what Rawls has called "reflective equilibrium."[34]

32 See Paul Chodoff, Stanford B. Friedman & David A. Hamburg, "Stress, Defenses and Coping Behavior: Observations in Parents of Children with Malignant Disease," *American Journal of Psychiatry* 120 (1964): 743; Ronnie Janoff Bulman & Camile Wortman, "Attributions of Blame and Coping in the 'Real World': Severe Accident Victims React to Their Lot," *Journal of Personality and Social Psychology* 35 (1977): 351.

33 In this respect her perspective appears to be similar to that of Bernard Williams and others who reject Kantian principles. Again, however, the latter is on such a different level of moral discourse than that which is relevant here that it is hard to connect them.

34 John Rawls, *A Theory of Justice* (Cambridge, Mass.: Harvard University Press, 1971), pp. 48–51.

I do not minimize the difficulty of differentiating between ephemeral sentiment and deliberative judgment. We have countless sources for the former, but in the nature of things reliable evidence of the latter is hard to find. In law, of course, one thinks of precedent, custom and legislation as sources of community values. These are ambiguous sources to be sure, and I would not claim they have any authoritative moral status. Nevertheless they are relevant evidence of community values, hence moral sentiment.

In the specific context of civil liability the tort law has been reluctant to recognize mere risk creation, but this undoubtedly reflects the fact that compensation for tort law has been traditionally regarded as a system for compensating harms that were (more or less) determinate. Within that framework the idea of anticipating harm simply did not occur to anyone as a *practical* function of the tort system until the rise of modern toxic torts involving widely diffused and frequently long-lived risks. It is not the case in any event that the refusal to recognize culpable risk creation alone as properly within the province of tort law reflected any *moral* qualms about condemning such conduct as wrongful without regard to any harmful outcomes. We have no moral qualms about imposing criminal penalties for attempts and conspiracies regardless of whether they are consummated. To be sure, there are differences between the penalties prescribed for such inchoate crimes and the completed offense. Conceivably this difference might reflect differential blameworthiness, though I doubt it. More likely it reflects an ambiguity in the circumstances in which the act took place which makes us uncertain how to judge the character and (probable) consequences of the conduct. Certainly we do not *excuse* the conduct in question merely because, by fortunate accident, particular harm did not occur.

There remains to be considered another objection to imposing civil liability for wrongful risk. It is an objection that goes less to the concept of moral wrongfulness than to the institutional character of tort law seen as a system of corrective justice. Ernest Weinrib has objected that liability for risk is inconsistent with the central premise of corrective justice, the existence of a juridical relationship between injurer and victim.[35] Echoing Judge Cardozo in the celebrated *Palsgraf* case,[36] Weinrib maintains that risk is not intelligible without regard to an identifiable set of perils and victims and these cannot be identified until harm materializes to a specific individual.

Weinrib's argument about risk is more or less incidental to a general theory of tort law as a system of corrective justice, in which Aristotelian formalism is married to Kantian deontological morality.[37] To be true to the requirements of corrective justice tort law must be conceived as "unitary," involving an "intrinsic," and symmetrical, relationship between plaintiff's wrongdoing and defendant's harm. For Weinrib tort law is simply incoherent as a system for instrumentalist aims – the enforcement of public standards or repairing accident losses. For instance he asks, on the instrumentalist account, why does the law not permit recovery where a risk dissipates itself without harm, as in Thompson's scenario of the careless but lucky driver; why is the amount of the award to plaintiff equal to his injury, as distinct from some punishment measured by the gravity of the offense?

Finessing for a moment the merits of Weinrib's general account of corrective justice, I am puzzled by his view that

35 See Weinrib, *supra* note 8 at 439–41. See also Weinrib's "Toward a Moral Theory of Negligence Law," *Law and Philosophy* 2 (1983): 37.
36 Palsgraf v. Long Island R. Co., 248 N.Y. 399, 162 N.E. 99 (1928). In *Palsgraf* Judge Cardozo held that there could be no duty of due care to unforeseeable plaintiffs. Whether foreseeability is properly regarded as a duty question or one of "proximate cause" or merely as an element of the negligence calculus itself is a fine point of tort law sometimes debated among scholars, albeit to rather little practical end. In fact the "Palsgrafian" condition, if I can call it that, is seldom a significant issue in tort litigation for the simple reason that the judicially defined realm of foreseeability is so capacious as to impose no practically important boundary on the scope of duty.
37 The theory is most fully developed in "Toward a Moral Theory of Negligence Law," *supra* note 35, and in "Legal Formalism: On the Immanent Rationality of Law," *Yale Law Journal* 97 (1988): 949.

the forms of corrective justice are incompatible with the conceptions of probabilistic causation or liability for wrongful risk creation. Nothing in Aristotle's forms of justice forbids defining causation or harm in terms of probabilities. And clearly nothing in Kant's conception of moral duty requires materialization of harm; quite the contrary, the whole idea of the categorical imperative is to exclude consequences from the calculus of moral duty just as we noted earlier in discussing "moral luck."

A central target of Weinrib's attack on instrumentalist theories of tort law is the intermixture of corrective and distributive justice purposes. Whether such an intermixture violates the required norms (forms) of justice, Weinrib's critique seems to me to exaggerate the degree to which those two purposes are in fact confused in the tort system, or in conventional explanations of the system. Tort liability is not imposed in order to allocate wealth in the name of equality or other criteria of moral deserts.[38] Admittedly, insofar as tort law permits and even encourages loss spreading through insurance, it is engaging in distributional aims of a sort. However, this distributional element is not a self-standing feature of the liability system. We do not willy nilly seek out "deep pockets" to bear the losses of victims; any concern for "distributional fairness" is interstitial and incidental to the purpose of correcting a wrong.

In any event nothing in the idea of liability for wrongful risk creation would alter the existing system in respect to purpose. Nor would it fundamentally alter the existing sys-

38 Weinrib's argument is confused on this point to the extent that it equates incidental distribution within the framework of redressing accident losses with more general objectives of wealth distribution. "Legal Formalism," *supra* note 37 at 984. A similar confusion can be found in Fletcher, *supra* note 23 at 547 n.40. Perhaps the best illustration of the point in existing tort law is the collateral source rule which forbids courts from considering a victim's collateral benefits or other "wealth" in measuring the compensation due. While some states have recently enacted statutes to alter this rule (as part of more general concerns about the burden of tort liability), I know of no law or court decision that has held that the victim's compensation is dependent on his wealth.

tem in regard to form. The juridical relationship between plaintiff and defendant that Weinrib insists on preserving would remain intact; liability would depend on a duty to identifiable victims[39] and a wrongful breach of that duty by the creation of an unreasonable risk of harm. True, in risk-based liability the relationship has not been "particularized" by fully determined harm, but that much is true in the present law, as I pointed out earlier: victims now recover not simply for presently manifest harm but for estimated future harms that may or may not materialize. Moreover, even manifest harms need not be the certain product of the injurer's actions to support liability under conventional tort rules; proof of causation – which Weinrib believes to be the linchpin of the juridical relationship – is inherently probabilistic.

I have argued that liability for risk conforms to essential features of the class corrective justice model, finessing the larger question whether the model itself is an attractive one. That larger question is too big for this essay, but in view of Weinrib's elegant critique of much of the contemporary thinking about risk and liability a few observations about his model are appropriate. Weinrib's model of corrective justice is part of a more general defense of legal formalism in which the forms of justice are seen as providing the core "internal" justification of the "moral rationality" of law. It is a conception of legal, *cum* moral, rationality that not only outlaws instrumentalist (external) justification but insists on the purest definition of the forms themselves. In his model the Ar-

---

39 Weinrib does not tell us how we should apply the "particularized nexus" requirement in cases involving injuries to a large and open-ended class of victims (for instance, users of asbestos). However, the way in which he talks about the relationship between "doer" and "sufferer" suggests a kind of one-to-one relationship that does not capture the reality of modern tort law in these cases. In fact, of course, the "sufferer" in these situations is no more than a "statistic" to the "doer," and the argument of "Palsgrafian" foreseeability no more than an actuarial calculation. If such situations still fall within Weinrib's corrective justice model, there is no reason why risk-based liability cannot do so. If such situations fall outside his model, one would have to say that his model is of no practical usefulness to the modern world of tort law.

istotelian forms of justice not only provide a way of thinking about legal purposes, they constitute the essential framework of legal justification; they provide the coherence – the "justificatory structure" – of law. Although the forms themselves have no substantive content (that is, no substantive political criteria of justice) they necessarily imply certain relationships and concepts (*e.g.*, equality, personhood) that give them commanding moral force. I noted earlier that Weinrib marries Aristotelian formalism with Kantian deontology; one could say that it is through the Aristotelian forms of justice that Kant's moral duty implements itself.

To say the least Weinrib's vision of the legal system is an exquisitely pure one. Form not only dominates social purpose, but circumscribes the character of moral discourse. The forms of justice (as he and Aristotle define them) provide the exclusive framework in which law can be rationally justified. On first acquaintance the argument is so single-minded in its defense of pure form one is tempted to see it as a semantic claim: if you want to appeal to concepts of "corrective justice" and "distributive justice," this is the correct way to use those terms. However, that seems not to be the limit of the argument (and in fact treating the claim as one of semantics unfairly trivializes it). The argument seeks not merely to define the use of terms but to define the basis for determining legal rationality and thereby to determine the realm of law itself, in much the way that Kant sought to determine the realm of moral duty: if you want to talk about the "moral rationality of law," this is the way you must talk about it.

Weinrib offers this as an "internal justification" of law,[40] though one would be hard pressed to distinguish it from transcendentalism. But no matter how it is styled the question that begs to be answered is, what is the point of internal justifications that have no connection to external purposes? Weinrib invites us to think about the logic of the law in the

40 Weinrib, "Legal Formalism," *supra* note 37 at 1014–15 n.132, perceives a parallel to Dworkin's attempt to construct an internal justification of the law in *Law's Empire*, though the two types of "internalist" arguments seem quite different.

340

same terms as we think about the logic of geometry.[41] But to what end? In other words (more or less those of Richard Rorty):[42] why should we talk this way about law? Or, at least, why should we talk this way about tort law? Weinrib repeatedly appeals to notions of "coherence" as if any other way of talking about law and justice were incoherent, almost literal nonsense. Such a claim seems exceedingly bold in the face of the fact that adoption of his model would require drastic change in the way contemporary lawyers, judges and legal theorists do in fact talk about law and justice. I do not say that tort law (or law in general) must be instrumentalist. Unlike Weinrib I do not find instrumentalist justification in general to be either incoherent or objectionable, but it is not my claim that instrumentalism is either a necessary or sufficient foundation for tort law. My objection to Weinrib's disembodied formalism is not that it is anti-instrumentalism but that it is too far removed from human aims to be meaningful as a moral theory. I shall not pursue the point further. To do so would distract from my central objective, which is to defend a conception of liability for tortious risk within the basic framework and rationales of the present liability system. In saying this, however, I necessarily invite questions about the *practical* limits of the tort system inasmuch as there cannot be much doubt that liability for tortious risk creation would extend the reach of tort law. Something further must be said about those limits.

V. RISK AND THE LIMITS OF TORT LAW

Beneath the often expressed concern about burdening courts with complex problems of proof in determining uncertain future events there lies a more basic anxiety that recognizing risk as a basis for liability would lead to overzealous prosecution of insubstantial or highly speculative claims. That concern is fed in turn by the growing suspicion that our society

41 *Id.* at 963.
42 See Richard Rorty, *Contingency, Irony and Solidarity* (Cambridge: Cambridge University Press, 1989), pp. 44–69.

has of late developed something of an hysteria about risk, producing a veritable avalanche of overly protective laws and regulations.[43]

In part this development arises as a consequence of increased epidemiological sophistication in identifying (or at least labeling) the hazards of modern life. These hazards are not all new, and those that are new may be no more significant than older hazards we have either surmounted or accepted. Indeed, given the steady increase in longevity, one would be hard pressed to make the case that life today is riskier than, say, fifty or even twenty years ago. However, many risks once thought to be inevitable, if not "natural," are now considered "artificial," and hence avoidable, by-products of modern social activity.[44]

It is a commonplace of intelligent discourse that not all avoidable risks should be avoided. I am quite prepared to acknowledge the force of this commonplace as well as the criticism that our legal and public institutions sometimes act to the contrary (by implication a comment on the intelligence of legal/public discourse). However, determining what risks are matters of legitimate concern is not pertinent here. I take it as given that the law makes the creation of certain risks subject to prevailing tort law standards. In that context the general question of the right level of risk control is one of specifying standards of care for risk-creating activity.

43 See, e.g., Mary Douglas & Aaron Wildavsky, *Risk and Culture: An Essay on the Selection of Technical and Environmental Dangers* (Berkeley: University of California Press, 1982).

44 Douglas and Wildavsky, *id.* at 36–37, insist that the modern concern about risk is only partly due to increased technological sophistication. More importantly they say it is a consequence of changes in cultural – and political – attitudes about moral responsibility (and accountability) for risky activity; "institutionalized mistrust," not technology, is the driving force of this new (and in their view lamentable) concern. It is almost tritely true that our modern view of risk is shaped by social and political attitudes. How far those attitudes are exogenous cultural artifacts (as Douglas and Wildavsky seem to imply) rather than the product of technological modernization is more controversial. So too is their polemical argument that the politics of risk are driven by extremists.

Whether those standards/levels are too high (or too low, or just right) is a matter of no consequence to the question whether risk-based liability is a useful concept. The relevant question here is how to enforce prevailing standards, whether to permit them to be enforced ex ante, against the creation of risk, or only ex post, when they become manifest as particularized harms. Actually, putting the question in terms of a choice between judging risks and judging harms is somewhat misleading insofar as the present system is in fact a mixture of both, as I have shown. It would be more accurate to formulate our question in terms of a shift in system orientation: how far should we expand *enforcement* of torts standards based on probabilistic measures of harm?

Recognition of risk-based liability would increase the number of claims filed and adjudicated, of course. For any given class of cases for which risk was recognized as a compensable event – say, the DES cases – we might expect increases, at least in claims filed, by several orders of magnitude. For those who believe the benefit–cost ratio of claims adjudication under the existing system is unfavorable, the prospect of such an increase no doubt will be frightful to contemplate. There comes a point where the expansion of liability to cover broad, ill-defined harms stretches the basic purposes of tort law beyond its historic purpose and beyond its usefulness. Tortious risk may become so diffuse and general that it merges imperceptibly into the common stock of risks that inhere in social life. At such a point tort law becomes an awkward vehicle for regulatory control and equally awkward as a means of reparation.

This objection is more focussed than the general concern about risk regulation previously noted and is by that token more directly pertinent to the question of private liability. However, I believe it is still off the mark.

There is a controversy of long standing about the role of tort law in the "administrative state." The increase in the ambition of tort law in America – most strikingly evident in the enlarged scope of liability for medical accidents, product-related defects and environmental harms – has given new

intensity to old doubts about the reliability of a private liability system for correcting and/or redressing accidental
injury.[45] Proposals to replace tort rules in favor of
administrative regulation and social insurance schemes are
now a standard feature in the academic literature and a common item in the agenda of social reformers as well.[46] I have
my doubts about the merits of such proposals, but there is
no need to explore the matter here. I need only note the
obvious: if the tort system has no role to play generally in
the control of and compensation for conventional accidental
harms, it has no role at the edges of the traditional system.
If a routine auto or a product-defect accident are not fit subjects for common law liability, then plainly the mere tortious
creation of risk is far beyond the pale. The question immediately relevant is whether there is something peculiar in the
nature of probabilistic judgments that should cause us to
make them the *exclusive* province of administrative regulators
or bureaucratic insurance mechanisms.

I stress "exclusive" to denote the fact that no one is suggesting that tort law should become the exclusive vehicle for
controlling unwanted risk or compensating those who suffer
from it; the arguments for legal change all run in the opposite
direction. The arguments for administrative preemption of
private liability rules typically make two related albeit distinctive types of claim. The first is a kind of Weberian claim
about the preeminent expertise of bureaucratic organizations;
the second is a claim about the need for comprehensive as
opposed to incremental decision making.

The first claim seems to me very weak unless it is joined
to the second. In other words the expertise of administrative
agencies lies predominantly in the realm of comprehensive
decision making. The ability to study risk in various forms,
over a range of situations, and to make global rules without

---

45   Peter W. Huber, *Liability: The Legal Revolution and Its Consequences* (New
     York: Basic Books, 1988), is fairly representative of popular critiques
     of the current tort liability system.
46   See, *e.g.*, Stephen D. Sugarmen, "Doing Away with Tort Law," *Cal-
     ifornia Law Review* 73 (1985): 555, 559–91.

regard to their fit with individual cases is decidedly the comparative advantage of bureaucratic organizations, not common law courts which must organize their activity around the disposition of individual cases. But in the disposition of any given case I doubt that agencies have any intrinsic advantage. The common assumption that agencies are populated with technical experts is much exaggerated, but in any event very misleading, for the pertinent point of comparison between agencies and courts is that of decision-making responsibility. In any particular case court and agency can command roughly equivalent technical information and advice. Given comparable access to such information and advice the question then is ability to comprehend and apply it. Do we have any reasons to think that courts – judges and juries – are generically inferior to administrative officials on this score? While there is no shortage of stories about judicial (I here include judges and juries) ignorance and even irrationality, that much can be said of administrative officials as well. The more important criticism of common law decisions is not that they are stupid, but that they lack a comprehensive view of the nature and consequences of general rules. In the nature of the common law process there are limits on the ability of courts to examine all of the trade-offs involved in global rules, and they are seldom confronted in any particular case with a full picture of the probable consequences of the decisions they make. This is the vice of incremental decision making generally.

This is also its virtue. One very large virtue of the common law is that it does not typically lay down rules for global orderings. Not being in a position to take "the long view" can be a distinct advantage if the error costs of coming up with the wrong long view are high. Not to be misunderstood on this point I should stress that I am not endorsing the claims that the common law *process* or the courts as an *institution* are inherently predisposed towards efficient outcomes.[47] Such claims seem to me fanciful, if indeed they are

47   These two types of positive (as distinct from normative) efficiency

even intelligible.[48] It is not necessary to embrace such claims in order to advance the more modest claim of relative competence – a claim that defends the current liability system on both efficiency and fairness grounds by inviting comparison with other social programs of regulation and reparation. To be fair the comparison should be made within the same perspective for each alternative: the "real" tort system against the "real" regulatory or social insurance programs. Unfortunately, reformers all too often choose to present the real tort system with all its warts against idealized regulatory/ insurance programs with all their warts removed.

At bottom the question of public judgment about competing systems or programs must formulate a set of reasonable aspirations constrained by realistic expectations. It may be that in this posture it is too much to expect that tort law could be extended as I have outlined without breaching the limits of those realistic expectations. I remarked earlier on

claims are quite different. The process claim rests on an "invisible-hand" type theory of legal evolution. Essentially the theory is that inefficient rules are more frequently litigated than efficient rules, a process that mathematically leads to the long-term extinction of the former in favor of the latter. See Paul Rubin, "Why is the Common Law Efficient?" *Journal of Legal Studies* 6 (1977): 51; George L. Priest, "The Common Law Process and the Selection of Efficient Rules," *Journal of Legal Studies* 6 (1977): 65. The institutional claim is distinctly not an invisible-hand theory insofar as it depends on self-conscious rule selection by judges. See, *e.g.*, Landes & Posner, *supra* note 16 at 19.

48 The process model assumes both that the litigants pursue strategies that are "efficient" to them and that these strategies yield socially efficient rules as well. If this is not tautological (what survives the process is definitionally "efficient"), it is undemonstrated by any showing that the rules do in fact conform to any clear and useful definition of efficiency.

The institutional model does not rest on any convincing theory of judicial motivation that would cause judges to seek out "efficient" rules. Essentially the judicial motivation is derived from an ex post judgment that the rules themselves tend to be efficient. However, that judgment requires both a highly stylized description of tort law rules (one that abstracts to a level that allows the variety and inconsistencies to be ignored as mere "detail") and an extremely simplified theory of efficiency. For an extended critique of both types of efficiency theories see, *e.g.*, Kornhauser, *supra* note 16.

346

the rising concern over the expanded role of tort liability; I suggested that concern is properly addressed to the substantive standards of liability – what kinds of risk do we want to control or compensate for within the liability system? Yet it may be that this question simply cannot be addressed head on but only indirectly through subordinate issues such as timing of recovery, or requirements for causal connectedness, or limiting compensation to fully manifested and particularized harms.

Certainly it would be disingenuous to claim that risk-based liability is an idea whose time has come. Traditional conceptions of the way tort liability should work have yet too strong a hold to make that claim. And there are daunting practical problems that I have only barely touched upon. Nevertheless, the potential benefits of early recognition and explicit evaluation of risk, coupled with the fact that risk assessment is an unavoidable feature in much of the present system, argue for further exploration of the possibility of innovation in the adjudication and control of tortious risk.

Part IV

Punishment

Chapter 10

Retributive hatred: an essay on criminal liability and the emotions

JEFFRIE G. MURPHY

> It's great to be back in Chicago where people still
> know how to hate.
> > Mike Royko, on returning home
> > after covering the 1972 Democratic Convention
> > in San Francisco

The critical legal studies movement has, in my judgment, raised at least one important issue for jurisprudence and moral philosophy. I am thinking of its claim that traditional moralistic jurisprudence errs in confining its inquiries to formal, abstract, and public doctrines and to the intellectual rationales for those doctrines. According to the "crits," a full philosophical grasp of law and morality requires an examination of the underlying causal forces that in part generate both the doctrines and the intellectual rationales for them. The person who seeks total enlightenment about morality and the law is invited to look, not just to the ideological superstructure, but to the underlying substructure that gives the superstructure at least a part of its point. This seems to me an invitation that those of us who practice traditional jurisprudence should accept.

I am particularly interested in the degree to which certain moral and legal doctrines are rooted in specific *passions* (feelings, emotions) and the degree to which a philosophical examination of those passions will have a bearing on an understanding and evaluation of the doctrines that they in part generate and for which these doctrines in part serve as rationalizations. Although not currently at the center of philosophical fashion, this type of inquiry has, of course, a venerable philosophical history. It was pursued not simply by Nietzsche, Freud, Marx, and other heroes of the critical legal studies movement, but also by such writers as Hume and Adam Smith – pursued in their case as an inquiry into "the origin of our moral sentiments." Smith, for example, believed that much of our idea of retributive justice had to be understood in terms of the passion of resentment; and it is this family of passions, in fact, that I propose to take as my object of inquiry for the present study.[1]

Speaking very generally, we may say that the criminal law (among other things that it does) institutionalizes certain feelings of anger, resentment, and even hatred that we typically (and perhaps properly) direct toward wrongdoers – especially if we have been *victims* of those wrongdoers. (The great symbol for such institutionalization in our literature is that of Athena, rather than banishing the Furies, making an honorable home in Athens for them and thereby transforming them into the Eumenides or "the kindly ones.") In the present age, most of us do not feel comfortable talking about the criminal law in such terms, for we are inclined to think that civilized people are not given to hatred and to an anger so intense that it generates the desire for revenge – that they are not, in short, driven by what (following Westermarck) I will call *the retributive emotions.*[2] We prefer to talk highmindedly of our reluctantly advocating punishment of criminals perhaps because social utility or justice demands it and tend

---

1 This essay was prepared for the conference "Liability in Law and Morals" at Bowling Green State University, April 15–17, 1988. It is a modified and expanded version of Chapter 3 of the book *Forgiveness and Mercy* (Cambridge: Cambridge University Press, 1988) by Jeffrie G. Murphy (Chapters 1, 3, and 5) and Jean Hampton (Chapters 2 and 4).

2 See Edward Westermarck, *Ethical Relativity* (London: Routledge and Kegan Paul, 1932), Chapter III. Westermarck's work on the moral emotions – particularly the retributive emotions – has been interestingly discussed in J.L. Mackie's "Morality and the Retributive Emotions" in his collection of essays *Persons and Values* (Oxford: Clarendon Press, 1985).

to think that it is only primitives who would actually *hate* criminals and want them to suffer to appease an anger or outrage that is felt toward them. Good people are above such passions or at least they try to be. Some would even say that this is a requirement of Christianity.

It has not been this way in all ages, of course. Consider for example, what James Fitzjames Stephen – the great Victorian judge and theorist of the criminal law – said about that branch of law and its relation to the retributive emotions. He was no doubt a devout Christian but he could, to use the current vernacular, really "get into" hating. Though often regarding criminals as rather like noxious insects to be ground under the heel of society, Stephen does not see the punishment of such persons as having merely extermination value. The criminal law, he claims, gives "distinct shape to the feeling of anger" and provides a "distinct satisfaction to the desire for vengeance." He writes:

> The sentence of the law is to the moral sentiments of the public in relation to any offence what a seal is to hot wax. It converts into a permanent final judgment what might otherwise be a transient sentiment. . . . [T]he infliction of punishment by law gives definite expression and solemn ratification and justification to the hatred which is excited by the commission of the offence. . . . The forms in which deliberate anger and righteous disapprobation are expressed [in the execution of criminal justice] stand to the one set of passions in the same relation which marriage stands to [the sexual passions].[3]

Stephen's point is a simple one: certain wrongdoers quite properly excite the resentment (anger, hatred) of all right-thinking people; and the criminal law is a civilized and efficient way in which such passions may be directed toward their proper objects – allowing victims to get legitimate revenge consistently with the maintenance of public order. This is not the criminal law's only legitimate and important pur-

3 James Fitzjames Stephen, *A History of the Criminal Law of England* (London, 1883), Volume II, pp. 81–82.

pose, but it is one of them. Passions such as resentment can, of course, provoke irrational and dangerous conduct (which passions cannot?), but this is no more a reason for condemning them in principle than it would be for condemning the sexual passions in principle. The case for the rational control and institutionalization of a passion must not, in short, be confused with a case for the utter condemnation and extinction of that passion – a mistake perhaps made by certain strands of Christianity with respect to both sexual desire and resentment.

In spite of the insights that I take to be present in Stephen's position, most contemporary writers reject it without argument – simply assuming that the passions of resentment and hatred (as desires for vengeance and revenge) are so obviously evil and corrupt that no acceptable social policies can be allowed to express them. In a recent essay defending retributivism, for example, Michael Moore argues that retributivism must be utterly severed from any foundation in these retributive emotions if the doctrine is to avoid automatic rejection.[4] Here Moore stands with most contemporary writers in assuming (contrary to Stephen's and my intuitions) that the burden of proof clearly lies on the one favoring these emotions and not on the one who would stand against them.

An important exception to this contemporary bias is to be found in some work by Jean Hampton.[5] Though she is in general very skeptical of the retributive emotions, she is not willing simply to assume their inherent evil. Apparently accepting that she may bear the burden of proof on this issue (or at least that it is just as fair to assign it to her as to the supporter of these emotions), she develops sustained and profound arguments against most forms of the retributive emotions – resentment and especially hatred. Since I have written extensively on resentment elsewhere,[6] I will in this

4 See Michael S. Moore, "The Moral Worth of Retribution," in *Responsibility, Character and the Emotions*, edited by Ferdinand Schoeman (Cambridge: Cambridge University Press, 1987).
5 See Chapters 2 and 4 of *Forgiveness and Mercy, supra* note 1.
6 See Jeffrie G. Murphy, "Forgiveness and Resentment," in *Midwest Stud-*

essay concentrate on what may appear to be the most unattractive of all the emotions in the family of emotions under discussion: the emotion of *hatred*. In trying to make a case for its legitimacy (mainly by attempting to meet arguments against its legitimacy), I will initially build on some of Hampton's discussion.

Hampton distinguishes three kinds of hatred: simple hatred, moral hatred, and malicious-spiteful hatred (Nietzsche's *ressentiment*). Simply having an aversion to someone because of some nonmorally objectionable quality (e.g., he is a bore) is nonavoidable and raises no moral issues unless one acts on the feeling in immoral ways. (Trying to avoid a bore at a party is permissible; killing the bore – though very tempting – is not.) Moral hatred is aversion to a person (e.g., a Nazi) because of the immoral cause with which he is identified and is coupled with a desire to triumph over him and his cause. There is no desire to hurt the person *simpliciter* but only a willingness to allow such hurt if unavoidable in the pursuit of victory over his immoral cause. Malicious or spiteful hatred, however, has as its very object the attempt to diminish and hurt another and thereby gain competitive advantage over him and his status; and it is this kind of hatred, argues Hampton, that is both irrational and immoral.

I am inclined to agree with almost everything that Hampton says – as far as it goes. However, there is, in my view, an important dimension of hatred that Hampton does not explore – a dimension that in some way combines elements of her categories of moral and malicious hatred and thus suggests that the moral phenomenology of hatred and resentment is even more complicated than her already very complex analysis indicates. Or so I shall argue.

The desire to hurt another, to bring him low, is not – in

ies in *Philosophy*, Volume VII, edited by Peter French *et alia* (Minneapolis: University of Minnesota Press, 1982), and Chapter 1 of *Forgiveness and Mercy, supra* note 1. See also Jeffrie G. Murphy, "Mercy and Legal Justice," *Social Philosophy and Policy*, Volume 4, Number 1, Autumn 1986, and Chapter 5 of *Forgiveness and Mercy*.

my judgment – always motivated by the competitive desire
to appear better than that person in some way. Sometimes,
I suggest, such a desire is motivated by feelings that are at
least partly *retributive* in nature – e.g., feelings that another
person's current level of well-being is undeserved or ill-
gotten (perhaps at one's own expense) and that a reduction
in that well-being will simply represent his getting his just
deserts. (This is no doubt the thought behind the old common law principle that no man shall be allowed to profit from
his own wrongdoing.) Take a case where Jones has injured
me, has taken an unfair advantage of me, has brought me
low, and is himself unrepentant and flourishing. I hate him
and want him brought low. My attitude here is like Hampton's spiteful hatred in that I want Jones to hurt. But it is
like her moral hatred in that part of the basis for desiring the
hurt is the desire to restore what (at least seems to me) is
the proper moral balance of whatever goods are in question,
and not a simple desire to look better than Jones on some
morally irrelevant scale of comparison. It is not the kind of
hatred felt by Saul for David (David inflicted no unjust injury
on Saul) but is a kind that might be felt, for example, by
former inmates of a concentration camp toward a former
camp commandant finally captured and put on trial for
crimes against humanity, or by those American soldiers now
dying of cancer toward those who recklessly exposed them
to radiation during atomic testing, or – on a less global scale
– by a man toward his wife and best friend when he discovers
that they have betrayed him and have been conducting an
adulterous affair behind his back, or by a woman toward a
rapist whose attack has left her forever terrified and sexually
insecure. The hatred felt by such persons will typically have
a *righteous* dimension – indicated by the fact that they, unlike
people motivated by petty envy or spite, are often willing to
avow publicly, as appropriate and as nothing to be ashamed
of, the true nature of their feelings and motives. Such people
often show up, for example, at criminal sentencing hearings
where, as crime victims, they want to influence the judge to
impose very harsh treatment on those who have harmed

them – sometimes ruined their lives utterly.[7] Even those who would argue that such appeals should not influence a judge must surely admit that the desires represented in the appeals are in some sense understandable, natural, and appropriate to the harm done to these people – that they involve something which is, even if not ultimately authoritative, at least more worthy of our attention and respect than petty spite or envy. I shall call the hatred present in such cases *retributive hatred* and shall suggest that, although in most cases it should be overcome, it still deserves a certain amount of respect. It is not obviously irrational or immoral. Indeed it is sometimes

7   It is common these days to hear the complaint that our society – particularly our legal system – is callous toward at least some victims of crime. One example of such callousness may be a refusal to respect the natural feelings of hatred that some victims may feel toward those who have harmed them – feelings that perhaps deserve more respect than simply being dismissed as irrelevant because "merely vindictive." There is – for reasons to be explored later – social and personal danger latent in such powerful feelings, but such danger might be minimized if these feelings – instead of being ignored – are institutionalized. (Athena, exhibiting the pagan world's healthy honesty about the passions, may have been on to something here.) Allowing victims some advisory role in criminal sentencing thus might be a legal practice that benefits both the community and the victims themselves; for the practice recognizes the validity of the hatred while placing important constraints on its excess. As such, it might even help to educate persons on the legitimate bounds of hatred. Of course, we hear much talk about crimes being offenses against the state or community as a whole – against the general rules of order in which all citizens have an equal stake. Because of this, it is often thought that all citizens have the same stake in demanding punishment for crime and that individual victims, therefore, should play no role. But this is too simplistic. The rapist (for example) may be a freerider on the legal compliance of all of us, but only some very unfortunate subset of us suffer from him in ways that seriously undermine our actual well-being. Is it absurd for such persons to think they have a special interest in seeing criminals get their just deserts? I do not think so. For an interesting exploration of the legal issues involved in allowing victims a role in criminal sentencing, see the 1987 Supreme Court case of *Booth v. Maryland*. In his dissent in that case, Justice Scalia does an excellent job of pointing out flaws in some standard arguments that purport to demonstrate that victims should have no such role. For further discussion of these issues, see Jeffrie G. Murphy, "Getting Even: The Role of the Victim," in *Crime, Culpability, and Remedy*, edited by Ellen Frankel Paul, Jeffrey Paul, and Fred D. Miller, Jr. (Oxford: Basil Blackwell, 1990).

both therapeutic for the victim and appropriately directed toward the wrongdoer and is not to be dismissed with a few pious clichés.

It is striking the degree to which those who wish to give hatred a bad name tend to focus on examples either of hatred that is not retributive or of retributive hatred that is clearly unjustified because the person hated is in fact (the hater's beliefs to the contrary) not really guilty of any unjust conduct. Hampton's example of David and Saul is of the former sort, as is her example of the mother who is above hatred and resentment of her child. (David did no wrong to Saul, and the child was not guilty of *responsible* wrongdoing.) An example of the latter sort is provided in the following passage from Simone Weil's *Gravity and Grace* (once quoted against me by Herbert Morris in protest of my sympathies for resentment and hatred):

> A beloved being who disappoints me. I have written to him. It is impossible that he should not reply by saying what I have said to myself in his name. Men owe us what we imagine they will give us. We must forgive them this debt. To accept the fact that they are other than the creatures of our imagination is to imitate the renunciation of God. I also am other than what I imagine myself to be. To know this is forgiveness.[8]

This is a dark passage, but I take it that at least a part of Weil's point is this: because of our pride, our vanity, our self-importance, we often project upon the world an illusion of what others owe us and thus quite improperly feel ourselves wronged when those others act in ways contrary to the illusion we have created. To this observation, I am inclined to reply as follows: *Of course* people sometimes fantasize hurts and *of course* any hatred based on such imaginary

---

8 Herbert Morris was the commentator when I presented a condensed version of Chapters 1 and 5 of *Forgiveness and Mercy* (*supra* note 1) at a symposium at the 1987 meetings of the American Philosophical Association, Pacific Division. My paper, Morris's comments, and a rejoinder by me will appear in a forthcoming issue of *Criminal Justice Ethics*.

injuries is totally unjustified – both irrational and immoral. But are we to conclude from this that there are no *real* moral injuries the perpetrators of which are quite rightly to be resented or even hated?

Surely the answer to the above question is a clear *no*. If a total case is to be made against hatred, it must be made against examples where the hatred appears at its best and most prima facie justified – examples where a person has in fact been treated very immorally, has been hurt badly by the immoral treatment, reasonably believes that the wrongdoer is totally unrepentant of the wrongdoing and is in fact living a life of freedom and contentment, and – *given all that* – hates the wrongdoer and desires that the wrongdoer suffer. Such cases may be rare, but – confessing that I firmly hold the unmodern view that there is such a thing as evil in this world – I believe that they do exist. For example: When the women victims in a recent series of vicious rape cases in Phoenix testified that they wanted "The Camelback Rapist," who had utterly shattered the lives of some of them, to be sentenced to the maximum term that the law allowed, many of them openly admitted that they were acting on anger and hatred.[9] They were outraged at the thought that this vicious man, utterly unrepentant, could soon continue to lead a free life given what he had done to their lives. I sympathized with their anger and hatred, having no inclination at all to call them petty or spiteful. I would have found it indecently insensitive and presumptuous had anyone charged them with the vice of failing to forgive and love their enemies or had anyone read them passages from Simone Weil on the tendency of human beings to imagine wrongs where there are no real wrongs – had, in short, anyone attempted to add to their already considerable burdens by making them feel guilty or ashamed over a reaction that was, given what was done to them, natural, fitting, and proper. My feelings (and

9 E. J. Montini, "Victims of 'Camelback Rapist' Pour Out Anger, Fear and Sadness," *Arizona Republic*, May 12, 1987, p. A2. (The word "Camelback" in this context refers to a region of the city of Phoenix.)

theirs) in such a case may be subject to criticism, but of one thing I am sure: *this* is the kind of case that must be discussed and made central in any comprehensive attack on the nature and justification of hatred, the kind of hatred I have called retributive in nature.

Resentment, I have elsewhere argued, is essentially tied to self-respect. It is an emotional defense against attacks on self-esteem and thus is, as both Nietzsche and Hampton suggest, a sign of weakness; for if one is certain of the value of one's self, it will not be truly threatened by attack from another and will not stand in need of defense. But of course one is never certain of such matters and thus some weakness or vulnerability in the area of self-esteem seems to me an ineliminable part of the human condition. We are, at least in part, social and socialized products – creatures whose sense of self is so much a part of our social setting that the idea of self-respect or self-esteem cannot be totally detached from a concern with how others (some others) regard and treat us, for – as Hume stressed – "men always consider the sentiments of others in their judgments of themselves."[10] To think otherwise is to fall victim to the liberal myth of atomic individualism in its crudest form. A truly strong person will have the resources to fight off attacks on his self-esteem when they are unjustified, but no person is so "strong" (so asocial) as to be totally indifferent to all such attacks – so indifferent that he does not even resent them. Hampton reminds us that Jesus set an example that it is possible to be otherwise, but Jesus – being divine – perhaps had certain advantages that mere mortals lack. It may not be too difficult to ignore insults and injuries from mere human beings if one, being the son of God, has a rather more impressive reference class from which to draw one's self-esteem.

Even supposing that what I have said about resentment is correct, however, it may not seem that it will help very much

10 David Hume, *A Treatise of Human Nature* (1739–40), Book II, Part 1, Section VIII. See also John Rawls's discussion of the social nature of the primary good of self-respect in *A Theory of Justice* (Cambridge, Mass.: Harvard University Press, 1971), pp. 440 ff.

in mounting a case for the justification for hatred – even retributive hatred. For the hater, unlike the resenter, is not simply engaged in protest and self-assertion. He also desires that the object of his hate be *hurt*. If hate is sometimes justified, then the desire to hurt another must sometimes be justified. But how can this be?

This is how: If it is morally permissible intentionally to do X (under a certain description), then it is surely permissible to *desire* to do X (under the same description). If there is any truth at all in retributive theories of punishment, then it is sometimes permissible that persons be hurt (punishment hurts) in response to their wrongdoing. It is thus sometimes permissible to hurt people for retributive reasons. Given this, it is sometimes permissible to desire to hurt people for retributive reasons.[11] Using Hampton's Sartrean idea that desires or emotions are strategies, we may say that retributive hatred is a strategy designed to see (and to let the victim see) that people get their just deserts; as such it is neither irrational nor immoral. The wrongdoer gets his just deserts (and what is wrong with that?) and the victim gets some personal satisfaction from seeing justice done (and what is wrong with that?). Deterrence values may also be served, for a person perceived as given to hatred and revenge is perhaps less likely to become a victim than are those who are not given to such passions. ("I'm Noko Marie, don't mess with me!" says a vindictive Kliban cat.) Retributive hatred is thus in principle vindicated as a permissible, if not mandatory, response of a victim to wrongdoing.[12]

11 Moore (*supra* note 4) seems to ignore the possibility that the feelings of resentment and hatred – and the desire for vengeance or revenge – might be legitimated if they can be analyzed in such a way that, instead of validating principles of retribution, they are themselves validated by such principles.

12 If reciprocal altruism is an adaptive evolutionary strategy, then it would seem that reciprocal retributive hatred might be as well. In this sense such hatred will properly be called a *natural* response to certain kinds of wrongdoing. On the evolutionary advantages of a strategy of "tit for tat," see Robert Axelrod, *The Evolution of Cooperation* (New York: Basic Books, 1984).
    The retributive theory of punishment is, in essence, the theory that

Does this then mean that we should all enter at full speed the wide and wonderful world of hatred – cultivating and nursing it in ourselves and teaching it to our children? I think not. Thus, having made the best case I can in favor of hatred, I shall now begin to consider what is wrong with it – why it perhaps deserves much of the bad press it has received and why, in general, we should seek to overcome it – and why the law, even when properly attentive to its legitimacy, should be very cautious in its institutionalization.

Note that what I have attempted to show thus far is that, in a certain restricted class of cases (cases of retribution), hatred is *in principle* vindicated or justified. But a showing that some response is in principle justified does not by itself show that the response is ever *in fact* justified, *all* relevant things considered; for to justify in principle is to justify for a pure and clear case, and it is always possible that the world never contains a pure or clear case – or that we are never in

people are to suffer punishment because they *deserve* it and not simply because social utility (e.g., crime deterrence) requires it. Critics often describe retribution as an obviously *pointless* infliction of suffering – as though future deterrence obviously has a point whereas redressing an injustice obviously does not. But this would surely need to be argued for; as it stands, it is simply question-begging. The retributive theory of punishment is, of course, controversial; and the complex arguments pro and con on the matter cannot be surveyed in the present context. Attempting to follow in the footsteps of Kant, I have in the past written extensively in defense of retribution's essential connection to some of our most basic moral ideas – our ideas of justice and fairness and our conception of people as morally significant in part because they are capable of the kind of responsible wrongdoing for which blame and punishment are appropriate (as they are capable of responsible rightdoing for which praise and reward are appropriate). I cannot possibly rehearse here the case I have attempted to develop in the past in defense of retributivism, and so I must simply content myself with referring the reader to my earlier writings – specifically my collection of essays *Retribution, Justice and Therapy* (Dordrecht: D. Reidel, 1979). The most persuasive brief presentation and defense of retributive thinking is to be found in Herbert Morris's classic essay "Persons and Punishment," *The Monist*, Volume 52, Number 4, October 1968. I have recently come to have some doubts about retributivism as a total theory of punishment and have expressed these in my "Retributivism, Moral Education, and the Liberal State," *Criminal Justice Ethics*, Volume 4, Number 1, Winter/Spring 1985.

a position to *know* if we are confronted with one. Given such a state of the world, it thus might always be a bad *policy* to exhibit the response no matter how in principle justified it may be. (Some people argue in a similar way about capital punishment – rejecting it, not in principle, but because they believe that the state can never administer it in a way that will not be arbitrary and capricious.)

With this pattern of thought in mind, consider what Kant – a staunch defender of a retributive outlook on punishment – says about hatred and revenge in his *Metaphysical Elements of Virtue*:

It is . . . a duty of virtue not only to refrain from repaying another's enmity with hatred out of mere revenge but also never even to call upon the world-judge for vengeance – partly because man has enough guilt of his own to be greatly in need of forgiveness and partly, and indeed especially, because no punishment, no matter from whom it comes, may be inflicted out of hatred. – Hence men have a duty to cultivate a *conciliatory spirit* (*placabilitas*). But this must not be confused with *placid toleration* of injuries (*mitis iniuriarum patientia*), renunciation of the rigorous means (*rigorosa*) for preventing the recurrence of injuries by other men.[13]

Consider also a couple of related passages from his *Religion Within the Limits of Reason Alone*:

We call a man evil, however, not because he performs actions that are evil (contrary to law) but because these actions are of such a nature that we may infer from them the presence in him of evil maxims. In and through experience we can observe actions contrary to law, and we can observe (at least in ourselves) that they are performed in the consciousness that they are unlawful; but a man's maxims, sometimes even his own, are not thus observable; consequently the judgment that the agent is an evil man cannot be made with certainty if grounded on experience.

13 Immanuel Kant, *Metaphysical Elements of Virtue*, translated by Mary J. Gregor (New York: Harper & Row, 1964), p. 130.

[People] may picture themselves as meritorious, feeling themselves guilty of no such offenses as they see others burdened with; nor do they ever inquire whether good luck should not have the credit, or whether by reason of the cast of mind which they could discover, if they only would, in their own inmost nature, they would have practiced similar vices, had not inability, temperament, training, and circumstances of time and place which serve to tempt one (matters which are not imputable) kept them out of the way of those vices. This dishonesty, by which we humbug ourselves and which thwarts the establishing of a true moral disposition in us, extends itself outwardly also to falsehood and deception of others. If this is not to be termed wickedness, it at least deserves the name of worthlessness, and is an element in the radical evil of human nature, which (inasmuch as it puts out of tune the moral capacity to judge what a man is to be taken for, and renders wholly uncertain both internal and external attribution of responsibility) constitutes the foul taint in our race.[14]

There is much that is puzzling in these passages, but in general they can be read as commentaries upon two well-known Christian teachings: "Vengeance is mine; I will repay, saith the Lord" (*Romans* 12:19) and "Let him who is without sin cast the first stone" (*John* 8:7). For Kant here seems to be making two main objections to hatred and to any action – even punishment – motivated by hatred:

(1) Human beings, given their cognitive limitations, are never in a position to know if another (whose essential character is, after all, inner) is evil to the degree that hatred of him would be justified. Such matters are properly left to God, who "knows the heart."[15]

14 Immanuel Kant, *Religion Within the Limits of Reason Alone*, translated by Theodore M. Green and Hoyt H. Hudson (New York: Harper & Row, 1960), pp. 16, 33–34.
15 Kant (ibid., pp. 60–61) speaks of God as being uniquely qualified to make ultimate judgment because He "knows the heart" of the wrongdoer – a theme whose implications I pursue more fully in my "Does Kant Have a Theory of Punishment?" *Columbia Law Review*, Volume 87, Number 3, April 1987. Note that if hatred and vengeance are permissible for God then there must be a sense in which these re-

(2) Each human being is himself so morally flawed as to lack proper standing to hate and despise other human beings and to seek to hurt or destroy them. If any human being is to be utterly banished from the realm of benevolent concern (as hate would so banish) then only a morally superior being, God, is in a position to take such a stand.

Both of these arguments are ways of raising the question "Who are *we* to judge and thus to hate?" (Given how little we know and how morally flawed we are, is it not presumptuous of us to judge and hate? Is this not a clear example of self-deception and a sin of arrogance or pride?) In my view, neither of the arguments is conclusive as it stands; and yet there is a profound *caution* against hatred being expressed in each. Let me try to indicate what this may be.

Do we know enough to hate? Kant claims that we can never know for certain if another being is truly evil; for his acts may be motivated by reasons (perhaps honorable, perhaps insane) that do not come to light – *cannot* come to light if Kant's metaphysical view that moral motivation lies in a nonphysical noumenal realm is correct. Suppose we grant this. What lesson are we supposed to learn? – that we should never judge or condemn others at all, that we should never have criminal trials, that we should open the doors of all the jails? Surely such a response would be drastic and irrational, and Kant himself never suggests it. Although we may not have knowledge (in the sense of Cartesian certainty) of human evil and responsibility, we surely are able to form *reasonable beliefs* about such matters and are surely sometimes justified when we act on such beliefs. If we waited for Cartesian certainty, we would never act at all – in any area of our life. And this would be suicidal – both socially and personally.

What then is the point of Kant's epistemological caution

sponses are *in principle* permissible – unlike, say, sadism, which would surely be wrong even for God. Note also that the passage from *Romans* 12:19, far from being an argument against the desire for vengeance, is a *promise* of vengeance.

against hatred? I think it is this: Even though the necessities of maintaining civilized life and schemes of just cooperation require that we sometimes make and act on our best judgments of wrongdoing and responsibility (that we have trials and jails, in short), we should be very cautious about over-dramatizing and overmoralizing what we must (regretfully) do here by portraying it as some righteous cosmic drama – as a holy war against ultimate sin and evil. Such a view would, among other things, tempt us to dangerous excesses – excesses that would harm others through our overly severe (and thus unjust) treatment of them and harm us through our own corruption – as one is always corrupted if one presumes to play God. We should always be vividly aware of our limitations as human beings – and never more so than in cases where we can do great evil if we are not aware. Such a caution is particularly appropriate when directed toward one who is (or believes he is) a *victim* of wrongdoing. For such persons (as Simone Weil noted) have a natural tendency to make hasty judgments of responsibility, magnify the wrong done to them, and thus seek retribution out of all just proportion to what is actually appropriate. (This insight into human nature lies behind the old common law maxim that a man is not to be a judge in any controversy to which he is a party.) People sometimes get such matters exactly right; but, more typically, they get them wrong – more and more wrong the more wildly angry and filled with hatred they become. Because of this lesson in humility, cautions against hatred and actions motivated out of hatred are surely in order.

Are we pure enough to hate? Kant is not concerned merely to make the epistemological point that victims, being interested parties, may have their perceptions and judgments too clouded to be reliable haters. He also seeks to raise this *moral* caution against hatred: Even if it were possible to be absolutely sure of the iniquity of another person, possible to know exactly how much suffering his evil deserves, no one of us is sufficiently better than that person to be qualified to demand or inflict the suffering. If a stone may be cast only by the morally pure, none of us can ever – without hypocrisy or self-deception – cast a stone.

But is this a genuine obstacle to all hating – to all desires to inflict retributive hurt? Suppose I hate Jones because he has spitefully damaged the favorite piece in my art collection, and I want to see him suffer for having done this. I pause and consider the principle "Let him who is without sin cast the first stone," note accurately that I have never spitefully damaged a favorite object owned by anyone, and thus feel perfectly free to cast away. I am not morally perfect, of course, for I have in my time done several unnice things – suppose, for example, I once committed adultery. But how could this be relevant here – given that the occasion of my present hatred is what Jones did to my treasure and not anything about his sex life? Given that I am totally innocent ("without sin") with respect to the kinds of wrongs germane to the present case, may I not thus indulge my retributive hatred without any fear that I am a hypocrite or am engaged in self-deception? Are not both Jesus and Kant adequately answered by such a process of reflection?

I think not. The above response is too shallow, for it fails to reflect the kind of serious moral introspection that Jesus and Kant are attempting to provoke. The point is not to deny that many people lead lives that are both legally and morally correct. The point is rather to force such people to face honestly the question of *why* they have lived in such a way. Is it (as they would no doubt like to believe) because their inner characters manifest true integrity and are thus morally superior to those whose behavior has been less exemplary? Or is it, at least in part, a matter of what John Rawls has called "luck on the natural and social lottery"?[16] Perhaps, as Kant suggests, their favored upbringing and social circumstances, or the fact that

---

16 See Rawls, *supra* note 10, pp. 65 ff. See also my "Marxism and Retribution," *Philosophy and Public Affairs*, Volume 2, Number 3, Spring 1973, reprinted in *Retribution, Justice and Therapy*, *supra* note 12.

they have never been placed in situations where they have been similarly tempted, or their fear of being found out, has had considerably more to do with their compliance with the rules of law and morality than they would like to admit. Perhaps if they imagined themselves possessed of Gyges's Ring (a ring which, in Plato's myth in *Republic*, makes its wearer invisible), they would – if honest with themselves – have to admit that they would probably use the ring, not to perform anonymous acts of charity, but to perform some acts of considerable evil – acts comparable, perhaps, to the acts for which they often hate others. If they follow through honestly on this process of self-examination, they will have learned another important lesson in moral humility.

One does not, of course, want to let natural lottery arguments carry one too far down this road of moral humility, for an utter absorption in such considerations would spell the end of moral responsibility and the moral significance of human beings that is founded upon such responsibility – would, indeed, spell the end of one's own moral significance. Does not each person want to believe of himself, as a part of his pride in his human dignity, that he is *capable* of performing, freely and responsibly performing, evil acts that would quite properly earn for him the retributive hatred of others? And should he not at least sometimes extend this compliment to them? Albert Camus expressed this concern very forcefully when he wrote:

> I do not believe . . . that there is no responsibility in this world and that we must give way to that modern tendency to absolve everyone, victim and murderer, in the same confusion. Sentimental confusion is made up of cowardice rather than generosity and eventually justifies whatever is worst in this world. If you keep on excusing, you eventually give your blessing to the slave camp, to cowardly force, to organized executions, to the cynicism of the great political monsters: you finally hand over your brothers. This can be seen around us. But it so

happens, in the present state of the world, that the man of today wants laws and institutions suitable to a convalescent.[17]

The lessons of moral humility are thus not to be regarded as fatal objections to all hatred in all cases; and that is why I have referred to them as *cautions*. But they are deeply important cautions. They should make all morally reflective persons pause and at least think twice about their hatreds and the courses of action on which these hatreds tempt them to embark. For to commit to a strategy of retributive hatred is to take on strong assumptions of moral epistemology and moral qualification – assumptions that may prove insupportable. If they do, then one's hatreds, however motivated initially by a righteous desire to defend one's moral worth against assault, will have in fact accomplished nothing but a diminishing of that worth. This would leave one open to *self-hatred* – an outcome that any rational strategy would surely seek to avoid.

If we consider retributive hatred as a strategy, as Hampton – following Sartre – invites us so to consider all emotions, additional cautions against it emerge. If retributive hatred involves a desire to hurt others in a way comparable to the hurt they have inflicted, then one who is driven by such hatred will remain unfulfilled until the retributive hurt is in fact inflicted. But there are often serious (sometimes fatal) obstacles in the way of such an occurrence; and thus the hatred, deprived of an outlet, begins to poison a person from within. (An appreciation of the self-destructive potential of hatred and resentment, deprived of an outlet and thus forced

17 Albert Camus, "Reflections on the Guillotine," in *Resistance, Rebellion, and Death*, translated by Justin O'Brien (New York: Knopf, 1961), pp. 230–31. In Friedrich Dürrenmatt's short novel *Traps*, Alfredo Traps derives enormous feelings of agency and pride when he is persuaded at a mock trial that he has performed, with full moral responsibility, an evil act. He has never had such feelings before but has always simply regarded himself as a "helpless victim of the age." He thus resists (to the point of executing himself!) all attempts to argue that he was not responsible and thus should not be hated and punished.

into sublimation, was one of Nietzsche's great insights.)[18]
We speak of persons who "nurse a grudge" and often regard
them with a mixture of contempt and pity. But people would
not have to nurse their grudges if they would simply act
them out – *get even* – and one may well wonder why grudge
nursers do not simply do this and get the poison out of their
systems.

There are, I think, three reasons why persons may sometimes fail to act out their retributive hatreds:

(1) *It is impossible to get even.* The person you hate may be
protected and unreachable or may be indifferent to whatever
evil you might seek to inflict on him. Or it may for some
other reason be impossible to inflict upon him exactly what
you think he deserves, and you might be unable to calculate
a proper equivalent. (Hegel, in what in another writer might
be taken for humour, asks how we are to exact an eye for
an eye and a tooth for a tooth if we are dealing with an
eyeless and toothless destroyer of eyes and teeth.) Perhaps
the evil of your enemy is of such magnitude that no punishment you could inflict would seem properly proportional.
Or your enemy might even be dead. Thus nothing that you
could do would ever count, in fact or in your eyes, as your
getting even with him. Here we have impotent hatred – an
emotional state that is potentially, as Nietzsche argued, very
self-destructive.

(2) *It is too costly to get even.* Spinoza, in writing of the fear
of death, does not argue that it is irrational to fear death. He
argues rather that it is irrational to be *led* by this fear. His
central idea, relevant to many emotions, is that a rational
person will apply a kind of cost/benefit analysis to his mental
life and will not pursue any passion to the extent that he

18 "The slave revolt in morality begins when *ressentiment* itself becomes
creative and gives birth to values: the *ressentiment* of natures that are
denied true reaction, that of deeds, and compensate themselves with
an imaginary revenge . . . *Ressentiment* itself, if it should appear in the
noble man, consummates and exhausts itself in an immediate reaction,
and therefore does not *poison*." Friedrich Nietzsche, *On the Genealogy
of Morals*, Essay I, Section 10 (pp. 36 and 39 of the Walter Kaufmann
translation; New York: Random House, 1967).

loses more than he gains in the satisfaction of that passion. How absurd, argues Spinoza, if one becomes so consumed by the fear of death that one misses out on the many joys and positive benefits that life offers. And thus he writes:

> A free man, that is to say, a man who lives according to the dictates of reason alone, is not led by fear of death, but directly desires the good, that is to say, desires to act, to live, and to preserve his being in accordance with the principle of seeking his own profit. He thinks, therefore, of nothing less than death, and his wisdom is a meditation upon life.[19]

So too for hatred. Imagine the costs in time and trouble that might be involved in planning revenge, tracking down, and then adequately harming the object of one's hatred. And imagine the costs in liberty or damage judgments if illegal means are required and the costs in safety if your enemy is powerful or has powerful friends. The whole process could, in some cases, become one's life instead of being a part of one's life; and the hater would pay a price for being led by this passion comparable to the one that Spinoza warns against with respect to the fear of death. Lucky indeed the person for whom the legal system will institutionalize a portion of these feelings. For feelings of hatred can, in many cases, consume one's entire self. Thus it might be seen as a blessing – perhaps even divine grace, if one is given to those sorts of metaphors – to have the burden of hatred lifted from one's mind. For this reason forgiveness can bless the forgiver as much as or more than it blesses the one forgiven.[20]

---

19 *Ethics*, Four LXVII. I have explored this thought in some detail in my "Rationality and the Fear of Death," *The Monist*, Volume 59, Number 2, April 1976, reprinted in my *Retribution, Justice and Therapy, supra* note 12.

20 Next to Heinrich von Kleist's classic 1810 novella *Michael Kohlhaas*, Fay Weldon's recent novel *The Life and Loves of a She-Devil* is the best portrayal I know of both the charms and dangers of retributive and other hatreds. Ruth, the central character, driven by hatred and a desire for revenge, takes extraordinary steps (including reconstructive surgery and a general change of her very identity) to bring her enemies (her former husband and his new wife) low. When it is all over, she

(3) *Constraints are imposed by moral decency.* Suppose that, in a particular case, you know that you can pursue hatred and revenge without incurring any of the costs noted above. Suppose you have your enemy totally in your power, can inflict upon him exactly what you think he deserves, and can do so with impunity. Suppose that you even know the degree of his guilt and exactly what suffering he deserves and further suppose that you know that, even with Gyges's Ring, you would never have committed the wrong for which your enemy now stands hated. Such a case is no doubt impossible in the real world, but let us suppose as a thought experiment that you find yourself presented with one. Is this at last a case where no cautions apply and where hatred and revenge may be freely and happily indulged?

Even here I have doubts. Sometimes it will seem that the only adequate (i.e., proportional) punishment for the evil that a person has done requires that one, in inflicting the punishment, perform an act that one finds intrinsically immoral; and thus one will balk at its performance even under the banner of just retribution. For example: There is a sense in which it seems that the only punishment adequate for a torturer and mutilator is torture and mutilation; and yet one might well have grave and even final reservations about performing such acts no matter how proportionally appropriate they seem. One's repugnance at taking advantage of a person's utter vulnerability to treat him in ways one regards as morally indecent may thus take precedence over one's hatred of that person and one's just desire for revenge. For one may find that one accepts, on the level of personal morality, something very like the United States Constitution's Eighth Amendment ban on "cruel and unusual punishments" or

has brought them as low as she had ever desired. But, given the costs she has borne, it is unclear that she emerges a total winner. Some of her hatreds also seem to be in Jean Hampton's category of malicious hatreds and illustrate Hampton's important point that the strategy of malicious hatred is irrational because, the moment it accomplishes its aim of bringing another low, it makes it impossible to take any competitive pride or satisfaction in being superior to such a low person.

Kant's injunction that the punishment of a criminal must be "kept entirely free of any maltreatment that would make an abomination of the humanity residing in the person suffering it."[21] Thus one's retributive hatred, driven by moral outrage against an injustice suffered and by a desire to make sure the perpetrator of the outrage gets his just deserts, may be doomed by one's own better nature to go forever unfulfilled – in spite of adequate opportunity for accurate fulfillment – because one's inherent moral decency blocks the steps necessary to attain perfect retribution. Thus the moral person may settle for less than perfect retribution or for no retribution at all.

This concludes my set of cautions against hatred. Since I regard retributive hatred as in principle the natural, fitting, and proper response to certain instances of wrongdoing, I do not regard the passion itself as either immoral or irrational. (It is not – like malice or spite – the moral equivalent of a phobia.) I do, however, believe that it is generally both ir-

21 Immanuel Kant, *The Metaphysical Elements of Justice,* translated by John Ladd (Indianapolis: Bobbs-Merrill, 1965), p. 102. I have explored Kant's theory and the constitutional ban on cruel and unusual punishments in my "Cruel and Unusual Punishments," in *Retribution, Justice, and Therapy, supra* note 12. A slightly revised version of this appears at the close of Chapter 3 (pp. 138–57) in Jeffrie G. Murphy and Jules L. Coleman, *The Philosophy of Law: An Introduction to Jurisprudence* (Totowa, N.J.: Rowman and Allanheld, 1984).

In John Irving's novel *The Hotel New Hampshire,* the character Franny attempts to deal with her trauma as a gang rape victim by continually telling herself that the rape never touched "the me in me." She never achieves any real peace, however, until she manages to get at least partial revenge against the leader of the gang who raped her. But her inherent decency prevents her from getting total revenge, as decency has a way of doing.

In *Wild Justice: The Evolution of Revenge* (New York: Harper and Row, 1983), Susan Jacoby suggests that legal punishment, in addition to protecting society from the dangers of private vengeance, also gives victims the benefit of not being forced to act out in full certain violent aspects of their natures. She writes (p. 43): "When the burden of revenge is assigned to lawful authority, victims still have the psychic satisfaction of seeing their assailants' punishment, but society is protected from the violent passions of unchecked avengers and avengers themselves are protected from a weight that frequently proves too great for the more gentle side of human nature."

rational and immoral to be *led*, to use Spinoza's phrase, by this very dangerous and often blind passion. I have called the case against hatred a set of cautions; taken together these cautions constitute a body of reasons so profound that instances where it is acceptable to proceed in spite of them are, in my judgment, rare. Thus rational and moral beings would, I think, want, not a world utterly free of retributive hatred, but one where this passion is *both* respected *and* seen as potentially dangerous, as in great need of reflective and institutional restraint.

Adam Smith, admiring retributive hatred when "graceful and agreeable" but realizing that this passion "must be brought down to a pitch much lower than that to which undisciplined nature would raise [it]," eloquently puts his balanced and measured case for the passion in words on which I could not improve:

> How many things are requisite to render the gratification of resentment completely agreeable, and to make the spectator thoroughly sympathize with our revenge? The provocation must first of all be such that we should become contemptible, and be exposed to perpetual insults, if we did not, in some measure, resent it. Smaller offenses are always better neglected; nor is there any thing more despicable than that forward and captious humour which takes fire upon every slight occasion of quarrel. We should resent more from a sense of the propriety of resentment, from a sense that mankind expect and require it of us, than because we feel in ourselves the furies of that disagreeable passion. There is no passion, of which the human mind is capable, concerning whose justness we ought to be so doubtful, concerning whose indulgence we ought so carefully to consult our natural sense of propriety, or so diligently to consider what will be the sentiments of the cool and impartial spectator. Magnanimity, or a regard to maintain our own rank and dignity in society, is the only motive which can ennoble the expressions of this disagreeable passion. This motive must characterize our whole style and deportment. These must be plain, open, and direct; free from petulance and low scurrility, but generous, candid, and full of all proper regards, even for the person who has offended us.

374

It must appear, in short, from our whole manner, without our labouring affectedly to express it, that passion has not extinguished our humanity; and that if we yield to the dictates of revenge, it is with reluctance, from necessity, and in consequence of great and repeated provocations. When resentment is guarded and qualified in this manner, it may be admitted to be even generous and noble.[22]

22 Adam Smith, *The Theory of Moral Sentiments* (1759; Indianapolis: Liberty Press, 1982), p. 38. Smith speaks of resentment; but, since he views this passion as involving a desire for revenge, it is closer to what I have called retributive hatred. Smith also gives a central place to concerns about rank and status, and this might prompt some to dismiss his account of justified resentment as simply bourgeois prejudice. This, I think, would be a mistake. The status in question may be viewed as moral status (and thus a clear object of legitimate concern) and such status, since we are social creatures, may in large part depend upon how others treat and regard us – may depend upon what John Rawls calls the social dimension of self-respect. We should not, in short, trivialize all status worries by assuming that they all must be on a par with, for example, such inane concerns as where one is to be seated at a formal dinner.

Of course, some persons (e.g., Socrates and Jesus) may claim that they derive their entire sense of their worth from non-social factors – in Jesus's case that he was the son of God and, for Christians perhaps, that they are created in God's image and that their true and ultimate worth – their destiny – is to be found in the hereafter. Such persons could then reject utterly the social status dimension of moral worth that I find present in such writers as Aristotle, Smith, Hume, and Rawls. There might, however, be a price for such rejection – e.g., could this degree of insulation from others be compatible with true love or friendship or with meaningful membership in any human relationship or community? Recall Jesus's remark to his mother (*John* 2:4): "Woman, what have I to do with thee?"

Sentiments similar to Smith's were earlier expressed by Aristotle – another thinker who is not overly quick in expressing total condemnation of any natural human passion: "The person who is angry at the right things and towards the right people, and also in the right way, at the right time, and for the right length of time, is praised. . . . The deficiency – a sort of inirascibility or whatever it is – is blamed, since people who are not angered [in this way] all seem to be foolish. For such a person seems to be insensible and to feel no pain. Since he is not angered, he does not seem to be the sort to defend himself; and such willingness to accept insults to oneself and to overlook insults to one's family and friends is slavish" (*Nicomachean Ethics*, 1125b ff., translated by Terence Irwin, Indianapolis: Hackett Publishing Company, 1985).

As both Smith and Aristotle make clear, it is not mandatory (only

In closing, let me briefly just note my awareness of one final concern that may be felt about the account of retributive hatred that I have been developing. Someone might argue that there is no point in discussing the rationality or legitimacy of such hatred because hatred is an *emotion* and it makes no sense to speak of emotions in terms of rationality or legitimacy – and certainly no sense to talk about them as if they could be brought under our voluntary control. No, such a skeptic might argue, the passions are simply *givens* – brute facts about our psychological nature that must simply be accepted and planned around but that can never be rationally assessed or rationally controlled.

I believe that this attack on my enterprise involves many deep confusions – e.g., a confusion of emotions with sensations. I have written on the issue of reason and the passions elsewhere and am doing some more work on the issue at the moment.[23] I do not have space to develop my ideas on this topic in the present context, but I hope to elaborate on them in print in the future. Although I have no doubt that my analysis of resentment and retributive hatred presupposes views on action theory and the philosophy of mind that are controversial, it is my belief and hope that these views are ultimately supportable. If they are not, then the reader is of course free to resent or even hate me for having wasted his time.

permissible) to inflict the hurt that will constitute the proper revenge. They also make clear that the hurt constituting the proper revenge must never exceed what is properly proportional to the injury and will often involve no more than the hurt feelings or embarrassment that the wrongdoer will experience when righteous anger or public rebuke is directed toward him. Another important point that they also make is that a person who is large of spirit will try to pass off minor injuries and insults and will indulge himself in retributive hatred only rarely and as a last resort.

23 See my "Rationality and the Fear of Death," *supra* note 17, and my forthcoming "Rejoinder to Morris," *supra* note 8.

Chapter 11

A new theory of retribution

JEAN HAMPTON

"One day, a serf-boy, a little boy of eight, threw a
stone in play and hurt the paw of the General's favorite hound. 'Why is my favorite dog lame?' He was
told that the boy had thrown a stone at it and hurt
his paw. 'Oh, so it's you, is it?' said the General looking him up and down. 'Take him!' They took him.
They took him away from his mother, and he spent
the night in the lock-up. Early next morning the General, in full dress, went out hunting. He mounted his
horse, surrounded by his hangers-on, his whips, and
his huntsmen, all mounted. His house-serfs were all
mustered to teach them a lesson, and in front of them
all stood the child's mother. The boy was brought out
of the lock-up. It was a bleak, cold, misty autumn
day, a perfect day for hunting. The General ordered
the boy to be undressed. The little boy was stripped
naked. He shivered, panic-stricken and not daring to
utter a sound. 'Make him run!' ordered the General.
'Run, run!' the whips shouted at him. The boy ran.
'Sick him!' bawled the General, and set the whole
pack of borzoi hounds on him. They hunted the child
down before the eyes of his mother, and the hounds
tore him to pieces. . . . Well, what was one to do with
[the General]? . . . "
"Shoot him!" Alyosha said softly. . . .
Fyodor Dostoevsky, *The Brothers Karamazov*

This essay is based on two chapters that I wrote in *Forgiveness and Mercy*,
by Jeffrie G. Murphy and Jean Hampton (Cambridge: Cambridge University Press, 1988). See in particular "Forgiveness, Resentment and Hatred,"
chap. 2, and "The Retributive Idea," chap. 4.

JEAN HAMPTON

In *The Brothers Karamazov* Alyosha Karamazov reluctantly admits that he, like his brother, is familiar with the desire to punish with pain the misdeeds of an evildoer, not simply to deter him or others from committing similar actions again, but also because the evildoer "deserves" it. Philosophers have called this reason for punishment "retribution." But they have been notoriously unable to satisfy critics of the idea that retribution is either a coherent or a justifiable reason for inflicting pain. In this essay I shall attempt a new interpretation of what we really want when we demand retribution. On a problem this hard, one hesitates to claim success at resolution, but I believe this new interpretation at least merits consideration as a promising approach to explaining and justifying retributive punishment.

I. THE PROBLEM WITH RETRIBUTION

In part because retributivists have been at a loss to explain their notion of desert, I have proposed, along with others,[1] that retribution may be nothing more than revenge. The retributivist's *lex talionis*, his "eye for an eye, tooth for a tooth" conception of punishment, sounds like a restatement of the kind of vengeance which victims frequently want. The wrongdoer inflicts one pain, the victim (or the society which represents him) reciprocates with a second. Aren't both parties violent, disrespectful of the other's worth, cruel? And if this is so, how can the second "vengeful" harmdoer be any less worthy of moral criticism than the first?

Jeffrie Murphy's justification of retribution as a kind of hatred plays into the hands of such critics.[2] If my call for the punishment of my offender is simply an expression of my hate for him, doesn't that show rather decisively that my

---

1 See my "Moral Education Theory of Punishment," *Philosophy and Public Affairs* (Summer 1984), vol. 13, pp. 208–238. And note that the Supreme Court Justices' decision in Furman vs. Georgia characterized retribution as "naked vengeance" arising from a need of our "baser selves" (408 US 238, 1972; see pp. 304 and 345).
2 See his "Retributive Hatred," this volume.

retributive sentiments are merely the sentiments of revenge, vindictiveness, abusive anger?

In response, Murphy presents us with victims of wrong-doings whose interest in harming their assailants does not seem, at least at first glance, spiteful or malicious in character. There is Franny, the character in Irving's *The Hotel New Hampshire* who can only achieve peace after suffering the trauma of gang rape by causing harm to the leader of the gang who raped her.[3] And there are the real-life cases of the victims of the Camelback rapist, who vigorously campaigned for his receiving the maximum sentence allowed by law, outraged at the thought that his punishment should be anything short of severe given what he had done to them. Murphy chides those who would criticize these women for such feelings, contending that, given what the rapist did to them, their demand that he suffer great pain is "natural, fitting, and proper."[4] Certainly we can sympathize with these women, and share their outrage at this rapist's deeds. And we may experience the same sort of outrage if we dwell on personal experiences in which others have badly wronged us. But people who angrily insist on the intense suffering of their wrongdoers do not strike us as *noble* or in any way exceptionally meritorious (in contrast, for example, to people such as Jesus when they "forgive from the cross"). Perhaps the only reason we are reluctant to criticize these victims for their hatefulness is because we believe they are already experiencing too much pain to make it right to inflict any more. Moreover, when Murphy describes what Franny wants when she experiences what he takes to be the retributive emotion, he uses the word "revenge,"[5] suggesting once again that her emotion is in fact malicious hatred which merits moral criticism.

Proponents of retribution maintain, in the face of such doubts, that there can be something profoundly ignoble,

---

3 Ibid., fn. 21, p. 373.
4 Ibid., pp. 359–360.
5 Ibid., fn. 21, p. 373.

even despicable, about someone who would block or deny the retributivist response following at least *some* crimes. Consider, for example, the story told by Ivan to his brother Alyosha in *The Brothers Karamazov*, quoted at the beginning of this chapter. How could even the most loving Christian saint resist the thought that a man who would set dogs on an innocent child and force his mother to watch the boy being torn to pieces should die? Turning the other cheek towards such a monster seems villainous in and of itself.

Does Christianity insist on such villainy? One might well think so if one notes Jesus's hostility to the *lex talionis*:

> "You have learned that they were told, 'Eye for eye, tooth for tooth.' But what I tell you is this: Do not set yourself against the man who wrongs you. . . . You have heard that they were told 'Love your neighbor, hate your enemy.' But what I tell you is this: Love your enemy and pray for your persecutors: only so can you be children of your heavenly father, who makes the sun rise on the good and the bad alike, and sends the rain on the honest and dishonest." (Matt. 5: 38–39, 43–46)

The sunshine and the rain are for us all, because God loves us as his children. If we are to follow the Lord's example, must we strive not to hurt those who are his beloved children, and our own spiritual brothers and sisters, no matter what they do to us?

Perhaps not. One must beware of presenting too saccharine a portrait of Christianity's requirements, given other things that Jesus does and says. There is the famous incident in which he angrily overthrows the tables of the money-changers in the temple in Jerusalem (Matt. 21: 12–13); there are his ruthless judgements of the scribes and Pharisees: " 'Woe unto you, scribes and Pharisees, hypocrites! For ye are like unto white-washed sepulchres, which outwardly appear beautiful, but inwardly are full of dead men's bones, and of all uncleanness' " (Matt. 23: 27–28); and there is his invocation of hell: " 'Ye serpents, ye offspring of vipers [said to the Pharisees], how shall ye escape the judgement of hell?' " (Matt. 23: 33). Doesn't the anger in these deeds and words arise from his judgement that these people are wicked and deserve to suffer, at least the fire of his words, and maybe even the fires of hell? (E.g., see Luke 13: 1–5, or Matt. 5: 29–30.)

As Dostoevsky appreciated, it is hard for even the most stalwart Christian saint to resist the pull of retribution, and Jesus himself may not have wanted that pull to be resisted. But those who worry about whether or not this idea is legitimate need to be reassured that they are not endorsing vengeful violence. And they have received little help in allaying those worries from philosophical defenders intent on explaining its legitimacy.

For example, it is common for such defenders to insist that there is no telos or goal behind the suffering retributivists want: it is simply desired, they say, because it is supposed to be "fitting" or "suitable" or "right." And in response to queries about *why* suffering is suitable for wrongdoers, such defenders commonly insist that this question has no answer. It is supposed to be bedrock intuition that, at the very least, those who are not guilty ought not to suffer pain, and more positively, that those who are guilty deserve to suffer in proportion to the pain they have caused. J.L. Mackie claims that such ideas have for us an "immediate, underived moral appeal or moral authority."[6] But those suspicious of retribution are generally unpersuaded by this kind of defense. Presumably they are the people who either do not find this firm "bedrock intuition" inside themselves or are suspicious of its authority (fearful that it may only be vengeance masquerading), and thus cannot be convinced by an unanalyzed appeal to it.

Accordingly, some retributivists have attempted to explain the supposed fittingness of inflicting suffering on a wrongdoer, with dubious results. For example, Nozick proposes that the punishment represents a kind of "linkage" between

---

6 J.L. Mackie, "Morality and the Retributive Emotions," *Criminal Justice Ethics* (1982), vol. 1, no. 1, p. 3.

the criminal and "right values."[7] But why is inflicting pain on someone a way of effecting this linkage? Why isn't the infliction of a pleasurable experience for the sake of the crime just as good a way of linking the wrongdoer with these right values? If Nozick explains the linkage of pain with crime by saying that the pain is necessary to convey to the criminal that his actions were wrong, then he has answered the question but lost his retributive theory, putting forward instead a variation of the theory justifying punishment as moral education.[8] Other philosophers, such as Hegel, speak of punishment as a way of annulling or cancelling the crime, and hence as "deserved" for that reason.[9] But although these words have a nice metaphorical ring to them, it is hard to see how they can be given a literal force that will explain the retributivist's concept of desert. As Mackie notes, punishment cannot eliminate crimes in any literal sense because future events never cause past events not to have happened.[10]

Mackie himself admits that there does not seem any readily understandable way of making conceptual sense out of retribution and proposes an evolutionary – and merely explanatory – derivation of it as a *feeling* that has evolved in our species. Even as dogs snarl and cats scratch at those who attack them, human beings, according to Mackie, also feel the emotional urge to "hit" those who hurt them. Such "hitting" is unreasoned and unreasoning – it is instinctive in just

7 Robert Nozick, *Philosophical Investigations* (Cambridge, MA: Harvard University Press, 1982), pp. 374 ff.
8 See Herbert Morris, "The Paternalistic Theory of Punishment," in J. Murphy, ed., *Punishment and Rehabilitation* (Belmont, CA: Wadsworth, 1985); and Hampton, "Moral Education Theory of Punishment."
9 See his *Philosophy of Right*, ed. T.M. Knox (Oxford: Oxford University Press, 1976).
10 See Mackie, "Morality and the Retributive Emotions," p. 4. Both Mackie and Herbert Fingarette (the latter in "Punishment and Suffering," *Proceedings of the American Philosophical Association*, 1977) review a variety of retributivist arguments in defense of the idea that wrongdoers deserve to suffer, all of which appear to come up short. Each also makes a positive proposal of his own. I consider Mackie's below and Fingarette's in footnote 26.

the way that a snarl or a bite following a harm is instinctive in other mammals. So we snap at relatives, verbally spar with colleagues, and some of us even physically attack those who have hurt us. Mackie argues that this emotional response exists within us because it encourages cooperation among human beings by introducing a negative sanction for non-cooperation that has been selected for and refined in our very social species. So this response is not something one engages in so that one might deter exploiters in the future; instead it is an instinct for attack following a harm which is engaged in for *no* reason, but which has been implanted in one as a member of the human species because of its deterring consequences. The instinct itself isn't teleological, but its existence in the human being is explained by the fact that it furthers this creature's goal of survival.

Mackie liked the way this explanation of retribution fit with advocates' defense of it as foundational while also making teleological sense of it. But appealing though the explanation is, I would argue that it is at best incomplete because it denies to retribution any cognitive content. And cognitive content is precisely what those who defend retribution must understand the response to have if retribution is to *justify* the infliction of harm on wrongdoers. A primitive urge, which is all the strike-back response could be in other mammals, cannot by itself justify anything. Mackie himself realizes this, and so justifies the harm which his retributive sentiment calls for by appealing to the evolutionary advantages of the sentiment's existence in human beings; so for Mackie *the sentiment itself* doesn't justify the harm. Yet traditional retributivists have insisted that retribution is an idea which does have justificatory force in and of itself: that wrongdoers deserve to suffer is supposed to be a good *reason* for inflicting harm on them.

So while I believe Mackie is right that there is a natural instinct for "striking back" at harmdoers that frequently accompanies (although need not accompany) our attempts to inflict pain on those who wrong us, I would also argue that he is not correct to think that this is *all* retribution is. The

383

concept of retributive desert, which is more than an instinct or feeling, and which animals do not have, has once again escaped analysis.

A different defense of retribution has been advocated by Herbert Morris.[11] On this view, retribution is understood as a concept linked to the idea of *distributive justice*. Laws are understood as constraints on behavior which society finds collectively beneficial; individuals who break those laws for individually rational reasons are subverting the system for private gain in a way that makes them similar to free riders – that is, people who derive gain from a collective good without paying any cost for that good. Punishment of these free riders is a way to "even up the score": the legal system takes, via pain, the benefit that these individuals derived from their lawbreaking. But what is this benefit? If it is the monetary gain from the crime, then compensation of the victim would be sufficient to take away the wrongdoer's benefit. Yet the retributivist would desire punishment over and above any compensation provided by, say, a thief to her victim. Moreover, on this view it would make no sense to punish unsuccessful offenders.

So perhaps the criminal's benefit which the punishment is supposed to take away is the elevation of utility that comes from being able to break off the restraints of society and pursue one's own good. On this view, the thief must be punished even after he has been made to compensate his victim in order to take from him the advantage that comes from the lawbreaking itself. One immediate problem with this position is that because all lawbreakers have benefitted in the same way and (it seems) to the same extent by throwing off the restraints of law, the position seems to require that all lawbreakers receive the same punishment. To avoid this problem an advocate of the position would have to develop a theory that explained how those who broke gravely important laws derived more benefit than those who broke

11 See Herbert Morris, "Persons and Punishment," in Murphy, *Punishment and Rehabilitation.*

384

less serious laws, so that the former deserved more punishment than the latter.

Suppose for the sake of argument that such a theory could be developed.[12] While there are some crimes which this position, supplemented by such a theory, might be thought to suit, e.g. thefts, embezzlements, and property crimes generally, there are other crimes which make the position look uncomfortably strange – even repulsive. Consider the crime of rape. Are we to understand that the reason we punish rapists is that we believe they derived a benefit from being able to rape (which is greater than that gained by those who merely rob cars or speed on the highway) that we wish *we* could have but which we prevent ourselves from enjoying because we believe such conduct, when performed on a widespread basis, is collectively disadvantageous? Or consider murder: do we envy the murderer his freedom to satisfy his desires through killing, and punish him merely because we seek to take from him the advantage of being unrestrained in pursuit of his murderous desires, where that restraint is one which we would willingly throw off but for our recognition that it is mutually advantageous? Such suggestions seem ridiculous. The idea that punishment is simply the taking away of the *advantages* which rapists or murderers have in virtue of being unrestrained presupposes that we accept that their actions (or the actions' consequences) are, at least in certain circumstances, inherently desirable and rational, and that we object to them only because, if performed by everyone, they would be collectively harmful. Hence it is a theory presupposing a position on the nature of criminal law and criminal acts which is too awful to be right.

But perhaps we can make it less awful.[13] Suppose we say, not that the criminal gets an advantage from his crime, but that when he commits a crime he isn't paying the *cost* that

12 See George Sher, *Desert* (Princeton: Princeton University Press, 1987), which tries to do this.
13 This line of argument was suggested to me by Richard Gale.

we are paying when we obey the law. Again, this makes him, in a different way, a free rider, because he enjoys the benefits of our cost-paying while not paying costs himself. But once again, although this theory may explain, in part, the nature of our condemnation of those who violate various sorts of property or tax laws, it does a poor job of accounting for the condemnation of those who violate persons. If I refrain from murdering you, am I really imposing a cost on myself for the sake of creating a collectively advantageous social order? If I become angry at you for murdering, is my anger solely or even primarily about the fact that you haven't paid the cost I've paid but have enjoyed the fact that I and others have paid it? Once again, such a view seems badly wrong.

But the fact that it is wrong teaches us something important: This theory of retribution fails in a fully adequate way to link our condemnation of a wrongdoer *to that which makes his conduct wrong.*[14] The *right* theory of retribution is one that will be able to do just that. Joel Feinberg has proposed that punishment has an expressive function.[15] I want to pursue that idea by developing a theory that explains retributive punishment as expressive of the wrongfulness of the criminal act being punished. However, in order to do that, we must have a theory that explains what it is that makes punishable conduct not merely harmful or injurious but also wrong. I will now try to develop such a theory.

II. THE MESSAGE IMPLICIT IN WRONGDOING

What is it that really bothers us about being not merely harmed but also wronged? It is not simply the fact that wrongdoings threaten or produce physical or psychological

---

14 Except perhaps for property crimes. The free-rider explanation might provide at least part of the reason why these sorts of actions are immoral, accounting for the plausibility of the theory when it is applied to them.

15 Joel Feinberg, "The Expressive Function of Punishment," *Doing and Deserving* (Princeton: Princeton University Press, 1970).

damage, or damage to our careers, interests, or families. However much we may sorrow over our bad fortune, when the same damage is threatened or produced by natural forces or by accidents, we do not experience that special anger that comes from having been *insulted*. When someone wrongs another, she does not regard her victim as the sort of person who is valuable enough to require better treatment. Whereas nature cannot treat us in accord with our moral value, we believe other human beings are able and required to do so. Hence, when they do not, we are insulted in the sense that we believe they have ignored the high standing which that value gives us. As Murphy notes,

> One reason we so deeply resent moral injuries done to us is not simply that they hurt us in some tangible or sensible way; it is because such injuries are also *messages* – symbolic communications. They are ways a wrongdoer has of saying to us "I count and you do not," "I can use you for my purposes" or "I am here up high and you are there down below." Intentional wrongdoing *insults* us and attempts (sometimes successfully) to degrade us – and thus it involves a kind of injury that is not merely tangible and sensible. It is moral injury; and we care about such injury.[16]

But to understand exactly what a wrongdoing involves, we must appreciate that there are various ways of being "lowered."

Consider Murphy's characterization of the message sent by the wrongdoer to his victim; the wrongdoer is saying that she is not *worth* enough for him to accord her better treatment. Now there are (at least) the following two ways that a victim can respond to this message: she can reject it as wrong and hence regard the action as inappropriate given what she believes to be her true (high) worth, or she can worry (or even believe) that the wrongdoer is right, that she

16 Murphy, "Forgiveness and Resentment," in Murphy and Hampton, *Forgiveness and Mercy*, p. 28.

really isn't worth enough to warrant better treatment, so that his action is permissible given her lower worth.

If she responds in the first way, she perceives herself to have suffered *no literal degradation* as a result of the wrongdoing. Her high value is, she believes, unchanged despite the action. But she is nonetheless *demeaned* in the sense that she has been forced to endure treatment that is too low for her. So there is a difference between being demeaned and being literally lowered in value. A prince who is mistaken for a pauper and who therefore fails to receive royal treatment will regard this treatment as demeaning not because he will believe or even worry that the treatment literally makes him into a pauper and so causes him to lose his princely status, but because he will believe that the treatment is too low for him *given* that princely status. It is because he believes that he is *not* lower in status that he regards the treatment as insulting. Similarly, a victim who is demeaned by an action believes he has experienced treatment which is insufficiently respectful of his value. Hence he finds the treatment insulting. The degree to which he is demeaned is the degree to which the treatment he experiences is too low for him.

Not to give people treatment appropriate to their value (i.e., not to give people the treatment they deserve) is to injure them. But this "objective" injury (an injury based upon what one takes the correct moral or societal facts about self-worth to be) is usually – although it need not be – associated with a subjective injury. If the person who has been wrongly treated *knows* this, then he will not *be* but *feel* insulted. Moreover, he will probably feel pain from the insult, a pain with which we are all too familiar. Why "dishonoring" treatment can hurt us like this is something for which I do not have a reason-based explanation. Perhaps it is not the sort of thing which admits of a reason-based explanation.

The objective injury may not, to an observer's eye, correspond with a victim's subjective experience of injury. The latter can be seen to be too great or not great enough, and criticism of it presupposes that one believes the victim has accorded himself the wrong value. Thus, our view, or the victim's view, of when he is demeaned depends upon the value which our, or his, "theory of human worth" accords him.

A theory of human worth tells one what sort of treatment is appropriate or required or prohibited for certain types of individuals on the basis of an assessment of *how valuable* these individuals are. Some philosophers follow Hobbes in thinking that any assessments of our value as individuals can only be instrumental; "The value, or worth, of a man is, as of all other things, his price; that is to say, so much as would be given for the use of his power."[17] Other philosophers insist that regardless of our price, the value which determines the kind of respect which we should be accorded as persons is non-instrumental and objective. For example, according to Kant, in virtue of having the property of rationality it is a fact that we are intrinsically valuable as ends-in-ourselves, so that we are all equal in worth, and have the same rank relative to one another.

But there are also objective theories of our intrinsic worth which do not accord all of us equal rank; consider, for example, views of human beings which propose that certain people, in virtue of being members of a race or caste or sex, are higher in value and deserving of better treatment than human beings who are of a different race, or caste, or sex. The fact that women are more frequent targets than men for certain kinds of violence shows that many assailants see males, but not females, as having a value that rules out the infliction of this sort of violence. And those human beings (e.g. blacks in America) who have suffered unequal treatment, even slavery, know what it is like to be accorded value and rank which are considerably lower than those bestowed on other human beings (and which, in extreme cases, can be more like those accorded to animals).

One's theory of human worth may also be non-objective, denying that there are any properties in virtue of which it is

17 Thomas Hobbes, *Leviathan*, ed. C.B. Macpherson (Harmondsworth: Penguin, 1965), chap. 10, par. 16.

389

a fact that we have a certain intrinsic value and rank among our fellows. A theory of this sort may see any existing notions of relative standing based on assessments of "intrinsic worth" as, in reality, a societal invention, connected with or perhaps even the same as social standing in that culture. Alternatively, it might be perceived as a ranking that reflects subjective assessments of instrumental value; or as a ranking which varies from individual to individual depending upon what properties each uses to construct it and his judgement of the extent to which individuals manifest these properties.

Theories of human worth can also differ in the *way* that worth is assigned. It can be assigned on the basis of certain criteria that are essentially non-competitive, as when a professor assigns grades to students by determining the "level" of their work according to certain criteria in such a way that it is possible in theory for every student to get an A. Or it can be assigned using criteria that are inherently competitive, as when a professor compares her students to one another and assigns a higher rank to those who do better in the comparison than to those who do worse. Similarly, theories of human worth may evaluate people to see whether or not they meet non-competitive criteria required for a certain value and rank (e.g., do they qualify as ends-in-themselves, as natural slaves?), or people may be assessed to see how far they are better or worse than one another, such that their particular positions can be determined on a scale ranking them in value. In what follows, when I speak of people losing "value" or losing "rank," I intend these phrases to be neutral between the two grading systems.

The evidence which one takes to count as determining rank is also part of one's theory of human worth. There are a variety of scales that measure us: e.g., tennis rankings, social rankings, intelligence rankings, rankings of work in a classroom. But such rankings need not be taken by us (or by others) to have anything to do with our worth as persons. For example, a prince might think he is equal in intrinsic worth to a pauper, but nonetheless insist that he receive treatment which recognizes his superior socio-political rank.

On the other hand a philosopher might take great exception to an action which he interprets as slighting his considerable rank in the philosophical community because he believes that rank measures his worth as an individual. Evaluations of our ability as a parent, or as an athlete, or as an artist, may or may not be regarded as relevant to the determination of our over-all value as persons, i.e., as an indication of the extent to which we are "important" or "impressive" as persons. What we take to be evidence of people's value is therefore part of our theory of what human value is.

Finally, whether or not we can gain or lose value (and thus rank) is part of this theory. Kant would insist that there is no way human beings can gain in value, and no way for them to lose their value unless their capacity to reason (and thus their very humanity) is badly damaged or destroyed. In contrast, Hobbes would insist that insofar as our value is instrumental, it is relatively easy for us to gain or lose worth since these gains and losses depend on the skills, traits, and abilities which we gain or lose and on how the market prices these skills, traits, and abilities.

Which theory of human worth is, properly speaking, a *moral* theory is controversial. People in this society are apt to think that only some version of an egalitarian theory of human worth (e.g. that of Kant) can qualify as moral. But regardless of whether or not any hierarchical theory of worth merits the label "moral," it is still the sort of theory which human beings tend to find enormously attactive and which exerts political and social pressure both in our society and in more consciously caste-based societies. Indeed, it may be that many of us are only paying lip service to the egalitarian theories of worth which we tend to commend as appropriate foundations for our moral theorizing.

So to summarize the discussion above: a theory of human worth involves, first, a conception of what it is for a human being to be valuable or of worth (e.g., is he of instrumental value? or intrinsically valuable?); second, a conception of how, in virtue of their value, human beings should be ranked relative to one another (e.g., must they be ranked as equals?

or should some be ranked higher than others?) where an individual's rank determines her "standing" relative to other people; third, a conception of how evidence for that value is to be ascertained such that rank can be determined (e.g., competitively? non-competitively? with reference to what other measuring scales – e.g., job performance, athletic prowess, degree of virtue?); and fourth, a theory of how (if at all) human beings can gain or lose value (and thereby rank).

A person's view of her value and relative rank among her fellows determines whether or not an action will be interpreted by her as demeaning. For example, she can feel demeaned by another's action if she believes that she is the superior of this person but has received treatment that accords her mere equality. A white person who is forced to sit next to a black person on a bus might believe this demeans her by making it appear that they are of equal rank and value, so that they should be accorded equal treatment. Alternatively, one's theory can prevent one from feeling demeaned by treatment which seems, given *our* view of her value, demeaning. A rape counsellor once told me of a woman who failed to tell anyone that she had been raped by a man she knew because she thought this was the sort of thing women had to "take" from men.

This rape victim is actually an example of someone who has suffered a more severe kind of injury than simply being demeaned. Prior to the rape she received treatment persuading her that her value as a woman did not rule out this treatment by men. She is like a princess who believes, after receiving treatment appropriate only for a pauper, that she really is a pauper. Such a person cannot feel demeaned because she has already suffered injury to her sense of self-worth. I will speak of this injury as the experience of *diminishment* following a wrongdoing. There are two ways in which one can feel, and believe oneself to be, diminished.

The first way, which I will call "revealed diminishment," involves a person taking the action as *evidence* that her value and rank are lower than she thought: this will lead her to worry that the wrongdoer's message may be right and that

she has incorrectly accorded herself a value and rank, associated with a certain level of treatment, which she does
not warrant. Note that she does not believe the action has
effected a lowering of value and rank (so that, once again, it
has not literally degraded her); instead she worries that it
has *revealed* a rank that is lower than she thought. So what
is lowered is her self-esteem.[18] Whereas someone who only
experiences what she takes to be demeaning treatment will
be quite sure that this treatment is too low for her, someone
who feels diminished in this sense has received treatment
that raises in her own mind the possibility that her estimate
of her own value and rank may be incorrectly high. The
higher the victim's degree of belief in this possibility, the
more severe the injury to her self-esteem. If her faith in her
own high worth is not completely undermined, she will still
have some degree of belief that the wrongdoer's treatment
of her was inappropriate given that high worth, and hence
will believe (to that extent) that she has been demeaned. But
to the extent that her sense of self-worth is shaken, any
emotional protest of the insult will be mixed in her with the

18 In "How to Distinguish Self-Respect from Self-Esteem" (in *Philosophy
and Public Affairs*, Fall 1981, vol. 10, no. 4, pp. 346–60) David Sachs
separates "self-respect" from "self-esteem." The discussion above
does not make use of that distinction; esteem and respect for oneself
are taken to be the same thing. One might separate them, however,
if one thought that a person could gain or lose self-esteem while
maintaining the same respect for herself as a human being. Note that
this way of talking presupposes a rather Kantian theory of human
worth which makes someone's value objective, permanent, and un-
changing for as long as she remains a person, but which makes her
achievements, e.g. on the job, or in her avocation, or her moral performance, that which determines her esteem for herself and which
can change quite considerably over her lifetime. On this view, such
measures of excellence are held to be irrelevant to the determination
of one's worth as a person and it is that worth which is what one
respects in oneself. To the extent that this sort of theory of human
worth is embraced by a community, Sachs's distinction makes sense,
but it need not be embraced. Hence in my discussion, I try to be as
neutral as possible and so refrain from making a distinction that some
theorists would find problematic: "self-esteem" and "self-respect" are
thus treated as synonyms. Each refers to one's assessment of one's
own value.

fear that the action wasn't an insult (or wasn't very much of an insult) after all.

The second way of feeling diminished, which I call "actual diminishment," involves taking the immoral action to have *done* something to *change* one's moral value, so that the action quite literally degrades one. For example, a victim can come to fear that he has lost value, and so rank, if he interprets the assault as a "loss" to the wrongdoer which makes him "not as good as" she is in the way that a boxer's loss to another in the ring will result in his being ranked lower than the victor. Or he may fear that the action effects his degradation through the physical or psychological harms it has caused. There are certain ideals current in our society towards which we strive: for example, being the ideal athlete, the perfect mother, a "real" man. Actions can rob us of properties necessary to realize these ideals. A man paralysed from the waist down by a gun-shot wound can feel that the paralysis robs him of his manhood, or destroys his athletic dreams. A woman whose injuries mean that she can no longer bear children can feel that she has become a biological failure as a female. Feeling lowered in quality (i.e., losing ground relative to one's ideal) as a result of these injuries does not, in and of itself, mean feeling that one has suffered a loss of value as a human being. But such injuries can be linked by these victims (falsely, most of us think) to their worth as persons; they may worry or even believe that the injury from the action which makes them less than their ideal thereby makes them less valuable as persons, so that they no longer merit the same kind of respectful treatment that they did before the injury. Once again, this form of diminishment comes in degrees. To the extent that the action has shaken one's confidence in that value and rank, it has also diminished one. If it destroys all such confidence, the diminishment is complete.

This second form of diminishment, which is the experience of having been literally degraded, is the subjective experience of something one takes to be objectively possible. Notice that if one accepts an egalitarian theory of human worth, one will not believe that such degradation can occur. So the objective injury (if it exists) may or may not go along with the subjective experience of such injury.

Is degradation or diminishment (in either sense) immoral? To answer this question, we need an analysis of what makes a human action not only a harm to a person but a *wrong*, and the preceding discussion provides us with one:

A person wrongs another if and only if (while acting as a responsible agent) she treats him in a way that is objectively demeaning.[19]

So on this definition responsible agents commit wrongs, as opposed to mere harms, if (but only if) doing these things is itself objectively *demeaning*, i.e., *objectively disrespectful of these individuals' worth*. And such disrespect must be measured by an objective yardstick. "Objective" here simply means "external, not based on the victim's subjective experience." Such a yardstick would be provided by one's theory of human worth. Doing something which creates in someone the subjective experience of being demeaned is not evidence that she has been treated immorally (witness the white woman's unreasonable reaction to the black man seated next to her on the bus). We shall also see later that not all diminishment qualifies as demeaning, and thus disrespectful, treatment. Indeed, I shall argue that retribution

19 This definition needs refinement. For example, the notion of responsibility needs spelling out. I shall pass over this thorny problem here. In addition, the definition does not adequately distinguish between intentional harming that counts as wrongdoing, unintentional harming that counts as wrongdoing (negligence), and unintentional harming that does not count as wrongdoing (e.g. accidents). Presumably, the first two kinds of action involve "objectively demeaning" treatment, but not the third; however, more analysis is needed to explain why this is so. Finally, note that on this definition a harm performed by someone judged not a responsible agent is not a wrong. Thus the harm committed by an insane person is a harm but not a wrong.

is a certain kind of diminishing treatment that can be morally required.[20]

III. RETRIBUTIVE IDEA ONE: PUNISHMENT AS A DEFEAT

Let us return to the development of a theory of retribution. To endorse retribution, we must be sure that it is an idea that makes sense as a legitimation of harm, and is importantly different from the vengefulness that emanates from malice. Even more ambitiously, I believe we must establish, *contra* Murphy, that *retribution is not a form of hatred at all*, so that (as Jesus may have been trying to say) the claims of love need not be violated by the claims of justice, or vice versa. This is not an easy task. As we have seen, the project of "making sense" of retribution in order to show how it is different from revenge has been attempted before and is notoriously difficult to pull off. Moreover, advocates of retribution who are convinced it is a bedrock intuition will believe I am foolish to try to analyze it since they regard it as a foundational moral idea which cannot be broken into pieces nor explained by something more fundamental.

I do not believe retribution is foundational. Instead I believe it gets its irresistible character by being the conjunction of two basic ideas mandating the harm of the wrongdoer as a means to an end. I will argue that those who want retribution want to inflict suffering that is taken (for two different reasons) to show that the action being punished was wrong. To put it metaphorically (but in a way that I hope is evocative), the punishment is the victim's value "striking back" and in this way proving itself. But why must a victim's value strike back via pain? And how does painful retaliation con-

20 This definition of a wrong need not commit us to assuming that any responsible agent who acts wrongfully is a wrongdoer. For example, a man who robs a bank because terrorists have threatened to kill his family unless he does so commits a wrong according to this definition, but we do not blame him for that wrong, and thus do not consider him a wrongdoer.

stitute vindication of the victim's worth? Just like Nozick, I must explain why pain effects a linkage between the criminal and what is true about a victim's value.

But before pursuing this idea, let me point out that because I will understand retribution as a communication about value, my analysis of it makes it presuppose a theory of human worth. As I just discussed, there are a variety of such theories, and what *kinds* of punishment a retributivist will recommend depends upon which theory she accepts (although the *point* of the retributive punishment will be the same, no matter what theory of human worth is presupposed).[21] For now, let me illustrate the theory using a Kantian theory of human worth, which makes people intrinsically, objectively, and equally valuable. Aside from the fact that I believe this is the theory retribution ought to presuppose, I will also maintain that it is the theory advocates of it generally do presuppose.

Those who wrong others, on the definition developed in the previous section, objectively demean them. They fail to realize or else do not believe that others' value rules out the treatment which their actions have accorded them; and they incorrectly believe or implicitly assume that their own value is high enough to make this treatment permissible. So criminals send a message when they behave immorally: implicit in their wrongdoings is a message about their value relative to that of their victims.

Now let us consider how a victim feels when he has had that message "inflicted" upon him. Take a child who has been victimized by a bully and who desires to beat him up because "he deserves it": This child's desire for punishment is a desire to establish that the bully is not someone who is elevated above him – or indeed anyone. The child wants to *defeat* the bully, and the defeat is supposed to be proof that the bully is not the "lord" which he has claimed to be. I take this child to be characteristic of someone who desires retrib-

---

21 However, although I am not able to develop this idea here, I am doubtful that those who hold an instrumental theory of human worth can make use of it to ground any kind of retributive response.

utive punishment. He wants to *counter with punishment* the insulting message sent by his offender.

The child's punitive action is an attempt at diminishment in the first sense defined above; i.e., he is attempting to diminish the wrongdoer by supplying evidence showing that this wrongdoer is not as exalted as he believes. Such diminishment is only wrong if a wrongdoer's value precludes it such that it can be considered demeaning treatment. But the child's attempt at diminishment is aimed at conveying what the child takes to be the truth about how valuable the bully is relative to himself and to others. And I am proposing that it is *not* demeaning to accord someone treatment designed to represent the *truth* about his value relative to others (assuming, of course, that it really does represent the truth).

However, the child is after more than diminishment in this sense. A retributivist's commitment to punishment is not merely a commitment to taking down hubristic wrongdoers a peg or two, it is also a commitment to asserting moral truth in the face of its denial. If I have value equal to that of my assailant, then that must be made manifest after I have been victimized. By victimizing me, the wrongdoer has declared himself elevated with respect to me, acting as a superior who is permitted to use me for his purposes. A false moral claim has been made. Moral reality has been denied. The retributivist demands that the false claim be corrected. The wrongdoer must be humbled to show that he isn't the lord of the victim. If I cause the wrongdoer to suffer in proportion to my suffering at his hands, his elevation over me is denied, and morality reality is reaffirmed. The purported master is mastered by me in turn, and in this way I show that he is my peer.

So I am proposing that retributive punishment is the defeat of the wrongdoer at the hand of the victim (either directly or indirectly through an agent of the victim, e.g. the state) that symbolizes the correct relative value of wrongdoer and victim.[22] It is a symbol that is conceptually required to reaf-

---

22 In what follows, I speak of there being victims of crimes, but I do not point out the way in which every member of a society can be consid-

firm a victim's equal worth in the face of a challenge to it. Thus the punishment has a telos, but the telos is not so much to produce good as it is to establish goodness.[23]

How does the infliction of pain constitute such a symbol? The answer is that pain conveys defeat – so that if defeat could be accomplished in some other way, presumably the victim would be just as likely to use it as he would to use pain. But *any non-painful method*, so long as it was still a method for *defeating* the wrongdoer, *would still count as punishment*. Indeed, if one considers the wide variety of experiences which count as punishment in our society but which are not inherently painful (e.g. requiring public service), one realizes that what makes any experience the suffering of punishment is not the objective painfulness of the experience, but the fact that it is one which the wrongdoer is *made* to suffer and which is an experience that represents his *submission* to the punisher. To use a phrase of Fingarette, punishment is an experience designed to "humble the will" of the person who committed the wrongdoing.[24] And such humbling is generally disliked and found to be painful, which perhaps explains why punishment is so often confused with the infliction of pain. A better synonym for punishment, according to Fingarette, is the infliction of *suffering*, one meaning of which, according to the O.E.D., is "to endure," "to submit," "to be subjected to," so that "in the respect that we suffer, we experience what we do not will, or in a stronger sense, we experience what is *against* our will."[25] But I propose that the most general and accurate definition of punishment is

the experience of defeat at the hands (either directly or indirectly through a legal authority) of the victim.

ered a victim of some sorts of wrongdoings (e.g. felonies). Were this idea to be incorporated into the discussion, wrongdoers would have to "pay" not only for what they did to particular people, but also for what they did to all of us.
23   I am indebted to Richard Gale for this way of putting things, and for pressing me about many of the ideas in this section.
24   See Fingarette, "Punishment and Suffering."
25   Ibid., p. 510.

If punishment is understood in this way, it appears morally problematic not only insofar as it may involve the infliction of pain, but more importantly because it *always* involves the attempt to master another human being. However, I want to argue that such mastery is only morally wrong, i.e., demeaning, when it aims to establish something false about the relative value of the one claiming it (i.e., the one whom we call *wrong*) and his victim; it is not morally wrong if the point of the mastery is to deny the wrongdoer's false claim to superiority and to assert the victim's equal value.[26]

But exactly how does punishment make this assertion? And why is this method the only, or even the best, way of vindicating the victim's worth?

Consider that retributivists standardly endorse the *lex talionis* as a punishment formula, or (as I would reinterpret it) as a formula for determining the extent to which the wrongdoer must be mastered. That formula calls for a wrongdoer to suffer something like what her victim suffered and is fre-

---

26 This defense of retribution sounds, in some respects, like Fingarette's, but it is worthwhile pointing out the difference between the two accounts. Like Fingarette I see punishment as the delivery of a defeat to the wrongdoer, as an experience of submission, of being dominated. But Fingarette justifies the delivery of this defeat *only* by a legal institution. And the point of its infliction is to make the wrongdoer recognize that she is required not to defy the law's imperatives, i.e., to see that the law (and not she herself) is "boss." This justification of retribution succeeds only so long as the law is a legitimate institution, and Fingarette offers no such justification for it. He also offers no justification of the punishment practices of non-legal institutions such as schools or families. So at best his is only a partial explanation of retributive thinking, specifically in legal contexts. Moreover, his account is a strikingly non-moral explanation of the retributive idea, one which Fingarette believes is necessary so that the law is not confused with morality. But surely retributivists such as Kant have taken retribution to be a deeply moral notion – perhaps even part of the bedrock of moral thought. To offer a non-moral explanation of it seems, therefore, to fundamentally misrepresent the idea. I am inclined to think his account might be right as part of the reason a legal system punishes, but is wrong as an account of retribution. My account of retribution tries to explain its moral core, which I believe a variety of institutions, including not only the law but also families and universities, make use of in pursuit of both moral and non-moral objectives.

400

quently mocked by those who point out that delivering to the criminal what she delivered to the victim can be either impossible or ridiculous or both in many instances. But the punishment formula does not seem quite so silly if it is interpreted as calling *only* for proportionality between crime and punishment. To inflict on a wrongdoer something comparable to what she inflicted on the victim is to master her in the way that she mastered the victim. The score is even. Whatever mastery she can claim, the victim can also claim. If his victimization is taken as evidence for his inferiority relative to her, then her defeat at his hands negates that evidence. Hence the *lex talionis* calls for a wrongdoer to be subjugated in a way that symbolizes the idea that she is the victim's equal. The punishment is a second act of mastery that denies the lordship asserted in the first act of mastery.

A critic might query this analysis by worrying that, even if retributive punishment is one way to achieve this end, it might not be the only way or even the best way. And if there is another way to reassert the victim's value that is as good as, or better than, the punitive method, then why shouldn't the retributivist sanction that method, and suspend the punishment of the wrongdoer – something which a "hardcore" retributivist would presumably never want to do?

But I contend that punishment is uniquely suited to the vindication of the victim's relative worth, so that no other method purporting to achieve vindication could be preferred to it.[27] Suppose we gave a victim a ticker-tape parade following the crime to express our commitment to his value. Still the fact that he had been mastered by the wrongdoer would stand. He would have lost to her, and no matter how much the community might contend that he was not her inferi-

---

27 But consider the fact that Martin Luther King, Jr., is considered the great champion of the rights (and thus the value) of blacks, and yet never inflicted punishment. Strategies such as civil disobedience might be almost as effective, in certain circumstances (maybe even as effective), as punitive defenses of worth. Still, one wonders whether King and others chose their non-violent method of fighting criminality because the superior, punitive method was denied them.

or, the loss counts as evidence that he is. Hence *the victim wants the evidence nullified* and punishment is the best way to do that. The evidence isn't made to vanish by punishment, nor made never to have existed. Instead it is explained away. Copernicus didn't make the evidence of the sun rising vanish, but he did nullify it in the sense that he showed it wasn't really evidence for that conclusion. Similarly, punishment undercuts the probative force of the evidence provided by the wrongdoer's action of his superiority. The wrongdoer can't take her crime to have established or to have revealed her superiority if the victim is able to do to her what she did to him. The punishment is therefore a second act of mastery that negates the evidence of superiority implicit in the wrongdoer's original act.

What is the retributivist's motive for wanting to reaffirm the equal worth of wrongdoer and victim?

His retributivist motive should not be confused with a variety of non-retributive motives which he might also have. Consider examples of non-retributivist motives: He might see the communication as having desirable deterring effects both for the criminal and for the larger society. Or he may believe that it can morally educate the criminal and the society, on the grounds that the wrongdoer's loss to his victim (or to that victim's societal representative) will force both parties to reassess their relative value. He may also desire to inflict punishment in order to benefit the victim, who may feel a resentment or hatred that is fed by a fear that the crime has revealed her to be or else rendered her lower.[28]

But the *retributivist* motive for inflicting suffering is to annul or counter the appearance of the wrongdoer's superiority and thus affirm the victim's real value. So even in a situation

---

28 Perhaps some of the impatience felt by victims towards people, such as myself, who have advocated punishment as a way of morally educating criminals stems from the fact that we have tended to see the suffering as helpful only to the one who did the harming or to society members tempted to do what he did, and thus have ignored the very real help to her injured self-esteem which the victim can and should get from the defeat of her assailant.

where neither the wrongdoer nor the larger society will either listen to or believe the message about the victim's worth which the "punitive defeat" is meant to carry, and where the victim doesn't need to hear (or will not believe) that message in order to allay any personal fears of diminishment, the retributivist will insist on the infliction of punishment insofar as it is a way of "striking a blow for morality" or (to use a phrase of C.S. Lewis) a way to "plant the flag"[29] of morality.

Recall earlier that I said an adequate theory of retribution would show how it was a response to what was immoral about the wrongdoer's action. This is precisely what the present theory tries to do. If punishment symbolizes the reassertion of the victim's value, it is desired by one who is responding to and who rejects the denial of that value by the criminal's action (where that denial is what makes the action immoral). And one's commitment to that value can motivate one to carry out that reassertion even when one is quite sure that the defiance will persist despite the message.

This reassertion is what Hegel might have meant when he spoke of the way punishment "annuls the crime." Of course it can't annul the act itself, but *it can annul the false evidence seemingly provided by the wrongdoing of the relative worth of the victim and the wrongdoer.* Or to put it another way, it can annul the message, sent by the crime, that they are not equal in value.

We might also use this approach to retribution to explain Kant's famous concern to punish criminals even when the society of which they are members is about to disband:

Even if a civil society were to dissolve itself by common agreement of all its members (for example if the people inhabiting

29 C.S. Lewis, *The Problem of Pain* (New York: Macmillan, 1944), p. 45. Quoted by Robert Nozick in his *Philosophical Explanations* (Cambridge, MA: Harvard University Press, 1981), p. 718n80. The complete passage is: "It plants the flag of truth within the citadel of a rebel soul." So expanded, it sounds a bit too educative to be a purely retributive sentiment.

an island decided to separate and disperse themselves around the world), the last murderer remaining in prison must first be executed, so that everyone will duly receive what his actions are worth and so that the bloodguilt thereof will not be fixed on the people because they failed to insist on carrying out the punishment; for if they fail to do so, they may be regarded as accomplices in this public violation of legal justice.[30]

I agree with Kant that we would be accomplices in the crime if we failed to punish its perpetrator because we would be condoning the evidence it gave us of the relative worth of victim and offender, or to put it another way, we would be acquiescing in the message it sent about the victim's inferiority.

These last remarks should make it clear that this analysis of retribution presents it as something other than a justification of punishment designed to convey a moral lesson to the wrongdoer or the larger society. Indeed, it may be that *part of what it is to take an action as immoral is to have the desire to reassert the victim's value through punishment.* But having made this proposal, I want to argue that such an assertion only makes sense (and only appears justifiable) if people are at least *able* to understand the symbolic significance of the punishment, albeit perhaps unwilling to do so. Imagine Kant's desert island suddenly hit by toxic fumes which mentally disable all but the victim; would the victim still believe he would be the accomplice of the wrongdoer if he desisted from punishing her? Wouldn't the punishment of an individual who can neither remember the crime nor understand what the punishment is about, in a community of people who are no better able than she to comprehend either, seem a meaningless cruelty? My point is that even if retributivists insist that their central reason for reasserting value through punishment is not to effect moral education, but to utter moral truth whether or not anyone bothers to listen, in fact one would only bother to utter it in a world where the truth

30 Immanuel Kant, *The Metaphysical Elements of Justice*, trans. John Ladd (Indianapolis: Bobbs-Merrill, 1965), p. 102.

can be comprehended. So the retributivist is concerned with education in an attenuated sense of the word insofar as he wants the moral truth to be heard, but is not intent on successful persuasion or criminal reform; he wants to annul the criminal's message and reassert the moral truth, but does not perceive punishment as a certain cure for immorality.

We have set the stage for another question: should one punish a wrongdoer who is unable to understand the assertion behind the punishment even if the rest of society is able to do so?[31] Here too I think a retributivist who appreciates what retributive punishment is for would refrain from inflicting it. Such punishment is supposed to be a defeat; but if a wrongdoer has changed so that he has lost considerable rationality and now cannot understand that he is defeated nor why that defeat has occurred, then the man who was able to, and who did, defy the facts of others' value no longer exists. That is, the agent of the crime no longer exists. Now it was that agent who implicitly claimed superiority over the victim through his action. He is therefore the one who must be defeated. But he is gone, and in his place is an individual whose value as a human being without agency may be problematic to assess. The time for punishment is passed, just as surely as if the wrongdoer had died.

Do these remarks raise problems for the retributive punishment of reformed criminals? No; one would only think so if one mistook retributive punishment for moral education. But retribution isn't about making a criminal better; it is about denying a false claim of relative value. The reformed and penitent murderer (who still retains the capacity to understand what he has done) is still (for moral purposes) the same person who committed the murder because he retains the agency which previously produced the murder (i.e., he is still the agent who chose to perform this action). Thus he is the one who implicitly claimed superiority over the victim

---

31 This question has contemporary relevance to those disturbed by some people's enthusiasm for the punishment of old Nazi war criminals who are now senile, and who ramble and drool through their trials.

through the crime, and he remains the one who must be levelled in order to negate the evidence of superiority provided by the crime. If he is truly penitent, he may be just as interested in seeing that claim denied as the family of the victim. It is not uncommon for remorseful wrongdoers to seek out punishment, seeing it as a way of making up for what they did to their victims. (Of course, there might be powerful reasons for being merciful toward such people and suspending or weakening their sentences; even if retribution is justifiable, it may not always be required.)[32]

Let us return to the retributivist's punishment formula. As I discussed, the retributivist's endorsement of the *lex talionis* is the insistence on proportionality between crime and punishment. And this makes sense if punishment is a defeat for the wrongdoer in the name of the victim which is intended to express the victim's value. The more severe the punishment, the more the wrongdoer is being brought low; and how much we would want to bring a criminal low depends upon the extent to which his actions symbolized his superiority and lordship over the one he hurt. The higher wrongdoers believe themselves to be (and thus the more grievously they wrong others) the harder and farther they must fall if the moral reality of the parties' relative value is to be represented properly. So the increasing severity of punishment symbolizes the increasing severity of the violation of the valuable entity. The value will "strike back" more severely against more severe trangressions of it.

So if the Camelback rapist, who used the women he raped for his own satisfaction as if they were his slaves, were to receive a light sentence, his victims would have effected only a small defeat. And this would be evidence not that they were his equals, but that they were his inferiors, able to do far less to him than he was able to do to them. Hence the man's victims fought for a severe defeat that would send a

---

32 I do not have time to explore the relationship between justice and mercy here, but that relationship is explored at some length in Murphy and Hampton, *Forgiveness and Mercy*, chap. 5 (written by Murphy).

message of their mastery over him sufficient to negate the evidence, provided by his crime, of their inferiority to him.

This retributivist theory is still not complete: a good retributivist generally wants limits placed on punishment sentences. Moreover, the retributivist would prefer that these limits not come from *outside* his theory (so that without modification by external moral considerations the theory would be taken to endorse, say, torturing torturers), but from *within* the theory (so that the theory itself has the resources to rule out torture, no matter what the wrongdoer has done). Retributivists have, however, generally despaired of being able to do this. They have instead tended to draft what seem to be morally-required *external* criteria for drawing the line between permissible and impermissible punishment.

I want to propose that we might be able to set the limits of retributive punishment by using the internal resources of the theory as I have interpreted it above, assuming a Kantian theory of human worth. Consider that on my analysis, genuinely non-malicious retributivists have as the aim behind the infliction of suffering not the vengeful diminishment of the criminal to a bestial level but the vindication of the victim's value. This aim means that the punisher must not do anything that would be interpreted as an attempt not merely to deny the wrongdoers' claim to superiority but also to *degrade* them, i.e., cause them in some way to lose value. Sometimes a crime is ghastly in the way that it portrays the victim as vastly lower than the criminal or in the way that it seems to reduce him almost to a bestial level: for example, mutilations, torture, enslavement. The *lex talionis* would license doing the same thing to the wrongdoer as a way of making the equal status of the victim manifest. But to one who is committed to the idea that the wrongdoer has an intrinsic value that is equal to the value of others, such treatment can be hard, if not impossible, to stomach. One cannot see the punishment as reasserting the moral facts if it involves doing something to the wrongdoer that either makes him, or else represents him to be, degraded below the level of human beings generally. Of course, the next question to be asked is: why isn't *every* punishment in violation of those facts insofar as it is an attempt to master a human being whose value is supposed to be intrinsic, permanent (for as long as he remains a human being), and equal to that of others? Retributivists can reply that there are methods of mastery that deny the criminal's claim to lordship, and that may be severe if the criminal has gravely mistreated his victim, but which are nonetheless not so severe that they are identical either to the treatments which are considered permissible only for entities far less valuable than human beings or to those which actually make them less valuable. Being made to pay a fine, or perform a public service, or to suffer confinement (under humane conditions), is to experience subjugation and defeat, but (at least arguably) none of these is treatment permissible only for something subhuman, nor do they make one subhuman. On the other hand, having an eye cut out, having to endure acid thrown in one's face, losing fingers, being tortured, are treatments that one would refuse to consider permissible for animals, much less humans, and which may damage people in ways that cause them to lose value. So the retributivist who is committed to reasserting moral truth must beware that her way of reasserting it does not implicitly deny for the criminal what it seeks to establish for the victim. Or alternatively, if the retributivist wants to establish the relative equality of victim and offender, he does not want to treat the offender in such a way that her value as a human being is denied. (So I would argue that one reason why capital punishment is controversial is that it is simply not clear whether execution does deny value or not.)

The *lex talionis* therefore cannot, by itself, be the appropriate punishment formula for the sophisticated retributivist because there is no upper bound on the amount of pain that it would require a wrongdoer to suffer in virtue of his crime, other than "what he did to his victim" – a bound that could well be far too high. A more accurate retributivist formula would call for comparability of punishments with crimes within certain limits that reflect the value of the wrongdoer, and a policy toward constructing punishments that would give the best expression possible of the value of the person hurt by the wrongdoer subject to these limits. To strike a blow for morality and thus for the idea that all human beings have great (and equal) value, the victim must make sure that she fights in a way that recognizes the wrongdoer's own very real value; she must, to use Kant's phrase, defeat him in such a way that she continues to "respect humanity in his person."

IV. RETRIBUTIVE IDEA TWO: VINDICATING VALUE THROUGH PROTECTION

The preceding argument was an attempt to explain a way in which the wrongdoer could be "linked up with right values," and his crime "annulled," by having punishment inflicted on him. The key idea in that argument was that punishment was the experience of defeat, designed to humble the wrongdoer and thus express his real worth relative to the victim. However, there is another way to make the connection between right values and pain. This connection is made when, for various reasons, *society*, rather than the victim, is responsible for carrying out punishments of wrongdoers.

No matter how else punishment is justified, its role as a deterrent is a central reason why societies inflict it on criminals. The way it works to deter crime is not dissimilar to the way in which nature affords protection to many of its plants and animals. Consider the lowly nettle. This is a plant that, to the naked eye, has no obvious protection against damage. There are no thorns visible, and no potentially-worrying sap on the leaves; it grows in readily accessible places rather than only in hard-to-reach crags or ravines, and it is ubiquitous in the summer. Yet anyone who touches it once is loath to do so again, because tiny hairs on the leaves secrete a chemical which reacts with human skin to produce a prickly burning sensation for several minutes. The nettle therefore enjoys a protective defense against human beings. It is a protection that does not stop someone from touching or damaging it (in the way that being encased in impenetrable glass would do); instead it is a protection that "strikes back" after any human interference with the plant, thereby deterring future interference.

Punishment is analogous to a nettle's sting. The threat of suffering punishment is like the nettle's protective secretion: a transgression activates an unpleasant experience such that future transgressions are deterred. Human beings, as I have already discussed, have an instinctive strike-back response which (as Mackie notes) may have evolved in us because of its desirable deterrent consequences. But reason as well as instinct directs us to harm wrongdoers in order to deter future crime.

As retributivists are fond of pointing out, this can't be the whole story behind punishment because victims see the punishment not only as a protection against the future, but also as an appropriate response to the past, one that is *deserved* in virtue of what the wrongdoer did. I now want to propose a second source of the retributivist notion of desert, one that is *derived from* punishment's role as a deterrent, but is itself quite different from deterrence.

Why should human beings have any kind of protection from attack, provided either by legal machinery or through social censure or ostracism? Clearly each of us has some ability to react against a transgressor, and some of us enjoy significant abilities in this area. But others of us, for instance, the new-born, the aged, the sick, or the just-plain-weak, do not. One way to understand our practices of punishment is to see them as a societal attempt to deliver for each victim a protective "sting" against a transgressor which he may be ill-prepared or unable to deliver for himself. But why should society want to afford each of us this protection? The answer to this question depends upon what theory of human worth one holds. One may believe that our worth derives from our ability to be of use to our fellows, so that society ought to protect each of us to the extent that we are instrumentally valuable to it. Or one may believe with Kant that human beings enjoy an

410

equal and intrinsic worth, so that a society should protect us equally. But whatever one's theory of human worth is, I am suggesting that societal punishment practices should be seen as created and designed to protect it. If society knew how to encase those it values in a substance that would protect them from all damage it would surely do so (assuming it could afford to do so). But since no such protection is possible, it protects us in the way that nettles are protected – via a kind of sting that is delivered after a transgression which is intended to deter future transgressions.

Societies also have limited resources. How should they use those resources to punish wrongdoers? In particular, should all human beings be accorded the same protection? If there are some who are more valuable than most, shouldn't society protect them by a legally or socially created sting that is greater than usual, and which is thus a better deterrent? And if there are people who are less valuable than others, shouldn't society protect them by a legally or socially created sting that is less than usual, thereby deterring less effectively? Not only are these grades of protection possible, but they exist in virtually every legal system that has ever been created, either officially or unofficially. Racist, sexist, or caste-based societies declare that some kinds of human beings are worth more than others; in these societies the punishment of those who injure the less valuable people is lighter than the punishment of those who injure the more valuable people. Statistics exist which support the view that killing a white man in the United States has historically been punished more severely than killing a black man.[33] Certain crimes against women by men in this and other societies have been lightly punished, and even condoned; e.g. rape or wife-beating. One also sees differences in treatment in response to social

33 See the discussion of racial discrimination in the application of the death penalty in papers by Wolfgang and Reidel, and Bowers and Pace, in Hugo Bedau, ed., *The Death Penalty in America* (3rd ed.) (Oxford: Oxford University Press, 1982).

status; the rich and powerful enjoy a more thorough and surer defense of their persons than do prostitutes, or drug addicts, or ghetto-dwellers.

Accordingly, how society reacts to one's victimization can be taken by one to be an indication of *how valuable* society takes one to be, which in turn can be taken to be an indication of how valuable one really is. This point is essential to understanding a societal component of the retributive idea. Of course a victim wants her assailant punished insofar as that punishment is one form of her defense against future crime. But she also wants her assailant punished by society in a way that is properly expressive of what she takes her value to be. *If legal punishment is a protection of one's value, then its infliction on a wrongdoer is a reflection of that value.* So because society's punishment protects those who are valuable, people who long for a high valuation may come to demand punishment not only because they want this legal protection, but also because they want the expression of what the legal protection symbolizes. (Compare a man who wants a high salary not only because he desires great wealth but also because he desires what great wealth in his profession symbolizes, e.g. career success, or great talent.)

Victims of criminals such as the Camelback rapist worry that if society allows the wrongdoer to suffer no painful consequences as a result of his action, he (and others) may conclude that the ones he transgressed against are not valuable enough for society to construct a significant protective barrier that exacts a (deterring) cost from one who would transgress it. So another idea behind victims' insistence that their wrongdoers shouldn't be allowed to "get away with it" is that society shouldn't allow the wrongdoers or the larger society to conclude, because of little or no protective response, that wrongdoers were right to believe their victims lacked value relative to them. The rage felt by the members of San Francisco's gay community after the light sentence given to Dan White, the murderer of Harvey Milk, was surely connected with their belief that the jury did not regard this homosexual as of sufficiently high value to punish his murderer severely. In their eyes the murderer *did* get away with something: namely, with the idea that as a white male heterosexual he was of more value than Milk.[34]

V. CONCLUSION

So now we have two ways to link the infliction of suffering following a wrongdoing to the expression of the victim's worth. Both arguments attempt to capture and explain Nozick's intuition that retributive punishment is a way to link up a wrongdoer with right values and Hegel's idea that punishment in some sense "annuls" the crime. Earlier I expressed puzzlement over why *pain* was required to effect such a linkage or annul the crime. But as we said in discussing the first idea, punishment is not so much the infliction of pain as it is the infliction of a *defeat*, which such non-painful experiences as community service can deliver just as well as pain (although because pain is commonly seen to represent defeat, it is a useful medium to symbolize the idea that the wrongdoer is not one's superior). And as we said in discussing the second idea, pain, or more generally, a humbling defeat which prideful wrongdoers will intensely dislike, can deter the commission of a crime against someone (or even something) having value; and the victim can come to see the value which the humbling defeat is meant to protect as symbolically expressed through the protection.

Some readers may have already noticed that if my analysis of retribution is right, it is not a species of hatred at all and hence not revenge (although it can still qualify as part of a sentiment if sentiments are understood to contain cognitive content).[35] Indeed someone can desire retribution and harbor

34 But I do not endorse this reading of the light sentence. Given that Mayor Moscone was murdered along with Milk, the jury cannot be taken to have made a statement about homosexuals with their verdict, and were probably confused by a bad California law on diminished capacity.
35 In order to present a complete account of how they are different, a thorough analysis of revenge is necessary. I develop such an analysis in *Forgiveness and Mercy*, chap. 2, and discuss the differences between revenge and retribution in chap. 4.

neither love nor hate towards her wrongdoer. She would simply be averse to the act and the message it carries, and desire to punish the wrongdoer in order to assert a different message implying that better treatment of the victim is required. Her attention is on the crime, and on the victim's value; it is not on the criminal himself except insofar as his defeat is the way in which the communication must be made.[36] Of course retribution may be accompanied by some form of aversion (perhaps quite considerable) towards the wrongdoer, but my point is that retribution itself carries no such opposition. The suffering is not meant as an expression of a con-attitude toward the criminal, but rather as a response that not only offers protection for the victim but also reasserts the victim's value. So parents who dearly love their children can administer retributive punishments because such punishment does not require or involve hatred. Moreover, one reason why retribution might seem like such a good posture for a government to take as it punishes criminals is that this is neither a loving nor a hateful posture (neither of which one might think a legal system ought to take).

The Greeks talked of the Furies pursuing wrongdoers, torturing them for what they did. Each of us hopes that there will be something like the Furies which will doggedly pursue those who wrong us. Retributive punishment is our name for the Furies, and at a fundamental level it is punishment which we desire because we see it, for the two different reasons discussed above, as our *value* striking back at those who harmed us, and so confirming the fact that we *are* valuable, that their actions were indeed wrong, and that it is required that we be treated with respect.

36 This way of putting things makes one wonder why the retributive theory as I have outlined it doesn't make punishment of a criminal "a mere means to an end" such that he is being used when he is punished. The argument of the last section attempts to show that retributive punishment, properly understood, never involves acting towards the wrongdoer in such a way that his value is demeaned – which is what I would argue Kant should have meant by "treating someone as a mere means."

Chapter 12

Punishment and self-defense

GEORGE P. FLETCHER

In working out his theory of retributive punishment, Nozick argues that self-defense should be treated the same as or at least equivalent to punishment. Specifically, he claims that if a defender inflicts harm on an aggressor in order to thwart the aggression, the harm suffered should be deducted from the punishment that the aggressor deserves for his criminal act.[1] To illustrate the point, let us suppose that the standard punishment for rape is seven years in jail. If the victim stymies the rape by cutting the attempting rapist with a razor blade, the pain that the offender suffers in the cutting should be deducted from the penalty a court may subsequently impose. The proper punishment will be seven years minus n, where n represents the harm inflicted in the victim's defensive effort to repel the rape. It is as though the injury is a 'down payment' on the penalty the offender deserves for his crime. As Nozick puts it: "One may, in defending oneself, *draw against* the punishment the attacker deserves ... ".[2]

Most people trained in the law would dismiss this claim out of hand. It is assumed that self-defense is one sort of thing and punishment, quite another. Self-defense expresses

---

This article first appeared in *Law and Philosophy*, vol. 8 (1989). © 1989 Kluwer Academic Publishers. Printed originally in the Netherlands. Reprinted by permission of Kluver Academic Publishers.

1 See R. Nozick, *Anarchy, State and Utopia* (1974) pp. 62–63. Nozick carries forward the argument and endorses his earlier views in R. Nozick, *Philosophical Explanations* (1981) p. 364.
2 R. Nozick, supra note 1, at p. 63 (emphasis added).

a right to defend oneself or others against aggression; its purpose is exclusively to prevent the threatened harm. Typically, punishment comes into play only after the aggressive act has made its mark – when it is too late for self-defense. The function of punishment cannot be to prevent the instant harm, but at best to sanction it and to induce others, by example, not to replicate the harmful act. Treating harm inflicted in self-defense as a 'down payment' on deserved punishment confuses harmful acts incident to preventing aggression with harmful acts undertaken deliberately to sanction criminal acts already passed. Nozick obviously remains unimpressed by this easily perceived distinction, and his thesis challenges us to find firmer ground for not deducting harm inflicted in self-defense from the punishment deserved for a completed crime.

There might well exist a legal system in which lawyers were genuinely puzzled about whether harm inflicted in legitimate self-defense constituted punishment. There is considerable evidence that in Talmudic jurisprudence, for example, the rabbis struggled with the problem. The scholars generating the laws of the *Mishna*[3] and the commentaries of the *Gemara*[4] confronted difficulties in assaying whether harm inflicted in self-defense should be treated as a form of punishment. Let us take a closer look at the Talmudic material. The relevant *Mishna* prescribes as law:[5]

> A housebreaker is judged according to his purpose. If the housebreaker breaks a cask and there is blood guilt for killing him, he is liable for the damage. If there is no blood guilt, he is exempt.

3　The *Mishna* (sometimes spelled *Mishnah*) is the first written version of the oral Torah. It was transcribed by Rabbi Judah the Prince, who died in 219 A.D. For a quick summary of this and background issues in Jewish law, see Finkelman, *Self-Defense and Defense of Others in Jewish Law: The* Rodef *Defense*, 33 *Wayne Law Review* 1257, fn. 2 (1987).
4　The *Gemara* consists of the first four hundred years' discussion and analysis of the *Mishna*. See Finkelman, supra note 3.
5　Babylonian Talmud, *Sanhedrin* 72a.

We can sidestep the metaphysical mysteries of 'blood guilt' and treat the expression as equivalent to 'lawful' or 'justified'; the presence of blood guilt as tantamount to 'unlawful' or 'unjustified'. The implicit reference to justification builds on the passage in Exodus 22:1, which holds that killing a housebreaker is justified (i.e., no blood guilt for the slaying) unless 'the sun has risen upon him'.

Although there are pitfalls in reading modern categories into the understanding of ancient texts, killing of the housebreaker seems to be a clear instance of 'self-defense'. The reference in the *Mishna* to judging the housebreaker 'according to his purpose' is clarified in the commentary to mean the justification of the killing is the personal danger to the homeowner. The breaking-in generates, as we moderns would say, a presumption of mortal danger to the homeowner. In those cases where the presumption loses its warrant, as when a father breaks into the home of his son (even with the purpose of taking property), there is no right to respond with deadly force.

The point of this *Mishnaic* rule is to exempt the housebreaker from civil liability for damage done during the period that he is subject to being killed lawfully and justifiably. It does not matter whether the homeowner in fact responds with deadly force. The fact that the homeowner could lawfully kill him is sufficient to exempt him from all civil liability for all acts that he might commit. It is as though by exposing himself to the homeowner's lawful response, he enters a twilight zone in which he is no longer liable for his acts.

No modern lawyer would even consider the possibility of exempting the housebreaker from liability for tort damage, whether as an intruder he is subject to being killed on the spot or not. What could have led the rabbis to formulate this curious principle of tort exemption for unjust aggressors?

The conventional explanation is that individuals should be liable only for the greater offense they commit and not for lesser included offenses.[6] Thus, if in the very act of stealing,

6　The principle reads, in Aramaic: *Kim Ley B'drabah Minah.*

a thief violates the Sabbath (e.g., by carrying the goods in the public arena) he is liable only for the latter, capital offense.[7] Applying this principle to the case of the housebreaker who breaks a cask implies that the tort of destroying property is considered, in Talmudic jurisprudence, as a lesser included offense committed in the course of the housebreaking.[8] Now the question becomes: why would lawyers think this way about the relationship between what we call tort and what we call crime? Don't they see that crime is one thing and tort, something totally different? We would never regard a tort, entailing a duty to pay compensation, as a lesser included offense in the crime of burglary. How could the rabbis have thought differently?

The answer, obviously, is that the rabbinic scholars did not work with the conceptual distinctions that govern our thought. They thought of all forms of liability as lining up on a single linear scale. For this single scale to take hold of their thought, however, they had to think of harm inflicted by the homeowner as a mode not only of preventing the break-in and protecting the life of the homeowner, but of

7 The *Gemara* or commentary to this *Mishna* distinguished between completing the theft by picking up a purse before carrying the purse into public and thereby desecrating the Sabbath by carrying an object outside of an enclosed space and picking up the purse at the very moment that one crosses the line between the enclosed and public space. In the event that the theft is complete prior to the desecration of the Sabbath, the actor is liable for both: if the desecration encompasses the final act necessary for the theft, then the actor is liable for the desecration. See Babylonian Talmud, *Sanhedrin* 72a.

8 This conventional explanation ignores a troubling detail, namely that if the housebreaker escaped he would not thereafter be prosecuted by a rabbinic court. At least, there is no source supporting such a prosecution. Therefore, one can not quite say that the greater offense of housebreaking displaces the lesser included tort. The only accurate description is suggested in the notion of the 'twilight zone' of legal responsibility. When someone is subject to being killed, lawfully, he bears no responsibility for acts that he commits. This way of putting the principle also explains the case put in note 7 of desecrating the Sabbath. Though the Sabbath-desecrator is not subject to being lawfully killed on the spot, see the *Mishna* in Babylonian Talmud, *Sanhedrin* 73a, he is liable to judicial execution, and therefore he is not liable for other acts committed in the course of his desecration.

sanctioning, imposing liability on the housebreaker for his aggressive act. For purposes of displacing the lesser included liability for property damage, the defensive act by the homeowner had to appear as of a piece with the community's imposing the death penalty on someone who had desecrated the Sabbath.

There is considerable evidence in the commentaries of the *Gemara* that the rabbis thought of killing the housebreaker as a sanction for his act. They were troubled, therefore, with procedural implications of this analogy; if certain procedural rules apply when a court metes out punishment, the same rule should presumably apply in the field when a homeowner decides to inflict harm on an intruder. For example, a Jewish court cannot carry out a decree on the Sabbath; therefore, it would seem that the homeowner should not be able to 'execute' an intruder on the Sabbath. It is obviously necessary, however, to allow the homeowner to protect himself, whatever day of the week it may be.[9]

A Jewish court will not execute anyone for homicide unless immediately prior to the deed, two witnesses warn the slayer that he is about to commit a capital offense and he responds that he plans to go ahead anyway. In the discussion of slaying the housebreaker, the question recurs: How can the homeowner use force if the housebreaker has not received the required warning that he is about to commit a capital offense? Today we would reject this question as irrelevant. It would be like asking how someone can use force in self-defense without first according the suspect-aggressor a jury trial. The procedures governing conviction have nothing to do with the use of self-defense to protect oneself against imminent aggression. At least that is the way it seems to us.

But the discussants in the Talmud reasoned differently. Instead of rejecting the analogical extension of the required warning, they recognized the problem and sought to explain why in the case of housebreaking the requirement was satisfied in spirit, if not in form. The function of the warning,

9 See the discussion of this point in Babylonian Talmud, *Sanhedrin* 72b.

they seem to reason, is to put the potential offender on notice of his capital liability. The housebreaker is also 'warned' although not by the words of witnesses. To be liable to a lawful response by the homeowner, the intruder must 'dig under' and 'break in' into someone else's private space; this act of breaking puts him on notice, the rabbis conclude, that he might be subject to a fatal response.[10] That the rabbis indulged in this reasoning, verging on legal fiction, reveals how seriously they took the conceptual links between official punishment and private self-defense.

The rabbinic institution of the 'warning' and the resulting self-imposed limitation on the capital jurisdiction of the rabbinic courts are taken to reflect the rabbis' passionate opposition to capital punishment. In a limited sense, this interpretation is correct. But the rabbis were not opposed to seeing offenders die for their deeds. They recognized liberal rights of self-defense, including the homeowner's right to slay the intruder.[11] They thought of aggressors and housebreakers as deserving death.[12] What the Talmudic discussants were concerned about, however, was a *court's* imposing the death penalty. There was nothing wrong with a private individual's killing an aggressor on the spot, but a court's assuming the power to execute an offender in the name of the entire community remained problematic.

Talmudic jurisprudence appears to have an anarchistic bent. It is a system designed to work on the basis of every male Jew's devoting his life to studying legal texts. If everyone knows the law and acts on the basis of his knowledge, judges and courts are superfluous. Of course, no legal system

10　See the discussion *id.*
11　In addition, the rabbis developed the elaborate principles governing killing a *rodef* even though there is no explicit biblical support for the institution. See generally Finkelman, supra note 3.
12　Rashi, the leading 11th century commentator, whose writings on the Talmud are regarded as authoritative and published in the standard editions in the margins around the *Mishna* and *Gemara*, interprets the phrase 'there is no blood guilt' in killing the housebreaker to mean: "the housebreaker is to you as though he has no blood (i.e., life) and it is permissible to kill him". Babylonian Talmud, *Sanhedrin* 72a.

can ever be fully self-administering. In some extreme cases, judges must intervene to resolve disputes and punish criminal offenders. But nonetheless, I would submit, the ideal of a self-administering system infuses Talmudic thinking. And an ideal self-administering legal system vests in potential victims the authority to kill offenders on the spot.

Given this ideal, the threatened homeowner functions as the primary judge of the housebreaker's deed. So far as I know, there is no mention in the Jewish legal source of judging and punishing a housebreaker after the deed is over and done. The homeowner responds and sanctions him or no one does. This is as far as one could go in realizing John Locke's conception of a right to punish in a state of nature.[13]

For purposes of understanding the foundations of Nozick's 'down payment' thesis, the point that we can derive from this discussion of the Talmudic law is this: the more jurists think of the state's punishing criminals as a practice of last resort, the more they are likely to regard acts of defense as the preferred mode of punishing aggressors. It is no accident, therefore, that Nozick develops his 'down payment' as an aspect of his general defense of a minimalist state bordering on an anarchistic, self-administering system.

By like token, those of us who readily reject the 'down payment' thesis presumably take the institution of state punishment as the primary form of legitimate violence. Self-defense then comes into focus as an ancillary institution, designed solely for the purpose of self-protection when state officials are not able to come to the rescue. Once state punishment becomes clearly institutionalized, philosophers are likely to think that this is the way things must be. A harmful act is punishment, as H. L. A. Hart claims, only if it is "imposed and administered by an authority constituted by a legal system against which the offense is committed".[14]

13 See J. Locke, *Two Treatises of Government* (Laslett, ed. 2nd ed 1967) §§ 7. For an effort to turn the private right to punish into a theory of self-defense, see Hurka, 'Rights and Capital Punishment', *Dialogue* **21**, 652.

14 See, e.g., H. L. A. Hart, 'Prolegomenon to the Principles of Punishment' in H. L. A. Hart, *Punishment and Responsibility* (1968) pp. 4–5.

Perceiving punishment as a legitimate expression of power by an 'authority constituted by a legal system' promotes the distinction between punishment and self-defense. What the state does is one thing; private self-help quite another.

That distinction firmly in place, we can begin to ponder other fundamental differences between the two practices. Inflicting punishment is an act of justice carried out in the name of the community. There is nothing untoward, therefore, in thinking of punishment as having the purpose of inflicting harm proportionate to the desert of the offender. By contrast, self-defense has the limited function of protecting the potential victim from aggression. The focus of the defensive act should not be on inflicting harm, but on thwarting the attack. The harm to the aggressor, as Aquinas appears to be the first to point out,[15] is merely an unfortunate but necessary side effect of the potential victim's securing his own safety. The defensive act, emanating from the defender's needs and rights, has no bearing on the aggressor's receiving just retribution for his criminal acts.

The assumption is that only the state is entitled to carry out acts of justice relative to its citizens. No individual is authorized to make this judgment about the just deserts of his fellow citizen. Why this assumption should be so obvious is far from clear, but for the purposes of discussion, I will accept it and explore its implications. The question arises, therefore: if individuals are not entitled to make judgments of justice in exercising self-defense, what are they doing? Is there some value or principle that is vindicated when an individual thwarts an aggressive attack? Of course, he furthers his own interests. But is there something more at stake? The answer is yes, but the matter is not so obvious, particularly to lawyers trained in the common law tradition. An act of self-defense, I shall argue, vindicates the entire legal order, or as Kant would put it, the supremacy of the Right.

15   See *Summa Theologiae* II–II q. 64a. 7.

SELF-DEFENSE AS AN INSTITUTION OF RIGHT

The concept of Right as developed in Kant's Theory of Right (*Rechtslehre*)[16] refers to a particular transpositive conception of Law. It is the Law as a set of enduring principles, binding by virtue of their intrinsic rightness. Unfortunately, the term is frequently and mistakenly translated as 'justice'[17] – a rendering that obscures the very distinction between Right and justice that I shall try to clarify.

According to Kant, the Right guarantees each individual the external freedom to express his choices, his *Willkuer*, provided that every person enjoy the same scope of external freedom.[18] As in Rawls's first principle of justice, each person is entitled to the maximum degree of freedom compatible with a like freedom in others. Acts of aggression encroach upon the external freedom to which all human actors are entitled, and therefore these aggressive acts violate principles of Right. This is the sense in which they are wrongful (contrary to Right) or unlawful. Defeating aggression, nullifying the intrusion, therefore, restores the Right. There is nothing mystical about this vindication of the Right: in clear concrete terms, defensive force terminates physical encroachment and reinstates the freedom of the attacked party.

Stressing the objective incompatibility of the aggressive act with principles of Right explains why desert is irrelevant to the harm that the aggressor justifiably suffers. In view of the distinction between justified and excused aggression, it need not be the case that unjustified or wrongful aggression is also unexcused and culpable. Wrongful aggression might well be excused on grounds of insanity, duress or mistake. Principles of legitimate self-defense apply to these cases of psychotic,

---

16 For a series of articles on Kant's legal theory, see the symposium in the *Columbia Law Review* **87**, no. 3.

17 See, e.g., I. Kant, *The Metaphysical Elements of Justice* (J. Ladd trans. 1965).

18 *Id.* at 34: "[Right] is therefore the aggregate of those conditions under which the will [*Willkuer*] can be conjoined with the will of another in accordance with a universal law of freedom."

coerced and mistaken-motivated aggression precisely as they cover the more typical cases of culpable wrongdoing. As the Model Penal Code acknowledges, the act triggering a legitimate defensive response need only be 'unlawful', and 'unlawful' is defined in the Code as compatible with cases of excused aggression.[19]

It is generally assumed that the event triggering a right to reply with defensive force must be a human act. Natural forces, animal acts and other threats of this kind do not generate rights of self-defense. A fetus endangering the health and well-being of its mother might be subject to abortion on grounds of necessity or lesser evils, but not on grounds of justifiable self-defense.[20] The fetus's growth, and not anything that could be called action, is the source of danger to the mother.

This view prevails in Western legal systems, but it is by no means easy to justify as a matter of principle. Note that requiring a human but not necessary culpable action occupies a middle position between applying self-defense to all human-based threats, at one extreme, and insisting on a culpable act of aggression as the condition for self-defense at the other. It is easier to defend either of these extremes than explain why a non-culpable human act should be necessary and sufficient to trigger the right of self-defense. Perhaps the explanation is no more sophisticated than the observation that by definition, only human acts jeopardize the legal order and the supremacy of the Right. Natural events cannot stand for the Wrong, for the denial of the Right, and therefore there is nothing about the fetus endangering its mother that represents a wrong against the structure of human freedom and social cooperation. Defending the interests of the mother against the endangering fetus may

19 Model Penal Code §§ §§ 3.04; 3.11
20 In some situations where an individual's body – not his action – endangers another, self-defense might be available as an excuse. On this distinct line of development, see G. Fletcher, *Rethinking Criminal Law* (1978) pp. 866–888.

be good for the mother, but it hardly appears to be a defense of the Right against the forces of wrongdoing.

This Kantian conception of self-defense generates a controversial corollary about the limits of defensive force. The problem is whether some principle of proportionality requires the defender to forgo defensive force out of concern for the interests of the aggressor. Need a property owner stay his response if his only recourse against a fleeing thief is to shoot him? The Kantian view, which has taken hold strongly in German criminal theory, is that if aggression threatens the 'principles of ordered liberty' implicit in the Right, then those who are threatened should be able to use all necessary force to frustrate the attack. It is important, however, to acknowledge that self-defense is a right, but not a duty. The property owner may let the thief escape, but whether he should or not, Kant claims, is properly reserved to the realm of ethics rather than law.[21] Whether one acts out of concern for aggressors resembles the question whether one should come to the aid of persons in distress. Though the categorical imperative requires rescue, principles of Right do not. Similarly, although morality may require consideration of the aggressor as a human being, the Right views the aggressor as a threat to the supremacy of principled order.[22]

Thinking of self-defense as a vindication not only of specific human interests, but of the entire scheme of social cooperation explains why the right of self-defense lends itself to universalization. Everyone is entitled to intervene and

21 I. Kant, *supra* note 17, at 41.
22 Philosophers writing about self-defense assume, without foundation, that there is no problem in cutting off self-defense when the cost of the defense intrudes too much on the interests of the aggressor. See Quinn, 'The Right to Threaten and the Right to Punish,' *Philosophy and Public Affairs* **14**, 327, 349–51. Hurka, "Rights and Capital Punishment," *Dialogue* **21**, 652. The argument seems to be that morality requires concerns for the interests of the aggressor. It is never made clear, however, why morality should act as a constraint on the theory of Right. Kant agreed that morality requires solicitude even for aggressors but insisted that morality should be a private matter – not a standard for controlling the scope of personal rights.

ward off the attack and vindicate the Right. The autonomy of one becomes the autonomy of all. It is tempting to equate this liberal conception of self-defense in domestic legal systems with the right to resist aggression in the international sphere. It is as though each person is an island and those who tread upon his territory risk a declaration of war. But international law does not recognize the right of everyone in the international community to intervene on behalf of an endangered member. Consent of the invaded party is necessary to legitimate intervention. That the theory of self-defense in domestic legal systems recognizes a universal right to resist aggression follows from self-defense as a vindication of the Right. Apparently, the relevant sense of Right obtains in domestic law, but not in international law.

Self-defense, it must be admitted, has some surprising features. In its pure liberal form, it directs our attention neither to issues of desert nor of proportionality. It reflects a dehumanization of the aggressor, treating him as hostage to the absolute demands of the Right. The indifference to questions of justice in the theory of self-defense appear even more striking as we elaborate the strong connection between the criteria of punishment and substantive justice.

PUNISHMENT AS AN INSTITUTION OF JUSTICE

It is difficult to imagine an operative system of punishment, even a nominally utilitarian system, that ignores that question whether the offender is fairly and justly punished. Admittedly, these questions of justice are confronted more explicitly in retributive systems. But even a utilitarian system must find a way to accommodate commonsense judgments of fair treatment.

The factors that bear on just punishment are the degree of the offender's wrongdoing (homicide is worse than larceny) and the degree of his responsibility for committing the wrong (intentional wrongs are worse than negligent wrongs).[23] The

23 These two factors reflect Nozick's formula $R - r.H$, where r stands

basic principle of equivalence, punishing measure for measure, expresses the kind of proportional relationship between deed and response that is absent in the liberal theory of self-defense. The basic punitive response may be modified by a diminution of the actor's responsibility (a case of negligence or mitigation), and these factors express a general theory of desert – also missing in the theory of self-defense.

Kant took the requirement of justice (not of Right, but of justice) in punishment so seriously that he wrote: "If justice [in punishment] perishes, then it is no longer worthwhile for men to remain alive on this earth".[24] However sure he was of justice as a commanding imperative, he had difficulty developing a specific theory of just punishment. Sometimes the argument is that punishment is a categorical imperative; any deviation from equality in punishment was apparently tantamount to using the offender as a means to some social end.[25] Sometimes the argument is simply that the *lex talionis* – an eye for an eye, etc. – is the only precise standard that the law could apply and still be law.[26] In the discussion of punishing theft, the claim is that punishment should represent a universalization of the actor's criminal maxim: Thievery becoming a universal practice means that

> he robs himself of the security of any possible ownership. He has nothing and can also acquire nothing, but he still wants to live.... [B]ecause the state will not support him gratis... he becomes a slave, either for a certain period of time or indefinitely....[27]

Imprisonment and forced labor, then, become the appropriate punishment for someone who demonstrates in his con-

for the degree of responsibility and H stands for the degree of wrongdoing.

24 I. Kant, *supra* note 17, at 100.
25 Note the example of the prisoner willing to undergo medical experimentation in return for shorter imprisonment. Kant condemns an arrangement of this as unthinkable – as selling justice for a price. *Id.* at 100–101.
26 *Id.* at 101.
27 *Id.* at 102.

duct that property rights are insecure. In an even more provocative claim, Kant invokes the biblical notion of blood guilt as a rationale for the duty to punish every offender. He imagines a community about to disband and argues that prior to the dissolution:

> The last murderer remaining in prison must first be executed, so that everyone will receive what his actions are worth and so that the bloodguilt thereof will not be fixed on the people. . . . [28]

The shifting bases of these arguments reflect some uncertainty about the proper grounding of retributive punishment, but as I shall argue later, the invocation of the seemingly archaic notion of blood guilt and the linking of just punishment with moral theory suggest a theme that captures deep intuitions about the duty to punish in response to heinous crimes.

The important omission in Kant's theory is that he does not ground the theory of just punishment in a defense of the Right. It is true that he writes of the state's right to punish offenders. But the reference seems to be not to the theory of objective Right – as we saw it invoked in the theory of self-defense – but to the personal right of the sovereign to punish those who have shown themselves unworthy to be citizens. [29] In contrast to Hegel's later, mysterious claim that punishment negates the wrong and reinstates the Right, Kant limits himself to arguments about the moral duty to do justice.

In this exposition of the distinctions between Right and justice, between self-defense and punishment, I have supposed that these practices are realized in their pure forms. The reality of the case law is, of course, more complicated. The recognition of the principle of proportionality in self-defense cases can best be understood, it seems, as an infusion of criteria of morality and justice into the analysis of rightful

28   *Id.* at 102.
29   *Id.* at 99.

self-defense. Yet formal principles of Right do not mix readily with substantive criteria of justice. And that explains why we have no systematic theoretical account of why the criteria of proportionality should limit the right of self-defense. Everyone seems to agree that a defender should be able to inflict more harm than he or she avoids by acting in self-defense, e.g., a woman threatened with rape should be able to kill to protect her sexual and bodily autonomy. The scales may be tipped in favor of the innocent victim and against the wrongful aggressor. And therefore the principles of lesser evils, or balancing competing interests, hardly account for the cutoff point dictated by the principle of proportionality. Yet no one knows how much more harm the defender may inflict on the aggressor, how much the scales may be tipped in favor of the person attacked, before reaching the point of perceived injustice. All we know is that at a certain point, we sense that the scales are so far out of kilter that criteria of justice displace our commitment to the Right and the sanctity of individual autonomy.

THE 'DOWN PAYMENT' THESIS REVISITED

Though Nozick's 'down payment' strikes contemporary legal theorists as counterintuitive, it is not necessarily wrong. A legal system that seeks to be self-administering would enthrone self-defense as the primary mode of suppressing aggressive intrusions. State punishment might then appear as a continuation of the repressive measures initiated by the threatened victim. If this were the prevailing view of self-defense and punishment, the 'down payment' thesis would come into focus as a tenable claim.

That the thesis is not regarded as plausible illustrates how far we have come in taking a number of distinctions for granted. It is not only that self-defense is viewed as radically different from state punishment, but that each of these institutions has come to stand for a particular conception of merit in using force against criminal acts. Self-defense defends and reinforces the rightful and lawful order of cooperation among autonomous individuals. Punishment goes beyond the maintenance of the lawful order by realizing an imperative to do justice – or, in Kantian terms, to avoid the injustice of suffering unsanctioned crime.